STRANGE EVENTFUL HISTORY.

The story of the saints of the Church of England.

Christopher Loveless.

ISBN 978-1-4716-4078-0

First published 2012

Acknowledgements.
Thanks are due to the Bodleian Library, Oxford, and to the
University of Chichester.
My brother, Jeremy Loveless, put me up in Oxford during key parts
of the writing.
The Diocese of Chichester gave me a sabbatical to research the book.
Mrs.Mary Spreadbury typed the manuscript.
My wife, Natalie Loveless, gave invaluable help in preparing the text
for publication.
Colin, Jill and Timothy Loveless read the first draft and made useful
suggestions for improvements.

For Benedict and Madeleine.

Contents.

INTRODUCTION.

To open a new diary for the first time is one of life's minor pleasures. The blank pages, yet undefaced by the scrawl of appointments and deadlines, foster the pleasing illusion that next year is free space, empty time when anything could happen. Yet a well-bred diary is not completely void of content. Already marked are a calendar of events, some familiar, others mysterious. Burns Night and Shrove Tuesday, United Nations Day and Muslim New Year, Corpus Christi and the Duke of Edinburgh's birthday: our sense of time is shaped by a wealth of traditional days and celebrations.

I early discovered that the Church of England has its own calendar, richer, more alluring and more mysterious than anything the modern diary affords. On Sundays in our village church, a small boy waiting for Matins to start, I would leaf through the calendar at the front of the Prayer Book, wondering about the strange names listed there. Who were Machutus and Evurtius, Agatha and Blasius? What did they do? What was Lammas Day for? Why did they need to Invent the Cross? What was Edward King of the West Saxons translated into? So in idle curiosity began what was to escalate into a lifetime of discovery. I started trying to find out more about the saints, to trace their stories and, where possible, to read their writings. A strange alternative history began to unfurl for me, which travelled in parallel to the secular history I learned at school, while hardly ever meeting it. Some names, Augustine, Edward the Confessor, Thomas Becket, Joan of Arc, Thomas More, belonged in both histories, but most of the saints seemed hardly to touch English History at all. Their achievements mattered somewhere else; their stories remained largely untold.

With the publication first of the Alternative Service Book, and then of its successor Common Worship, the church's calendar was greatly extended. In particular many more names from the eighteenth, nineteenth and early twentieth centuries appeared. But modern though these new arrivals proclaimed themselves by their dates to be, they were often scarcely less obscure than the early martyrs and hermits who had perplexed my boyhood. Somebody had obviously decided that Octavia Hill, Isabella Gilmore and Apolo Kivebulaya were worth remembering year by year, but they were not exactly household names; many did not even warrant an entry in the Oxford Dictionary of the Christian Church. So I continued to collect facts and biographies and books, searching second hand bookshops and carrying away in triumph a set of sermons of Francis de Sales or a biography of Geoffrey Studdert Kennedy.

It soon struck me that the world of sanctity, like so many others, was a very small world. So many saints seemed to know each other; many in fact were related to each other. St.Basil the Great had a saint as grandmother, a saint as brother, a saint as sister and a saint as best friend at university. Saints clustered together as they worked on common projects: the writing of the creed, the conversion of Northumbria, or the transformation of the squalor of Victorian London. This interconnection of saints was obscured by many of the standard reference works, which tended to list saints either alphabetically, or in the order in which their feast-days occur in the year, so that each person was presented in a self-contained article, sealed off from their relatives, rivals and inspirations. This made it curiously hard to get a sense of how saints fitted in to any pattern bigger than their individual biographies, and without that sense it was hard to see what their contribution was, or why they mattered.

So the idea for this book was born. I decided I wanted to tell a continuous story, the story of the saints, which would also be the story of the Christian faith. I gave myself two rules. Every feast day in the Anglican calendar would be included, and the order of chapters would be broadly chronological. As well as the calendar of 'Common Worship' I have also included the feasts of the Book of Common Prayer, which first whetted my appetite so long ago, and various local additions made to the calendar within my own diocese, Chichester. I found that many of these local extras had become such good friends that a book about saints which omitted them was unthinkable.

The book is unlike a general History of Christianity, because the discipline of arranging the material following a defined set of church feast days meant that a shape was dictated rather different from that of the standard histories. Experts on particular periods will find peculiar omissions. It was a challenge to write about the early church without Origen or Tertullian; about the Middle Ages without Gregory VII or Innocent III; about the Reformation without Erasmus or Zwingli. The Anglican calendar becomes more local as it gets more modern, so the reader will find a lot about nineteenth century England, very little about post-Reformation Catholicism, surprisingly little about Scotland, virtually nothing about the Orthodox churches, an account of the new churches of Africa and Asia which is largely confined to the British Empire.

The book is not a comprehensive work of reference. I have aimed to give a sketch of each person which captures the essence of what made them unique or loveable. Where a list of church positions held and charity committees sat on bored me, I saw no reason to suppose it would not bore my readers. Where a person is valued for his or her writings, I have attempted to review briefly the principal works, but have not given substantial quotations; such resources are readily available in anthologies, and to quote usefully would have made the book too long. I have looked out for good stories. Although I have been diligent in indicating where these are apocryphal or legendary, they were often an important cause of a saint being loved or remembered by future generations, and it seemed joylessly purist to omit the best tales in the name of historical accuracy. St.George keeps his dragon, St.Catherine her wheel and St.Cuthbert his otters, and none the worse for that. Finally, I have attempted to connect my story with more generally known history, by highlighting any connections between my saints and other famous people and events, in a way most of them would have considered grievously worldly-minded; and where relevant, I have indicated the artistic conventions by which the saints can be recognised in painting and sculpture. Their contribution was not just to the Christian church but to human history and culture.

I wish the reader joy as he embarks on this strange, alternative history of the world, a history dominated by attempts to escape from time into eternity, and yet by extraordinary efforts to transform the passing world and bring about the Kingdom of Heaven on earth.

ALL SAINTS DAY. 1st November.
What is a saint? In the New Testament, the saints are simply the people of God. When Paul writes to the saints in Corinth, he is not writing to those in Corinth who are good, still less those who are

good and dead; he is writing to all the Christians there. They are called saints, holy ones, not because of their virtue, but because God has called them and set them apart to be his special people. Every Christian is a saint by virtue of God's calling.

Nevertheless, from earliest days, certain individuals have been remembered and revered because they manifested the holiness of God in particularly striking ways, either by their life, or by their death, or by their writings. In time, these loved people came to be allocated by the church special days, usually the date of their death, on which they would be commemorated. In some traditions, the saints thus honoured are regarded as praying for those who remember them, and their friendship and intercession is sought. The Church of England, officially at least, does not recommend more than that these special people be remembered, so that their example may inspire us on our own spiritual journey.

How do you become a saint? The earliest method was by popular acclaim. When a great Christian died, his or her anniversary of death would be kept as a local festival, and the tomb would become a place of prayer and pilgrimage. Overwhelmingly, in the early centuries, those whose memory was thus preserved were martyrs. In the early Middle Ages, they might also be founders of churches, or people whose prayer was strikingly holy – why should a little accident like death prevent someone so good at praying from continuing the service to the community she loved?

As the church elaborated its systems and regularised its authority, it was inevitable that an official process for declaring a person a saint should be established. By about 1300, the Roman church was claiming a monopoly on the right to confer sainthood. Popular acclaim was no longer enough; experts must examine the life and writings of a claimant, and the Pope, in a special ceremony, must canonise him. Among the criteria for canonisation is the requirement of two posthumous miracles, performed when the saint was asked to intercede for a sufferer. The miracle shows that the saint has successfully passed through Purgatory and is indubitably in heaven, enjoying eternal bliss, and in a position to pray successfully for those who remember and honour her on earth. Only Christians who die in communion with the Roman Catholic Church can be thus canonised.

The Church of England since the Reformation has never developed a procedure of canonisation, not surprisingly, since Anglican doctrine has no space for Purgatory and therefore no interest in defining which Christians have or have not arrived in Paradise. As a result, the Anglican calendar remained for several centuries the modified medieval calendar which survived at the beginning of the Book of Common Prayer, with the thirteenth century Bishop Richard of Chichester the most recent name to be commemorated by Anglicans. In 1980, when the Alternative Service Book provided modern equivalents of the Prayer Book services, the calendar was extensively revised and enlarged, and the names of many persons of the modern era were added. The Anglican and Protestant figures selected had not of course been officially canonised; they were chosen because their lives and writings were felt to have a lasting power to inspire their successors. In 2000, the Alternative Service experiment was consolidated and the books of Common Worship produced, and with these books came a further extension of the calendar, which now offers 248 names of people or events worthy of commemoration. Nineteen of the more obscure saints in the Prayer Book calendar are not included in the revised calendar, although the Prayer Book calendar remains legal and in some indefinite sense normative for the Church. Each English diocese is also at liberty to add extra names to the calendar for local observance; my own diocese, Chichester, has twenty names in its local calendar which are not found in the national list. As a general rule, people are not eligible to be included in the calendar until they have been dead for fifty years, as a guard against passing fashion; this rule has been waived in the cases of three modern martyrs.

Acclaimed by the love and tears of those who knew them; canonised by the Pope and Curia after due process; voted onto a list by a Church of England committee – these three routes give us the 287 chapters of this book, which together give an account of the amazing variety of ways by which God has called men and women to follow Jesus and, in the process, to become holy, to be saints.

PART ONE. THE WORD BECOMES INCARNATE.

ANNE & JOACHIM. 26th July

The city of Jerusalem is filled with pilgrims. From all Judaea, from Galilee, from the thousands of synagogues scattered throughout the whole world, faithful Jews converge on the Temple, the place the Lord has chosen, the only place where offerings can be made to God. Among the pilgrims, waiting to offer sacrifice, one day c.25BC, is a party from the city, full of spirits, throwing jokes and mockery back and forth. Among them is Joachim who is waiting with a smile on his lips, but grief in his heart. His wife Anne is barren and, in a society where fertility is a sign of God's blessing, the lack of a child is a constant torment to Joachim. As he steps forward to make his offering, a neighbour, half joking, half in cruel earnest, holds him back. 'You! The barren man! Wait until last; you are cursed by God!'

The remark draws Joachim's secret grief into the open, touching the vulnerable spot with intolerable clumsiness. Joachim leaves the Temple in tears, returns home, and without attempting to speak to his wife, withdraws to his farm on the hills. Here he lives in self-imposed exile, considering himself accursed and praying to God for mercy. His wife Anne, meanwhile, remains solitary at home, weeping in her daily prayer and grieving over her starved womb.

Were they called Joachim and Anne at all? Their names first come to us two hundred years after the event, in stories evidently shaped by the many biblical tales of barren women whom God chooses for unexpected joy by miraculous conception. But these stories have given to the unknown parents of the Virgin Mary identities and characters, by which the church delights to remember them.

THE CONCEPTION OF THE VIRGIN MARY. 8th December.

Staying away from home, lamenting your lot and refusing to sleep with your wife is not perhaps the best way to overcome the curse of childlessness. God takes a hand, sending an angel simultaneously to Joachim hiding in his sheep folds and Anne forsaken at home, ordering them to set out and meet each other, reconnect, recommence their poisoned marriage. The estranged couple meet at the Golden Gate, kiss, embrace, smile, lead each other home. They vow that if their long prayers are answered, they will give the child to God as (most unJewish of vows) perpetual virgin. Mary is conceived that night. Roman Catholics believe that this conception of Mary was marked by a high miracle, the intervention of God to permit an immaculate conception, a child free of all stain of original sin, prepared as a fitting shrine for the Son of God. Mary of the Immaculate Conception is portrayed in art as she appeared to St Bernadette so many centuries later at Lourdes, standing on the world God made and trampling the serpent which has bound it by sin.

Most other Christians cannot in conscience call Mary's conception 'immaculate' but rather regard her as conceived just as any other child might be conceived. This means that in a church calendar dominated by virgins and celibates, 8th December is the only day in the year when we are encouraged to contemplate as something holy and God-given, the ordinary act of conjugal love by which a new life is formed.

THE BIRTH OF THE VIRGIN MARY. 8th September.
Nine months to the day after the conception – our liturgical tradition assumes an admirable regularity in the bodily functions of holy women – St Anne is brought to bed and brings forth the longed-for child, Mary. This is one of the three births commemorated in our calendar, and in each case a birth is connected with promise, hope, fulfilment. The longing of a couple for a child parallels the longing of God's people for redemption and points too into the heart of God himself, who (in a scriptural image) groans like a woman in childbirth,[1] so intense is his longing to see his purposes fulfilled and the his people set free to live and act in his image and likeness. These feasts of the childhood of Mary speak to us of careful divine preparation for the fulfilment of divine promises.

The embroiderers of legend, so eagerly fleshing out the tantalisingly little we are told about Mary in scripture, portray Joachim and Anne bringing three year old Mary to the Temple in

---

[1] Isaiah 42.14.

fulfilment of their vow to dedicate her to God. Mary toddles forward and climbs unaided the steep staircase at the top of which the priest waits to receive her. So great is her infant longing to do God's will.

A popular artistic tableau shows St Anne teaching the young Mary to read, an image of motherhood as the passing on of wisdom. Pious supposing, imaginative reconstruction, meet our need to know more about this young girl who is growing towards womanhood in the quiet village of Nazareth, all unsuspecting the unique role which is about to be thrust upon her.

JOSEPH. 19th March.
It is time to meet Joseph, the carpenter of Nazareth, who is engaged to be married to Mary. The legend-makers said that Joseph was chosen by miracle as Mary's husband. The priests who were her guardians commanded all her male cousins to present wooden rods, which were locked in the sanctuary overnight, and Joseph's rod, like Aaron's before him, flowered the next morning. The betrothal of Mary was a matter of some delicacy as her husband was expected to respect and protect her eternal virginity, and this is why Joseph is portrayed in art as a very old man: nobody younger and more virile could be expected to keep such a pledge.

But Joseph and Mary as we meet them in scripture appear as an altogether less complicated couple. Their betrothal was nearly broken by the unexpected pregnancy of Mary, but Joseph's loyalty and love stood the test and the very ordinary young carpenter took on responsibility for his very extraordinary stepson.[2] There is no reason to believe that Joseph and Mary did not enjoy perfectly normal conjugal relations after the birth of Jesus, and that the four brothers and unspecified number of sisters mentioned in the gospel[3] were not the children of Mary and Joseph. With at least seven children and a few teenage apprentices, the life of the holy family must have been considerably less tranquil than some devotional literature would have us believe.

---

[2] Matthew 1.18-end.
[3] Mt.13.55-56.

Joseph does not appear in the stories of Jesus' adult life, so it is presumed that he died during Christ's youth.

THE ANNUNCIATION (Lady Day). 25th March.

From her birth Mary has been prepared for the astonishing encounter related with such simple beauty by St Luke[4], and made famous by innumerable paintings and stained-glass windows. Her unremarkable routine, tending her mother's house and preparing for her imminent marriage, is broken into by a vision of the Angel Gabriel, who hails her as the one chosen to be the mother of God's Son. Mary does not for a moment understand the theological implications of this and we shall see as our story progresses how many great theologians will labour to unpack the meaning of this meeting of an angel and a girl in Nazareth. But she responds with generous courage to the angel's message, and conceives her Son by the direct action of the Holy Spirit. This moment of Incarnation, of God's taking our human flesh, is both the pivotal point of human history (symbolised even by our dating system) and the source from which everything else in our story flows.

THE VISITATION. 31st May (2nd July BCP).

Mary's first action after her encounter with the angel was to leave home and journey to visit her cousin Elizabeth[5]. Why did she do this? The simplest answer is that Elizabeth's experience had been offered to her as a validation or parallel of her own. Elizabeth too had conceived a child beyond nature, after she and her husband had resigned themselves to barrenness. If an angel offers you a sign, it is prudent to go and look for that sign. But Mary must also have been aware that by making this journey she was buying time, time to become accustomed to the miraculous change within her, time to put off the painful confrontations with her parents and with Joseph, time to spend with the one person who, because she herself had experienced pregnancy as miracle, would understand her predicament and share her joy.

---

[4] Luke 1.26-38.
[5] Lk 1.39-45.

St Luke relates the great gladness with which these expectant mothers met and gives us Mary's song, the Magnificat[6], still recited every day at Evening Prayer as a celebration of the Incarnation. Mary rejoices at God's choice of her and, by extension, of every poor, humble, powerless person to be bearers of his glory and recipients of his grace.

THE BIRTH OF JOHN THE BAPTIST. 24th June

Mary arrived at Elizabeth's house during the sixth month of Elizabeth's pregnancy and stayed with her for three months; it is likely therefore that she attended her cousin during her labour and was among those who celebrated the birth of the child John.

Elizabeth's husband Zechariah had been given angelic promises about the role his son would play in preparing Israel to meet its Saviour – the shock sent the poor man dumb[7]. At the child's birth, Zechariah confirmed in writing 'His name is John'[8] and at once recovered his powers of speech to utter the great Morning Prayer canticle, the Benedictus[9], like Mary's song a celebration of God's faithfulness to his promises. Songs, promises, angel visits and joyful births are being woven together in these early stories to create an atmosphere of holy wonder. The birth of Jesus himself will be the expected climax of this series of domestic marvels.

Artists have delighted to show the little boys, Jesus and John the Baptist, playing together. In fact, we know nothing of John's early life and will not meet him again until he is sent forth into the wilderness to prepare the way of the Lord.

THE NATIVITY OF CHRIST (Christmas Day). 25th December.

The story of the first Christmas is one of the few Bible stories that everybody still recognises, at least in the decorated, magical version which is presented in nativity plays and at carol services. Mary and Joseph are called from home, travel to Bethlehem, the town where kings are born, and find themselves destitute there, so that the Son of

---

[6] Luke 1.46-55.
[7] Lk 1.18-20.
[8] Lk 1.63.
[9] Lk 1.67-79.

God is born in total poverty, adored by the humble beasts of the farmyard and by poor shepherds from the hills.

There are certain difficulties with the traditional story. St Luke believed that the reason Joseph had to travel to Bethlehem was to take part in a census[10]. But Quirinius, who organised the census, only became governor of Syria ten years after the death of King Herod, in whose reign Jesus was born[11]. So was there an earlier census or did Joseph have entirely different business in Bethlehem? Some have speculated that Joseph, as a descendant of David, had actually been born in Bethlehem, David's town, and that the famous manger was not in the stable of an inn, but in the lower room of his parents' two-storey peasant house. Did Mary go to Bethlehem to visit her in-laws? She was presumably glad of an excuse to leave Nazareth and have her baby quietly, away from the gossip and the calendar-counting calculations of neighbours. And once there, mother and baby were moved into the quiet of the lower room, away from the noise of family life upstairs. (Like her mother, Mary gives birth nine months to the day after her child was conceived).

The beauty of St Luke's story, and the Christmas saga which has been embroidered out of it, will always win the battle for hearts and minds against such well-argued reductionism. Saints in every age have drawn the pure water of God's love from the fountain of this story of heaven come to earth, God born in poverty, joy manifest in winter cold and a king in the rags of an outcast child. 'Let us go to Bethlehem and see this thing which has come to pass'[12]. The shepherds came first; the procession of pilgrims who followed them has never ceased.

THE CIRCUMCISION OF CHRIST. 1st January.

St Luke devotes one verse to a brief notice that Jesus was circumcised like every other Jewish boy on the eight day after his birth[13]. At first sight this does not make a very inspiring theme for a church festival. In the medieval calendars, important feasts had

[10] Lk 2.1-2.
[11] Matthew 2.1.
[12] Luke 2.15.
[13] Luke 2.21.

octave days a week later, which recollected the main celebration, often with a slightly different emphasis. The Circumcision is the Octave Day of Christmas. Common themes for meditation are Christ's obedience to the Law of his people throughout his life; the giving of his name, Jesus, meaning Saviour; the first occasion when his blood was shed; and, on New Year's Day, the call to each of us to be circumcised spiritually in our hearts.

THE PRESENTATION OF CHRIST (Candlemas). 2nd February.

A second rite of passage for the newborn Jesus was his presentation in the Temple, which took place when his mother had completed her forty days of ritual seclusion and was ready to be ceremonially cleansed from the uncleanness of childbirth. The festival, duly celebrated forty days after Christmas, is sometimes called the Purification of the Virgin, in memory of these rites. This would be the first time Mary appeared in public and would be her opportunity to give thanks for the birth of her Son. At the same time, Jesus, as a first-born son, would be ceremonially offered to God and a sacrifice made (in this case, the poor man's sacrifice of pigeons)[14] to redeem his life. This commemorated the terrible miracle by which God rescued Israel from slavery in Egypt by slaying all the Egyptian firstborn; the first-born of Israel henceforth belonged to God and must be bought back by the sacrifice.[15]

There is some irony in imagining these rites being performed for the holy family: Mary, the pure virgin, must undergo ritual purification, and Jesus, born to redeem the human race, must himself be ritually redeemed.

St Luke relates how these simple family observances were interrupted by two ancient prophets, Simeon and Anna, who had waited all their lives to see the Messiah and now recognised him in the child Jesus.[16] Simeon's prayer of thanksgiving, the Nunc Dimittis, is the third gospel canticle in daily use in the church, from early days in the night prayer Compline, and since the Reformation in Anglican Evensong.

---

[14] Lk 2.24.
[15] Exodus 13.3,12.
[16] Lk 2.27-38.

The feast is popularly called Candlemas because of Simeon's recognition of Jesus as the 'light to lighten the gentiles'. In the Middle Ages people brought candles to church to be blessed on this day. In recent liturgical revision Candlemas has assumed a new importance as the 'hinge' festival which brings the celebrations of Christmas to an end and, by its emphasis on Christ's being offered to the Father, points us forwards to his cross. For Mary, Candlemas is a day of foreboding as well as joy; Simeon warns her that 'a sword shall pierce your own heart also,' and out of this hint a whole body of literature, music and art has been developed expressing the poignant grief of the Virgin as she shares her Son's sufferings.

EPIPHANY. 6th January.

St Matthew gives a quite different account of Christ's birth, with no shepherds or manger, and all angels confined strictly to dreamworld. Instead another strand of miracle and legend is introduced, the story of the wise men from the east who follow the star to Bethlehem and present to the child gifts of gold, frankincense and myrrh.[17] Later traditions, drawing on the prophecies in Isaiah and the Psalms of how kings would come to offer gold and incense,[18] made the wise men kings and gave them the names of Caspar, Melchior and Balthasar. They are buried in Cologne Cathedral.

The Christian tradition has effortlessly accommodated the wise men as Act Two of the Christmas story, although scholars often regard the whole story as one invented for devotional purposes, and orthodox Christians manage not to notice the story's apparent endorsement of astrology as a means of discovering truth.

The wise men were the first gentiles (non Jews) to worship Christ and the feast of Epiphany (a word meaning 'revealing' or 'manifesting') introduces a season of meditation on the progressive revelation of Christ to the unbelieving world. Twelfth Night, its popular name, is properly the evening of 5th January, as 6th January is the thirteenth day of Christmas. Most English Christians associate the feast entirely with the Three Kings, and it is traditional to replace

---

[17] Mt 2.1-13.
[18] Isaiah 60.3,6; Psalm 72.10.

the figures of the shepherds with those of the wise men in Christmas cribs on this day. In the Eastern churches, Epiphany is a festival more wide-ranging in its focus than this one incident, and a complex celebration includes also Christ's baptism and first miracle, as key moments of revelation. This richer emphasis is being rediscovered in English churches.

THE HOLY INNOCENTS. 28th December.

Matthew relates the tragic aftermath of the visit of the wise men.[19] Their coming alerted King Herod the Great to the messianic rumours emanating from Bethlehem and he acted to scotch them by massacring the boy babies of the little town. However Joseph, warned in a dream, had already escaped with his wife and son to the next door province of Egypt. This kingdom was under direct Roman rule and Herod, a client king of the Roman Empire, had no jurisdiction there.

The massacre entirely accords with the ruthless nature of Herod's rule which we know from non-biblical sources. The little children of Bethlehem who died are honoured as martyrs, because despite their ignorance and innocence, they died for Christ.

THE BAPTISM OF CHRIST (Sunday after Epiphany)

After a luxuriously detailed celebration of Christ's birth, the church calendar is remarkably restrained in its commemoration of incidents from his adult life. Just as Christian art and music is supremely dominated by the two mysteries of Jesus' birth and death, so the liturgical year is strung between the two peaks of Christmas and Easter.

After thirty years of obscure life in Nazareth, Jesus was drawn to the River Jordan, where his cousin John the Baptist had begun a new religious movement, proclaiming the coming of the Messiah and calling his fellow Jews to prepare for this by being baptised. The ritual was normally offered only to non-Jews wishing to convert, and John's invitation to those born and brought up as God's covenant people, marked his urgent sense that the coming of the Messiah

---

[19] Mt 2.13-16.

meant a break with the old world which had become corrupt. The Qumran scrolls, discovered in the desert where John preached, have shown us that other Jews at this time were withdrawing into the desert to create new pure societies.

Both the gospel writers and later theologians have been perplexed as to why the sinless Jesus submitted to a ritual which symbolised forgiveness of sins. Reading between the lines, we may speculate that Jesus was at first a disciple of John the Baptist and that his emergence as the leader of a new religious movement was resented by some of John's other followers. Like many others, he came to be baptised out of desire to be ready for the coming Kingdom of God. As presented in the gospels, Jesus' baptism was a big moment in his developing self- awareness. Jesus experienced the descent of the Holy Spirit upon him and heard God's voice declaring him to be 'my beloved Son'.[20] Whether or not he had previously suspected it, Jesus now knew that he would have a key role in bringing in the kingdom for which John's preaching had been preparing.

This experience of being called 'Son' by the Father lies at the heart of the mystery of Jesus. His central awareness of God was as his loving father, and this gave him the unique vision out of which he preached and performed his saving acts.

ASH WEDNESDAY AND LENT

Following the extraordinary day of revelation of his baptism, Jesus withdrew into the desert for a prolonged period of fasting, prayer and self-examination. There were strong biblical precedents for this – Moses, Elijah and other prophets had withdrawn into the desert at times of spiritual crisis.[21] The period of forty days which Jesus spent there is in the Bible a symbolic round number, meaning 'a long time' but has gradually been established as a period of prayer and fasting for all Christians in preparation for Easter.

The stories of Jesus' temptation in the wilderness[22] portray in the form of parables which might well have been told by himself, his

---

[20] Mark 1.
[21] Exodus 34.28; 1 Kings 19.8.
[22] Mt 4.1-12.

inner struggles as he tried to come to terms with his destiny. Three times Jesus is tempted to adopt an easy, popular way of being the Messiah. Each temptation is rejected and Jesus chooses the hard way of humble service and eventually painful self sacrifice on the cross.

THE APOSTLES

Jesus returned from the desert and began his ministry of preaching and healing in about 27AD. He travelled as a wandering rabbi about the hills, lanes and villages of Galilee, announcing the coming of the Kingdom of God. Jesus does not appear to have made any strategic effort to capture places and people of influence – Sepphoris, the principal city of Galilee, only five miles from Nazareth, is never mentioned in the gospels, nor did he ever visit the luxury lakeside resort of Tiberias. But as he began to attract crowds by his earthy, challenging teaching, he did do one thing which shows he was consciously founding a new Israel. He chose twelve apostles to form the inner ring of his disciples. The lists of the twelve apostles in the different gospels do not entirely match and the subsequent careers of most of them are deeply obscure. It was not the identity of the individuals which mattered as much as the number – twelve, the number of the tribes of Israel. These were to be the founding fathers of Jesus' new community, which would one day be called the church.

We may summarise briefly what is known about most of the apostles; there will be more to say about Simon Peter and about John.

ANDREW. 30th November.

Andrew was a fisherman from Bethsaida on the north-west shore of the sea of Galilee.[23] Like Jesus, he had been drawn south by reports of the preaching of John the Baptist, and at the Baptist's prompting, he was the first to follow Jesus and ask to be permitted to stay with him.[24] Andrew brought his brother Simon to Jesus and the two of them were called more formally to the life of wandering evangelists when Jesus called them from their nets.[25] Despite this symbolic separation from their old life, Simon and Andrew continued

---

[23] John 1.44.
[24] Jn 1.35-40.
[25] Mark 1.18-20

intermittently to make money by fishing and their house in Capernaum was a base for Jesus.

Andrew is said to have preached the gospel in Greece where he was martyred by crucifixion on a diagonal cross, which is his emblem in art. He became patron saint of Scotland, not because he ever ventured so far north, but because his relics were brought in 732 to the town which now bears his name. Oengus II, a Pictish king, subsequently vowed to dedicate Scotland to St.Andrew if he was victorious in battle; according to legend, he saw the St.Andrew's Cross in the sky on the day of his victory.

JAMES THE GREAT. 25th July.

At the same time as Andrew and Simon, Jesus called two other fishermen, brothers, James and John, the sons of Zebedee. Their mother, Salome, also became one of his followers; she is thought to have been the sister of the Virgin Mary, so that James and John were first cousins of Jesus.[26] The brothers were the closest of all Jesus' friends. He nick-named them 'Sons of Thunder', indicating a fiery, passionate temper. James is the only apostle whose death is recorded in the New Testament[27]; he was beheaded in 44AD by King Herod Agrippa I. This early martyrdom did not prevent him becoming patron saint of Spain – he certainly never went there, but his body was miraculously delivered there in an empty boat and his shrine at Compostella was regarded as the third holiest in Christendom during the Middle Ages. During the re-conquest of Spain from the Moors, the humble Galilean fisherman was believed to be leading the Christian armies in full armour. Zebedee and Salome would have been very surprised to be introduced to the fearsome Santiago di Compostella.

---

[26] This theory is arrived at by a combination of Mark 15.40 , which states that Salome, James and John's mother, was at the cross, with John 19.25, which attests the presence of Mary's sister. Salome and the un-named sister are presumed to be the same person.

[27] Acts 12.2.

JOHN THE EVANGELIST. 27th December.

John is usually assumed to have been the youngest disciple because of the very late traditional date of his death. As the 'disciple whom Jesus loved', his personal memories are behind the Gospel of St John, even if he did not write the gospel as we have it. Scholarly consensus has tended to date the gospel late and to regard it as unreliable, but it is the only gospel which claims to be written by an eye-witness and John often reveals details which help us make sense of the narrative in the other three gospels. The discovery of a fragment of papyrus dated to the last decade of the first century proves that John's gospel was circulating in Egypt by that date. The gospel was therefore written earlier than has been supposed, and it is entirely plausible that the direct memories of John lie behind the book as we have it.

MATTHEW. 21st September.

Matthew was a tax-collector, responsible for collecting customs dues on the lakeside in Galilee. As such, he was regarded as a traitor for his collaboration with the occupying Roman forces, and as a sinner for participating in a notoriously corrupt profession. Jesus called him from his tax office and shocked his righteous neighbours by accepting hospitality in his house.

Matthew certainly did not write the gospel which bears his name. This gospel is clearly based on St Mark's account and it is most improbable than an eye-witness and an apostle would subordinate his own memory to the writings of a second-hand authority. However, both Matthew and Luke have another source of Jesus' teaching in common, a lost document or tradition often referred to as 'Q' and this collection may well have been compiled by Matthew the tax collector who must, by his trade, have been one of the more literate disciples. In Mark's and Luke's account, Matthew is called Levi, but he is manifestly the same person.

PHILIP. 1st May.

A brief account of Philips's early call by Jesus is given in John[28], but all we know of him is that he was a native of Bethsaida. His name is

---

[28] John 1.39.

Greek, which suggests that he came from a background culturally open to the world outside Judaism, and indeed, when Greek pilgrims wanted to meet Jesus, it was Philip whom they chose as intermediary.

BARTHOLOMEW. 24th August.

About this apostle we know for certain nothing more than his name. Traditionally he is equated with Nathanael, the friend of Philip from Cana in Galilee, whose initial cynicism about a prophet from Nazareth was overcome when Jesus proved able to read his mind.[29] Bartholomew is said to have preached in Persia where he suffered the peculiarly horrible martyrdom of being flayed alive. His emblem in art is a butcher's knife.

THOMAS. 3rd July. (21st December BCP)

Thomas is called Didymus (or Twin) but his brother is nowhere mentioned and may have died in infancy. It is tempting to attribute to this his melancholy approach to life – all the sayings of his which are recorded reveal bewilderment and a willingness to believe the worst. He is most famous for his 'doubting Thomas' encounter with the risen Christ. Tradition has it that he was a builder by trade and that after the resurrection he travelled as far as India preaching the gospel. Certainly, when Portuguese explorers arrived in Goa in the sixteenth century they found the 'Mar Thoma' Christian community, which had existed quite isolated from the rest of the church for many centuries.

JUDE. 28th October.

Jude is of all the apostles the most obscure, the patron saint of lost causes. In Matthew's and Mark's lists, he appears as Thaddaeus or Lebbaeus; there is no way of telling if we have two names for one man or two different people. John records one telling question put by him at the Last Supper[30], and he is traditionally the author of the epistle of Jude, although this author refers to the apostles as if he were not himself one of them[31].

---

[29] John 1.39ff.
[30] John 14.22
[31] Jude 17.

SIMON. 28th October.

Simon is called the Zealot, and that is all we know. The Zealots were the radical Jews, who offered armed resistance to the Romans, assassinating tax collectors and collaborators and dreaming of a free Israel. It must have been a dramatic change of direction for Simon to follow a teacher who preached non-resistance and to find himself an equal partner with Matthew the tax collector.

JAMES THE LESS. 1st May.

Finally, we consider the other James. Traditionally, this apostle James has been equated with James the Lord's brother, who played a central part in the life of the earliest church. The fact that James the apostle is called 'Son of Alphaeus' may make this identification unlikely, but the reasoning goes as follows; Alphaeus could be an alternative form of Cleophas. Cleophas was the husband of Mary, who is said to be the sister of the Virgin Mary and mother of James. Given that Joachim and Anne are unlikely to have called both their daughters Mary, Mary the wife of Cleophas was most likely the Virgin Mary's sister-in-law, Joseph's sister. Joseph and Alphaeus/Cleophas were thus brothers-in-law and Jesus and James were cousins. Jesus did have an actual brother called James but he, like all Jesus' brothers, seems to have disapproved of Jesus' eccentric and controversial lifestyle and mission[32].

If tradition is right, it was James the Less who wrote the Letter of James, a letter which certainly seems 'Galilean' in tone, with its close verbal echoes of the Sermon on the Mount[33], and appeals to traditional Jewish piety rather than to specifically Christian themes.

James, the Lord's brother, who became leader of the church in Jerusalem, was the rallying point for all those Jewish Christians who were uneasy at the way Paul and others were opening up the church to non-Jews and risking the loss of the Jewish roots of Christianity. According to Acts, James was personally sympathetic to Paul and used his influence with the conservative wing of the

---

[32] Mark 3.21; John 7.5.
[33] James 5.12; cf.Mt.5.37.

church to maintain unity[34]. He is said to have been stoned to death by unbaptised Jews in 62AD.

THE BEHEADING OF JOHN THE BAPTIST. 29th August.

After the death of Herod the Great, his dominions were divided into four tetrarchies, each of which was bestowed by the Romans on one of his sons. Archelaus, ruling in Judaea, was soon deposed as untrustworthy, and that southern part of Palestine came under the direct rule of a Roman procurator, at the time of Christ's ministry Pontius Pilate. Galilee, the native province of Jesus, was ruled by Herod Antipas, who displeased his orthodox Jewish subjects by marrying his brother's wife, after a scandalous divorce. John the Baptist was fearless in denouncing this immorality in high places, and was locked up for his pains, traditionally in the Dead Sea fortress of Machaerus. The gospels relate how his death was eventually brought about by Herodias, the adulterous wife, and Salome, her daughter by her first marriage, who manipulated Herod into a public promise to give Salome the head of the Baptist[35]. The death of his cousin seems to have shaken Jesus, and coming as it did just as his own fame was beginning to rise, led to repeated speculation that Jesus actually was John the Baptist, either escaped from prison or miraculously raised from the dead.

THE CONFESSION OF PETER. 18th January, CDC.

What did the apostles think they were doing, leaving their homes and livelihood and following a homeless preacher around the countryside? The gospels present them as oscillating between a bold faith in Jesus and a confused fear of the future. Certainly they imaged that the kingdom Jesus proclaimed would be a political kingdom, a free Israel with a king like David – Luke says they were still hankering after this as late as Ascension Day[36].

Certain incidents are recorded which mark decisive steps forward in the apostles' understanding of the kingdom. Jesus seems to have made deliberate efforts to escape from the crowds of

---

[34] Acts 15.13ff; 21.18ff.
[35] Matthew 14.1 ff.
[36] Acts 1.6.

sensation-seekers, who followed him hungry for miracles, and to get away to teach the apostles more intensely. Mark shows him constantly on the move, often beyond Jewish territory. During a stay in the Syrian town of Caesarea Philippi, north of Galilee, Jesus asked his disciples the fateful question 'Who do you say that I am?' Peter's classic answer was, 'You are the Messiah, the Son of the living God.'[37] What exactly he meant by this has been endlessly debated, but quite clearly Peter did not envisage the peculiar messianic role which Jesus was beginning to develop – that far from being a conqueror, the Messiah must willingly choose suffering and death as the path by which salvation would come. Peter and the others resolutely blanked Jesus when he tried to share this vision. The Confession of Peter, as it is called, reveals how Jesus was moving away from the idea of the Kingdom as something whose coming he was called to proclaim, and towards the idea of the Kingdom as something he personally must induct by his death. From this point he turned his face resolutely towards Jerusalem, where death was waiting for him.

MARY MAGDALENE. 22nd July.
How did Jesus and the apostles support themselves during their travels? Thirteen young, labouring men, scandalising the pious by their marked disinterest in fasting, needed regular meals, no matter how strong their faith in the God who feeds the birds. There are scattered hints in the gospels that the apostolic band was supported by a larger circle of disciples, who did not abandon their homes but sustained Jesus with money, food and hospitality.

Mary Magdalene was one such supporter, a woman from the lakeside town of Magdala, who was healed by Jesus when he cast seven devils from her[38]. Does that indicate, in our terms, mental illness? Traditionally Mary Magdalene was assumed to be the un-named sinful woman who gate-crashed a dinner party to fling herself at Jesus' feet and wash them with her tears[39]. Mary Magdalene is also supposed to be the same person as Mary of Bethany, who with

---

[37] Matthew 16.13ff.
[38] Luke 8.2-3.
[39] Luke 7.36ff.

her sister Martha offered Jesus hospitality[40] and, just before he entered Jerusalem for the last time, anointed Jesus with costly oil, which he told her to keep for his burial[41]. The stories which are unquestionably about Mary Magdalene describe her faithfully following Jesus to the foot of the cross, when the male apostles had fled, and then going on Sunday morning to anoint his body, only to become the startled first witness of the Resurrection[42].

As with James the Less, we therefore have possibly three different women who have been combined by popular devotion to form the powerful image of the Magdalene, passionate in sin, in repentance, in devotion to Christ, the only person in the gospels who repeatedly offers him intimate physical care. Mary Magdalene's intense love for Jesus has made her an object of romantic curiosity, spawning a variety of legends about her secret marriage to Christ and providing the 'love interest' in countless musicals, passion plays and films. In recent years, as the 'apostle to the apostles', the one who announced the resurrection to the church's first leaders, she has become an icon for supporters of women's ordination. It seems a pity, as the calendar has done, to prise apart pedantically the strands of biblical tradition which make up this richly inspiring figure.

MARY, MARTHA AND LAZARUS. 29th July.

When it was assumed that Mary Magdalene was the same person as Mary of Bethany, her sister Martha was honoured on the octave day of her feast. St Martha's Day has now become the feast of Mary, Martha and Lazarus, the family at Bethany, thus firmly prising apart Mary Magdalene form the Bethany Mary as somebody quite different.

Bethany is two miles from Jerusalem, and Jesus used Martha's house as his southern base, a safe haven for him near the dangerous holy city. The story of how Martha became exasperated doing housework while Mary (Magdalene or no) sat at Jesus' feet and listened to him, has become proverbial, and the two sisters were used as types of the active and contemplative life in medieval preaching.

---

[40] Luke 10.38-42.
[41] John 12.1-7.
[42] John 19.25; 20.1-18.

St John tells the story of their brother Lazarus's sickness and death, which occasioned the most spectacular of all Jesus' miracles, when Lazarus was raised to life four days after he died[43].

After the resurrection, we are told that Mary, Martha and Lazarus sailed across the Mediterranean to Gaul to preach the gospel there. Martha tamed a dragon in the wilderness near Arles. Lazarus was martyred and was buried (this time for good) at Autun. Mary Magdalene survived her siblings and lived a solitary old age in the wilderness lamenting her long ago sins and being fed by angels. She is buried in Vezelay in Burgundy, a church of spectacular beauty whose shrine was suspected of being a fake for pilgrims even in its medieval heyday. The Bethany family was accompanied on this mission by Joseph of Arimathea, who forged on further north to plant his staff on the hillside at Glastonbury, where it flowered into a hawthorn, and to hide the Holy Grail there for King Arthur's knights to find it. This was not the first time Joseph of Arimathea had been to Britain. As a tin merchant, he went often to Cornwall to trade with the miners, and he took with him his teenage nephew from Nazareth, whose feet, in ancient time, thus walked upon England's mountains green. All of these legends ought to be true and, when one visits Glastonbury or Vezelay, it is easy to think they might be.

THE TRANSFIGURATION . 6th August.
Only one other incident from Christ's adult life is commemorated in the calendar; the mysterious experience of the Transfiguration.

Matthew, Mark and Luke all relate how Jesus withdrew to a mountain for prayer, with only his three closest disciples, Peter, James and John, for company. The three apostles saw him transfigured by an inward light, witnessed his conversation with the long dead Moses and Elijah and heard the voice of God proclaim, 'This is my beloved Son. Listen to him'[44]

For Jesus, this intense spiritual experience seems to have been a preparation for the ordeal that awaited him in Jerusalem. For icon

---

[43] John 11.
[44] Matthew 17.1-7.

painters and mystical writers ever since, the Transfiguration has provided a rich store of images for exploring the depths of prayer.

The feast of the Transfiguration in August has been rendered somewhat redundant by the new lectionary, which in effect makes the Sunday before Lent into the feast of the Transfiguration, thus emphasising the incident's significance as a glimpse of glory preceding the darkness of Christ's sufferings.

THE PASSION OF CHRIST

There would be no Christianity if Jesus of Nazareth had not died on a cross. The story of Jesus' suffering, death and victory has been told, retold, preached about, painted, dramatised, filmed, made the subject for endless devout meditations for two millennia, and remains inexhaustible. Every incident, every character in the gospel accounts has been analysed and argued over – the motives of those who arranged Jesus' execution, the significance of the various trials, the nature of his tortures, and above all, the question, why? Why did Jesus' enemies find it necessary to kill him? Why did Jesus himself believe that he must die?

The celebration of Easter is by far the oldest Christian festival, apart from the weekly observance of Sunday as the Lord's Day, which became established almost immediately among the apostles and their followers. In the earliest centuries, the entire sequence of Jesus' betrayal, sufferings, death and resurrection was commemorated in one night of vigil, Holy Saturday, leading into the baptism of converts and celebration of the Eucharist at dawn on Easter Day. Gradually, the ritual was elaborated and extended back through the week before Easter to produce the current highly dramatic arrangement of a Holy Week, following day by day the events of Jesus' passion, prepared for by the forty days of Lent and followed by the fifty days of Eastertide.

PALM SUNDAY

From his base, the home of his faithful Mary and Martha at Bethany, Jesus made deliberately provocative preparations for his last entry into the holy city of Jerusalem. At a prearranged signal, a donkey was produced on which he rode into the city. Was he consciously fulfilling the prophecy of Zechariah – 'behold your king comes to you, meek and lowly, riding on an ass'[45]? Was he making a statement about the nature of his kingship, one of humble service, rather than the triumphant warfare which a stallion might have symbolised? He cannot have been surprised by the reaction he provoked. It was Passover, the Jewish festival of liberation, and the city was thronged with pilgrims whose minds and imaginations were filled with dreams of freedom from slavery. The Palm Sunday welcome, with branches being torn from trees, to make a carpet for Jesus to ride over, may have been improvised but was entirely forseeable. The whole affair marked Jesus as dangerous; dangerous to the Roman garrison, keeping order at a notoriously volatile time of the year; and dangerous to the priests who administered the Temple, the sacrificial heart of Judaism. They had a delicate line to keep, retaining the trust of the Roman government and thus maintaining, in appearance at least, their right to independence in religious affairs, while at the same time performing the ancestral rites which were the focus of passionate loyalty for the crowd of pilgrims who hated the Romans and resented the apparent subservience of their leaders to the pagan tyrants. Jesus had alienated significant numbers of the Pharisees, the popular pietist movement, by his casual approach to matters of ritual purity, his compromised observance of the Sabbath, his neglect of traditional fast days. He had alienated the zealots by his preaching of forgiveness of enemies and his willingness to show friendship to the Romans and their collaborators. Now he appeared, posing deliberately as a king, in a week when all the efforts of the government were directed to keeping the streets quiet and free from fanatical happenings.

Quietly, the authorities began to plan his destruction

MAUNDY THURSDAY

Jesus spent the first part of the week teaching and disputing openly in the Temple; such were the crowds of his supporters that nobody dared attempt an arrest. The intervention of Judas Iscariot therefore

---

[45] Zechariah 9.9.

was crucial. His offer to lead the Temple police to where they could arrest Jesus without public notice sealed Jesus' fate.

Jesus seems to have taken precautions to ensure that he could spend his last night alive quietly with the apostles without fear of interruption. A secret signal was arranged so that a room could be prepared for his Last Supper without Judas finding out in advance where it was[46]. St Mark believed that the Last Supper was held on Passover night[47], but John, the eye-witness, says that the following day, the day of Christ's death, was the day of preparation for the Passover[48]. Some have believed that he says this simply to be able to make a symbolic parallel; in his gospel Jesus dies on the cross just as the lambs are being killed in the Temple for the Passover feast. If, however, Mark is right, and Thursday night was Passover night, it seems odd that the chief priests were so eager to get the bodies taken off the crosses before nightfall on Friday, to avoid defiling the Sabbath, yet were happy for the crucifixion itself to take place on Passover, one of the holiest days in the year. Moreover, the crowd would request the release of the Passover prisoner surely on the day before the feast, so that the released prisoner could celebrate his freedom at the Passover meal with his family. For these reasons, I believe John is right and that, while Jesus kept the Last Supper as a Passover, he was in fact pre-empting the festival by twenty-four hours.

Jesus gave the traditional Passover blessings new meanings which reveal what he thought he was doing by offering himself to death. The bread and wine which were blessed at every meal became his body and his blood – imagery which must have shocked and alarmed the apostles.

After the Supper, Jesus led them outside the city to the Garden of Gethsemane, where, with iron courage, he held his party steady while he prayed and awaited the inevitable. When Judas brought the guards to arrest him, Jesus forbade his followers to fight and willingly handed himself over. After this, it is not surprising that the apostles panicked and fled.

---

[46] Luke 22.10-12.
[47] Mark 14.12.
[48] John 19.31.

Maundy Thursday, when Jesus' last supper and arrest are commemorated, gets its name from the Latin 'Mandatum' a commandment, in memory of Jesus' saying at the supper 'A new commandment I give you; love one another.'

GOOD FRIDAY

Although arrested and charged by the Temple authorities, Jesus was condemned and executed by the Romans, as a political rebel against the empire. Pontius Pilate, the governor, is represented as having grave doubts about the justice of a guilty verdict; he tried to evade the responsibility of taking a decision by referring the case back to the priests, passing it to the court of Herod Antipas, and offering Jesus as the Passover prisoner to be released by acclaim from the crowds. In the end, it was the threat of mob violence which forced his hand and Christ was condemned.

His sufferings were terrible and have been portrayed over and over again in Christian art. Crowned with thorns in mockery of his claim to be bringing in God's kingdom, flogged with the ghastly lead-studded Roman whips, forced to carry his cross out of the city and finally crucified with nails through arms and feet, Jesus died willingly, submitting himself to God's will and speaking only to pray for his executioners, to comfort his mother and another man dying with him and, in prayers taken from the psalms, to express his sense of abandonment, and his final returning confidence in God.

Joseph of Arimathea rescued his body from being flung onto a rubbish tip and gave him decent burial in a sealed cave.

EASTER DAY

Now comes the turning point from which the whole of the rest of our story draws its power. Jesus' shattered followers rested on the Sabbath, but early on the next working day, Sunday, Mary Magdalene and others visited the grave of Jesus, only to find it broken open and his body gone. The gospels record the confused and confusing events which followed. In their inconsistency and incoherence, the Easter stories read plausibly as deriving from eye-witness attempts to make sense of a happening which no one had foreseen and no one could at first understand. Attempts to reconstruct 'what really happened' are legion, ranging from devout Christian synthesis of the biblical accounts to militant atheist dismissal of the whole story as a nonsense made up several decades later to express what the early Christians would like to have happened. What is indisputable is that by the end of the forty day period in which 'appearances' of the risen Christ were experienced, a band of 120 persons had been formed, all of whom were convinced that they had seen Jesus alive and that God had raised him from death. Jesus had not 'come back to life' as Lazarus and others who were miraculously raised had done; rather he had been taken by God into a new life in which his physical life (and his actual body) had become the vehicles for an indestructible and eternal being 'at the right hand of God'. The New Testament writers struggle to find ways of putting this transformation into words, but without it, it is impossible to make sense either of the New Testament or of the history of Christianity. Christian faith is built not on the teaching, nor the example, nor the personality of Jesus, but on his followers' conviction that 'this Jesus whom you crucified, God raised to life'[49].

Easter is the name of an Anglo-Saxon spring-goddess, and the use of her name in the Christian calendar is one of the most audacious borrowings from the early English pagan culture by the Anglo-Saxon church. In most romance languages, the festival of Christ's resurrection is called 'Pasch' reflecting the close links between Jesus' death and the Jewish Passover; much of the imagery of the exodus from Egypt is used by early Christian writers to bring out the significance of the cross.

ASCENSION DAY
The forty day period, during which the followers of Jesus experienced his physical presence among them, was brought to an end by the Ascension. The apostles experienced Christ being received into the clouds and they understood that they would not again see him with their physical eyes. Of all the stories of Jesus, the Ascension is the hardest for a modern imagination to comprehend. Even in the first century, educated people did not literally believe that

---

[49] Acts 2.32.

heaven was a place above the sky to which you could fly upon clouds. The physicality of the ascension is the puzzle; how could Jesus' risen body be taken up into heaven, which is not a place in the physical universe? This is only the supreme of the many unanswerable questions about the nature of Jesus' existence after the resurrection. His body served as the means by which his friends recognised him, yet clearly it was no longer physical in any ordinary meaning of that word. Jesus is taken up into God, so that the Ascension is the day of his triumph, and he leaves behind promises, that he will be with his church for all time, that the apostles will shortly be clothed with power from on High, and that at the end of time his followers will once again see him as he returns to judge all things. The rest of our story will show how these promises were fulfilled.

PART TWO. THE APOSTOLIC CHURCH.

ST MATTHIAS.14th May (24th February BCP)

The apostles returned to Jerusalem where they seem to have been living a common life, perhaps in the house where the Last Supper had been celebrated. Their state of mind can be imagined. They had shared the trauma of Jesus' arrest and murder, and with it the collapse of their hopes of a swift arrival of an uncomplicated kingdom where justice and freedom could be restored to Israel. They had then experienced together the inexplicable phenomena of Christ's resurrection appearances, which had convinced them that death had not conquered their leader, but left them utterly perplexed as to what they should do next. What sort of kingdom was Jesus in fact ushering in, and how did he expect them to act?

At Peter's prompting the believers chose by lot a man to fill the vacant twelfth place in the apostolic band left by the treachery and suicide of Judas[50]. The apostles seem to have been clinging on to Jesus' appointment of them as the twelve founders of the new Israel. Did they at this stage anticipate that the college of the twelve would be perpetually renewed by fresh elections, so that Jesus' people would always be led by twelve apostles? Such a design was never realised. As we have seen, most of the original twelve remained personally obscure, while the term apostle came to be applied much more generally to missionaries and founders of churches, losing its original connotations of a personal friend of Jesus and witness of his resurrection.

About Matthias as an individual no more is known than that he had followed Jesus during his earthly life and was elected by lot to be the twelfth apostle.

PENTECOST

After the apostles had waited for ten days, praying together daily, there occurred the first and greatest of those powerful experience of revival which are called Pentecostal after the name of the Jewish

---

[50] Acts 1.15ff.

feast on which the gift was given. The believers felt themselves to be filled with the Holy Spirit, an experience which is described in the imagery of wind and fire. The effect of this was to provoke the whole group to loud prayer and praise and to an outburst of preaching in the streets. Luke tells us that pilgrims from every land heard the apostles speaking in their own languages[51]. Was this a miracle of speaking, so that Thomas the carpenter from Capernaum and Andrew the fisherman from Bethsaida suddenly found themselves speaking fluent Cappadocian? Or was it a miracle of hearing, so that the urgency, joy and excitement of the Holy Spirit were brought home to the hearers, transcending language barriers? Whatever the precise nature of what happened, this day is regarded as the birthday of the Christian church. Neither the word Christian nor the word church was used on the day – the friends of Jesus did not yet think of themselves as founding a new religion. They were Jews who knew that in raising Jesus from the dead, the God of their ancestors had revealed the Messiah. Even the Phrygians and Pamphylians were Jews from abroad, returning as pilgrims to the Holy City. But from this day, when the good news that Jesus had been raised began to be proclaimed, the kingdom which Jesus preached was no longer a future hope, but was made visible, however imperfectly, in the human society soon to be called 'Ecclesia', the people called together, the Church.

THE NAME OF JESUS. 7th August BCP.
What sort of society was this new church which, impelled by the conviction of the Resurrection, was now coming into being? Entry into the community of believers was by baptism, which the apostles took from their old association with John the Baptist, giving it a new meaning by connecting it with their new conviction that Jesus was alive. Baptism was now given 'in the name of Jesus'. It meant forgiveness of sins and new life as the believer was incorporated into the risen life of Christ. The name of Jesus was now a name of power, rapidly acquiring some of the aura of the old Hebrew name of God, I am who I am. In the name of Jesus, the believers met and shared a

---

[51] Acts 2.6.

common life of prayer and the pooling of money and resources. In the name of Jesus, Peter and John performed the first miracle of the church, setting a lame man on his feet to dance in the Temple courts. In the name of Jesus, this little group of Jews was slowly but inevitably edging towards a new identity, defined by their allegiance to the crucified carpenter, rather than by their heritage of covenant, law and prophets. The authorities and those who had colluded at Jesus' death took note and took steps to prevent people acting or speaking in the name of Jesus. The new movement was however, unstoppable.

The feast of the Name of Jesus become popular in the fourteenth century and it survived in the reformed calendar of the Church of England. It does not feature in 'Common Worship' and much of the resonance of the feast has been transferred to the 1st January, the Circumcision and Naming of Jesus.

CORPUS CHRISTI
Along with baptism, the other distinguishing mark of the new community was the regular celebration of the rite Jesus had given them at the Last Supper, the sharing of bread and wine 'in remembrance of me'. In these early days called simply 'The breaking of bread', the memorial was still embedded in an actual meal. The believers met to share food and at the end of the meal bread and wine were passed round in honour of Jesus, the invisible host at this 'love feast' as it was called. Paul's First Letter to the Corinthians shows some of the tension which began to surface at these affairs, where drunkenness and snobbery defaced expression of the simple fellowship[52]. Within the first century, steps were being taken to prevent the breaking of bread being defiled by these excesses, and something very similar in structure to our Communion service was being established as normative.

The Feast of Corpus Christ (Latin: The Body of Christ) was a much later medieval devotion, designed to spread belief in Christ's real presence in the bread and the wine. Abolished at the Reformation, the feast has been reintroduced as an optional

---

[52] 1 Cor 11.20-22.

observance. We shall see as the story proceeds how this meal given by Jesus to his followers as a sign of unity has been the cause of tragic divisions among Christians. At this early stage, it was a simple ritual which linked Christians as the movement spread through the Roman Empire, and enabled them to meet and recognise each other as brothers and sisters.

STEPHEN. 26th December.

As the little community grew, it became, inevitably, more difficult to administer. New believers contributed their wealth to a common fund, from which a growing number of widows and orphans were supported. When tension began to arise between natives of Jerusalem and converts from outside about alleged unfairness in the way this largesse was distributed, the apostles organised the appointment of seven deacons, administrative officers to oversee the church's funds and leave the apostles free to preach and baptise[53]. Of these seven, the dominant character was Stephen – clever, unafraid of conflict, and with a 'face like an angel'[54]. It was not long before Stephen clashed with Jews opposed to the new Jesus movement. Brought, like Jesus before him, before the Council, he defended himself by an uncompromising attack, claiming, as the distinguishing mark of his own Jewish people, a perpetual, wilful misunderstanding of God's will, and announcing that because of Jesus the Temple and its sacrificial cult were redundant (the apostles themselves were still attending Temple services at this time). Outrage grew into anger and Stephen was lynched, being dragged outside the city and stoned to death. The first martyr (reverting to the angelic side of his nature) died forgiving his murderers.[55]

THE CONVERSION OF ST PAUL. 25th January.

Among those who witnessed the death of Stephen was a young Pharisee who had come to Jerusalem to study from his native city of Tarsus. Saul quickly became one of most energetic activists in the campaign to stamp out the new movement, yet within a very few

---

[53] Acts 6.3-4.
[54] Acts 6.15.
[55] Acts 7.60.

months of Stephen's death Saul of Tarsus would himself be asking for baptism in the name of Jesus. His conversion was an event second only to the resurrection of Jesus in ensuring the success of the young Christian movement and the shape it would ever afterwards bear.

The story of Saul's conversion is told three times in the Acts of the Apostles[56] and alluded to frequently in his own letters. Leading an expedition to Damascus to arrest followers of Jesus there, Saul was suddenly struck down by a seizure which blinded him. He heard the voice of Jesus asking 'Why do you persecute me?' and was led a broken man into Damascus. There he was visited by a Christian, Ananias, who prayed with him, restored his sight, and baptised him.

Saul always maintained that his meeting with Jesus at the gate of Damascus was no vision or inner experience but an actual encounter with the risen Christ, on a level with the Easter experiences of the twelve, and constituting a direct commission to him which gave him the same apostolic status as those Jesus had called in his lifetime[57].

In natural terms, the physical mechanism by which the revelation was made seems to have been a sudden seizure which had a permanent ill effect on Saul's eyesight, despite the partial cure effected by the prayers of Ananias. We find from his letters that he was humiliated in Galatia by an illness connected with his sight[58] and that when he wrote himself rather than dictating (his usual course) he had to form unusually large letters[59]. Many people think that this recurring problem with his sight was the thorn in the flesh from which he three times besought the Lord to deliver him[60].

Although the conversion itself was so sudden and dramatic as to become proverbial, it was followed by a prolonged period of obscurity in which Saul attempted very little. He spent time in Arabia and when he did try to take part in preaching and public

---

[56] Acts 9.1ff; 22.1ff; 26.12ff.
[57] 1 Cor 15.8-10.
[58] Galatians 4.13-15.
[59] Gal 6.11.
[60] 2 Cor 12.7-8.

activity was politely but firmly sent home to Tarsus where he could do little damage[61]. At this stage, the Christians were not all sure that they wanted Saul to be converted. His energy and vision, at all stages of his life, made things difficult for those called to be his companions.

LAMMAS DAY. 1st August BCP.
The persecution launched by Saul and others did not cease with Saul's conversion. The Christian community was scattered from its base in Jerusalem and little groups were beginning to be established all over Syria (including, as we have seen, Damascus). In Jerusalem itself the apostles continued to meet in the house of the Last Supper and the church continued to grow.

In 44AD Herod Agrippa I made a bid for popularity among his Jewish subjects by becoming active in the fight against the new movement. This Herod was a nephew of Herod Antipas, the king who beheaded John the Baptist, and had been educated at Rome as a client prince and hostage, along with the future Emperor Claudius. Now that Claudius was emperor, Herod returned to his country strong in imperial favour. We have already seen how he arrested and beheaded James the brother of John, and he proceeded to strike at the heart of the church by arresting Peter himself.

Peter had become the undoubted leader of the church, fulfilling Jesus' promise that he would be the rock against which the gates of hell would not prevail. His arrest was a severe blow to the little community. His miraculous rescue from prison is related in Acts 12, after which Peter soon disappears from the New Testament story. He appears to have left the Jerusalem church in the care of James the Less and to have travelled to Antioch, which was the third greatest city of the Roman Empire and rapidly becoming the most dynamic of the Christian churches. We shall meet him again at the end of his life in Rome.

The chains with which Peter was unsuccessfully bound become objects of reverence in later centuries; Gregory the Great liked to send filings from them enclosed in little gold keys to his

---

[61] Acts 9.30.

favoured connections. A day in honour of the chains was established, Vinculamas (Vincula being Latin for chain) which became popularly shortened to Lammas. At the beginning of August, it became an agricultural feast of first fruits, when the first sheaf of the new harvest was presented in church. Lovers of English country lore have made periodic efforts to revive its observance, but for the majority of supermarket shoppers, one harvest festival a year seems to be enough, and Lammas Day is unlikely ever to be more than a footnote in the calendar.

BARNABAS. 11th June.

We have seen how Saul was not exactly welcomed with open arms into the Christian church. Some doubt was natural; very few groups would welcome a notorious persecutor into their inmost councils without suspicion. Saul was sponsored by a remarkable man, Joseph of Cyprus, known to all the Christians by his nickname, Barnabas, Mr Helpful.

Barnabas was one of the earliest converts after Pentecost, and sold his estate in Cyprus to give the proceeds to the apostles[62]. He was a natural team player, gifted at seeing and bringing out the potential of others. When news came to Jerusalem that the church in Antioch was baptising gentiles (non-Jews) and admitting them as Christians without requiring them to keep the Jewish law, the first great division in the church opened up. The earliest followers of Jesus assumed that they would continue to live as Jews and the thought of people claiming to be Christians while making no effect to conform to Jesus' own Jewish culture was profoundly disturbing. In these circumstances, it was to Barnabas that the apostles turned. He had the tact, the skill and the vision to visit Antioch, assess what was going on, and to give it the approval of the mother church – though this battle was far from won. As he watched the exciting growth of the Antioch church, Barnabas remembered the controversial convert Saul who had been sent home to Tarsus and realised that his gifts

---

[62] Acts 4.32.

were needed in Antioch. He brought Saul to the city, stood his sponsor and together with him became a leader in the church[63].

It is not entirely clear how leaders were appointed at this early stage. Like Saul/Paul, Barnabas is referred to as an apostle, a term which was now being applied beyond the original twelve to describe church leaders and particularly the missionary founders of churches. But appointments were not being made from the top down. So rapidly was Christianity spreading that institutions and leadership patterns were being improvised as need arose, although such developments were usually reported back to Jerusalem for apostolic approval. The churches of Antioch and Rome were both founded by unknown persons, presumably Christian merchants and travellers, although they received visits from apostles once they were established to confirm them in their Christian identity

The church leaders in Antioch now commissioned two of their number, Saul and Barnabas, to be missionary travellers and they were sent off, taking with them a young cousin of Barnabas, Mark.

These missionary journeys were not completely blind leaps into the unknown. As practising Jews, Saul and Barnabas could be sure of a welcome at synagogues wherever they went and existing Jewish communities were nearly always the places where new Christian groups were seeded. What is more, the apostles tended naturally to go where they had contacts, so the first missionary journey began by returning to Barnabas' home province, the island of Cyprus. It was on this island that the missionaries had a great coup, converting the governor, Sergius Paulus, the first member of the Roman ruling class that we know of to become a Christian.

It has been plausibly argued that this conversion not only determined the direction the missionaries next took but also holds the key to the mystery of why Saul suddenly became known as Paul, as he does halfway through the story of his visit to Cyprus. Sergius Paulus had family estates in Galatia, now part of Turkey, and it was to the obscure cities of Lystra, Iconium and Derbe, that Paul and Barnabas now headed, precisely the area where clients and tenants of Sergius Paulus would be ready to receive them. Could it be that Saul

---

[63] Acts 11.22-26.

was adopted or in some way legally associated with his eminent convert, taking his name as a means of opening up Roman society for his message?[64]

The mission to Galatia established Christian churches against fierce opposition from Jews who could not accept the new teaching. So tough was the going that young Mark abandoned the mission and returned to Jerusalem. This was the beginning of a rift between Paul and Barnabas, for when, after their return to Antioch, Paul suggested revisiting the churches they had founded, Barnabas, ever one to give a second chance to an outsider, wanted to take Mark again. For Paul, the man had proved his untrustworthiness and he objected strongly to taking the weakling. So the apostles went their separate ways and, as the Acts of the Apostles follows Paul, we lose sight of Barnabas. He and Mark returned again to Cyprus and there, in about 61AD, Barnabas is said to have been martyred. His tomb can still be visited, but as it is in the Turkish part of the island, there is no local Christian community to tend it. A caretaker will unlock the gate for you to descend into the little vault and will sit on the steps and smoke while you look at the unmarked, unhonoured slab which marks the resting place of the man whose generosity of spirit determined the very name by which he is remembered.

MARK. 25th April.
What became of Mark, the failed missionary, who was the cause of the split between Barnabas and Paul? His connection with the church went right back to the earliest days, for his mother, yet another Mary, owned the house in Jerusalem, almost certainly the house of the Last Supper, where the apostles and the first Christians met[65]. Indeed, some have speculated that Mark himself was the mysterious young man, only mentioned in Mark's gospel, who followed Jesus to the Garden of Gethsemane and ran away naked when the guards tore his linen robe off him[66]. We have seen how Mark accompanied his cousin Barnabas on the first missionary journey and how he felt

---

[64] See Robin Lane Fox 'Pagans and Christians' p.293 for a detailed examination of Paul's relations with Sergius Paulus.
[65] Acts 12.12.
[66] Mark 14.51.

unable to complete the task. After he returned to Cyprus with Barnabas, we catch three glimpses of him, two in scripture and one in tradition.

It is good to know that he made peace with Paul and was one of those who visited him during his last imprisonment[67]. We also find him working with Peter in Rome[68] and it is here, according to tradition, that he wrote his gospel, basing it on the memories of Peter. The book was written about 68AD shortly after the death of Peter and is usually regarded as the earliest of the four gospels.

After this, Mark is supposed to have travelled to Alexandria, in Egypt, one of the greatest cities in the Roman Empire, where he was one of the founders of the Christian church there, and where he was martyred and buried. When the city fell to the Muslims, centuries later, Mark's bones were rescued and brought to Venice, where they now rest in the basilica which bears his name.

Mark's gospel is his lasting gift to the church. A short book, written in abrupt, unliterary Greek, he tells the story of Jesus' ministry and death with great rapidity, emphasising Jesus' restless wanderings and the bewilderment of the disciples and others as they tried to make sense of this astonishing man. Mark's account of the crucifixion is stark; Jesus is portrayed as abandoned by everybody, even God; and Mark's account of the Resurrection is ambiguous. The women meet a young man at the tomb and, having heard his message, they leave filled with fear. The sense of awe at the mighty things God was doing in Jesus dominates the gospel.

TIMOTHY. 26th January.

The dispute about the right place of gentiles within the church had not been resolved by the diplomacy of Barnabas or even by the visit of Peter himself to Antioch. When Paul and Barnabas returned from the first missionary journey they went up to Jerusalem to take part in what later became known as the Council of Jerusalem, the first time the whole church met together to settle a controversy. The issue provoked strong feelings. To gentile converts, it seemed self evident

---

[67] 2 Timothy 4.11.
[68] 1 Peter 5.13..

that they had been baptised into Jesus Christ and had received a new freedom as children of God, a freedom which had its own validity, irrespective of any tradition or code of customs, however venerable. The Jewish Christians of Jerusalem, on the other hand, were appalled to see centuries of loyal obedience to God, customs for which Jews had laid down their lives in martyrdom, the way of life which had safeguarded the holiness of the people of God over generations, all about to be jettisoned for the doubtful gain of welcoming into the church people with no moral or spiritual tradition, who must compromise the purity of the movement and make it harder for Jews to accept what God was offering his chosen people through Jesus. The issue was decided by Peter's strong words in support of the gentile Christians, the practical testimony of Paul and Barnabas about the work of the Holy Spirit in non-Jewish lives and the decisive intervention of James the Less, the leader of the Jerusalem church and champion of the traditionalists[69]. Agreement was reached that while Christian Jews would continue to live in the way of their ancestors, keeping the food laws and observing the customs like circumcision and the Sabbath, no such requirement should be laid on gentile converts, who were only required to abjure idolatry, observe the taboo against eating blood and accept Jewish standards of sexual morality.

Like most compromises, this one, while it succeeded in the short term in holding together the church, was quickly overtaken by events. The church would shortly be dominated by gentiles who would become increasingly intolerant of any remaining Jewish customs; the Jews who rejected Jesus hardened their resistance to the Nazarenes so that it became difficult and finally impossible for Christian Jews to worship in the synagogue, and the unhappy story of mutual distrust and hatred between the sister religions was launched.

The attempt of the apostles to create a society where two groups, each pursuing different ways of life with a good conscience, could live together as brothers and sisters, was defeated by human obstinacy, intolerance and fear. It would not be until modern times that similar experiments would be tried; for most of Christian history

---

[69] Acts 15.

it would be assumed that unity meant uniformity, and this assumption made persecution a fatally attractive option.

We return to Paul who, after his separation from Barnabas and Mark, made his way back to Galatia to revisit his converts there. At Lystra, he met a young man who was both to provide a test case for the compromise agreed at the Council of Jerusalem, and would also be one of Paul's dearest friends for the rest of his life. Timothy was the child of a mixed marriage. His Jewish mother and grandmother had brought him up with a thorough knowledge of the scriptures[70], but his pagan father appears to have vetoed his proper participation in Judaism; in particular, Timothy had never been circumcised, an operation which the Greeks and Romans regarded with peculiar disgust. Paul had just fought, and fought hard, for the right of the gentile converts not to undergo this painful rite. Nevertheless, as Timothy was Jewish, Paul made sure that at his baptism, he was circumcised[71].

Timothy appears in the writings of Paul as young, inexperienced and lacking in self-confidence. Nevertheless, the older and the younger man became devoted friends and Timothy was one of Paul's most trusted lieutenants. As Paul travelled through Asia Minor and Greece, founding and supporting an ever-expanding network of little congregations, he needed people he could rely on to carry messages, assess the nature of problems, adjudicate disputes and bring back news to Paul. These duties Timothy loyally performed, while giving the celibate apostle the human companionship he needed. Paul calls him his son and loved him as such.

When Paul was imprisoned, Timothy was left in charge of the church in Ephesus, where he received two letters of guidance and encouragement from his friend. He is supposed to have been martyred in that city.

---

[70] 2 Timothy 1.5.
[71] Acts 16.1-3.

LUKE. 18th October.

Another of Paul's closest allies was the physician Luke, who may well have first come to know him as doctor for his perennial eyesight problems. Luke is the writer, not only of the gospel which bears his name, but also of the Acts of the Apostles, from which much of our knowledge of these earliest days is derived. Unobtrusively, he marks out the events of which he himself was an eyewitness by three accounts of journeys in which the narrative switches from 'they' to 'we'. The first of the passages occurs when Paul has made his way through Asia Minor to Troas on the Hellespont[72]. We may assume it was there then that Paul and Luke first met, and that Luke accompanied Paul on his historic journey across the narrow strip of sea into Macedonia. For the first time the gospel was preached in Europe, the continent destined to be the heartland of Christianity. Luke accompanied Paul as he preached in the great Greek cities, Athens and Corinth, places of unrivalled cultural status within the Roman empire. He was with Paul too on his final voyage back to Judaea. Always preoccupied with the problem of maintaining unity between the old Jewish Christians in James' Jerusalem and the new congregations he had founded all round the Aegean, Paul had made a collection from his Greek churches to assist the poor in Jerusalem. How the Jerusalem Christians came to be so poor we do not know. It is tempting to speculate that the early idealistic days of communal living, when Stephen distributed money to the poor and Barnabas sold his estates, had left the church with no capital and a large number of members used to regular free meals. For Paul, the collection was supremely important; it was to be a practical demonstration that for all the divergence of their traditions, the gentile churches loved and revered the mother church in Jerusalem.

Unfortunately, the plan backfired. After a cautiously friendly welcome from James, Paul's presence at worship in the Temple caused a riot and Paul was arrested for his own safety. He remained in prison in Caesarea for two years while a complicated legal wrangle ran its course, with the Jewish priests seeking to have him tried in the religious courts as a blasphemer, the Roman governor using delaying

---

[72] Acts 16.10.

tactics in the hope of being handsomely bribed by all parties, and Paul, knowing that he could not expect a fair trial in Jerusalem, exercising his right as a Roman citizen to press for his case to be heard in Rome.

All this time Luke was with him. What was he doing during these two years? At the beginning of his gospel he states that he had been careful to speak to eye-witnesses. It seems probable then that during his stay in the land where Jesus had lived and died, he met and interviewed as many people he could find who had known Jesus. In particular, from earliest times, it has been believed that he met and spoke to the elderly Virgin Mary, thus gathering the memories he worked up into those wonderful stories, unique to Luke, of the Annunciation, the Visitation, the Christmas shepherds, Simeon and Anna. Luke was even supposed to have painted Mary's portrait, thus becoming patron saint of painters as well as doctors; several churches claimed to possess this portrait from life, but sadly all the works have proved to be much later, Byzantine pieces.

Another person Luke must surely have met, as implied in Paul's letter to Timothy, was Mark, for Mark's gospel has clearly been used by him as a principal source for his own writing. Luke combined Mark's work with the lost collection of Jesus' sayings called 'Q' (deriving, as we have seen, perhaps from an Aramaic book by Matthew) and enriched his work with the other information he had gathered. As well as the Christmas stories, we owe uniquely to Luke such key parables as the Prodigal Son and the Good Samaritan, together with the story of Jesus having his feet washed by the sinful woman who might not have been Mary Magdalene.

Luke's gospel gives the gentlest and most lovable portrait of Jesus, always stressing his compassion, his love for women, children and the poor, and his role as the one who ushers in the age of the Holy Spirit. The Acts of the Apostles, which continues the story, has sometimes been called the Acts of the Holy Spirit, for Luke's conviction was that the same Jesus who taught and healed in human form in Galilee, now continued his work through the Holy Spirit in the life of the church.

Luke accompanied Paul again when his case was finally referred to Rome, shared with him in a dramatic shipwreck off Malta, and arrived with him in the capital city of the Empire, where he was allowed to attend to his patient under a fairly gentlemanly house arrest.

PAUL. 29th June.

Since his conversion, we have followed the exploits of Paul through the eyes of his companions and fellow labourers. It is time to assess more fully the achievement of this remarkable man, who deserves to be called the second founder of Christianity.

From the day of his conversion, Paul was devoted to the spread of the Christian gospel throughout the world. His were the gifts of a pioneer; he was always eager to press on into unknown territory, starting a church where no church had ever been. But even if that was his primary calling, he soon became caught up in an increasing burden of pastoral work as his Christians wrote to him asking for his guidance and adjudication on matters of controversy. He was a man on fire, utterly absorbed in his task and inclined to be short with those whose zeal did not match his own. He never married and supported himself on his travels by plying his trade of tent-making. He is described in tradition as a short, bandy-legged man with a big nose and gleaming black eyes.

Throughout his ministry, Paul fought with passionate anger two linked battles. One was for the right of gentiles to be accepted as full members of the church, and in this battle he became increasingly hardline about his own Jewish heritage, analysing with growing radicalism the shortcomings of religion based on law, and exploring the freedom bestowed by the Holy Spirit on those who had been born again into new life in Christ. Again and again he emphasised the utter newness of Christian living, so that no previous loyalties, whether of race, social class or religious tradition could bind a Christian: 'Owe no man anything but to love one another, for love is the fulfilling of the law'[73]. Most radically of all, Paul argued the primacy of faith as the judge of conduct. If someone acted with good conscience, believing sincerely that what they did was pleasing to Christ, then their actions could not be called sinful, however many

---

[73] Romans 13.8.

man-made regulations and customs were breached. On the other hand, 'whatever does not proceed from faith is sin'[74], so that a person who disobeyed their own conscience out of respect for institutions or fear of criticism was sinning, even if those about him described his action as virtue. Not even Paul himself dared face full on the implications of this rejection of law for the way religious institutions are run. His vision of society was essentially a conservative one, in which people gladly accepted their traditional roles and a community was held together by deference and obedience. There is, therefore, a continual tension in his writings between his exhortations to his Christians to be law-abiding and dutiful, and his radical conviction that anyone set free by Christ is no longer bound by any law except the law of love. This tension has led to a bitter irony. In the modern era, in successive centuries, subjects of absolute monarchies (17th/18th century), slaves (18th/19th centuries), women (19th/20th centuries) and gay and lesbian Christians (20th/21st centuries) have sought the liberty which Paul proclaims with such radiant force: 'neither Jew nor Greek, slave nor free, male nor female – but you are all one in Christ Jesus'[75]. In each struggle, the forces of conservatism have rallied behind verses of the same St.Paul to express their belief that God wills the status quo. When Paul said that he wanted to be 'all things to all men'[76], this was probably not what he had in mind.

Those among the early Christians who were disturbed by Paul's teaching attempted to undermine it by personal attacks on the apostle. He was not, after all, of the number of those who had known Jesus personally, and his claims to be an apostle were therefore, they said, spurious. Paul's second battle, therefore, was a constant maintaining of his own authority, of the divine authenticity of his vision at Damascus and of his right to expect obedience from his converts. His passion gets the better of him at times, but we must recognise that what was at stake was not his personal prestige, but the promotion of his teaching, his interpretation of what the death and resurrection of Jesus really meant, the very liberty of the human race, which the Son of God had died to purchase and which timorous

---

[74] Romans 14.23.
[75] Galatians 3.28.
[76] 1 Cor 9.22.

souls, obsessed with controlling people's ritual observances, were trying to claw back and destroy.

Paul was a complex man with little of the direct, simple beauty of character of Jesus, and it is fashionable in many Christian circles to dislike him and avoid grappling with his message. But the heart of the man is not to be found in his battles and controversies, but in his shining conviction that in Christ God has saved, not the world simply, but even him, the worst of sinners. His love for Christ, his awe-struck delight in the miracle of regeneration worked by the Holy Spirit, his selfless dedication to the way of love, these are the themes which recur again and again in his writings; 'Far be it from me to glory except in the cross of our Lord Jesus Christ, by which the world has been crucified to me and I to the world'[77]. 'We are joint heirs with Christ, provided we suffer with him in order that we may also be glorified with him'[78]. 'I count everything as loss because of the surpassing worth of knowing Christ Jesus my Lord'[79].

His letters are the oldest documents in the New Testament, written twenty or thirty years after the Crucifixion. They are not theological treatises, but real letters, written in response to pressing, topical problems, and gems such as those we have quoted arise out of often obscure arguments. The letters to the Thessalonians, Galatians, Corinthians, Romans and Philippians are universally accepted as being by Paul; the other letters may be by him or by imitators or disciples. Philippians was written from prison as he waited to be tried for his life, and of all his letters is most consistent in its sense of joyous trust in Christ and deep love for his church family.

Paul was finally tried at Rome in 66AD, the year of the great fire which destroyed much of the city. The Emperor Nero was popularly accused of starting the fire deliberately so that he could 'fiddle while Rome burned', and was glad to deflect blame onto a group even less popular than himself: the Christians. Paul, as a Roman citizen, was granted the comparatively civilised death of being beheaded by a sword, and his body is buried in the basilica which bears his name.

---

[77] Gal 6.19.

[78] Romans 8.17.

[79] Philippians 3.8.

TITUS. 26th January.

Among the many helpers of St.Paul mentioned in the New Testament, one more is honoured with a feast day, Titus, whom Paul seems to have met at an early stage in his career. He accompanied Paul to the Council of Jerusalem and as a gentile convert was an early beneficiary of the liberty granted not to be circumcised[80]. He seems to have been reliable and discreet, and was later of great help to Paul in his negotiations with the Corinthian church.   This church had among its members a large number of strong characters and individualists, and the congregation exercised great gifts of the Holy Spirits, which led to various leaders claiming extraordinary authority. When Paul had to intervene to excommunicate a member who was living a life of flagrant immorality, Titus became a sort of shuttle diplomat, bringing the parties together[81].

When Paul was imprisoned, Titus began an apparently unrewarding period as leader of a difficult church in Crete. Appointments such as this show how by the end of the apostolic period, patterns of church leadership were solidifying.   It was increasingly common for each church to be led by a single man, supported by a college of elders and now usually called the Overseer or Bishop.

THE VIRGIN MARY. 15th August.

We only catch one glimpse in the New Testament of Mary after her Son's resurrection from the dead. She is last seen praying with the apostles as they wait for the Holy Spirit at Pentecost[82]. On the cross, Jesus with his dying breath had commended her to the care of John, the disciple whom he loved, and tradition asserts that Mary accompanied John to Ephesus, where he preached in his old age. Mary's house, on the hills above Ephesus, can still be visited. It is the only place in the world where Roman Catholic and Muslim places of prayer are accommodated under the same roof; for Muslims, while denying the godhead of Jesus, believe in the virgin birth of the last prophet before Mohammed, and give great honour to the Virgin

---

[80] Gal 2.3.

[81] 2Cor 7.6-7.

[82] Acts 1.14.

Mary. It is quite an experience to pass from the ornate gaudiness of the Christian chapel through the plain doorway into the austere mosque, and to reflect on how different history would have been had Christians and Muslims always been able to co-exist so harmoniously

Traditions diverge as to whether Mary died in Ephesus or in Jerusalem, where the cave where she died can be viewed at the foot of the Mount of Olives. It was early believed (and is now a doctrine of faith for Roman Catholics) that she was granted the same privilege as the prophet Elijah and was taken body and soul into heaven, thus being exempted from the need to be raised from the dead on Judgement Day. Catholic countries keep 15th August as the Assumption of the Virgin Mary, and around this pious belief another marvellous set of legends accumulated. Gabriel brought Mary a palm branch from Paradise as a sign that the end was near. The apostles were miraculously transported from their various mission fields back to Jerusalem to attend her funeral. The celestial palm branch was carried in front of her coffin as protection against the malice of the Jewish authorities; an officer who attempted to stop the ceremony had his hand miraculously stuck to the coffin until he was released by a touch of the palm branch. The next day, the apostles found Mary's tomb empty and full of roses. Predictably, it was Thomas who refused to believe that she had been raised until granted a vision of Mary seated in the heavenly places; she gave Thomas her girdle as proof, and this was in great demand by pregnant woman, as by binding it around their waists they might hope to ease their labour pains.

Whatever may be thought of this highly coloured account, it is certain that no one has ever attempted to show bones of Mary for veneration Something of her distinguished career after death will be traced in what follows. She has appeared many times to give advice, or warning, and in doing so has initiated places of pilgrimage. The most famous of these in England is Walsingham, where just before the Norman conquest the lady of the manor, Richeldis, was directed by Mary to build an exact replica of her house in Nazareth. The replica was itself reproduced in the twentieth century and is still the focus for pilgrimage and prayer. In modern times, Mary has appeared at Lourdes, at Fatima and at Medjugorje, always in remote mountainous areas, and always to children. For many Christians, her motherly love is a source of spiritual strength second only to the love of Jesus himself.

PETER. 29th June.

We are drawing to the end of the apostolic age, and return to two others who knew Jesus best and were loved by him most intimately.

We have already seen much of Peter's achievement both before and after the crucifixion. On the night of Jesus' arrest, his nerve failed him and he denied three times that he even know Jesus; the incident is one of the very few related in all four gospels, and clearly left a permanent mark of shame on Peter. We may speculate that it was this experience of being broken, and then restored by the risen Christ, which transformed Peter from the rather bumptious spokesman for the apostles we meet in the gospels, self-reliant (and nearly always wrong), into the spirit-filled, steady, trustworthy leader portrayed in Acts.

We know that Peter visited Antioch and was attacked by Paul there for his lack of resolution in maintaining the rights of Paul's beloved gentiles[83]. Tradition makes him the first Bishop of Antioch, and the cave where he supposedly preached and baptised can still be visited in the old city – the way up to it is filled with rubble and weeds, but the present writer was guided unerringly by some local children, who also displayed the gigantic carved head of the Virgin in the cliff face.

Leaving Antioch, Peter travelled to Rome, where he led the church for several years, only to meet a martyr's death in the same persecution of Nero which brought St Paul to the block. A much loved legend tells how Peter was urged by the church to leave the city until the persecution had died down. But outside the walls, he met Christ carrying his cross and asked him 'Quo vadis? Where are you going?' The Lord replied, 'To Rome, to be crucified a second time in your place.' Peter took the hint and returned to the city and his death. As a peasant lacking the privileges of citizenship, he was sentenced to be crucified. His response was, 'I am not worthy to die in the

---

[83] Gal 2.11.

same way my Lord died', and the executioners with brutal wit turned his cross upside down.

Over Peter's tomb on the Vatican hill, a huge shrine has been built, housed within the massive grandeur of the Basilica. The contrast of all this pomp with the humble life of the fisherman turned preacher is striking, but modern tests carried out on his bones have made it plausible to believe that they are indeed the remains of Simon called Peter from Bethsaida in Galilee.

ST JOHN BEFORE THE LATIN GATE. 6th May BCP.

In the Prayer Book calendar, St John is given a second feast day, which commemorates the traditional beliefs about what happened to him in his old age. Legend tells that Nero, having dealt with Peter and Paul, brought John too to trial. At the Latin Gate of Rome, the apostle was sentenced to be boiled alive. But by miracle, the water refused to hurt John, whose sentence was commuted to banishment on the island of Patmos. Nero's agents attempted to poison him, but John prayed over the cup and the poison did him no harm; it is for this reason that he is often shown in art charming a snake from a chalice.

The Bible certainly presents John as an old man living in exile on Patmos and this was the site of the extraordinary series of visions recorded in the Book of Revelation. The Book combined coded attacks on the persecuting Roman empire with thrilling visions of God's glory in heaven and Christ's victory shared by those called to die as martyrs.

We have already looked briefly at the controversy over whether John was the author of the gospel attributed to him. Similar questions hang over the authorship of Revelation, not least because the differences in style between the Gospel and Revelation are so extreme as to make it hard to imagine both coming from one pen. John's gospel was written in the last years of the First Century when the apostle was a very old man. While the narrative reads plausibly (as it is claimed to be) as the account of an eye-witness of Jesus' life, the teaching is a profound meditation on the meaning of Jesus. Taking favourite images from Jesus' parables (the good shepherd, bread of life, the vine), John draws out from them dialogues which touch at the very heart of the mystery of Christ. No book has had a more searching effect on the meditations, prayers and theology of later Christians than the gospel of John.

Of all the twelve apostles, John is the only one who did not die a martyr's death. He lived to extreme old age in Ephesus and it is said that when he was too frail to preach anything approaching a sermon, he would have himself carried into the congregation and would say simply, over and over again, 'Little children, love each other.'

PART THREE. BIRTH OF AN ILLEGAL RELIGION.

CLEMENT (died 100AD) 23rd November.

With St.John died the last of those who had known Jesus in the flesh. The second Christian century was one in which the foundations laid by the apostles were built upon, always in the shadow of threatened persecution. We get the impression of little Christian groups meeting throughout the empire, secretly in larger houses of the members, yet manifesting an impressive unity and power of organisation.

One of the believers whom Paul commended to his Philippians, was a young man named Clement[84], who went on to became Bishop of Rome. To call him Pope at this stage would be an anachronism, yet it is clear that at Rome, as in most of the larger Christian communities, an ordered succession of leaders had emerged by the end of the first century. Each bishop was consecrated for his duties by the laying on of hands of other bishops, and each led his church with the support of a college of presbyters supported by deacons who (like Stephen) assisted the bishop in practical tasks of church maintenance. Most bishops only cared for the church in one town, so their knowledge of their people was much more intimate than that of modern bishops, who guide dioceses the size of counties. The bishop would preside at the Eucharist every Sunday and would personally baptise all the converts of his church, at this time overwhelmingly adults.

All we know for certain of Clement is what we can deduce from his surviving letters to the Corinthian church. He writes exhorting them to unity and to mutual love. Certain passages are remarkably similar to the famous hymn to love which St Paul wrote to the same church a generation before, and it is disappointing to see that the same problems were still emerging despite such apostolic intervention. Clement's action in writing to the Corinthians shows how the bishops, as well as leading their own churches, supported each other and felt free to intervene in the life of other churches. Certain large churches, notably Rome, Antioch and Alexandria were already being looked to for leadership in their areas and it is on such

---

[84] Phil 4.3.

acknowledged primacy that the modern claims of the papacy were built.

According to legend, Clement was banished to the labour camps on the north coast of the Black Sea, where he was martyred by being tied to an anchor and drowned. It was believed that every year, on the anniversary of his death, the sea was miraculously parted so that pilgrims could visit the underwater shrine, built by angels (mer-angels?), where his body rested. Jacobus Voragine, in the thirteenth century, comments rather disingenuously that the miracle had ceased to occur by his time, he presumed because of the sinfulness of the inhabitants of the Crimea[85].

IGNATIUS OF ANTIOCH   (35-107) 18th October.

A few years after the death of Clement, there arrived in Rome a bishop of Antioch named Ignatius. He had been sent in chains across the empire to stand trial in Rome and be thrown to the lions in the amphitheatre.

The Roman authorities found it hard to understand what they were dealing with in Christianity. They were tolerant of the religions of their subject peoples unless, as with the druids, who practised human sacrifice, they found aspects of their cult disgusting. They had been particularly tolerant of the peculiar, monotheistic religion of the Jews. Several things made them uneasy about Christianity once they realised that it was not merely a variant form of Judaism. It was not an ancestral religion but a new faith; it did not belong to one tribe but claimed converts from all peoples. Nor was it a personal philosophy which the convert could happily hold in conjunction with the religion of his ancestors; Christianity claimed the absolute loyalty of its people and this meant that every convert was expected to make a violent break with his family and city. To understand what this meant, it must be remembered that pagan religion permeated every aspect of life; every significant moment was marked by traditional sacrifices and rituals. A Christian convert could no longer go out to dinner (where the menu would consist of animals sacrificed to the gods); go to the theatre (plots based on pagan mythology); hold

---

[85] The Golden Legend ch 171.

public office or join his family for celebrations such as birthdays, weddings or funerals. Nobody minded the Jews holding themselves aloof from the world around them, but when decent families were torn apart by this arrogant sect, it was no wonder people got worried. What is more, Christianity was a secret religion; only the baptised learned the mysteries of faith. In a world without weekends, Sunday worship took place very early in the morning or late at night before or after work, and, when the neighbours learned that at these secret meetings the members shared a kiss of peace with their brothers and sisters before eating the body and blood of Jesus, sinister rumours of incest and cannibalism gained a terrible plausibility.

Although Christianity was proscribed as an illegal religion, we should not think that persecution was unremitting. The Roman empire lacked the efficiency and ruthlessness of a modern totalitarian regime; there was no police force and no public prosecutor. It was up to individual governors to press for implementation of imperial decrees, which they did with more or less conviction. Individuals might bring accusations before the courts, but if Christians were well liked by their neighbours and ruled by lazy or tolerant governors, they had a remarkable if precarious freedom to live their faith fairly openly.

The career of Ignatius illustrates the curious mixture of threat and liberty under which the early Christians lived. During his journey to death from Antioch to Rome, he was entertained openly and with great honour by the Christian community in every town he passed through. The letters he wrote to encourage his fellow believers still survive; he appears to have had no difficulty writing them and having them delivered despite being surrounded by an armed guard whom he compares to ferocious leopards[86]. Ignatius' letters, like Clement's, reveal a church steadily consolidating its position and with an increasingly uniform hierarchy of leadership. A bishop himself, Ignatius urges obedience to the bishop as to Christ, and compares the presbyters to the apostles, whose authority they inherit, while the deacons in their servant ministry are signs to the people of Christ's living presence. All this was going on under the

---

[86] Ignatius Letter to the Romans 5.

noses of officials responsible for conducting Ignatius to his execution, yet no organised attempt was made to identify or round up the many who in the eyes of the law shared his guilt.

Ignatius' attitude to his coming death was remarkable. Both he and the Christians who cheered him on his way saw martyrdom as a victory. His faith in Christ and the resurrection was so intensely real that he had no fear and no regrets; to him martyrdom was a privilege, a guarantee that, being worthy to share Christ's sufferings, he would certainly share his resurrection. He even wrote ahead to the Roman church forbidding them to attempt to win him a reprieve. 'I want the lions to grind me with their teeth, that I may be found pure bread.[87]' This astonishing joy in the face of death struck many spectators with awe and was responsible for many conversions.

Ignatius died as he longed to, mauled by the lions as entertainment for the Roman crowd.

POLYCARP (died 155) 23rd February.

The next notable martyr was St Polycarp, the aged bishop of Smyrna. He was eighty-seven years old and like Ignatius appears to have been brought up a Christian from birth. Smyrna was one of the seven churches around Ephesus in Asia Minor to whom St John had addressed the Revelation, and as a child Polycarp had heard John preach. Now, as the authorities picked off leaders of the new sect, the old man was arrested and put on trial. The governor was anxious to obtain a public recantation and pleaded with Polycarp to save his life by offering sacrifice to the pagan gods. He replied, 'Eighty-six years I have served him, and he never did me wong. How can I blaspheme my king and my saviour?'[88] His sentence was to be burned alive, and he was escorted to the stake by a triumphant crowd of Christians. It seemed to eye-witnesses that Polycarp's body turned gold in the fire and that the flames were reluctant to consume him. But consumed he was, and when the soldiers had dispersed, a bizarre scene of devotion ensued as Christians scrambled to collect his ashes and charred remains as relics. Again, this took place publicly and no

---

[87] Ignatius, 'Letter to the Romans' 4.
[88] Martyrdom of Polycarp 9.

attempt was made to arrest the Christian rank and file. If the plan was to terrorise humbler believers by making savage examples of the bishops, it was backfiring spectacularly.

JUSTIN (died 150) 1st June.
Apart from bishops, most early victims of persecution were prominent people who drew attention to themselves. One such was Justin, who in Rome brought himself to official notice by presenting a reasoned defence of the new faith to the emperor.

Justin was a philosopher, whose baptism came as the climax of a lifetime of questing for the meaning of life. He studied in Athens, which had for the Romans about the same combination of heritage, old-world class and academic excellence as Oxford, Cambridge and Stratford-Upon-Avon do for an American. Athens was the faded but still loved home of philosophy, drama and the arts. There Justin studied progressively in the schools of Stoicism (an ethical philosophy designed to develop the virtues in order to live with integrity); Epicureanism (the philosophy that our efforts should be applied to what will make us truly happy); Pythagoreanism (an attempt to prove the immortality of the soul, combined with belief in reincarnation and numerology); and Platonism (the doctrine that the unseen world of spirit and ideas is more real than the material world, which is simply a transient shadow of things eternal). In none of these could Justin find rest. A chance meeting with an old man on a beach introduced him to the Christian church; he was entranced by the antiquity and wisdom of the Hebrew scriptures and impressed by the seriously virtuous life of the Christians, and accepted baptism.

Disappointingly, Justin could not be regarded as a philosopher of the first class. His writings have considerable importance, however. He is the first in a long line of Christian thinkers to attempt to marry New Testament Christianity to Platonism, then the dominant way of thinking about the world and to most contemporaries the noblest of the philosophies. Justin reflected on the first chapter of John, with its teaching that it was the Word, eternally with God, through whom all things were made, which became incarnate in Jesus. This Word (in Greek, 'logos') seemed to have affinity with Plato's theory of forms, the eternal truths which were imperfectly reflected in the actual good, true or beautiful things we can see. If everything is made through the Word, then everything has some power to reveal the nature of the Word to the world. What was exciting about Christianity was that it was available to all. Plato and his followers assumed that aristocratic leisure would be essential for the arduous intellectual exercise of learning to contemplate the forms, so that the spiritual world became more real to your soul than was the physical world to your senses. But thanks to the incarnation of the Logos, the philosophers' hidden world of truth was made accessible to everybody in the human life of Jesus. Workmen, slaves, women, children, all could be philosophers by being baptised into the eternal life of the Word made flesh.

The second reason why Justin is important lies in his immersion in the backstreet world where ordinary people were living the life of the Word made flesh. He wrote an apology – a defence of Christianity – and sent it to the Emperor. In it he attempts to dispel the wilder rumours which were circulating by describing in some detail what actually happened in Christian worship. So we learn that just a hundred years after the death of Jesus worship had already assumed the shape which is still familiar to us today. The services began with the singing of psalms, reading of scripture and preaching. The deacons then took a collection and led the people in prayer. After this, the un-baptised left the church while the committed Christians greeted each other with a sign of peace and celebrated Holy Communion. Justin also described a baptism, still at this stage performed by full immersion and normally with adult candidates. We gain a vivid impression of these little, illegal house churches, meeting after dark with intense joy and excitement to share the common life of Jesus.

Justin's apology not only failed to impress the emperor but led to his own arrest. As a Roman citizen and member of the upper classes he was granted, like St.Paul, death by beheading.

IRENAEUS (130-200) 28th June.
The martyrdom of Justin coincided with one of the periodic flare-ups of persecution in which serious attempts were made to round up large numbers of Christians. In 177, a purge of Lyons in the South of Gaul

brought death to the bishop and scores of other Christians. One important member of the Church escaped with his life for the simple reason that he happened to be away on business in Rome, and so was not at home when the soldiers called. So banal an escape emphasises how fitful and inefficient the Roman persecution was, for all its savagery. The lucky presbyter was Irenaeus, and once the persecution had died down he was ordained bishop by the Bishop of Rome and sent back to Lyons to rebuild the stricken church.

Irenaeus found himself Bishop of one of the largest cities in Roman Gaul – the amphitheatre where his predecessor had perished was proudly named 'The Theatre of the Three Gauls', so certain were the citizens that nowhere else in the province would be found an entertainment complex of such magnificence. Irenaeus' most pressing task was to reassemble and put fresh heart into the Christians scattered by the persecution, but he soon found that his principal opponents were not the Roman authorities but Christian heretics. His great book 'Against the Heresies' was written to confound that strange spiritual movement, in its day as influential as Christianity itself, called Gnosticism.

The word Gnosticism is a Greek word meaning knowledge; it is the opposite of 'A-gnosticism', lack of knowledge. Gnostics might or might not think of themselves as Christian (those Irenaeus knew about probably did) but their spirituality was built around the belief that a secret knowledge had been revealed to them which enabled them to transcend the world of sense which those without the knowledge fondly supposed to be the real world. Irenaeus uses (a modern reader might feel) an excessive amount of space laying out the beliefs of the different Gnostic movements. We may summarise some of their common characteristics.

Just as Justin had begun to explore connections between Christianity and Platonism, the dominant philosophy of the day, so the Gnostics were heavily influenced by Plato's belief that the spiritual world of ideas was more real than the physical universe. They had elaborate mythological accounts of how from the pure abyss of being, chains of Aeons with abstract names (Silence, Light, Church, Father) constructed a bridge of connections to the world as we know it. At some point in most of these myths a terrible break in the bridge occurred, as one of the aeons (often Sophia, 'Wisdom') refused to accept its allotted place in the chain and rebelled, causing a dislocation, so that Sophia herself and those whose spiritual reality derived from her, found themselves lost in a world of sense. This world had been created, by accident or malice, by a being called the Demiurge (a Platonic word meaning Craftsman or Maker) who wished his created subjects to remain in ignorance of the chain of aeons above him and to worship him as the supreme God. Christian Gnostics believed that this Demiurge was the God of the Old Testament and, like too many modern Anglicans, saw the two Testaments as opposed to each other, with the vindictive, narrow God Jehovah being opposed by the altogether 'nicer', more spiritual Father of Jesus Christ. For Jesus was emphatically not the Son of the God of Abraham and Moses. He was a spiritual being who had descended from the realm of the aeons to enlighten with his teaching those in whom some sparks of the broken aeon Sophia remained. The enlightened were given secret teaching, supposedly derived from Jesus, which enabled them to rediscover their true selves, transcend the evil world of matter, and ascend into the realm which was their true home.

Regarding matter as evil, the Gnostics rejected any idea that the pure Jesus could have been contaminated by a physical existence. They regarded his appearance on earth as a pious charade. Jesus appeared to have a body but was in fact pure spirit, and the doctrines of his incarnation, crucifixion and resurrection the Gnostics regarded as disgusting, and looked upon their fellow Christians who believed such things as deluded persons still awaiting the inner enlightenment which would free them.

Gnosticism was to have a long history as the 'dark twin' of orthodox Christianity. Today Gnostic myths appeal largely to those who believe that 'the authorities', (the Demiurge and his servants, Christian bishops) are constantly busy suppressing dangerous truths, which a chosen band of secret initiates must keep alive. The recent so-called gospels discovered in Egypt (Thomas, Judas etc) are Gnostic texts dating from Irenaeus' lifetime and purporting to reveal truths about Jesus which the New Testament dared not tell. Gnostic ideas and a Gnostic attitude to the Church undergird such popular novels as Pullman's 'His Dark Materials' and Dan Brown's 'Da Vinci Code.'

Irenaeus opposed the Gnostics negatively by exposing the contradictions in their many and elaborate mythologies, and positively by stating energetically the Christian account of how the world came to be and the connection between the creation and the coming of Jesus.

Against the confusing medley of Gnostic belief, Irenaeus set the impressive unity of Christian faith throughout the world. All bishops, all churches, proclaimed the same truths. Irenaeus' summary of these truths is close to what we now call the 'Apostles Creed', which over the next two centuries would achieve its status as the normative summary of Christian beliefs. In particular, Irenaeus appealed to the authority of Rome as the mother church of the West with her impressive pedigree of bishops reaching in unbroken line back to the apostles Peter and Paul, all of whom had taught the same unvarying gospel. What room was there for a secret gospel which Peter had not known? The gospel he transmitted must be the true Christian faith. Unfortunately, there remained after Irenaeus at the very most a hundred years in which the unity of belief of Christian bishops could plausibly be appealed to as edifying. Ever since, bishops have been notorious for their disagreements with each other. Indeed 'committed' Christians today often bolster their sense of identity by a shared perception that their bishop is unorthodox or even heretical.

Irenaeus' positive restatement of the Christian gospel was profoundly creative. Despite its unhappiness, cruelty and sin, he had no hesitation in believing that this world was a good place, created for good purposes by a good God. God created Adam and Eve and placed them in the world so that they might grow into perfect happiness. Their failure to do this, and their choice of sinful ways instead, led to the incarnation of Christ, who as the second Adam recapitulated or relived the experiences of Adam, this time choosing the way of obedience to God which Adam had rejected. Irenaeus enjoyed drawing out the details of this scheme – Mary, the second Eve, listened to Gabriel instead of the serpent; Jesus, like Adam, was brought to a tree, the cross, but won life there instead of death. His vision of God's dealing with humanity is essentially an optimistic one; his most famous line is 'The glory of God is a human being truly alive.'

Irenaeus' version of the Adam and Eve story has acquired fresh resonance since the church came to terms with evolution as a scientific account of the beginnings of our race. He sees the first humans not as perfect beings living in a perfect world, which is then corrupted by sin, but as children created with the potential for perfection, a potential which is tragically not achieved because of the devil's deceit. Moreover Irenaeus does not see the incarnation as a rescue attempt, a mission which only became necessary once the perfect race had deviated from God's path. Rather it had always been God's intention to lead his human creatures to a point where a perfect union with himself could take place, and the incarnation would have happened (albeit less traumatically) had Adam and Eve never sinned.

This account of the beginnings and purpose of human life is much easier to harmonise with a Darwinian account of gradual growth and development than what was later regarded as the 'classic' version of the story, as preserved for example in Milton's 'Paradise Lost.'

Irenaeus is traditionally honoured as a martyr but there is no actual evidence that he met a violent end.

PART FOUR. MARTYRDOM.

THE EARLY MARTYRS
It will already be clear that most of the earliest Christian saints met a martyr's death. During the formative centuries of the church, martyrdom was the experience above all others which defined what it meant to be a Christian. We have seen how those who watched Polycarp burn eagerly collected his ashes for veneration. Similar scenes took place wherever martyrdoms occurred. The bodies of the victims were buried with great honour and their tombs became the focus for prayer and annual celebrations on the anniversary of their deaths. Each community cherished the legend of its own martyrs, who provided a direct link between themselves in their struggle after holiness and the heavenly kingdom where the martyrs rested victorious after their conflict. It was not long before martyrs were believed to intercede for their communities as heavenly patrons, and miracles were expected and experienced at their tombs. Much of the cult of the saints derives from this experience of vivid continuing contact between martyrs and their churches.

It is not surprising then that a high proportion of the best-known and best loved saints in the calendar are those who died under Roman persecution in the three centuries culminating in the terrible purge of Diocletian (303-304), the last attempt by the emperors to eradicate the new religion before the Empire acknowledged itself beaten and accepted Christianity as its official creed. The stories attached to these martyrs vary enormously in historical reliability. They include eyewitness accounts, descriptions in near-contemporary anniversary sermons and highly coloured stories worked up centuries after the events they affect to portray. The romanticising of martyrs is particularly marked in the case of women. The ingredients of a good martyr story were as formulaic and predictable in the Middle Ages as those of a Mills and Boon romance today. Readers knew what they wanted and writers made sure that they got it – endless variations on the tale of a young, beautiful, nobly-born girl, vowed to perpetual virginity and victorious in the midst of the wiles of treacherous suitors and the unbelievably sadistic cruelty of Roman governors. It is impossible to know how many of these tales derive from actual women of the Roman Empire who suffered for their faith.

In the accounts that follow we shall first look at two well-attested martyrdoms in Carthage where the writings of the victims themselves survive: then we shall summarise the martyrdoms of Rome where a high number of the remembered martyrs died; and finally we shall take a Cook's tour of the Empire from West to East. Although the historic personalities of these early heroes of the faith are hidden from us for ever by their legends, these are the stories which have fed the faith of millions over the centuries.

PERPETUA AND FELICITY(Died 203). 7th March.

Roman North Africa was one of the most prosperous regions of the empire, as its huge Roman remains, sticking up in the midst of the desert sands, still attest. It was then a well-wooded area, fertile enough to be second only to Egypt in importance as a supplier of grain to the capital. The principal city of the region was Carthage, and it was there that a group of Christians were martyred in 203. One of them, a young married woman named Perpetua, wrote an account of her experiences in prison, and this was supplemented by an eye-witness description of the death she endured, together with her slave Felicity, her brother Satyrus and two other male Christians. The 'Acts of Perpetua and Felicity' is interesting not only for its insight into the minds of the early martyrs and those who supported them, but also because of what it tells us of the way the Roman Games were organised. Perpetua's party were imprisoned under sentence of death for many weeks, waiting for a suitable festival for which they might provide the entertainment. Their situation was desperate. Perpetua had with her in prison her baby son whom she was breast-feeding; Felicity was heavily pregnant. Perpetua received visits in prison from her father, the only member of her family not a Christian, begging her for the sake of her family, to renounce her faith and come home. Curiously, her husband does not feature in the account. All the prisoners were filled with the same passionate enthusiasm as St Ignatius. Their only anxiety was that something might occur to prevent their acquiring the joy and honour of martyrdom. Perpetua records her dreams in prison. In one she climbed a ladder set with sharp knives, to find herself face to face with Jesus in a beautiful garden. She was able to wean her son and send him away with her father; her milk dried up the same night. Felicity, who as a pregnant woman would not have been allowed to be executed, gave birth prematurely a few days before the show, and she was able to give her baby to a Christian couple to be adopted, sure of her place in the execution party. These events were regarded as great answers to prayer.

We tend to assume that at the Games a good number of lions, tigers, gladiators and Christians were set loose in the arena to see who would be left standing at the end of the afternoon. The 'Acts' makes it clear that what spectators were actually offered was a carefully planned programme in which the species of animal each prisoner would face was advertised, together with the number of attacks they would be expected to endure. Those who survived their maulings were taken to sit in a 'safe area' called the Gate of Life. This was a formality for Perpetua's party, as all survivors were executed by gladiators at the end of the entertainment. It would be interesting to know if those at the Gate of Life were ever actually released. Presumably the interest for the spectators was seeing who survived what; no doubt bets were taken.

Perpetua and Felicity were first on, stripped naked and hung in nets to be tossed three times each by a mad cow. The crowd protested at seeing a noblewoman and a woman with the full breasts of recent childbirth dishonoured by nakedness and they were taken off and dressed. Nobody however protested at the cow. Both women survived their tossing and were taken to the Gate of Life where their hymns and cries of encouragement heartened the men.

Satyrus, for some reason, had a particular fear of bears and had prayed earnestly to be spared an encounter with one. His prayers were answered when the bear refused to come out of its cage to maul him. A leopard was substituted which ripped his arm off and caused him to lose so much blood that he died instantly.

Brought back for the grand finale, the survivors had their throats cut. Perpetua's gladiator was a novice and botched his first stroke, causing her to scream in pain. She took the sword point and guided it to a place in her throat where death would be quick and certain.

The joy and lack of fear displayed by these martyrs made a vivid impression on all who watched their end.

CYPRIAN (200-258) . 15th September (26th September BCP)
If the story of Perpetua and Felicity is a well-attested account of the sort of behaviour we all wish to be true when we remember the early martyrs, the career and struggles of St Cyprian, our other Carthaginian martyr, provide a sobering reminder of the less noble reaction of many early Christians to persecution.

Cyprian came to faith in middle age after a distinguished legal career, and became a Bishop of Carthage surprisingly quickly after his baptism. The election of a bishop was becoming an intensely political affair, especially in the large cities like Rome and Carthage. Election was genuinely democratic, with all the baptised choosing their favoured candidate by a show of hands. Whenever somebody like Cyprian, with local prestige and proven qualities as an administrator, became a Christian, election to a bishopric was a strong possibility.

In 250, shortly after Cyprian's election, the Emperor Decius launched the most organised and ruthless persecution the church had yet faced. Bishops were targeted and led off to martyrdom; Christian books and sacred objects were confiscated and burned; the entire population was required to obtain from the magistrate a certificate (or 'libellus') stating that they had performed their civic duty and sacrificed to the gods of the state. Faced with this unprecedented pressure, Christian morale collapsed in many places. We read of whole congregations led by their bishops reporting to the governor to offer the required sacrifices. Cyprian was persuaded by those about him to leave Carthage and lie low in the country. When Decius was killed in battle with the Goths and the persecution abated, Cyprian returned to his duties, to find that he had lost his ascendancy over his people.

During the persecution, many had apostatised by making sacrifices; others had purchased peace with the authorities by co-operating in handing over the scriptures; others had used bribery or friends in high places to obtain fraudulently their 'libelli', thus saving their lives while technically avoiding the sin of idolatry. Many of those whose courage had failed were now abjectly seeking readmission to the Church. On the other hand, there were groups of confessors, those who had not given way and had suffered imprisonment for their faith. These were now regarded as living saints and they claimed to speak in the Church with the direct authority of the Holy Spirit. Their prestige was far higher than that of Cyprian, the official leader of the Church, who had been prudent rather than heroic.

The early Church had so far failed to develop any mechanism for dealing with serious sin after baptism. It was a problem that was not supposed to exist. Paul had said that if anyone is in Christ, he is a new creation, and the expectation was that a baptised Christian, possessing the Spirit of Jesus, would be supernaturally enabled to live a perfect life of devotion to Christ. Baptism declared the complete forgiveness of the sinner, but a sinner who returned to his sin after baptism was a problem. How could the forgiveness of Christ be available for those who had deliberately violated the covenant by which that forgiveness was bestowed?

The confessors of Carthage felt empowered by their suffering and by the Holy Spirit within them to offer a generously liberal answer to this question. Cyprian found that they were freely distributing letters of pardon and reconciliation to the remorseful lapsed. Cyprian imposed a much tougher policy, obliging the sinful to remain in a state of permanent penitence. They were allowed to attend Christian worship, but had to sit on special seats near the door and appeal with tears for the prayers of the faithful. Not until their deathbeds were they readmitted to communion and sent on their way with some hope that God might have forgiven their betrayal of his Son.

Cyprian's vision of the Church was a holy society of persons freed from sin and bound together by mutual obedience to their bishop. 'Without the church, there is no salvation', he announced. 'No-one can claim to have God as his father who does have the church as his mother.' Hence he opposed those, like the confessors, who tried to lead the church by appeal to private judgement, however

Spirit-filled, and in opposition to their bishop. On the other hand, he stood vigorously for the right and duty of each bishop to lead his own church without interference from outside; he rejected attempts by successive bishops of Rome to claim jurisdiction over his own province of Carthage. Nor was he any more lenient towards the sins of bishops; those who had apostasised during the persecution were as guilty as any other lapsed Christian and could not safely continue in office, for if by apostasy they had lost the gift of the Holy Spirit, how could they bestow that Spirit on others in baptism and ordination?

Cyprian's church, ethically pure, united in loyalty to its bishop, suspicious of interference from outside and especially from Rome, and certain that on the spiritual worthiness of its ministers, depended the validity of its sacraments and corporate life, would after his death fall a natural victim to the greatest and most tragic of ancient divisions within the church, the Donatist schism, which convinced the majority of North African Christians that they and they alone were the true church, bound in duty to reject any common life with the rest of Christendom.

Cyprian and his clergy won the love and trust of their people by their heroic devotion during a terrible plague in Carthage and he bequeathed a strong and devoted, if narrow and puritanical church, to his successors. When persecution began again, there could be no further question of withdrawing from the conflict. Cyprian remained at his post, was arrested and endured his trial with dignity and a firm refusal to compromise. He was beheaded.

THE MARTYRS OF ROME

NICOMEDE (C200). 1st June BCP.

Nicomede was a presbyter who brought himself to the attention of the authorities by his persistence in giving Christian burial to the martyrs. He is believed to have perished in the arena.

The Christian burial tunnels in Rome, the famous catacombs, are still being excavated and are a popular place of pilgrimage. It is of course unlikely that everyone buried in these labyrinths died as a martyr, but the wall paintings and other remains bear eloquent testimony to how the Roman church literally 'went underground' during the worst persecutions. Secret worship took place here when even a backstreet house church was no longer safe.

CECILIA (c230). 23rd November.

Cecilia is supposed to have been a noble lady who had vowed perpetual virginity. This vow occurred on her wedding day, when she was entranced by the heavenly music which drowned out the words of the ceremony. Her husband (Tibertinus) was not unnaturally taken aback when Cecilia announced her decision after the guests had gone home, especially as he was not himself a Christian. However, Cecilia converted both him and his brother and the three were martyred together.

Cecilia is the patron saint of musicians because of the music she heard at her wedding and is portrayed in art with an organ, an instrument she certainly never played, as it had not been invented in her lifetime.

LAURENCE (238). 10th August.

Rather better attested than St Cecilia's is the legend of St Laurence. He was one of the seven deacons of Rome and, like the original seven appointed with Stephen, had responsibility for the administration of the church. Despite having no legal standing, the huge church of Rome had in fact accumulated a large amount of property and a fund out of which were maintained widows and orphans, girls vowed to virginity and a wider circle of poor and needy persons. The Roman State had no system of social security and the church's pioneer work in bringing organised relief to those whom society ignored, was one of the things which impressed and moved converts. When the Bishop of Rome went to martyrdom, Laurence is said to have cried out, 'Father, where shall the bishop go without his faithful deacon?' To which the bishop replied, 'In two days, you shall follow me.' So it proved, for the deacon was in turn arrested.

It was intimated to Laurence that his life would be spared if he surrendered to the Prefect of the City the church funds of which he was the administrator. Laurence asked for time to collect the money and spent the night distributing the funds to the poor, asking each recipient to be in the forum the next morning. When the Prefect asked where the treasure of the Church was, Laurence gestured towards the great crowd of paupers and exclaimed. 'There is the treasure of the Church, the poor whom she loves and feeds in the name of Christ'.

Refusing to accept that this was more than a subterfuge, the Prefect had Laurence tortured to extract from him the real hiding place of the missing funds. Traditionally, Laurence suffered by being roasted on a gridiron (his emblem in art) and his last words were, 'You can turn me over now. This side is done.'

VALENTINE (268) 14th February.

Valentine was Bishop of Terni and was executed on the Appian Way half way between his diocese and Rome. Nothing is known about him which would help solve the riddle of how his name became associated with true lovers, a class of persons with whom as a celibate bishop he presumably had little in common. It is often stated that the day of his martyrdom coincided with a pagan early spring festival of courtship and fertility, but the connection is complex. Although Valentine's Day features as a motif in medieval and renaissance love poetry, the custom of sending Valentine's messages only took off in a big way with the birth of the greetings card industry.

PRISCA (date unknown). 18th January BCP.

Almost nothing is known of St Prisca, whose name survives in the church dedicated to her in Rome where her relics are preserved. It may be that she was the owner of a house on the site used as a meeting place by the Christians. She is listed as a virgin martyr and, if she was, she was presumably young, beautiful and nobly born.

FABIAN AND SEBASTIAN (250/288) 20th January BCP/CDC

Fabian was a Bishop of Rome who died in prison while awaiting martyrdom in 250.

He is rather overshadowed by the altogether more glamorous St Sebastian who, though martyred on the same date, in fact suffered some years later in 288. Sebastian was a soldier who became a Christian. Such converts were always faced with a peculiarly acute tug of loyalties; not directly because of the call of Christ to pacifism, although the Church in the early centuries believed, much more strongly than most Christians do today, that warfare was incompatible with discipleship and, as late as the tenth century, Christian soldiers were expected to confess death they had caused in battle among their sins. The more immediate challenge for men like Sebastian was the pagan culture of the legions, whose morale and identity was moulded by reverence for the emperor's statue and the standards of the legion. A man who felt unable to revere these symbols could hardly continue a military career.

If his legend is to be believed, Sebastian was one of those Christians so fanatical that he not only made no attempt to hide his faith, but proclaimed it as intolerantly as possible so as to court the privilege of martyrdom. After he had interrupted a pagan sacrifice by shouting out Christian slogans, he was arrested and his fellow soldiers used him as a target in their archery practice.

Sebastian survived this ordeal and, to the amazement of his officers, presented himself at the steps of the regimental shrine the next day, still defiantly proclaiming his faith in Christ. He was therefore beheaded.

Christian bishops had to take strong measures to restrain their more enthusiastic followers from offering themselves for martyrdom in this way. It was established that, while unsought martyrdom was an honour, a suicidal quest for death was a sin. Sebastian however was revered as a true martyr. He was a favourite subject with painters, for whom he provided a respectable opportunity to attempt the male nude, and is always portrayed as a beautiful and naked young man, pierced rather decorously with two or three token arrows.

PANCRAS (304) 12th May CDC.

Pancras was only fourteen years old when he perished in the last great persecution organised by Diocletian and his western colleague Maximian. His mother was brought to trial and the boy accompanied her to her interrogation. Maximian is supposed to have said, 'I am certain that a fine lad like you, with a great career ahead of him, has no time for this superstition, fit only for women or slaves'

But the boy proudly stood beside his mother and proclaimed his Christian allegiance. His death moved many because of his youth and noble birth and many churches are dedicated to him.

AGNES (304) 21st January.

Another young person who perished in the same persecution was Agnes, who was only twelve when she was led out to have her throat cut as a Christian. Although the ancient writers who commemorate her write about her with a positively Dickensian sentimentality, mourning her childish innocence, we should recall that twelve was the marriageable age for Roman girls and that Agnes, like all teenage girls then and now, would have regarded herself as quite adult enough to make her own decisions. Nevertheless, such unflinching courage in the face of death in one so young moved and appalled her contemporaries, including her judges, who spent a long time earnestly entreating her to save her life by offering the required sacrifice.

Of all the virgin martyrs, Agnes is the one whose death is best attested by near-contemporary sources. Her emblem in art is a lamb, both because of the similarity of her name to the Latin 'Agnus' (a lamb), and because of the animal's associations with innocence, youth and sacrifice.

We have now examined the martyrs of Rome and shall next survey those who suffered for their faith in the provinces. We shall, incidentally, be able to see how the gospel was spreading throughout the Roman world.

THE MARTYRS OF THE EMPIRE.

ALBAN (250) 22nd June (17th June BCP)

The most remote outpost of Roman power was the island called Britain whose first martyr was an army officer stationed in Verulamium.

Alban gave shelter to a priest on the run and, during the time the holy man was hidden in his house, conversed with him and asked for baptism. When the priest was tracked down, Alban took his hooded cloak and allowed himself to be arrested in the other's place. The governor was amazed to see someone so highly placed brought before him but Alban proudly announced his new faith, was led out of the city and beheaded. His executioner was converted, refused to do his duty, and promptly became the second martyr of Britain. At the place where Alban's blood fell, a miraculous spring is said to have gushed forth, and the town where he suffered is now known by his name.

DENYS (c250) 9th October.
As we have seen, the Christian faith was well established in the southern provinces of Gaul, now France, but there was no steady church in the more barbaric north. St Denys was sent from Rome charged with the apostolic task of founding a church for the northern Gauls. He established his base at Lutetia, now Paris, then a small city entirely confined within the island where Notre Dame now stands.

Denys is another of those saints whose legendary identity has been forged by the accidental confusion of persons sharing the same name. He is certainly not the same person as Dionysius the Areopagite, the Athenian philosopher converted by St Paul two hundred years earlier. Nor is he the strange Christian mystic now called Pseudo-Dionysius by scholars, whose mysterious teaching about angels was once so influential. Our Denys founded his church, but the mission was not well received and the local tribes conspired to destroy Denys. It is interesting that though Gaul had been a Roman province since the time of Julius Caesar, Denys is represented as effectively being lynched by ignorant barbarians rather than tried in a Roman court. Either this is an anachronism in the legend or imperial power was wielded with a light touch so far from home.

Denys is supposed to have been beheaded on the hill now called Montmartre (Martyr's Mount) in his honour. The expected spring predictably gushed forth, but a more spectacular miracle took place when the saint picked up his severed head and walked two leagues to what is now the abbey of St Denys, thus indicating where he wished to be buried. When the abbot of St Denys told this story to Voltaire's friend, the Marquise du Deffand, she, with rather charming cynicism, remarked 'La distance n'y fait rien; il n'y a que le premier pas qui coute'[89] (the distance is immaterial; it is only the first step which counts).

Entranced by the more exotic splendour of Sacre Coeur, the huge marble church which now dominates Montmartre, the Parisians seem to have forgotten the miraculous spring. It is marked by a statue of St Denys carrying his head under his arm, but the spring itself has become a drinking fountain in a children's playground and no particular attention is paid to it.

SYMPHORIAN (180). 22nd August CDC.

Further south, in the much more markedly Roman city of Autun, Symphorian met his end. A procession was taking place in honour of the mother goddess Cybele, and Symphorian denounced the proceedings offensively enough to have himself arrested. His mother leaned from the walls and encouraged her son not to lose courage as he was marched to execution.

Autun, at that time one of the most important cities in Gaul, is now a lovely market town. It still has its Roman walls and you can see where Symphorian's mother stood to watch his death. His actual shrine was destroyed in the French Revolution.

FAITH. 6th October BCP.

Further south still, in the province of Aquitaine, a beautiful young virgin called Faith (St Foi in French) was martyred on a gridiron, which is her emblem in art.

CRISPIN and CRISPINIAN (287). 25th October.

Finally, among the early French martyrs, we notice the cobbler brothers Crispin and Crispinian. They were not really cobblers, but noblemen who had fled persecution in Rome and, having lost their estates, were forced to work for a living. They died at Soissons. Curiously, they are supposed to have fled even further and to have cobbled for a time in Faversham in Kent, where there is a strong local tradition of the French saints living there for a time. This tradition is

---

[89] Quoted by Voltaire in a letter to Jean d'Alembert.

probably to be explained by their relics having been taken to Faversham after their deaths.

They are the patron saints of shoemakers.

VINCENT (304). 22nd January.

The first martyr in Spain is considered to be Vincent, a deacon of Saragossa. He was arrested with his bishop, but being the better public speaker of the two, was entrusted with the lion's share of the defence and thus became the more famous martyr. The authorities, clearly beginning to catch on how to deal with uppity deacons, destroyed him too on a gridiron.

LUCY (304). 14th December.

Sicily is honoured by two virgin martyrs, the most famous of whom, Lucy, died in Syracuse. Terrible efforts were made to undermine her obstinacy and her chastity. She was exposed for sale in a brothel but her preaching converted all her would-be clients, an incident Shakespeare borrows for 'Pericles, Prince of Tyre.' She was then locked in a steam bath which was deliberately overheated so that she might suffocate, but when this torment failed to hurt her, an executioner was sent in to finish her with the sword.

Lucy's name, which means light, and her December feast day, in the darkest days before Christmas, have made her a powerful symbol for poets and painters of the light of Christ; she features in this role in the 'Divine Comedy'. She is sometimes shown in art holding her eyes on a tray as a sign of the illumination she brings. This convention led to a particularly revolting variant of her legend; when a pagan suitor wrote her a poem complaining that he could not live without the light of her eyes, Lucy plucked them out and sent them to him, thus demonstrating her terrifying indifference both to him and to sensual pleasure.

In Sweden, where winter darkness is a force to be reckoned with, St Lucy's Day is a great celebration. The youngest daughter of the family is dressed as Lucy with a crown of candles (in these degenerate days of health and safety, the candles are usually battery-powered). Traditionally children go and sing hymns in praise of St

Lucy under the windows of their teachers and are rewarded by special spiced biscuits.

AGATHA 5th February BCP.

Sicily's other virgin martyr, Agatha of Palermo, has also been the victim of an error in painting. She was tortured to death by having her breasts cut off by shears and so is shown in art carrying her breasts on a plate. Medieval Christians, deceived by the similarity in shape, believed these breasts to be bells and so Agatha became the patron saint of bell-ringers.

Agatha left behind her a miraculous veil which is believed to have diverted the flow of lava from Mount Etna and saved her native town.

MARGARET OF ANTIOCH (304) 20th July.

Moving into the Eastern empire to the great city of Antioch, we meet one of the best loved virgin martyrs, St Margaret, although her legend is so late and the lack of near-contemporary reference to her so marked that some have questioned whether she actually existed.

Margaret was the daughter of a pagan priest; was converted by an old slave-woman and secretly baptised. Her father in fury banished her from the house and sent her into the country, hoping to cure her of her madness. This detail at least rings true, for Christianity at this time was very much a religion of the cities. The very word 'pagan' means 'country-dweller' and Margaret's father may well have thought some time away from Christian influence would be salutary.

His hopes were disappointed, for a young nobleman, Olybrius, out hunting, spotted Margaret keeping her father's sheep, fell in love with her and proposed. When she refused on the grounds of her religion, Olybrius in jealous rage reported her to the authorities and her fate was sealed.

In prison Margaret was subjected to terrible temptations, culminating in the appearance of the devil in her cell, taking the form of a ferocious dragon, which swallowed her alive. Margaret however made the sign of the cross in the dragon's stomach and it burst asunder so that she was able to emerge to have her head cut off in the usual way. Taken literally, the story is ludicrous, but as a parable of the struggle between despair and faith, it portrays in fanciful imagery what must have been a grim reality in many a martyr's cell.

St Margaret's image in art is her dragon, and she became patron saint of women in childbirth because of her ability to emerge unscathed from within a belly. This patronage explains the large number of churches built in her honour; faced with a wife having a difficult delivery, many a desperate nobleman must have promised a church to St Margaret in return for a safe birth.

In the East Margaret is also known as Marina. A church dedicated to her in Athens is built on a steep slope, down which it is considered good luck for women seeking children to slide.

LUCIAN OF ANTIOCH (304). 8th January BCP.

A more historically reliable, though far less popular, contemporary of St Margaret's was the philosopher and theologian Lucian, who also perished in the great persecution of Diocletian.

Lucian was an early exponent of what became known as the Antiochene school of theology. In a world where biblical study was dominated by (often fanciful) methods of allegorical interpretation, as developed by the great Origen in Alexandra, the theologians of Antioch favoured a plainer, more literal approach to the text.

Lucian for example was interested in the gospel evidence that Jesus Christ grew, changed and matured during his earthly life; that far from being eternally wise and holy, he had to learn the way of obedience to God like any other human being.

Very few of Lucian's writings survive, because he was the tutor of Arius, the notorious heretic of the next generation, and his work was considered suspect in consequence. In one sense, he was lucky to have been martyred, for had he survived the persecution, he might well have been excommunicated. A charming legend tells that Lucian's body was thrown into the sea, but brought back to the shore for burial by some friendly dolphins. It would be nice if this were true.

COSMAS and DAMIAN. (304) 26th September CDC.

Cosmas and Damian were twin brothers of Syria, who practised as doctors. Because of their Christian faith they offered treatment free of charge to the poor. After their martyrdom, they were invoked for healing, for obvious reasons. The practice arose of sick people sleeping in their shrine, hoping to be given a dream which would point the way to a cure; connected with this practice is one of the best tall stories about the early martyrs. A man with a cancerous leg slept in the shrine of Cosmas and Damian. In his dream he saw the twin doctors standing over him. 'We need to give this man a new leg,' said Cosmas. 'But the only leg available belongs to the negro who died yesterday,' replied Damian. The brothers agreed to use the leg in the operation. When the sick man woke up in the morning, he found that his leg was healed, but had become black, and on opening the negro's tomb, they found that the body now had the white, cancerous leg.

BLAISE. (310) 3rd February BCP.

Armenia was the furthest east of all the Roman dominions. For many years it was an independent kingdom, buffeted by the power politics of the great empires of Rome and Persia, which played out their rivalry by proxy in Armenia, supporting rival heirs to the throne. The greater part of the kingdom eventually was incorporated into the Roman empire, and the Christian church there is ancient, according to legend reaching back to the time of Christ himself, for the king of Edessa fell sick and wrote to Jesus asking him to come and cure him. After the Resurrection, Philip went to Armenia and healed the king by showing him the holy handkerchief of Veronica, on which Christ's face had been miraculously imprinted during his journey to death. Be that as it may, by the time of Diocletian, there was certainly a strong Christian presence in Armenia and during the great persecution, its Bishop, Blaise, and his people took refuge in the caves of the mountains. Discovered, he was brought to trial and executed by being combed to death with iron combs which were dragged across his throat and chest.

Because of this horrible end, Blaise is the patron saint of all who suffer diseases of the throat and on his feast, in some places, candles are still blessed and held to the throats of sufferers seeking a cure.

GEORGE (304) 23rd April.

We have reserved until last in our survey of the early martyrs the two most exotic and famous legends of all, the martyrs of Egypt and Syria, George and Catherine.

St George was a native of Syria, serving in the Roman legions, and on his conversion he resigned his commission, conceiving the profession of arms to be incompatible with Christian discipleship. From then on he was a marked man and Diocletian had him arrested and killed with every refinement of torture.

His most striking accomplishment was of course the destruction of the dragon, which lived in a lake in Libya and was appeased by a daily gift of sheep. When the local people ran out of sheep, a girl was chosen by lot for the daily sacrifice and, at last, it was the turn of the king's daughter to die. The Princess was tied to a stake near the dragon's lair but George, passing at just the right moment, saved her by piercing the dragon with his spear. It then became as meek as a lamb, so that the Princess was able to lead it into the market square bound by her girdle. There, St George killed it and proceeded to baptise the entire population.

The story, the best known of the legends of the saints, may be read as an allegory of the Christian martyr's victory over evil. More prosaically, it may be supposed that what George did was to bring to an end a cult of human sacrifice to the sacred crocodiles.

George is buried in Lydda where his shrine is revered by Muslims as well as Christians. Indeed George has quite a place in the local Muslim folklore, and he is supposed to lie behind the Arabic legend of a heroic warrior which John Buchan used as the base of his story 'Greenmantle'. He clearly never went anywhere near England and was adopted as patron saint of this land by English crusaders who believed that he led them to victory armed with his famous red cross shield, which now inspires nothing more savage than the perpetual quest for an English victory in the World Cup.

CATHERINE OF ALEXANDRIA (304). 25th November.

Our final martyr is Catherine, who, like Margaret of Antioch, is one of the best-loved and least historically attestable of all virgin martyrs.

The Alexandrian church had grown since the time of St Mark to be one of the largest and most influential in the East. The city also hosted a large Jewish community and was famous for its wealth and learning; the famous library of Alexandria drew scholars from all over the world.

Catherine is supposed to have been converted by a priest to whom her family gave shelter and, when she was arrested, her beauty made such an impact on the Emperor Maxentius that he made every effort to turn her from her ways so that her life might be spared. Fifty pagan philosophers were gathered to refute her arguments in favour of Christ but such was Catherine's wit and learning that she out-argued them all; all fifty were baptised and promptly executed.

In prison, Catherine was visited by the empress but she and all her ladies in waiting were also converted and martyred.

Catherine was brought out to face death on the famous Catherine wheel, a monstrous engine of four spiked wheels designed to roll together over the saint's body. However the wheel was never used as angels split it apart, so Catherine was eventually despatched by the sword.

The angels then carried her body to the foot of Mount Sinai where the monks of St Catherine's monastery guard it to this day.

PART FIVE. MAKING THE CREED.

HELENA (died 330). 21st May.

The heroic legends of the martyrs have always attracted the admiration and love of Christians. However, their sufferings, which dominate our view of these earliest centuries are not the whole story. During these three hundred years, the Christian church was steadily growing in numbers, in influence and reputation, at the same time as the Roman Empire, unconquered mistress of the world for seven hundred years, was at last showing signs of faltering. In the capital, the power of the senate had been weakened by repeated struggles for imperial power and by the tacit acknowledgement that it was the legions at the frontiers, not the senators, who held the real power to elect a new emperor. During the third century, barbarian invasions from the north breached the sanctity of the Roman frontiers and, when those were contained, a lethal series of civil wars between the heirs of Diocletian weakened the empire by draining it of troops and reduced the prestige of the emperors. The provinces were demoralised by a stagnant economy and burdensome taxation. In such circumstances, it was no wonder that such bitter persecution was visited upon the Christians, who seemed to be opting out of their civic and military duties, breaking the age-old covenant of loyalty between the gods and Rome and doing all they could to bring about the collapse of society and the end of the world, which they did of course preach as the greatest of future happinesses.

Diocletian had attempted to lessen the burden of empire and regularise the succession by dividing the empire in two and having each of the two emperors choose a Caesar as his heir presumptive who would inherit the throne bloodlessly and peacefully. The scheme, elegant on paper, never worked in practice but repeatedly broke upon the ambitions of the emperors and caesars.

The Caesar of the west was one Constantius Chlorus who, while making a tour of duty in the province of Britain met and married a Christian girl named Helena. She, according to scurrilous rumours, was the daughter of the ostler who rubbed down Constantius' horses, and, according to romantic legend, was the daughter of Old King Cole, the tribal ruler of Colchester. Either way, the marriage did not last. Although Helena gave her husband a son, Constantine, he divorced her as his political career demanded an alliance with the daughter of the Emperor Maximian. Helena lived some years in obscurity as a wealthy divorcee in Trier, when her quiet life was shattered by the news that her son Constantine had become Emperor and was summoning her to Rome and to the honours of Empress Dowager. Not only this, but Constantine had changed the history of Christianity and the world by becoming a Christian.

Constantine was proclaimed Emperor in York in 312. Advancing through Gaul and Italy, he was faced with a decisive conflict with the Emperor Maximian at the Milvian Bridge. On the night before the battle, Constantine dreamed that he saw a cross held up across the sun and heard a voice saying 'In this sign conquer.' Taking his dream as an omen, Constantine had his men paint crosses on their shields and advanced to what was indeed a magnificent victory. The new emperor entered Rome convinced that Jesus Christ was a god who won battles and for the rest of his life he was an enthusiastic patron of the Christian church.

Constantine himself was not baptised until he was on his deathbed, but this does not mean he was an uncommitted Christian. As we have seen, the early church remained unconvinced about the possibility of forgiveness for serious sin after baptism, and so at this time there was a tendency to delay baptism until such a time as the candidate could be relatively certain that he or she could not be tempted into major wickedness. Constantine, who was certainly responsible for as much treachery and murder as any other Roman emperor, probably reasoned that as it was impossible to be an effective emperor without politically necessary sin, he had better not be baptised until he was ready to exchange his earthly, for a heavenly, crown. Whatever the reason for his hesitation, it did not prevent him taking an enthusiastic part in the life of the church, of which he conceived himself to be the thirteenth apostle.

Under Constantine's patronage and freed from fear of persecution, new magnificent basilicas began to be built throughout the Roman world, replacing the old hidden worship of house church and catacomb. Helena was an enthusiastic promoter of this trend and devoted her old age to the rediscovery of the holy places in Palestine.

This task was not as hopeless as it might seems, although the Jerusalem which Jesus and the apostles knew had vanished without trace. Following a final Jewish rebellion against Rome in125 the Emperor Hadrian had had acted with ruthless violence to destroy all vestiges of Jewish nationalism. Jerusalem was razed to the ground, so that only the few stones of the 'wailing wall' survive of the great Temple where Jesus taught and prayed. A new city, Aelia Capitolina, was erected on the ruins, a city into which Jews were forbidden on pain of death to enter. The Jews were dispersed throughout the empire and their country was renamed Palestine in memory of their ancient enemies the Philistines. The Jews were not again to have a homeland of their own until the founding of modern Israel in 1948, and the story of their experiences as the wandering people makes one of the least edifying pages in church history.

Christians however continued to make pilgrimages to Aelia and to pray at the sites of the crucifixion and resurrection. To stop them doing this, a large Temple of Venus was built on top of the site. Paradoxically, this made Helena's task as an amateur archaeologist easier. All she had to do was demolish the temple, and the hill of the cross and Joseph of Arimathea's cave were revealed.

Helena industriously discovered many other sites connected with Jesus, using local tradition, intelligent guesswork and the assistance of dreams and visions. The cave of the Nativity at Bethlehem was excavated. As each site was identified, Helena's strategy proved how far in spirit she was from a modern archaeologist or preserver of historic heritage sites. Our instinct would be to restore the sites to make them appear as closely as possible as they would have done in the time of Christ. Hers was to build a huge church on top of each one. Her architects reduced the mount of the crucifixion, and the cave of the resurrection, to a cube of stone each and a church was built to house the two cubes in one building.

The art of building churches was a new one in the new world of legalised, privileged Christianity. The model most often used was that of the basilica or law court. At the end of the hall where the judges sat, a semicircular apse provided seats for the bishop and clergy, with the altar in the middle of the semi-circle. The people stood facing east in a great pillared hall, often crowned with a dome. Helena's budget for adorning the Holy Land with these structures appears to have been unlimited.

SYLVESTER (died 335). 31st December BCP.
In the time of Constantine, the bishop of Rome, whom we might now venture to call the Pope, was Sylvester, a conscientious man who did not play a leading part in the theological disputes of the time. He and his clergy must have experienced a certain amount of disorientation as the victorious Constantine took possession of their city. Where only fifteen years before terror had surrounded the Christian community, as young St Agnes and her fellow martyrs perished, now the survivors were summoned to the court to receive legal privileges, generous tax breaks, the opportunity to debate theology with the emperor and the reverence of courtiers who had suddenly discovered, with Constantine's conversion, that Jesus was the way, the truth and the life even for the upper classes and those with ambitious career plans. There can seldom have been such a transformation in one generation.

Constantine, however, was not planning to stay long in Rome. As soon as he had brought the civil wars to an end by dethroning his imperial rivals in the east, he planned a new start for the empire. The adoption of Christianity as state religion was to be symbolised by the building of a new Rome at the centre of the empire, on the straits which divide Europe and Asia. The new city was named, naturally, after the thirteenth apostle: Constantinople. From now on, imperial power would be exercised from there, leaving the still largely pagan senate to a ceremonial pretence at exercising power in the west, and the real concentration of prestige, influence and ability to make things happen in the hands of the Pope.

Sylvester is most famous for something which never happened. Constantine is supposed to have suffered from leprosy, to have been cured by the prayer of Sylvester, and in gratitude to have put into his hands a document bequeathing the western Roman empire to the heirs of St Peter for ever. This so-called Donation of

Constantine was believed to be genuine throughout the middle ages and was the foundation of papal claims to universal government. It was only at the Renaissance that the Donation was conclusively proved to be a forgery.

All of this was, of course, unknown to Sylvester, who must have wondered as he watched the imperial architects constructing his superb Lateran palace, and the grand shrines to enclose the remains of Peter and Paul, whether he was not in fact dreaming and would shortly wake to find himself back in the catacombs.

THE INVENTION OF THE CROSS. 3rd May BCP.

While Constantine busied himself among the foundations of the new capital, Helena crowned her work in Jerusalem by discovering the true cross.

Guided by a dream, she found[90] in a cistern the three crosses on which Jesus and the two robbers had died. But which of the three was the Saviour's? A test was devised. The three crosses were laid in turn upon the body of an unfortunate dying woman. Naturally the cross which effected a miraculous cure was hailed as the true one.

Again Helena demonstrated a spirit alien to ours once she had her treasure. She cut the cross into pieces, keeping a part for the new bishop of Jerusalem, and sending parts to the Pope and to her son at Constantinople. The emperor also received a miscellaneous parcel of treasures, including the crown of thorns, the boards on which Pilate had written 'King of the Jews' and the nails which had pierced Christ, one of which he made into a bit for his horse's bridle.

The wood of the cross was gradually shaved off into splinters as gifts for favoured pilgrims and potentates, so that it now only exists in tiny fragments, any number of which may or may not derive from the wood Helena found.

The heritage industry had been born.

ANTHONY OF EGYPT (251-356). January 17th.

The conversion of Constantine had radically changed the church, and not all the changes met with the favour of the 'old guard', the faithful

---

[90] Latin 'Invenit', hence the 'Invention of the Cross'.

Christians who had held firm to Christ through the terrible years of persecution. To be a Christian had been to take the hard way of the cross, withdrawing from the sinful pagan world, risking the hatred and scorn of neighbours, facing joyfully the liberation and victory of martyrdom. That tough, simple call to holiness was now in a generation being transformed into something a lot more comfortable, following fashionable crowds into the new marble basilicas, joining in worship led by robed choirs and gorgeously dressed clergy, who carefully tailored their sermons to please the ears of emperors and governors and their moral teaching to accommodate the lifestyle of the wealthy women whose donations would enable the church to continue living in the style to which it was rapidly becoming accustomed. Instead of standing against the world, it seemed that the church was entering into alliance with the world, and losing its soul in the process.

The martyr was established as the icon of a Christian losing all for love of Christ. But there would be no more martyrs. Christians who still wanted to give up everything for the kingdom of God needed to find a different way to holiness. They found it in the monastic movement being pioneered by, among others, Anthony of Egypt.

Anthony was a rich young man orphaned in his teens. At the age of eighteen, he arrived late at his village church; the gospel was being read as he entered, and it was Mathew 19.21: 'If you would be perfect, go, sell what you have and give it to the poor and come, follow me.' The text came to the young Anthony as a personal call from Jesus. He left the church and the next day put his house and lands up for sale, retaining only enough capital to get his sister a decent lodging with a local community of Christian women. Then he began his life anew. At first he lived on a small-holding at the edge of the village, giving himself to prayer and growing his own food – but the demands of the gospel pushed him towards solitude and total poverty. He built a cell in the desert at the verge of where human life was sustainable, worked at basket-making, lived on water and vegetables, slept as little as possible, tried to pray continuously and give his whole life to God.

The life of a hermit was not one of absolute solitude, although silence and solitude were regarded as essential if the task of allowing your soul to be re-made in Christ was to be achieved. Anthony had his periodic trip into market to sell his baskets and buy what he could not grow for himself. He met to consult and pray with other hermits engaged in the same quest. Gradually a loose community of men grew up, each battling his own demons in a solitary cell, but meeting on Sundays for the Eucharist. Above all, Anthony was beset by pilgrims, people who, from all over Egypt and beyond, came to stare at the marvel of a man living the life of angels while still in his mortal flesh, and to consult the wisdom of a man who, through his living death to sin, had become an oracle of the Holy Spirit.

Anthony was not the first to devote himself to this solitary life of desert prayer, but among the monastic pioneers he was much the most influential, for two reasons. One was his immense age; he lived to 105, with his faculties and ardour for God undimmed to the last. The other was the impression he made on his younger contemporary, Athanasius, Bishop of Alexandria, who wrote his biography, a book which became a best-seller.

The desert hermit replaced the martyr as the ultimate Christian hero. Hundreds of people who had become disillusioned with the easy, compromised church life of the cities, undertook this arduous way of self-denial, hoping to find their true selves. In Egypt and Syria, they went to the desert, not to find a peaceful place 'away from it all', but because the desert was the home of evil spirits, and like Jesus himself, they wanted to meet Satan in his strongholds and by the power of their prayer defeat and destroy the enemy. Anthony experienced severe inner turmoil, and his temptations, personified in a grotesque array of goblins and monsters, are a favourite topic for artists.

In the wider church, admiration for the hermits was widespread even among those who had not the courage to choose such an extreme way for themselves. For the next 1200 years, it would be universally believed that the celibate monk or nun, living in poverty and prayer, represented the closest a human being could get in this world to living the perfect life of Jesus Christ.

Anthony's emblem in art is a pig, because in the middle ages the pigs of the friars of St Anthony had special liberty to feed on common ground. He carries a bell, the sign of exorcism, in allusion to his battles with evil spirits.

ATHANASIUS (296-373). 2nd May.

Constantine had hoped that by supporting the Christian Church, with its impressive empire-wide network of bishops and churches, united in one baptism and in a common creed, he would find a means of rejuvenating and reuniting the empire itself. He was soon disillusioned. No sooner had his civil wars ended (324) and he attained unchallenged power, then he discovered that the church, which was emerging from the catacombs under his patronage, was riven by theological disagreement.

The most serious rifts were being caused by the teaching of an Alexandrian priest named Arius, the pupil of St Lucian of Antioch. As with all the great heretics, we only have access to the thought of Arius through quotations preserved in the writings of his opponents, and it is notoriously hard to establish exactly what he was trying to achieve. But broadly, Arius was questioning the traditional teaching that Jesus Christ, the Son of God, was one with his Father. To the Greek mind, formed by Plato as much as by the New Testament, it seemed clear that God must, as a perfect being, be beyond time and chance, unchanging and not subject to passions or suffering. Jesus on the other hand, clearly lived, as any human being must, a life of growth, toil, suffering and intense emotional experience. It seemed clear to Arius therefore that Jesus could not have been in the fullest sense God. He did not deny that in him was incarnate a divine being, the Logos or word of God, but that Being must himself have been part of the created order: the firstborn of all creation perhaps, God's instrument for reconciling his world to himself certainly, but still not God. This doctrine has the merit of clarity, and it has to be said on Arius' behalf, that many popular orthodox accounts of Jesus, then and now, have been guilty of making it sound as if Jesus was not a human being at all, but God dressed up as a man. Nevertheless, Arius shocked most ordinary Christians, who had been brought up to believe that in Jesus, God had done for them what they could not do for themselves. God was in Christ reconciling the world to himself. If Jesus, the Son of God, was not himself God, how could he be the source of salvation for others?

Arius had a lively mind and won supporters by his cleverness and by his ability to popularise complicated and abstract ideas. The sailors on the docks in Alexandria sang hymns Arius had written for them, incorporating his catchphrase, 'There was a time when he was not.' (It is snappier in Greek: *en hote ouk en.*)

Constantine was determined that his church should be a united church, and in 325 he summoned a council to Nicaea, with the brief of finding a formula to describe Christ and God which would hold all Christians together. About three hundred bishops attended the council, but the two most influential members were not bishops. One was the notorious Arius himself, and the other was a young deacon in the entourage of the Bishop of Alexandra, named Athanasius.

Athanasius had already made his name as a theologian by a short treatise called 'On the Incarnation of the Word.' In this work he outlined elegantly and with force his central convictions about our salvation. God had acted in Jesus to take our nature upon him and so redeem it. God had taken a human soul, mind and body and thus made divine every human soul, mind and body united with Christ. Each baptised person shared the divine life of God himself, and was thus guaranteed immortality and eternal happiness. But this could only happen if Jesus was truly divine, for only God himself could divinise our human nature by uniting it to himself.

On this simple assertion of the divinity of God's son, 'He assumed our humanity so that we might share his divinity', Athanasius was to take his stand and hold his position 'contra mundum' (against the world) for the whole of his long life.

The debate at the Council of Nicaea centred upon the relationship of the Son of God to the Father. While many opposed Arius, the bishops from Syria and Asia Minor were concerned that too simplistic a statement that the Son is God would open further problems, making it appear that 'Father' and 'Son' were merely modes or masks worn by God as he desired to perform various tasks. Eventually, Constantine himself intervened in the debate and suggested a defining word: 'homoousios', of the same substance. If the Son was described as 'of the same substance as the Father', this would make clear his full divinity while clearly differentiating him from his Father. The fact that the creative theologian was also master of the world and ran the imperial police had its effect; eventually all but two bishops signed the new formula and Arius found himself isolated and defeated. The Nicene Creed is still recited in our churches at Communion and its central clauses, describing the Son – 'God from God, Light from Light, true God from true God, begotten not made, of the same being as The Father' – still stand as a bulwark against Arius' attempts to reduce Jesus to the status of a creature.

At the time, however, the eternal truth of the Nicene formula was less than apparent. Many theologians distrusted the word 'homoousios' because it was not a biblical term and appeared an innovation. Moreover its use seemed to them to betray a failure to conceive of Father, Son and Holy Spirit as separate persons within the godhead. No sooner had Constantine got his signatures than a campaign began to revoke the decisions of Nicaea. Against the all-powerful Thirteenth Apostle, nothing could be directly attempted, and during Constantine's lifetime lip-service continued to be paid to the Nicene Creed, but its opponents began to discredit and isolate its champions.

Three years after the council, Athanasius became Bishop of Alexandria. Head of one of the oldest and richest churches, Alexandria's bishop had enormous power over the population of Egypt, and his influence in rural areas was buttressed by the increasing numbers who, following Anthony's example, were adopting the monastic life in the Egyptian desert. Athanasius' enemies began to collect evidence against him. He was opposed not only by the supporters of Arius, but by the Meletians, a group who, like the Donatists in Carthage, had emerged to oppose their bishop over issues to do with the purity of ministry in the aftermath of the persecution. In 335 Athanasius was accused of all sorts of high-handed behaviour, most sensationally of having murdered a Meletian bishop and used his body for black magic. In a coup worthy of Agatha Christie, Athanasius' defence team were able to confound the persecution by producing in court the supposedly murdered bishop alive and well, but when it was suggested to the Emperor that Athanasius was holding back the Egyptian grain fleet, thus threatening the prosperity of Constantinople, Constantine's heart was hardened and the bishop was exiled to Trier in Gaul. In all he was to face five separate periods of exile as imperial politics ebbed and flowed for or against Arianism. He never ceased to campaign unflinchingly for the Nicene Creed, and while distrusted and disliked by his fellow bishops became ever more deeply loved by the monks and common people of Egypt.

On Constantine's death, Athanasius was permitted to return to his diocese, but the Arian party had great influence on Constantine's son and successor Constantius. So long as Constantius' brother Constans, who ruled the Western empire, still lived, Athanasius had a protector, for the Latin-speaking church was always inclined to support the godhead of the Son in what seemed to the Arians a simplistic way. In 350, however, Constans was assassinated and after a period of turmoil Constantius became, like his father before him, sole emperor of the Roman world. Now Athanasius' enemies pounced. Old charges and new were piled up against him and Constantius was persuaded that, doctrine apart, the bishop of Alexandria was a dangerous person whose power needed to be checked. However deposing him was not going to be easy, entrenched as he was in the affections and loyalty of the Egyptian people. In February 355, imperial troops invaded the church where Athanasius was keeping a night vigil. In a shocking scene, members of the congregation, including several nuns, were trampled underfoot, crushed and killed as they attempted to screen their bishop from arrest. Athanasius escaped and simply disappeared. For the next six years he lived as an outlaw in Egypt, moving from house to house, monastery to monastery, always eluding capture. His people remained loyal and he was never once betrayed to the authorities.

On one occasion, pursued up the Nile by imperial agents sent to arrest him, a police boat drew up alongside the boat taking Athanasius to safety. 'Is Bishop Athanasius on board?' demanded an officer. 'No!' cried back the bishop himself in the dusk. 'He is hiding on the boat following us.' The police stopped to search the wrong boat and Athanasius made good his escape to Upper Egypt, where hidden in the desert monasteries he was untraceable.

The Arian bishops obtruded into the see George of Cappadocia, a venal and unscrupulous man who used his position to become rich, and who was only maintained in his place by military force. Meanwhile, the Arians were busy throughout Christendom. With Athanasius gone, those bishops who held to the Nicene formulae were isolated and picked off, some on charges of corruption or impropriety under canon law, others by being browbeaten and out-argued at successive church councils. At last, at the fatal council of Ariminum (Rimini) in 361, the Nicene Creed was neutered. Although formal respect continued to be paid to the work of the great Constantine, the 'homoousios' 'of one substance' was removed and a much vaguer term substituted. The Son was now only 'like' the Father. On this occasion, in the memorable phrase of Jerome, the 'whole world groaned and awoke to find itself Arian.'

To modern readers, these controversies, to which the bishops of the time devoted such passionate and angry energy, can seem very abstract affairs, and it is easy to lose patience with the endless pedantic wrangling over the mysteries of God's eternal being. Under the surface of the controversies, however, really important ideas about the nature of God and the way in which he deals with his world were being mapped out. The years from 325 to 461 were formative for Christian theology, and of an importance second only to the years in which the New Testament was written.

Athanasius did not live to see the triumph of the orthodoxy which he had championed and for which he had suffered. But, by the time of his death, a new generation of leaders had begun to emerge, Basil and Gregory in the East, Ambrose in the West, by whom orthodox Christianity would be further elucidated and would eventually be established.

The Creed called 'Athanasian' is not in fact by Athanasius, but is a later document built on the truths which Athanasius devoted his life to defending.

NICHOLAS (326) 6th December.

After surveying the stormy, controversial life of Athanasius, it will be a relief to turn to the lives of three of his contemporaries who will remind us in their different ways that other things were happening in the fourth century church as well as the hammering out of doctrines and dogmas.

St Nicholas of Myra was a perfectly ordinary bishop. He had lived through the persecutions without displaying any extraordinary heroism. He attended the Council of Nicaea the year before he died, where he manifested a suitably ferocious attitude towards the Arians. But he was loved and remembered for neither of these things. He is the first Christian to be venerated as a saint, not for a heroic martyrdom, nor for learned contributions to the development of theology, but simply because he was a good person who loved the people entrusted to him with unselfish generosity.

All that remains to us of this man who died as the unremarkable bishop of an unremarkable town, are legends of his miraculous goodness. Once, passing a house, he heard the three daughters of the place lamenting that their father's debts would compel him to sell them into slavery. Knowing the man would be too proud to accept open charity, Nicholas returned at night and rolled three bags of gold through the window into the shoes of the sleeping girls, thus furnishing each with a dowry. On another occasion he stood on a headland watching a ship about to be wrecked in a storm. Such was the intensity of the prayer he put forth, that the sailors believed they had seen Nicholas flying around their ship protecting it from winds and waves and bringing it safe to harbour. The most gruesome story concerns an innkeeper who had murdered and pickled three small boys so that he could feed them to his guests. Sensing the evil in the house, Nicholas made the sign of the cross over the pickle barrel and the boys emerged unscathed. Fortunately, this miracle is certainly a misunderstanding of a picture showing the saint blessing children in a baptismal font.

Nicholas has acquired an impressive portfolio of responsibilities; he is patron of children, sailors, thieves (known as St Nicholas' clerks in the middle ages) and pawnbrokers (whose sign is the three golden balls with which he saved the debt laden maidens).

He is also of course, and most famously, Santa Claus, the bishop who comes from over the sea to bring Christmas gifts to good children. He is still recognisable as a bishop in Holland, but universally elsewhere he has acquired, via Nordic mythology and nineteenth century whimsy, the magic reindeer, white beard, red cape, North Pole palace and toy-making elves which ensure that he is more venerated than all the other saints in the calendar put together.

The love given to the historic Nicholas is a salutary reminder to us that the church in its golden age was growing not just because of the brilliance of its theologians, but because of the humble faithfulness of priests and people to the daily life of worship and mutual love.

EPHRAIM OF SYRIA (306-373) 9th June.

Another young man who sat quietly on the back benches at the Council of Nicaea while the great names fulminated against Arius, was Ephraim, who had accompanied his bishop all the way from Nisibis in Mesopotamia, the furthest east of all the Roman dominions. Ephraim had been thrown out of home by his pagan parents at the age of eighteen when they discovered that he had been baptised, and was virtually adopted by his bishop, St Jacob. He grew up to become one of the greatest Christian poets.

Nisibis was in the territory so endlessly and fruitlessly disputed by the Roman and Persian empires. Three times in Ephraim's lifetime the city was besieged by the Persians. In 363, the Emperor Julian the Apostate was assassinated while on campaign against Persia, and his successor Jovian bought a breathing space by ceding Roman Mesopotamia to the enemy. Many Christians left Nisibis rather than live under pagan rule, and so Ephraim came to Edessa, where he lived for the rest of his life.

Like so many others of his generation, he was drawn by the hermit's life and made his home in a cave outside Edessa. However, he was far from isolated, taking an active part in the life of the local church, preaching and teaching, and above all writing the wonderful hymns for which he is still remembered.

Ephraim's language was Syrian, which explains why his work is little known outside the middle east. He wrote hymns to be sung at all the church's major festivals, strong, strange, haunting pieces worked out of allusive imagery and tangled, intricate metaphors, reflecting with passionate artistry on the central themes of the faith – Christ's virgin birth, his death, his resurrection, the work of the Holy Spirit like wine, like fire, like a plant covering the world with its blooms. His hymns are still sung in the liturgy of the Syrian church, and his indirect influence helped to bring singing and hymnody into a central place in Christian worship.

In the last year of his life, famine struck Edessa and Ephraim was incensed to discover that some who were hoarding grain gave as their excuse the impossibility of distributing it fairly. The ancient hermit offered his services to the city and was universally praised for the wisdom and justice of his decisions, which preserved many from starvation. Worn out by his exertions, he withdrew to his cave and died a month after the famine had subsided.

CYRIL OF JERUSALEM (315-386) 18th March.
By the middle of the fourth century, Jerusalem was becoming a very influential place. After its reconstruction by Constantine and Helen, pilgrims began arriving from all over the world, anxious to see with their own eyes the places where Christ suffered and died. We have a description of the city by a Spanish pilgrim, Egeria, who visited Jerusalem at the time when its bishop was St Cyril.

Cyril did his bit in the controversy over Arius – like Athanasius he was in exile for over half his episcopacy. He also engaged in a frankly tedious campaign to persuade the Emperor to give Jerusalem the status of a Patriarchal church and free him from the supervision of the Bishop of Caesarea. But, like Nicholas and Ephraim, he is remembered principally for the work he did as pastor of his church and by extension for the whole Christian world.

Most of Cyril's surviving writings are sermons delivered to his baptismal candidates (or catechumens) during their final preparation in Lent. Baptism was not treated lightly. The candidates had already attended church as enquirers for three years, during which time they were not permitted to witness the sacrament of Holy Communion; after listening to the sermon and prayers they left the building. It was after the departure of the un-baptised that the believers reasserted their love for each other by sharing the kiss of peace and proceeding together to celebrate the sacrament: this is the reason why the Peace occurs in the middle of the Communion service, in a manner which many 'traditional' worshippers find so disconcerting.   Now, formally anointed and catchumens, the candidates were expected to attend church every day in Lent, to be exorcised and to listen to Bishop Cyril's teaching.

Cyril taught them a structure of doctrine similar to the Apostles Creed, together with the Ten Commandments and instructions on Christian living.   His sermons convey vividly the great difference which baptism was expected to make in a person's life. Baptism, taught Cyril, was the way provided by God by which a believer made his own the experience of Christ's death and resurrection.   Christ underwent death in reality, the baptised only symbolically and in imitation, but the spiritual reality of freedom from sin, eternal life and adoption as God's children would be granted them if they received the sacrament with repentance and faith.

It must have been an extraordinary experience to sit in the Church of the Holy Sepulchre and hear Cyril speak about the cross and the empty tomb, when the very rocks on which the drama was acted out stood visible before you.

The celebration of Easter was built around baptism. Cyril and his community used their unique access to the sacred sites to build an extraordinary re-enactment in liturgy and ritual of the whole story of the Passion. On Palm Sunday there was a procession from Bethany over the Mount of Olives to Jerusalem. Maundy Thursday featured an all night vigil in the Garden of Gethsemane, while Good Friday was an exhausting day of fasting and prayer at the rock of Calvary.

On Saturday a further vigil took place all through the night, while the Old Testament scriptures were read and commented on. Just before dawn on Easter Day, the baptismal candidates were led into the pitch dark room, stripped naked and required to affirm their faith. They were then taken to the font, submerged totally in water three times and led out into the light to receive white robes, an anointing with oil as Christ's priestly people, and a kiss of peace from Cyril. As the sun rose they joined for the first time in the celebration of Holy

Communion. Given that this exhausting week of worship and sleep deprivation took place in the context of serious and prolonged fasting, some of the candidates must have had difficulty remembering where they were by the time they made their first Communion.

Pilgrims like Egeria were impressed and excited by Cyril's Easter ceremonies, and they took reports of what happened back to their home churches. Imitations of the Jerusalem Holy week soon became common, so that Cyril of Jerusalem may really be said to have invented Holy Week as it is now commonly celebrated.

HILARY OF POITIERS (315-367) 13th January.

While throughout the Christian world churches were built, liturgies and hymns composed, new converts were prepared by baptism and communities cared for the poor, the Arian controversy with all its poison of division and hatred continued to perplex the church. In Gaul, the foremost champion of orthodoxy is Hilary, bishop of Poitiers, known as the 'Athanasius of the West.'

Hilary became a Christian after a familiar period of disillusionment with pagan philosophy and its inability to deliver any certain knowledge of God. His first reading of John's gospel struck him with amazement and his baptism followed soon afterwards. He was married at the time of his conversion, but after he was elected Bishop of Poitiers, he and his wife lived in celibate friendship, and he persuaded his daughter to embrace a life of perpetual virginity. Slowly the monastic ideals were permeating the church, making married Christians afraid that their way of life was very much a second rate holiness.

We have seen how Constantine's son Constantius became convinced that Arianism, rather that his father's Nicene faith, would unite the divided church most effectively. In the east, it is true, that the majority of the bishops were 'semi-Arians.' That is to say that they were infinitely more worried by the theology of Athanasius than of Arius. To the semi-Arians, Alexandrian theology seemed to involve a crude blurring of the distinctions between Father, Son and Holy Spirit. Athanasius said bluntly that the work done by Jesus and the Holy Spirit within this world was being done by God: Did that mean that the transcendent God, utterly other, utterly holy, was compromised by contact with a world of change and suffering, beliefs which could only lead to a trivialised vision of God, an idolatrous shrinking of God into human categories? Against such risks, the dangers of Arianism seemed comparatively worth running. The Son and Spirit, doing God's work in the world must be clearly seen to be subordinate to God and in an important sense distinct from him. The situation was not helped by the fact that different theologians used different terminology. The word 'ousia' or 'being' was used as a synonym for 'hypostasis' a word indicating the role a particular person might play, the way in which their essential being expressed itself in action. To say Jesus had the same nature as the Father was very different from saying that Father, Son and Spirit were all the same role.

To Christians in Latin speaking Gaul, these anxieties seemed idle. Latin, with its definite logical structure, is ideally suited for expressing law and system; Latin speakers followed with difficulty controversies expressed in the more fluid, nuanced Greek. To Hilary, it seemed clear that the Son must share his Father's substance as all children share the nature of their parents. He opposed the semi-Arians and was exiled in 356 to Phrygia. He remained there for three years, during which he wrote his twelve volume 'De Trinitate' (About the Trinity), attempting to oppose Arius, while maintaining a real separate identity for the three Persons of the Trinity. His ideas would be developed by St Basil the Great and would form the basis of the eventual refinement of the Nicene doctrine which emerged as orthodox theology.

During Hilary's exile, his people refused to allow a replacement bishop to be elected, and Hilary ran his diocese from a distance. After his return, he continued to be energetic in the theological councils of the day and to oppose Arianism.

MARTIN (316-39) 11th November.
In 353 Hilary of Poitiers was visited by a man who was destined to eclipse him entirely in fame. This was Martin, a young soldier who had left his regiment under a cloud. He had inherited his military career from his father: at this time classes and ranks in the Roman Empire were steadily ossifying and it was becoming impossible for a

man not to follow his father's profession. While on garrison duty at Amiens, Martin had the encounter which defines him in popular legend. On a cold winter's day he met a naked beggar at the city gates. As he had no money on him, Martin cut his military cloak in half and gave part to the beggar, enduring mockery as well as cold for the unsoldierly figure he then cut. But that night, he dreamed that Jesus showed his torn cloak to the angels, saying 'Martin has covered me with this cloak.' In serving the beggar he had served Christ. He awoke and at once sought baptism.

Although the empire was now Christian, it was still felt that the profession of soldier was unfitting for a Christian and Martin sought to resign his post. As the barbarians were threatening Gaul, he was charged by his commander Julian (later the apostate emperor) with cowardice. Martin steadily refused to bear arms but refuted the charge of cowardice by offering to stand naked and alone in front of the barbarian host as it advanced. His bluff was never called as the barbarians retreated, and he secured his discharge. He had now come to Poitiers to seek ordination.

Moved by his story, Hilary ordained him, and on his return from exile granted him land at Limoges to follow his heart's desire, which was to live as a hermit. However he did not lead his life of solitary prayer for long. Invited to the city of Tours to pray (as he thought) at the bedside of a dying man who had asked for him, Martin found himself the victim of an amiable deception, and was seized and forcibly consecrated bishop. He accepted his new vocation, but was never able to reconcile it with his desire for hermit solitude. He refused to live in the bishop's palace, and instead built a hut at an inaccessible spot where the banks of the river Loire were closed in by steep cliffs. This place later became the abbey of Marmoutier. Hundreds went to join Martin in his spartan solitude; the diocesan officials and those who regularly needed to see the bishop on business were presumably less enchanted by his inaccessible retreat.

Martin toured his diocese conscientiously, making every effort to stamp out pagan worship. He demolished shrines and cut down sacred trees with a confident intolerance we should find it hard to admire today. On one occasion a pagan priest agreed to have his shrine tree cut down if Martin would stand under it as it fell. The saint accepted the challenge and the tree miraculously swerved and crashed to the ground beside him doing him no harm.

Much more likely to earn Martin approval from modern readers was his conduct during the persecution of Priscillian. In 384 a scandal occurred for the first time in Christian history. A Christian bishop had a fellow Christian executed for heresy. The victim was Priscillian and Martin was horrified. He at once excommunicated the persecuting bishop and interceded with the emperor to save the lives of Priscillian's followers.

A story less well-known than that of the beggar and the cloak illustrates Martin's mad, unworldly generosity even better. On one occasion he was preparing to lead worship at Tours when a beggar came to the church to ask for help. The archdeacon impatiently waved him away, but the beggar, who knew his man, went round to the vestry door and spoke directly to the bishop. In the church people were beginning to wonder why the service was starting so late. The archdeacon went to the Bishop's vestry and knocked. Without opening the door, Martin called out, 'One of Christ's poor is waiting to be clothed. I cannot go into church until this duty of charity is fulfilled' Furious at his bishop's unworldly stubbornness, the archdeacon went and bought the meanest set of second hand clothes he could find, returned to the church and threw them into the vestry. His humiliation was completed when Martin emerged to celebrate mass wearing this same shabby set of second hand clothes. He had of course stripped himself to give his bishop's robes to the beggar and now performed his duties in clothes his clergy considered adequate for a poor man but shocking draping the person of a bishop.

When he died, the clergy wanted to put him into a bed with sheets, but he answered 'It becomes not a Christian to die otherwise than upon ashes. I shall have sinned if I leave you any other example.'

THE TRANSLATION OF MARTIN. 4th July BCP.
The Prayer book calendar gives Martin a second feast, the date of the translation or moving of his relics. The term suggests a stately procession with chants and incense. The reality was scandalously

different. When a dispute arose over where Martin should be buried, the people of Tours sent a boat up the Loire by night. The crew broke into the hermitage at Marmoutier and carried Martin triumphantly back to Tours, where he was buried in a new shrine which survived until the French Revolution.

The story illustrates how much value was being given already to the bones of departed saints. Contact with their bodies was believed to connect the worshipper also with their holiness, and miracles were expected and received. It is a salutary reminder of the complexity and unpredictability of human society that Martin, with his rustic struggles against magic trees, was an exact contemporary of the sophisticated philosopher-bishops whose learned quarrels make up the history of doctrine in the late Roman Empire.

BRITIUS (Died 444) 13th November BCP.
Martin was succeeded as Bishop of Tours by Britius or Brice, a disciple of his but not a promising one. In fact Brice, like the archdeacon in the story above, found it hard to sympathise with his master's otherworldly impracticability. Once someone asked him where Bishop Martin was. 'In the church' replied Brice. 'gazing up to Heaven as though he were crazy.' Martin prophesied that Brice would succeed him and once remarked ruefully. 'If Christ could tolerate Judas, surely I can put up with Brice.'

Brice, once duly elected, proved an arrogant and unpopular bishop and no-one was sorry to see him removed from office after being falsely accused of seducing a nun. He spent seventeen years in exile in Rome, and must have spent them well for, when he was restored to his bishopric, he is said to have governed with exemplary holiness and humility. Nevertheless, it is hard to imagine that he would have become a saint if it were not for his connection with the well-loved Martin. Martin would no doubt be amused.

EVURTIUS (date unknown) 7th September BCP.
In the Prayer Book calendar, an early bishop of Orleans, a contemporary of Martin, Evurtius, is commemorated. He was sent from Rome to consolidate Christian mission in northern Gaul. So little is known of Evurtius, that it is believed his feast day only got

into the Book of Common Prayer because it was the birthday of Elizabeth I, which her subjects wished to keep as a holiday after that monarch's demise.

BASIL THE GREAT (350-379) 2nd January.

We return to the east and to the Arian controversy, which was about to be settled by three great men, known collectively from their province of origin as the Cappadocian Fathers. Basil the Great, his brother Gregory of Nyssa and his friend Gregory Nazianzen, had a incalculable effect on the development of Eastern Christianity.

Basil, his sister Macrina, and his brother Gregory, all saints, were brought up as Christians by their grandmother St Macrina the Elder. The family was aristocratic and wealthy and Basil, as eldest brother, inherited vast estates in Asia Minor. He was a child prodigy who had a brilliant career at the university of Athens, where he met his life-long friend Gregory Nazianzen.

In 358, the year of his father's death, Basil was baptised, sold much of his property and proposed to his family a simple life of study and prayer. However, his great scholarship, dominant personality and strong desire to 'get things done' meant that he was never going to resign himself to the quiet routine of a scholar monk.

When the bishopric of Caesarea, in Cappadocia, fell vacant in 370, Basil, with none of the bashfulness shown by other saints on similar occasions, campaigned vigorously to secure his own election. He was a born organiser and under his direction Caesarea became a model diocese. Using family money, Basil constructed the 'Basileion', a powerhouse of practical Christian charity, where the sick were nursed, children educated, the poor given work, and important new experiments in monastic living were successfully attempted.

Basil's organised mind was disturbed by the anarchic traditions of monastic withdrawal established by Anthony of Egypt and his followers. Men went off to be monks following their own whims, and although many became saintly, self-denying persons, many others became frankly nuisances, claiming the authority to intervene in church affairs, acknowledging no authority other than their own fancies, and competing in often grotesque forms of self-denial. Basil drew up a rule of life for monks, obliging them to live together in community, to devote themselves to regular patterns of worship and work, and to live under the authority of their bishop (Basil himself, as it happened). The rule of St. Basil has remained the model for monastic living throughout the eastern church.

As a theologian, Basil made an important contribution to the solution of the Nicene/Arian controversy. Although a firm friend and ally of the elderly Athanasius, he could appreciate the anxieties which the semi-Arians were trying to allay. Working along the same lines as Hilary of Poitiers, he established a definite difference of usage between the two controversial words 'ousia' and 'hypostasis'. For Basil, 'ousia' would always mean the essential nature of God, the 'godness' which makes God God, and this word is translated in Latin theology as 'substance'. 'Hypostasis' Basil used to describe the particular mode of being which makes the Father, the Son and the Holy Spirit different from each other, and this word is translated as 'person'. The three Persons of the Trinity share the same substance, rather, in Basil's favoured analogy, as three individual men are united by their common humanity. This analogy has its own problems – it comes dangerously close to saying that Christians do in fact worship three gods – but the neat use of terminology made is possible for most Christian now to edge towards agreeing that 'homo-ousios'. 'of one substance' was a respectable way to describe the relation of God the Father and God the Son. Reconciliation between Nicenes and Semi-Arians could not long be delayed and the surviving Arians were isolated and in decline. The picture of the three Persons, three identical young men, sitting at table together, is a favourite subject for icon painters. Basil, however, though he was convinced of the full godhead of the Holy Spirit, could never work out a way of describing the Spirit's relation to the Father which would not duplicate the language used of Jesus and make the Spirit ' a second Son.'

Basil's love of mastery and his administrative skill were manifested less attractively by the manoeuvres he executed to win a power struggle for the independence of his see. To enhance the importance (on paper at least) of Caesarea, he exalted several rural outposts into suffragan bishoprics and put in his friends as bishops.

His brother Gregory accepted his place as Bishop of Nyssa, but Gregory Nazianzen despised the whole scheme and never would go near his tiny posting-station diocese of Sosima. His lifelong devotion to Basil never came closer to cracking than on this occasion, but when Basil died in 379, he and Gregory of Nyssa both preached inspirational eulogies at the funeral of the man who does truly deserve to be called Great.

GREGORY NAZIANZEN (330-390) 2nd January.
Gregory was the son of the Bishop of Nazianzus, and a much gentler, more self-doubting man than his energetic friend Basil of Caesarea.

As we have seen, the two men met as undergraduates at Athens University, the top university of the day, and fell for each other with the sort of passionate friendship bordering on romance which young men sometimes experience. Basil's was the stronger character and Gregory was usually happy to play Patroclus to his Achilles.

Gregory was ordained by his father and assisted him in the running of his diocese. We have seen the disgust he felt when his dear friend foisted on him the non-job of Bishop of Sosima; although consecrated in 372 he never visited the village, and, as we shall see, this manoeuvre of Basil was later to cost his friend dear.

Despite his quiet life in Nazianzus, Gregory established a huge reputation by the brilliance of his preaching and by his incisive theological gifts. It was he who solved the dilemma of how to describe the divinity of the Holy Spirit, by proposing the term 'proceeding.' Whereas the Son alone was begotten by the Father, the Holy Spirit proceeded, a term which perhaps does not mean much more than 'derives from,' but ensures the full divinity of the Spirit is recognised.

It is unfortunate that later the eastern and western churches were to be divided over the question of the Procession of the Holy Spirit – the east maintaining he proceeds from the Father alone, the West from the Father and the Son – a technical dispute which is still the formal reason why the orthodox and Roman Catholic churches are not in communion with each other.

With such a reputation and with the great Basil's backing, alarming things happened to the retiring St.Gregory in 378, when the Emperor Theodosius ascended the throne. He was the first emperor since Constantine to be uncompromisingly pro-Nicene and anti-Arian, and hopes were high that an orthodox bishop might be appointed for the capital, Constantinople, which had been Arian since 351. Gregory Nazianzen was persuaded by the orthodox party to come to Constantinople as an alternative bishop. All the church buildings of the capital were held by the Arians and Gregory began a preaching ministry in a little house called 'Anastasis' or 'Resurrection.' His eloquence drew vast crowds and at Easter 379 Gregory and his congregation were physically assaulted by the resentful Arians. His life was further complicated by the machinations of Peter, Bishop of Alexandria, the successor of St Athanasius. Alexandria, which regarded itself as the senior church of the east, cherished a permanent jealousy towards Constantinople, the new town which because of its political status claimed ecclesiastical pre-eminence as well. Peter desired to place a protégé of his own on the bishop's throne at Constantinople. An apparently friendly and supportive Egyptian, Maximus the Cynic, began to attend services at the Anastasis, and the naïve Gregory accepted him as the friend he appeared to be. But one night, Egyptian bishops were smuggled into the city on the grain fleet, Egyptian sailors took possession of the Anastasis, and Maximus was secretly consecrated bishop while Gregory and the city slept. Outrage at this trick was almost universal and the Alexandrians had to retire to Egypt in a hurry. It would not be the last time that Egyptian jealousies would cause trouble for the Bishop of Constantinople.

The Emperor Theodosius in 380 declared himself the foe of the Arians. Throughout the empire their churches were confiscated and their bishops banished. Gregory's position as bishop was now secure. At Theodosius' bidding a council was summoned to Constantinople, under Gregory's chairmanship, to settle the doctrine of the church and end the Arian controversy.

Gregory, so eloquent and brilliant in the pulpit, was a terrible chairman. He had not a political bone in his body and his reaction to the infighting, negotiations and alliance-building of a great council was one of disgust, self-doubting panic and fretful anger. The council got bogged down adjudicating the position of rival bishops of Antioch, people tried to score points by undermining Gregory, some claiming that his translation from the wretched diocese of Sosima to Constantinople was illegal under canon law, some maintaining the rights of the treacherous Maximus. Gregory cracked under the strain and in the middle of the council resigned his Bishopric, abandoned his work and fled to the calm of a monastery, where he ended his days. His successor led the Council of Constantinople to the resolutions towards which Gregory and Basil had worked all their lives; the Cappadocian formula, that God is three Persons in one substance, was adopted as the official doctrine of the church, and has remained ever since the orthodox description of the Trinity, God's inmost being.

The Cappadocian theology proposed the absolute equality and identity of the three persons. They were consubstantial, co-eternal, and shared together in effecting all the works of God. Older pictures of God the Father as 'senior partner' sending the Son and the Spirit to do his work, conceded too much to the Arians. The whole Trinity was involved in every work of God as equal. The only difference between the Persons was in their relation. Each Person had a characteristic way of relating to the other two. The Father begets, the Son is begotten, the Holy Spirit proceeds.

This statement may seem abstract to the point of meaninglessness. It may be an elegant distillation of all the factors in the controversy which preceded it, but it seems bloodless compared with the vigorous dynamic account of God's ways given in the New Testament. But the Cappadocian Fathers had correctly perceived that the essence of God's being as Trinity is relationship. It would be left to later thinkers to reconnect their diagram of God with the primal truth that God is love, and in their explorations to discover that the doctrine of the Trinity, abstract though it may seem, is actually the map of a wonderful country, where God's riches are revealed to those who travel with faith.

GREGORY OF NYSSA (330-394) 19th July.

The third of the Cappadocian Fathers, Basil's little brother Gregory, never made the same impact on his contemporaries. Basil and Gregory Nazianzen are counted as two of the four father of the Eastern Church; Gregory of Nyssa never achieved that honour. Yet today his work is more read than either of the other two.

As a young man, he declined to join his brother's family commune, instead getting married. His family nickname was 'the Orator', because he preferred classical studies to Christian ones. He certainly grew up to be a great orator, most in demand at the funerals of great men. Basil, as we have seen, made him Bishop of Nyssa as part of his strategy of building a power bloc around himself, but he always considered Gregory rather a light-weight and never trusted him with any important work.

Gregory's writings however reveal him as anything but a light-weight. In his hands the abstract discussions about the nature of God which so pre-occupied his age are taken up into the service of a mystical vision. His most approachable work in his 'Life of Moses.' In this, he takes the biblical story of Moses and uses it as a structure for examining the life of prayer. Moses' first experience of God is one of new light, the burning bush which illuminates his soul. Following established Christian tradition Gregory relates the Exodus story to the salvation we receive in Christ – the Passover lamb represents Christ's sacrifice, the Red Sea baptism, the manna in the desert Holy Communion, and so forth. Then Moses arrives at Mount Sinai and is summoned to meet God, not in further light but in a cloud. For the person of mature faith, God is actually less clear, less defined, than for someone still in the foothills. Faith pushes us to the top of the mountain, where in the darkness of the cloud we have to recognise that God is beyond our ability to understand, to imagine, to conceive. All we can do is stand with him in our ignorance and worship.

This quest for the God who is greater than all human images and concepts was to preoccupy mystics and saints for centuries. Gregory's vision is an important counter-balance to the intellectual certainties of the doctrine formulated in his age.

MACRINA (Died 379). 19th July.

We remember finally a female member of the extraordinary family of Basil. Macrina was the eldest child, a woman of great spirituality, given to prayer and asceticism, an enthusiastic member of Basil's family commune. Virtually all we know about her comes from the writing of her little brother Gregory of Nyssa, to whom she had been a second mother. He describes the time he spent with her when she was dying, and how she ended up comforting him by her noble and well-reasoned account of the victory which death is for a Christian. Some scholars (many of them male) have supposed that much of this discourse was composed and put in the mouth of Macrina by Gregory. Other scholars (many of them female) have seized on this teaching which, although refracted for us through the writings of a man, gives us a rare glimpse of the theological heights to which women in theology's golden age could attain. Secluded, veiled and obliged to accept silent and submissive roles in the life of the church, women like Macrina were just as inspired by the call to Christian holiness as the male bishops whose writings preoccupy later readers.

NINIAN (360-432) 16th September.

In 394, the year of Gregory of Nyssa's death, the aged Martin of Tours ordained and commissioned one of his disciples to return to his native land and spread the gospel. The disciple was Ninian, the apostle of the Picts, and his life illustrates how Martin's vision of dedicated groups of missionary monks moving out into the pagan countryside, was beginning to transform northern Europe.

Southern Britain had now been a Roman province for over three hundred years, but the Romans had never been able to establish a permanent authority over the wild Picts who lived in what is now Scotland; famously the Emperor Hadrian had built a great wall of defence against them, creating a definitive northern frontier for the empire. It was across this wall that Ninian felt called to go. He discovered a barbaric, tribal society, and he and his companions settled to live among them very much according to the pattern of holiness he had learned from Martin. A church was built, called Candida Casa, the White House, a name which perhaps reflects the awe of the Picts at one of the first stone buildings to be constructed in their land. Here Ninian and his monks fasted and prayed, and from here they made missionary journeys throughout Galloway.

At a time when Roman political control in Britain was beginning to falter, a faith shaped by the Roman empire was establishing itself among Rome's enemies.

AMBROSE (339-397) 7th December (4th April BCP)

While in the eastern empire the Cappadocian fathers worked out their elaborate theological reconciliations, in the western empire the true heir of Hilary of Poitiers was emerging, a man who would end the Arian schism in Italy and by the force of his personality set the pattern for relations between church and state for centuries to come.

Ambrose was born in Rome, the son of a noble, wealthy and Christian family. The Pope used to call on them quite often, and when he was gone the child Ambrose would shock and amuse his sisters by imitating the Pope's pompous walk and the way he stretched out his hands to be kissed. Despite the Christian culture of his childhood, Ambrose was not baptised and was destined for a career in public life.

The city of Rome was rich, Christian and decadent. Political power had gone east, to Constantinople; military power had decamped northward, so that the emperor could be nearer the ever-growing threat of barbarian invasion from the frontiers. Milan and Aquileia were the imperial cities in Italy now, and Rome was left to the senate, many still pagan, faithfully going through the motions of governing the Mistress of the World, and to the Pope, who, with the support of the leading Christian families, was cheerfully filling power vacuums as they opened up.

Ambrose, the career bureaucrat, followed the people who mattered to Milan, and one of his duties in 374 was to supervise the election of the city's new bishop. No obvious candidate dominated the election, and during the debate Ambrose was horrified to hear a child cry out 'Ambrose for Bishop.' The cry was taken up and Ambrose was elected. His protest that he had not been baptised was swept away, and the new bishop underwent the sacraments of baptism, first communion, and ordination into all three orders of ministry, within a fortnight.

Accepting his new fate, Ambrose decided he had better acquire some theology and underwent a crash course of reading. He was a keen reader and one of the first people to possess the skill of reading silently. In the ancient world, one always read aloud, even when alone, and people found Ambrose's silent reading uncanny and fascinating. They used to tiptoe into his room at watch him at it. Among the authors devoured by the new bishop was Basil of Caesarea; a correspondence with the great bishop of the east followed, and the result was that Ambrose became a convinced enemy of Arianism. He had gained great personal influence over the young emperor Gratian, Theodosius' western colleague, and a few months after Gregory Nazianzen's Council of Constaninople in 381, Ambrose held his own western council at Aquileia where Arianism was decisively condemned, to the secret fury of Gratian's mother, a comitted Arian.

When Gratian died, his brother Valentinian was more inclined to listen to his mother than to his bishop, and granted the Arians one church in Milan for their worship. Tolerance was not accounted a virtue in those days, and Ambrose acted decisively to prevent the pollution. He and his congregation occupied the church (it was quite a small one, tactfully situated outside the walls) and refused to surrender it to the heretics. During the siege Ambrose kept up his people's morale by teaching them hymns to sing – his were the earliest sung in the West, though unfortunately the tradition that he wrote the 'Te Deum' is a legend only. The Emperor decreed his banishment, but the people would not let him go. Ambrose's prestige was enhanced by the fortuitous, miraculous discovery of the bodies of the martyrs Gervase and Proteus, a sure sign that God was blessing his rule over Milan. When Valentinian's senior colleague Theodosius leaned on him, the emperor and his mother were obliged to give way. Ambrose had demonstrated that the power of the Catholic church was equal to that of the failing empire.

Theodosius himself experienced the Ambrose effect, when this normally just Emperor perpetrated an atrocity, revenging a rebellion in Thessalonica by organising an indiscriminate massacre of the citizens as they attended games in the amphitheatre. Ambrose was horrified at the crime and wrote immediately to protest.

Theodosius was barred from receiving communion until he had done public penance for his misdeed. The spectacle of the all-powerful emperor kneeling at the church door like any common sinner was one which inflated the imaginations of bishops for a very long time.

Although he is the first of the four Latin doctors of the church, Ambrose was not really a scholar, but a man of action in the best Roman tradition. His writings, sermons, letters and commentaries, were written in haste while the bishop's attention was on more urgent practical tasks. He left behind him the memory of what a bishop could achieve if he was resolute and kept the love of his people.

JEROME (342-420) 30th September.
Among those distinctly unmoved by the passing of the great Ambrose was a priest resident in Bethlehem, named Jerome. He had borne Ambrose a grudge for years because of his failure to stand by him in one of the many controversies which dogged his life. Few saints can ever have nursed their grudges as warmly as Jerome. He deserves at least second prize for the most unpleasant church father to attain sainthood. (The unspeakable winner of the first prize will be introduced to the reader in a few pages.)

Jerome was born in Illyria and went as a student to Rome, where he appears to have led a fairly dissolute life, although his extraordinary intellectual genius was already apparent. The young Jerome then experienced a violent conversion, offered himself for baptism and left Rome to travel to Syria, where it was his ardent desire to live the life of a hermit.

The penance of Jerome in the desert is a favourite subject with painters; he is shown nearly naked beating his chest with a rock. It is disappointing to relate that Jerome was a total failure as a hermit. The giveaway was that he took his entire library of books with him, and he appears to have devoted much more energy to reading and writing then to fasting and praying. Within two years he was back at Rome, with a lasting sense of shame that the hermit's life, which he so admired, was beyond him. His true vocation was that of a scholar, and the most important thing he had done in Syria was to find a rabbi to teach him Hebrew. Almost uniquely among the leading churchmen of the day, Jerome could read the Old Testament in its original language.

In Rome, he found congenial work as the secretary of Pope Damasus, at whose command he began his lifelong task of translating and commenting on the Bible. Like all new translations, Jerome's work was at first met with scorn. There already existed an Old Latin translation, made from the Greek, and when Jerome attempted to point out and correct the many inaccuracies of this much loved version, he was fiercely attacked by traditionalists. With a constant genius for making enemies, Jerome retaliated to every criticism in scorching, virulently personal attacks, written in some of the finest Latin prose ever penned.

His undoing came about not through his scholarship but through his continuing ardour for asceticism. In the wealthy Rome of Pope Damasus, many upper class Christian women were discovering the emptiness of large palaces and society functions, and seeking to give themselves whole-heartedly to Christ. To many of these Jerome became a sort of spiritual director; prickly as he was to men, he always got on very well with women. Upon Paula and her daughter Eustochium, he poured his advice on living the life of penance – their stately mansion became an unofficial nunnery, their days filled with fasting, prayer and bible study, and their fortunes dedicated to alms-giving. We have already seen how veneration for the state of virginity was growing in the church; with Jerome, the ideal of perpetual celibacy was an obsession, the centrepiece of any Christian life worthy to be called Christian. Whenever he got into conversation with any young woman, he would attempt to persuade her to renounce marriage, so notoriously so, that mothers anxious to see their daughters marry well would forbid them to go to houses where they might meet Jerome. As the craze for asceticism swept fashionable Rome, a backlash was inevitable. It came when a young woman under Jerome's influence died unexpectedly. The cause of death is disputed, but popular rumour was not slow to accuse Jerome of causing her death by starvation, with his inhuman insistence on fasting. He had gone too far and lost all his support. Rome was no longer a place for him.

Jerome and Paula left Rome, making elaborate arrangements to avoid any appearance of travelling together, and made their way to Jerusalem. There they spent Paula's entire fortune (which was vast) in founding and maintaining a religious house at Bethlehem. Jerome was happy at last. He devoted himself to the direction of Paula and the other nuns and to his translation. The Vulgate, as it is called, remained the standard Bible translation in Latin speaking countries until the Reformation. Jerome's devotion to Hebrew led him to make one decision which has affected Bible study ever since. For the first four centuries, Christians had read the Old Testament in the Greek translation called Septuagint, which contained several books not found in the Jewish, Hebrew canon. Jerome denied full scriptural authority to these books, setting them apart from the Old Testament as 'Deutero-canonical' or 'Aprocryphal.' During the Middle Ages these apocryphal books continued to be read, as they always had been, as scripture, but at the Reformation, the Protestant reformers decided that Jerome had been right, and adopted his canon. That is why English and German bibles (which dominate the world of bible study) have a different Old Testament from that found in Roman Catholic and Orthodox bibles.

Jerome did not become any less fierce in old age, and continued to attack his perceived enemies intemperately in brilliant writings. A priest called Jovianian wrote a work defending marriage as a respectable context for holy living, and went so far as to point out that the Virgin Mary herself had had many children by Joseph. Jerome was incandescent. He hurried into print to prove with all the scholarship at his command that whatever the gospels may seem to say, Mary was in fact a perpetual virgin; he then added vicious attacks on Jovinian's personal morals and denounced marriage, calling on all married Christians to cease marital relations and seek the more perfect way. Most moderate Christians were embarrassed by this outburst, but Jerome's devotion to celibacy was the orthodoxy of the future. A later bishop was famously to declare that the only good thing about marriage was that it produced more virgins.

Many legends have attached themselves to Jerome's stay in Bethlehem, the most famous being that of a lion from whose paw the saint took a thorn. In gratitude the lion joined the monastery, and everyday used to guard Jerome's donkey as it grazed. One day the lion fell asleep and the donkey was stolen, In penance, the lion did the donkey's work, wearing panniers and carrying home firewood for the community. A few years later the beast suddenly threw off its panniers and hurled itself with furious roars at some passing merchants. They took refuge in the monastery, where the lion continued to menace them until they confessed the theft of the donkey (which the lion had recognised) and restored it to its rightful owner.

Jerome is portrayed in art with his lion, wearing a cardinal's hat, an anachronistic reference to his close links to Pope Damasus.

MONICA (332-387) 27th August.
Among the many people who approached St Ambrose asking for his advice, was a woman from north Africa, who had come to Italy looking for her son. She was perplexed that in many respects the customs of the Roman and Italian church differed from her home church, and she wondered whether she should continue to observe the patterns of prayers and fasting she had always known. Ambrose gave her the celebrated advice, 'When in Rome, do as the Romans do.'

This anxiously pious woman was St Monica, and the runaway son she was looking for was the great Augustine. Monica was a Christian but her husband Patricius was not, and their children were not baptised. Monica had set her heart on seeing Augustine a Christian, and to this end all her prayers and formidable energies were directed. Augustine, like many sons of formidable women, spent much of his youth trying to get away from his mother, but this story is really his and it is to him that we now turn.

AUGUSTINE OF HIPPO (354-430) 28th August.
Apart from St Paul, no single Christian writer has had more of an effect on Western Christianity than St Augustine. Catholics and Protestants alike have drawn from the inexhaustible well of his genius. In recent years it has become fashionable to dwell on the dark side of his legacy and Augustine has been blamed for the Inquisition, Calvinist predestination, and Christian guilt about sex. But there is much more to Augustine. He was one of the earliest

human beings to be seriously and perceptively interested in the way people's minds work. He was one of the fathers of liberal political theory. And above all he wrote, with a passion and clarity that has never been rivalled, about what it means to love God with all your heart and to make the search for God the centre of your life.

Augustine narrates the story of his early life in his most widely read book, the 'Confessions.' He was a lover of books, early marked out for an intellectual career, and relished his school contact with classical literature; he later blamed himself for weeping more over the death of Dido in the 'Aeneid' than over the death of Christ in the gospels. He began a teaching career in Carthage where he represents himself as having been extremely wicked. It is true that he took a mistress, who became mother of his son, Adeodatus, and was his companion for many years, but he does not appear to have been promiscuously debauched by the standards of today's universities. He eventually decided that his career would be furthered by a move to Italy and he departed, taking with him his mistress and son, but carefully not informing his domineering mother, St Monica. She however followed him anyway, anxious not only to see him baptised, but to find him a suitable heiress to marry, so that he might advance his career. Conversation between Monica and the mistress, whose name we never discover, must have been worth overhearing.

All this time Augustine had been engaged on an inner journey, searching for meaning and for peace. He was for some years a Manichee; this sect, descended from Persian Zoroastrianism and bearing some similarity to the Gnostic sects opposed by Irenaeus, proposed a universe starkly and eternally divided between two equal powers, one good, one evil, and offered its adherents a way to safety on the side of light, if they would despise their bodies, which were inherently evil, and cherish their souls, in which faint sparks of light remained. This world view left its mark on Augustine even after his conversion to Christianity. He was also permanently affected by his studies in philosophy, particularly the spiritual interpretation of Plato offered by the philosopher Plotinus. From him Augustine derived a sense of the unimaginable beauty and harmonious order of the spiritual world, from which human beings found themselves exiled.

On arriving in Italy, Augustine gradually exposed for himself the weaknesses of these systems and knew that if he were ever to belong to any organised religion, it would be the Catholic Church. He met and was greatly influenced by St Ambrose; he read and learned to love the Christian scriptures. But still he hesitated. He knew that if he became a Christian at all, he would seek uncompromisingly the highest and holiest paths, and he did not want to sacrifice his career or his illicit family (it does not seem to have occurred to him that he might marry his poor mistress rather than repudiate her). He took a country house outside Milan, and withdrew with some dear and trusted friends to spend time in prayer and reflection. Sitting in the garden one evening, he heard a child singing 'Tolle, lege!' 'Take and read.' He obeyed, took up the Bible next to him and opened it at Romans 13: 'Put on the Lord Jesus Christ, and make no provision for the flesh.' The words came to him as a direct message from God. He returned to Milan, sought baptism from Ambrose, and prepared for a complete change in his way of life.

As he prepared to return to Africa, he was movingly reconciled to his mother, who had seen her dearest wish fulfilled as her son became a Christian. The 'Confessions' contains an account of their last long conversation as they waited to take ship, and of Monica's Christian death. Augustine went home alone.

He attempted to live a retired life of prayer and study, but on a visit to the small town of Hippo he was acclaimed by the people and elected as their bishop. He remained there for the rest of his life.

Augustine's letters paint a lively picture of the life of a bishop at the beginning of the fifth century. The Roman state was slowly but surely breaking down. Its arteries were clogged by an inflexible and corrupt bureaucracy, its commerce and towns choked by merciless taxation, but the authorities nevertheless found it harder and harder to maintain the armies of the frontier and control the ever increasing incursions of barbarians. In provincial towns virtually the only institution which exuded confidence and competence was the Christian church. A bishop like Augustine found himself administering large sums of money, in effect running the city's welfare programme, and adjudicating cases which were brought to him because his judgement was perceived to be quicker and fairer than that of the official law courts. In the midst of all this business he preached daily, ran a household which resembled an unofficial monastery, and wrote incessantly. More of his words survive than from any other ancient author. His style is lucid, passionate, somewhat addicted to word-play and oratorical contrasts, often repetitive, and utterly convinced of the urgency of the message he has to convey.

In his sermons and letters we see Augustine at his happiest, encouraging Christian pilgrims along the path to Paradise. Those on a journey, he wrote, do not stop to enjoy the passing scenery, but press on to reach their home. Union with God, the vision of God in Paradise, fills his imagination and in the most ardent terms he kindles the desire of his hearers. For Augustine was the great preacher of love. For him will was led by desire and desire was love. Only a person who had been gripped by the great love of God could possibly choose the arduous path of salvation, but once the vision of God's love had entered a person's heart, their desire would draw them and make every obstacle light.

It is characteristic of Augustine that when he came to write about the Trinity, he re-imagined the abstract concepts of the Cappadocians in terms of human personality and love. If, he argued, man is made in the image of God, and God is Trinity, then we should find within ourselves something similar to the Trinity. Human self-consciousness was the key. A man does not only exist; he knows that he exists and he loves himself as he exists. Do these activities within a human brain resemble faintly the activities of the Persons of the Trinity within the being of God? Augustine opened the way for thousands of Christians to find in the doctrine of the Trinity, not a mathematical conundrum, but a description of a relationship of mutual knowledge and love right at the heart of God, a relationship which the believer is invited to share, through baptism into Christ's sonship and through receiving the Holy Spirit of love.

This is the Augustine who has inspired so many to desire God; his emblem in art is a heart set on fire with love. Tragically, this is not the whole story of this talented, tormented, ultimately flawed man.

In 410 Alaric the Goth sacked the city of Rome. These Goths were not the naked savages of legend; they had been living within the Empire's borders as allies, learning Roman ways, for some time, and they sacked the city not as an act of war, but out of frustration that their subsidies were not being paid regularly. Nevertheless, the burning of the city sent shockwaves throughout the empire. For seven hundred years Rome had been unconquered mistress of the world, and her violation symbolised the end of civilisation. All those whose lives we have been following were affected. The senate abandoned the province of Britain as too costly and distant to run, and Ninian found himself cut off from Christian culture as his imperfectly converted Picts swarmed over the now useless Hadrian's Wall. In Gaul, provincial bishops like Brice wondered how much longer the vestiges of Roman ways could be maintained as everywhere law and order broke down. In Bethlehem, Jerome, Paula and Eustochium were moved to tears by the crowds of once wealthy people, whose houses in fashionable districts of Rome they had once visited, now arriving in the east as refugees, begging for charity. The catastrophe brought into focus the discontent of those still loyal to the old ways, who had seen in ninety years the Empire turn Christian and then collapse. The sack of Rome proved to them that Romans had been wrong to abandon the old gods, and that the Christians were to blame for everything.

Augustine wrote in response to this calamity his biggest and arguably his greatest book, the 'City of God.' This work, seeking to justify the God who had allowed Rome to be burned, reveals how far Augustine had moved from the classical civilisation in which he had been educated, and whose collapse he was witnessing. In many ways he was already a man of the coming Middle Ages as much as of the departing glory of Greece and Rome. In the 'City of God', he argues that there have always been two civilisations, two cities. One is built on earth by human beings who ignore or defy God. For all its splendours it is built on a lie, that man does not need God, and it is doomed to fall and perish, as over and over again its manifestations have perished, Babylon, Nineveh, Tyre, Egypt and now Rome. The other city is eternal, unseen, a pilgrim city for those who know that their true home is God, and that city will stand for ever. The book is still read by students of politics, as the ideas Augustine puts forward were to prove fruitful in later centuries, helping people develop the modern, liberal ideal of a secular state separate from the church and religious institutions; not perhaps the end for which Augustine was aiming as he wrote. It is a vast work, full of incidental fascinating information about pagan religion, the life of the church of the time, and the curious observations of Augustine's ever lively mind: for example, he takes time to praise the existence of nipples on men as a sign that God cares for beauty as well as utility in his creation.[91]

As the world darkened around him, Augustine's mind too darkened. Throughout his episcopate he had worked to end the Donatist schism in North Africa, the division, dating from the persecutions, which held the majority of African Christians aloof from Christendom in a parallel church which they believed alone to be pure and undefiled. In his work against the Donatists, Augustine developed one important doctrine, and one which was very terrible. The important doctrine was that the sacraments of the church do not depend on the worthiness of the ministers for their efficacy. The Donatists believed that the Catholic church was unable to deliver salvation, because its clergy had been contaminated, having been ordained by bishops who had failed to keep the faith during the persecutions. Augustine argued, in effect, that sacraments like baptism and Holy Communion were gifts of God given to a believer receiving them by faith. If the priest administering the sacrament were immoral or heretical, that would not prevent God's grace reaching the person who wished to receive it. But when reasoned argument did not succeed in reconciling the Donastists, Augustine's heart was hardened, and he fatally condoned the use of force to bring them back to communion. He quoted the parable of the banquet in Luke's gospel; 'go out into the highways and compel them to come in, that my house may be full.' The great preacher of desire now wanted to see people forced against their consciences to attend worship, because it was good for them. This set a dire precedent for the bishops of the Middle Ages.

---

[91] City of God, Bk.22, Ch.24.

Even darker was the controversy which obsessed Augustine in old age. A British monk called Pelagius taught sunnily the doctrine which British Christians have always in their hearts believed, that God sent Jesus to tell us how to live, and that we, now we know, have got to try our hardest to be good, so as to be worthy of heaven. For Augustine, this was dangerous nonsense. He knew from his own experience that a human being has no power to turn to God except the power which God in his mercy gives. We cannot make ourselves good, but must rely utterly on the grace given us through Jesus Christ. So far, so good. But as the controversy raged, Augustine was forced back into positions which, however logical, were terrible. If human beings were incapable of saving themselves, they must be born sinners, and un-baptised babies should justly go to hell. If a person only turned to God when God called him, then the only reason for a person not turning to God must be that God had chosen not to call him, had in fact predestined him for God's own, inscrutable, good reasons, to burn for ever in hell. Trying to defend the God with whom he had fallen in love, Augustine succeeded in painting him as a monster, who would haunt the consciences of Christians for generations to come.

As the bitter old man lay dying in Hippo, distant flames could be seen along the coast. The Vandals had forced their way through Gaul and Spain and were now over-running Roman North Africa. The empire in the west was being destroyed. The Christian church remained, and for good and ill, in the west it would be a church shaped by Augustine.

JOHN CHRYSOSTOM (315-386) 13th September.

In 398, seventeen years after the resignation of Gregory Nazianzen, and as Augustine was commencing his labours at Hippo, the see of Constantinople was again filled by a saint and once again in a manner which earned the enmity of the Bishop of Alexandria. The new bishop was John of Antioch, already well known for his preaching in his native city, and he was chosen above the preferred candidate of Theodosius, patriarch of Alexandria. The hereditary feud between Alexandria and Constantinople was set for another round.

John is named Chrysostom, or Golden-mouth, for his preaching eloquence was indeed extraordinary, even by the high standards of his generation. Her sermons continue to be highly readable, for he was comparatively uninterested in the complex theological debates of the day and concentrated rather on applying the lessons of the gospel to practical conduct plainly and forcibly. He had a great ability to bring bible stories to life, so that the characters came before the listener as real people, and he insisted, with all the brilliance of his rhetoric, that Christians must be people of simple lives, spending their efforts principally on serving Christ in his poor. Unfortunately, in moving to Constantinople, he found himself preaching to a congregation obsessed with wealth, privilege and the lovely, silly things that people with seriously large amounts of money can buy.

The old patriarch of Constantinople had been hospitable, easy going and tired. John dismissed the palace servants, sold the gold dinner services, lived and ate as simply as possible, never entertained and gave the income he saved to the poor. He forbade monks to visit great houses to give spiritual consolation and confined them to their monasteries. He attacked the culture of luxury and beauty which pervaded the church. 'You deck out Christ's house with golden pillars and silken hanging, while Christ himself is dying of hunger at your gates.' The common people loved him, but influential persons began to think enough was enough. His especial enemy was the Empress Eudoxia, who considered some remarks about Jezebel, makeup and attendance at Sunday race meetings particularly ill-judged.

In 402 there arrived in Constantinople some Egyptian monks, who had been driven from their native land by Patriarch Theodosius. John took an interest in their case and Theodosius attacked. He arrived in the capital with his retinue of monks, pointedly ignored the Bishop and set about forging links with all who bore grudges against John. A synod was convened at the Oak, a villa across the Bosphorus, at which, with blatant injustice and some brilliant political manoeuvres, Theodosius secured the deposition and exile of John.

The people of Constantinople rioted in protest, demanding the return of their beloved bishop. So great and prolonged was the disturbance that the empress was compelled to bring John back and reinstate him. He however had learned no tact whatever from the experience and preached his most notorious sermon, on the death of John the Baptist: 'Again Herodias dances, again she demands the head of John….' The listeners had no doubt who Herodias was, and neither had the Empress Eudoxia. This time there would be no reprieve. John was hustled away to exile in the Taurus mountains, while his furious congregation burned down the Basilica and the senate House, destroying in the process a priceless collection of Greek art.

The malice of the empress allowed John no rest. He was taken ever deeper into the mountains, while his strength forsook him. Sleeping on the floor of a little chapel, John saw in a dream the local martyr, St Basilicus, who invited him to join him tomorrow. The guards tried to hustle him on, but he had no more energy. They laid him on the floor of the chapel, and his last words were 'Glory to God in all things.' John Chysostom is the last of the four Greek Doctors of the church, joining Athanasius, Basil and Gregory Nazianzen.

CYRIL OF ALEXANDRIA (444) 27th June.

In 412 the unscrupulous Theodosius died, and in his place was elected his nephew Cyril, who inherited all his uncle's ruthless determination. He is probably the nastiest person ever to be venerated as a saint.

As we have seen, the Bishop or Patriarch of Alexandria was a formidable person, able to rely on the absolute obedience of his clergy and people, and above all buttressed by the hordes of fanatical monks, always ready to terrorise the enemies of the patriarch into submission.

Some examples will give the tone of Cyril's episcopacy. There still remained a large Jewish community at Alexandria, and during a street disturbance a favourite of Cyril, one Hierax, was harassed by angry Jews. The situation escalated and culminated in Cyril unleashing his faithful monks. Overnight, every synagogue in the city was burned to the ground and organised Judaism ceased to exist in Alexandria.

At another scene of disturbance a monk threw a stone and bloodied the forehead of the city Prefect. The man was arrested and executed for riot. Cyril had his body carried to the Cathedral, where he ordered him to be venerated as a martyr.

Cyril's most notorious victim was the philosopher Hypatia. One of the few women of the day to achieve success in public life, Hypatia was a pagan who lectured to her students from behind a curtain to preserve her modesty. Her influence was resented; she was dragged from her carriage by the monks, and battered to death with roof tiles, after which the monks dismembered her and carried her bleeding limbs through the streets in triumph. By such means did Cyril maintain and extend his influence in his diocese.

It was not long before this disreputable bishop found himself reopening for the third time in thirty years the vendetta of Alexandria against Constantinople.

In 428 history repeated itself, when once again a priest of Antioch with a reputation for fiery preaching was elected Bishop of Constantinople, Nestorius, unlike John Chrysostom, was determined to intervene when he smelt heresy, and his anger was aroused by a new popular trend in worship, that of hailing the Virgin Mary as the Mother of God (Theotokos). Ever since the Council of Constantinople had established the full and absolute divinity of the Son of God, conceptualising the life of Jesus of Nazareth had been very hard.

The heretical Apollinaris suggested that when the Word was made flesh, God the Son took the place of a human mind and soul within Jesus: Jesus in other words was a human body directed by a divine soul. But this denied that Jesus was in any real sense a human being at all. The whole of a human being, body, mind and spirit, must have been united to God the Son. Both before, during and after the incarnation Jesus had two natures, Man and God, and these two were never mingled but remained each perfect. The result of such thinking was a schizoid Jesus, whose actions were divided between his divine and human natures – the man fell asleep in the fishing boat, while the God quelled the storm; the man wept at the grave of

Lazarus while the God raised him to life; the man bled and died on the cross, while the God remained impassible and incorruptible.

It was within this climate of thought that Nestorius made his protest against Mary, mother of God. Mary, he said, had been the mother of the man Jesus, mother of Christ, but not mother of God, for God the Son existed before all ages. 'It is ridiculous to suppose.' cried Nestorius, 'that God could be a child of one day old, could cry and suckle his mother's breast.' But this of course is exactly what ordinary Christians attending Christmas carol services have always loved to suppose. Popular piety was against Nestorius, and Cyril of Alexandria saw that he could harness popular piety to humiliate once again an upstart Bishop of Constantinople.

A Council was called at Ephesus in 431. Cyril conducted it and his behaviour shocked even his own contemporaries. Cyril's own Egyptian clergy would vote for him, as would most of the Bishops of Asia Minor. Nestorius could probably count on the support of the Bishop of Antioch, where emphasis had always been laid on Jesus' real humanity, and on the delegates from Rome, which had a long tradition of veneration for the two natures. Cyril did the maths and realised that he would have to cheat. He opened the Council early, before the arrival of the delegates from Antioch and Rome; squads of Egyptian monks ensured that waverers voted in the right way; Nestorius was condemned and Mary's right to be called Mother of God was established. Various counter-attacks were made upon Cyril, but in his Egyptian fastness he was impregnable, and he died still Patriarch of Alexandria.

If we ask how such an unspeakable man can be remembered and venerated by the church, there are two answers. The Council of Ephesus, despite its irregularities, did much to enhance the status of the Virgin Mary, already the object of intense love and devotion among ordinary Christians. Cyril thus stands as the Virgin's champion, and it as such that he is portrayed on the walls of countless Lady chapels and Marian shrines. The second reason is that Cyril, while he was a bad man, was a superb theologian. In his hands the difficult doctrines of Trinity and Incarnation, so painfully hammered out, came to life as with deft and delicate masterstrokes he shows how the life of the Trinity was acted out in the historical events of

Christ's life and the Spirit's coming. To read Cyril of Alexandria is to enter a different world from the sordid political record of his life. He may have been no saint himself, but his writings have enlightened and guided many souls holier than his own.

LEO THE GREAT (died 461) 10th November.
While in the East Christians thus disputed the natures of Christ in relative security, in the west the Roman Empire had virtually ceased to exist. Britain was being over-run by Angles, Saxons and Jutes; Gaul by Franks; Spain by Visigoths; and Africa, as we have seen, by Vandals. In Italy itself some measure of control had been re-established by imperial troops, but imperial tax-collectors were almost as much feared by the impoverished country folk as the barbarians themselves.
It was in these disastrous circumstances that Pope Leo I was elected in 440. His strength of character, immense integrity and simple theological wisdom made him the man of the hour. With dwindling resources and little help from the eastern Emperor, Leo enhanced the spiritual leadership of his office even as the political authority of Rome was disappearing.
    In 451 Attila the Hun invaded Gaul. The self-styled 'Scourge of God' brought terror everywhere he went with the ferocious warriors he had led from the borders of China. He was deflected from Paris by the prayers of St Genevieve and eventually forced to retire by the Patrician Aetius, who maintained the honour of Roman arms in a hopeless situation. The following year however Attila invaded Italy and it was the turn of the imperial city to cower before his advance.
    Leo went out to meet the conqueror, preceded by the clergy in procession and by the young women and children of the city dressed in white and imploring pity. According to legend, Attila was dumbstruck by the appearance of the apostles Peter and Paul above the city, but even if such supernatural aid is discounted, what followed was one of the classic show-downs of history. Unarmed and defenceless, the dignity and determination of the Pope had their effect on Attila. He allowed himself to be persuaded to retire and

leave Rome un-sacked. He died within a year of this celebrated confrontation.

Leo's attempts at protecting his city were less successful in 455, when Genseric King of the Vandals, now firmly ensconced on the ruins of Augustine's Africa, launched a naval raid on Rome. Again the city was defenceless; again Leo went out to plead for mercy; but all he could obtain was a promise that there would be no indiscriminate sack or slaughter. He watched helplessly as for seven days the Vandals systematically looted the city, carrying off all the portable wealth they could find, together with members of the imperial family and other prominent people worth holding to ransom. Throughout this era of dis-ease, Leo held his people together, preaching strong, confident sermons, encouraging people to put their trust in God and renewing for them the inner vision which could sustain them.

In 451, as if the invasion of the Huns did not give him enough to do, Leo intervened decisively in the great Council of Chalcedon, held to attempt a definition of the person of Christ. At the meeting the so-called Tome of Leo was read out, in which the Roman allegiance was stated to the formula 'Two natures in one person.' 'Rome has spoken' cried the assembled bishops and the formula was adopted. The doctrine of Christ thus holds together two paradoxical truths – one the one hand, Christ was perfect God and perfect Man, with neither nature in any way mixed, changed or altered; on the other hand, Christ was one unified person, not two people held together. It has been well observed that this formula of Chacedon merely lays out the limits within which any true account of Christ must be worked out. Some leeway was allowed by a doctrine of 'exchange of properties' whereby it was permissible to transfer any statement about one of Christ's natures to the other. Thus one could properly say, 'God was born of a virgin,' 'God died,' and 'Jesus was with God from eternity,' 'Jesus is at the Father's right hand.' The popular belief which is always the bedrock from which theology is hewn was thus safeguarded.

The Council of Chalcedon did not command universal assent. The Nestorians mostly went into exile in Persia and by missionary activity spread as far as China. The Egyptians (Copts) rejected the doctrine of Christ's two natures and as monophysites (one nature believers) broke off communion with the rest of the church. A complex monothelite heresy (Christ had two natures but one will) further fractured Christian unity in Syria. By the time the Muslims invaded the Eastern empire, most Christians in the area were more alienated from the government in Constantinople than they were from the Arab newcomers.

Nevertheless, Leo's intervention secured agreement between Rome and Constantinople and greatly enhanced the papacy's claim to leadership of the church.

PART SIX. THE DARK AGES.

ST BENEDICT (480-550) 11th July (21st March BCP)

In the terrible times of disruption and collapse to which Western Europe was now subjected, the life of a hermit or a monk, for so long held up as the ideal life of a Christian, became irresistibly attractive to many. Where all hopes of order and security in this life were so uncertain, it was the merest prudence to seek for the heavenly kingdom and make of this life of toil a whole-hearted preparation for another, better life.

Benedict of Nursia was only one of many young Italians of his generation who fled from the world to find peace in solitude, but he was destined to have greater influence on the life of future generations than any of them. With all the idealism of youth, the teenage Benedict gave himself up with almost mad enthusiasm to the hermit's life. He went to live at the bottom of a chasm, from which his only contact with the outside world was a basket on a rope, by which a friend sent down his meagre rations. Solitude did not deliver peace: as Benedict faced his demons, as his young body craved sexual fulfilment, he would sometimes hurl himself naked into bramble bushes and roll among the thorns in his efforts to subdue the flesh.

He emerged from his solitude having gained self-knowledge, self-mastery and perhaps a measure of the wisdom of maturity, for he seems tacitly to have acknowledged that such excesses were not the way to holiness. At any rate the rest of his life was devoted to forming communities of prayer built around a rule of life which combined strenuous search after God with practical common-sense about the needs of a community living together.

Hermits and monks tended to live a fairly anarchic existence. When each person acknowledges no authority but the Holy Spirit within him, problems are bound to arise, for there are few people whose spiritual life is so firmly based on self-knowledge, so sensitively attuned to the voice of God, that they do not allow a great deal of fantasy, self-aggrandisement and wishful thinking to pass for 'What God wants me to do.' In such a spiritual culture, restlessness prevails; whenever boredom or frustration sets in, each would-be saint fancies God is calling them to go somewhere else, start a new project, pour their energies into something new. And where everybody is convinced that his pet project has been revealed by the Holy Spirit of prophecy, quarrels intensify, for who gets so angry as the person who is convinced that by refusing to co-operate with *him*, his fellow believers are defying the living God?

Benedict saw all this, and knew much of it from his own experience, and set about to write a rule by which the monastic ideal might be safely and wisely pursued. What he wrote has stood the test of time and has been the foundation for nearly every monastic rule in Western Europe.

Benedict's monks took three vows. The first was stability of place. They vowed to remain in one community, not running away to a more satisfying or exciting place when things became difficult, but trusting God to reveal himself in this one place, among this one group of people. The second vow was to conversion of life. The monk renounced all personal property, committed himself to celibacy and directed his efforts to the good of the community. The third, and to Benedict by far the most important, was obedience. Benedict believed that the essential requirement for anyone seeking to make spiritual progress was the renouncing of self-will. Obedience to the abbot and to the community set each monk free from the craving to impose his own desires on others, broke the obstinate inner belief that oneself is the most important thing in the universe, and opened each humbled soul to the grace of God.

How did the monks actually fill their days? They met for prayer seven times a day, and this common prayer was largely built around the reciting of psalms. Each monk was also expected to meditate, a practice much less elevated than it sounds. With the collapse of Roman urban society, literacy rates were tumbling and the cost of books was soaring. 'Meditation' for the early monks was learning by heart: learning the psalms and gospels so that their meaning would penetrate the soul, and so that without books they could join in the daily singing of the psalms. Finally a great deal of manual work was done; each community grew its own food and aimed to be self-sufficient, with doctors, teachers and craftsmen all being provided 'in house.'

Benedict's first attempt at community was a disaster. The monks he gathered together, each accustomed to choosing his own way, found Benedict's emphasis on common life and obedience intolerably restrictive. It was not long before a plot was made to poison the abbot, but this was foiled when he made the sign of the cross over the poisoned cup, which instantly burst. For this reason he is shown in art with a chalice from which he is charming a poisonous snake. Other emblems are the raven which is said to have brought him food in his solitude and a copy of his rule open at the first words 'Ausculta, O fili,' 'Listen my son.'

After the poison scandal Benedict left the rebellious community and began again to lead a solitary life at Subiacum. Here disciples gathered and were eventually organised into twelve monastic houses of twelve monks each. When these were flourishing, Benedict moved once more, and founded his greatest monastery at Monte Cassino, which still stands, despite the battering it received in 1944 during the allied invasion of Italy.

Benedict's achievement was to set a norm for monastic life, demanding enough to satisfy the longings of the many who were searching for God, flexible enough to be adapted to different circumstances. During the Dark Ages, it was Benedict's monasteries, with their tight, self-sufficient life of prayer, study and hard work, which preserved order, scholarship and hope among the peoples of Europe. It is for this reason that he is regarded as the patron saint of Europe.

SCHOLASTICA (480-543) 10th February.
Benedict had a twin sister, Scholastica, who followed her brother into vowed religious life, and ran a house of nuns at the bottom of the hill where Monte Cassino was situated. Once a year, Benedict would leave his monastery and go to spend a day with his sister.

In the year Scholastica died, the day had been a particularly pleasant one and when the time came for Benedict to leave she begged him to stay longer. Benedict refused, for it was of course an unbreakable rule that monks must be back in the monastery by nightfall. Scholastica bent her head and prayed. At once a terrible storm broke. Scholastica looked up from her prayer and said 'As you would not hear me, I turned to the Lord. Now go, if you can; go back to your monastery.' Indeed the rain was so severe that Benedict could not leave the convent and was obliged to stay the night. The brother and sister sat up all night talking and praying, and at dawn Benedict left. He never saw Scholastica again, for she died within the week.

PATRICK (390 – 460) 17th March.

While Benedict in Italy patiently built the communities which would have the resilience to survive through the Dark Ages, the church in Britain was in tumult. We have seen how in 410 the Roman legionaries had been withdrawn and the island left to its own devices. The Roman civilisation took a hundred years to die, but die it did. Picts from the north, Scots, confusingly, from Ireland, Angles, Saxons and Jutes from Germany, all descended upon Britain and dismembered it. Christianity in what we now call England virtually ceased to exist, but in Wales, Cornwall, Cumbria and Strathclyde Christian churches continued to minister to the shattered remains of the Romano-Celtic culture.

While these national tragedies were being played out, an altogether more personal trauma was engulfing a young lad called Patrick, who lived, depending on which authority you believe, either in Strathclyde or in Wales. Irish raids were for him not an abstract problem but a reality, when at the age of sixteen he was kidnapped and sold as a slave in Ireland. Patrick was already a Christian, and as he tended his master's herds, he prayed to God, not only for his freedom, but for power to make Ireland Christian.

Ireland had never been reached by the Romans, and despite a strong tradition of sea-faring and good trade links with the Empire, it remained very much another world. Classical urban civilisation had no part in the Irish way of life. They were rural people, living on small-holdings, owing a personal rather than legal obedience to their chiefs, incessantly at war, and filling their evenings with the music of the harp and the tales of wonderful deeds done by kings long ago.

Patrick was eventually able to make his escape and he travelled to Gaul, now becoming France, where the Christian culture was proving more resilient to barbarian assault than that in Britain. There was to grow up a long tradition of sending British boys to be ordained in France. Patrick was trained and ordained by Germanus, bishop of Auxerre, and around 430 he returned to Ireland as a bishop, determined to win the island for Christ. He never again left the place of his former imprisonment, which had now become his home.

On arrival in Ireland, Patrick's first priority was to establish Christian worship, and he built himself a chapel, where he proceeded to keep Easter. In that particular year, Easter coincided with the pagan Irish Festival of Tara, a celebration of the sun's power to renew life at the spring equinox. As part of this Festival, all fires were extinguished overnight, and a new fire was lit at daybreak. Patrick, knowing nothing of all this, kept his Easter vigil, with the traditional bonfire and Paschal candle. His flames were seen from Tara, and Leoghaire, the High King of Ireland, summoned him to answer for his sacrilegious breach of the Festival customs. Patrick immediately preached the Christian gospel; it is on this occasion that he is supposed to have picked a shamrock and used its three leaves on one stem as an analogy for the Trinity. The king was impressed enough by the power which emanated from Patrick to spare his life, but he was not immediately converted. The encounter had at least given Patrick a platform and some notoriety, and over a period of patient years his message began to bear fruit.

He employed what would now be called 'friendship evangelism', loitering in public places and striking up conversations. In this way Leoghaire's daughters were converted as they came to draw water from a well where Patrick and his followers were praying. In all Patrick is said to have ordained 450 clergy and received the vows of hundreds of monks and nuns. His mission was powered by love, a love which the Irish people have always reciprocated. He was buried at Down, where his shrine and relics were destroyed during the religious wars of the sixteenth century.

Patrick is supposed to have banished all poisonous reptiles from Ireland. The hymn 'St.Patrick's Breastplate' is actually written by him and expresses well his spirituality, in which a consciousness of unceasing spiritual warfare is balanced by the ability to see God in all things, and by a conviction that Christ was with him as guide and protector wherever he went.

BRIGID. (date unknown) 1st February.

Among those converted by St.Patrick was the household of a chieftain named Dubtach, who had an illegitimate daughter, Brigid or Bride. As a child she was taken to hear Patrick preach, and fell asleep during the sermon. Legend tells that, seeking to avoid the marriage her father had arranged for her, she prayed to be made so ugly that her bridegroom would shrink from her, and her prayers were answered by a disfiguring illness which blinded her in one eye. Her sight was restored when she became a nun.

If she was disfigured in youth, she must have recovered beauty as well as sight, for once a hermit, who had seen the Virgin Mary in a vision, declared that the Mother of God exactly resembled Brigid. For this reason, she was often called 'Mary of the Gael.' Like the Virgin, as her reputation grew she took on many of the attributes of a mother goddess. The stories told of her are the tallest of Irish tall stories, but all breathe an atmosphere of gentle delight in the goodness of God, who hedged his saint around with miracles. When Brigid gave away butter to the poor, the pats were miraculously replenished before her grudging stepmother checked them. When the bishop called, she milked one cow, and produced enough milk for his whole retinue. She hanged her cloak on a sunbeam to dry, charmed a white wolf out of the woods, and when she sat at the side of the lake, all the ducks and geese would swim to her and nestle in her lap.

Behind this charming web of whimsical miracles lies the reputation of a woman who won all hearts by her generous kindness. A holy fire was kept burning on her tomb in Kildare, until it was extinguished as superstitious in 1220.

REMIGIUS (438-533) 1st October.

By this time, the former provinces of the Roman Empire were irrevocably lost and new kingdoms were arising as the barbarian conquerors consolidated their gains. In northern Gaul, the new masters were the Franks, soon to give their name to their new territory of France.

Despite the conquest, the Christian civilisation founded by St Denys continued to flourish. The barbarians had a love-hate relationship with the Christian church and the Roman culture with which it was associated. They were in awe of the magnificent cities even as they burned them; the church, with its high written culture, beautiful traditions of craftsmanship, and international system of government by synods and councils, intrigued and attracted them even when they found the gospel itself incomprehensible. So it was that Gaulish Christians found themselves free to practise their faith under their pagan masters.

Remigius, early distinguished by his learning, became bishop of Rheims at the age of twenty-two and was soon fast friends with Queen Clotildis, the wife of Clovis King of the Franks, and herself a committed Christian. Her efforts at converting her husband were thwarted by family tragedy. Her first two children were both baptised and both died in infancy, which convinced the King that baptism was a dangerously unhealthy practice.

His views changed when he was confronted with an invasion by the Alemanni. In the heat of battle, when defeat seemed certain, Clovis cried out for help to 'Christ, whom my wife calls Son of God.' The resulting victory convinced Clovis that Jesus had something to recommend him after all, and Clotildis secretly sent for Remigius, bidding him strike while the iron was hot.

Remigius instructed the warrior king in the Christian faith, and the story of Jesus had a profound effect on Clovis, especially the crucifixion. 'Would I had been there with my brave Franks,' said the King, rather missing the point of the story. 'The Jews would not have dared to treat him thus.'

Clovis was convinced, but did not believe that his people would lightly abandon their old religion. However, when Remigius addressed a meeting of the Franks, he was met with loud shouts of approval; and when Clovis was baptised in 496, he was followed to the font by 3,000 of his nobles and people.

According to later legend, Remigius also crowned Clovis as first King of France. The anointing oil for the ceremony was brought from heaven by a dove and was ever after kept in the cathedral at Rheims, until the phial was smashed during the French Revolution.

LEONARD (c.540) 6th November

Among the three thousand Frankish nobles baptised by Remigius was St Leonard, who went on to have a highly exciting, if legendary, Christian life.

Experiencing the inevitable call to live as a hermit, Leonard abandoned the court and went to live in the forest of Limoges. When Clovis and Clotildis went hunting in the area, the Queen went into labour. Leonard was at hand and his prayers and ministrations preserved the life of mother and child. The grateful king offered Leonard a reward, and he asked for as much land as his donkey could ride around in a night. On this land he built the abbey of Noblac (now St Leonard) and ruled the new community as abbot. He spent the monastery revenue in ransoming prisoners of war and buying back those enslaved for debt; he is thus patron saint of prisoners and is shown in art holding broken chains.

According to Sussex legend, St Leonard visited England, landing at the town which bears his name and spending time and prayer in the Forest of St Leonard. There he was attacked by a fearsome dragon, which he eventually slew. The blood which he shed in the fight fell to the ground and from it grew lilies of the valley, which can still be picked in St Leonard's Forest.

Leonard became a very popular saint in the Middle Ages, and many crusaders taken prisoner attributed their safe return home to his intercession.

GREGORY THE GREAT (540-604) 3rd September (12th March BCP)

While the kingdom of France was thus being established as a Christian land, the situation of Italy was still deplorable.

The northern part of the country was now a barbarian kingdom, Lombardy, while the south was still nominally part of the Roman Empire. The great Justinian and his general Belisarius had made a counter attack following the invasions of the Huns and Vandals and for a few more years Rome's imperial status was preserved. The exarch, representing the Emperor of Constantinople, maintained a precarious authority at Ravenna and along the Adriatic coast. Rome itself was governed for all practical purposes by the Pope, who alone retained any authority in the shrunken city.

If Jerome and Paula could have returned a hundred and fifty years after they left Rome, they would have been appalled at what they saw. It is estimated that the population had fallen to one tenth of what it had been in the high days of empire. Vast tracts of the city had simply been abandoned, and until the nineteenth century tourists could still expect to see the ruins of temples, bathhouses and circuses miles out in the country around Rome, the remains of what had once been prosperous urban districts. All the aqueducts had broken down, so that the aristocracy had abandoned their luxury villas on the summits of the seven hills and had moved downhill to be closer to the river and the wells. Under Christian pressure the gladiatorial games had been abandoned, and the great amphitheatres left to rot. The city paid taxes to Constantinople but got virtually nothing back in terms of public services or military protection. All that was left was the prestige of its name, still envied and feared by all the barbarian kings, and the church of the Popes.

To the rule of such a city was elected in 590 one of the greatest men ever to wear the papal crown. Gregory was born into one of the richest landowning families in Rome, and it is clear that even at this bleak époque, the very rich were cushioned by a still existent wealth. When Gregory turned to Christ and began to look for a simpler, more contemplative life, he was able to endow seven monasteries in Sicily with his estates, and to establish an eighth in Rome itself in his family's town house. Gregory himself did not take monastic vows – he sensed correctly that a man with his gifts needed to serve Christ in the world – but he lived a disciplined life of prayer and study within the monastery he had founded. When he was ordained, he spent several years as the papal envoy in Constantinople, where, curiously, he seems neither to have learned Greek nor to have made any contact with the theological writings of the east. When he returned to Rome the city, to add to its other woes, was in the grip of a terrible plague, and Gregory's election as Pope plunged him into a deep depression. His early letters breathe a sense of despair at the challenges which faced him. But Gregory was not a man to remain for long the passive victim of events.

Gregory called the people together to pray for an end to the plague; his measures were not sensible from a modern medical perspective, for he called the entire population in seven parties to process about the city, calling on God for deliverance. An eye-witness account related the unbearable earnestness with which the people offered their prayers, although even as the procession wended its way, participants were falling dead. The Litany was composed for this mournful act of prayer, and was always used as a processional form of prayer until the Reformation

When the plague abated, Gregory took every possible measure to restore prosperity and confidence to the ailing city. He proved a painstaking steward of the papal estates, which were very large, and devoted his increased income to repairing the city's fortifications, rebuilding churches, and giving relief to the many poor and sick inhabitants of Rome. Whatever his private anxieties, he exuded confidence from the pulpit and reinvigorated the faith of his clergy and people. By careful diplomacy, he was able to punch above his weight in the complex politics of the day and hold at bay both the Lombards, the local dukes and princes, and the imperial tax-collectors. Realising that the exarch of Ravenna was unable to offer any real protection to Rome, Gregory organised, trained and paid for troops of his own to man the defences – we are now far enough into the Middle Ages to have left behind the scruples of George or Martin about the fitness of soldiering as a profession for a Christian.

By his strong government Gregory was building for the papacy the sort of authority which later Popes would use to claim dominion over Christendom, but he was well aware of the dangers of power and his preferred title was the humble one which has ever since been borne by the popes: 'Servant of the servants of God.'

In the midst of all this practical work for the good of his city, Gregory did not neglect his spiritual duties as pastor and teacher. His sermons and other written works are severely practical: of his writings the one with the most lasting influence was his 'Pastoral Rule', a handbook for clergy which remained the standard training manual throughout the middles ages, and which is still relevant today, thanks to its shrewd observations as to how easily power and leadership can be misused.

It is slightly disconcerting to lay alongside the 'Pastoral Rule', with its level-headed practical wisdom, Gregory's 'Dialogues', a collection of stories which he made to strengthen the faith of his flock. In another sign of how much closer to the Middle Ages than to classical Rome this great Pope was, the dialogues report with absolute credulity the most astonishing series of miracles, involving demons, the relics of saints and the consecrated host. Gregory clearly set great store by what to us seem old wives' tales.

He was a great admirer of St Benedict, wrote his biography and encouraged the adoption of his rule in the monasteries of southern Italy.

Three legends about St Gregory were often retold in later years. The first told how on one occasion as he was celebrating mass, the bread in his hands took on the form of a child, thus demonstrating the real presence of Jesus in the sacrament. The mass of St Gregory is a favourite theme with artists.

Another legend, generous in spirit if implausible in incident, tells how Gregory grieved greatly for the pagan Emperor Trajan. It seemed unjust to him that so good a man, the most upright emperor Rome ever had, should be condemned to hell because he lacked baptism. At his prayer Trajan was miraculously restored to life for just long enough for the Pope to convert and baptise him, and the Emperor's place in Paradise was thus assured. Although the machinery of the tale is quaint, it is interesting as early evidence that Christians were finding it hard to reconcile themselves to the cruelty and injustice which were produced by too logical an application of the doctrine of hell-fire. The legend reassured that God's mercy is paramount, especially when Christians pray.

But the best known story about Gregory, and the most likely to be true, comes from the period before his elevation to the papal throne. He was walking though the slave markets when his attention was drawn to some fair-haired children of exceptional beauty. Gregory asked where these poor children had been brought from and was told they were Angles, from Britain. 'Not Angles,' said the witty saint, 'but angels.' He bought the boys and had them educated in his monastery. Later his mind reverted to the lost island of Britain and he resolved to organise its re-conversion.

But before we too, with the Pope, direct our attention to the Angles, we must return to the the west of the island, the land of Ninian and Patrick, and discover the doings of the Celtic Christians who had survived the Anglo-Saxon invasion.

PART SEVEN. THE CELTS.

DAVID (601) 1ˢᵗ March.

Thanks to St Patrick and St Brigid, Ireland was a Christian country, though isolated from the rest of Christendom and developing its distinctive traditions. Almost equally isolated, cut off by the bloc of Anglo-Saxon heathen kingdoms, were the Celtic churches of Wales, Strathclyde and Cornwall. So great was the resentment caused by the Anglo-Saxon invasions, that no attempt seems to have been made by the Celts to convert the Germanic intruders. But as we shall see, the Celtic church produced saints, who with their peculiar tradition of wandering, of pilgrimage through this world, did much to keep faith alive beyond their own hillsides.

The greatest of the Welsh saints was David, and it is frustrating that so little is known about him. Despite the wishful thinking of one chronicler, he was certainly not the uncle of King Arthur, whose resistance to the Saxons was staged about a hundred years earlier, and the tradition that the leek became the national plant of Wales because David gave leeks to the knights of the Round Table to wear as they charged the Saxon, is as devoid of truth as any of the other stories ingeniously devised to explain the Welsh love of this vegetable.

David is supposed to have been dedicated to God as a baby and brought up in a monastery school. He travelled widely as a youth. Celtic monasticism knew nothing of Benedict's humble determination to be rooted in one place; the monks of Wales and Ireland were travellers, always engaged in a paradoxical double quest, on the one hand for islands, mountains and headlands remote enough for a prayer of utter solitude, on the other for new places where churches could be built and people baptised. Their travelling symbolised their detachment from all earthly loyalties, while their poverty expressed their trust in God, who would supply their needs as they went. They were exactly the sort of monks that most irritated St Benedict.

Thus David travelled to Glastonbury, to the Isle of Wight, some say to the Holy Land itself. He returned to become a bishop and an abbot, and as such attended the synod at a place now called

Llandewi Brei (chuch of David the Bellower) in memory of him. Here he is said to have been the only speaker whose voice carried so that everyone present could hear him; he probably accomplished this feat without the hill which tradition says miraculously rose under his feet as he spoke.

In all David founded twelve monasteries, poor places without resources, where the monks pulled their ploughs by hand for lack of oxen. He died radiantly expecting heaven, surrounded by his weeping brothers.

MACHUTUS (died 640). 15th November BCP.

The Book of Common Prayer commemorates another Welsh travelling monk, Machutus or St Malo, who crossed the Channel in a coracle and founded in Brittany the town which bears his name. There were and are close cultural links between Wales, Cornwall and Brittany; they were all strongholds of the Celts after the barbarian invasions. Brittany is properly 'Little Britain', the sister of the island 'Great Britain'.

KENTIGERN (St Mungo) (died 603) 13th January.

St Kentigern was a native of Strathclyde whose nickname 'Mungo' or 'Darling' reveals that he, like Patrick and Brigid, was loved by the people who cherished his memory. He is the founder of the church and city of Glasgow, and his legend has all the Celtic hallmarks of wonder and sweetness.

His mother was raped and then abandoned by a nobleman; the cruel customs of the time blamed the victim as much as the perpetrator of rape, and Enoch, heavily pregnant, was set adrift in an open boat and abandoned. The boat drifted up the Firth of Forth, where a hermit called Servan rescued Enoch, tended her during her delivery, and adopted her son when she died. Kentigern was brought up by Servan, who loved him so tenderly that he aroused the jealousy of his other pupils. One day they tried to discredit Kentigern by killing the pet robin of Servan and blaming Kentigern for the cruelty. 'Give the bird to me', said the boy, 'and I will prove my innocence.' Gently he stroked the robin and restored it to life. The robin now appears on the arms of Glasgow.

Once grown up, Kentigern proved the worthy heir of St Ninian, building a community on the site of what is now Glasgow, and spreading the faith of Christ by prayer and love. He continued to have a way with animals. A wild boar guided him through the forest when he was lost; stags came out of the woods and drew his cart when his horse died. When a woman came to him crying because her husband would not believe she had dropped her wedding ring in the river, and accused her of giving it to a lover, Kentigern asked a salmon to swim to the bottom of the Clyde and bring back the ring. This salmon also appears on Glasgow's coat of arms.

Such stories, naïve though they are, reflect the Celtic belief in a God whose providence takes care over every detail of our lives. They are also images of the renewal brought about by baptism. As our alienation from God is ended through Christ, so our alienation from the world of nature and from the animals ends too, and paradise is restored.

COLUMBA (521-597) 9th June.

While at work on the foundation of Glasgow, Kentigern visited the islands off Galloway, and especially the holy island of Iona, where, returning the benefits conferred by St Patrick, an Irish monk had founded a community to help with the mission to the Picts.

This was Columba, who had founded Iona initially as an act of penance. The story of his crime illustrates intriguingly how the traditional warrior ethos of the Celts was uneasily joined to their new found passion for the gospel. In that world where books were fabulously expensive and rare treasures, Columba, already the founder of several monasteries, laboured for many months making his own copy of the Bible from a precious manuscript in another abbey, where he stayed as a guest. However, when the time came to leave, the abbot declared that copies made from his library remained the property of the abbey and could not be taken outside, and in this he was supported by the local king, whose judgement was 'the calf belongs to the owner of the cow.' Furious at being cheated, Columba raised his clansmen and a bloody battle ensued, in which many were killed. Columba was excommunicated, a sentence he accepted, being filled with remorse at where his passions had led him. The excommunication was lifted in return for a penance Columba imposed upon himself, namely to sail to a land where Ireland was no longer visible, and to remain there until he had converted as many pagans as the number of his fellow countrymen who had perished in his war.

Iona was the first island which Columba's little ship touched at after the shore of Ireland had sunk below the horizon, and it was here that he and his companions built the wattle huts which were to house their new community. From Iona, the monks spread out, making missionary journeys around the western isles and the lowlands of Scotland.

His fiery spirit now chastened, Columba became renowned for his extreme gentleness; his ministry centred on spiritual direction and on the giving of advice to people in trouble. Those who wished to consult him went to Mull and called until a monk brought a boat across to ferry them to Iona. Women trapped in unhappy marriages, farmers perplexed about their crops, kings of the Picts and bishops, scholars and travelling monks, all made their way across the narrow straits and all found themselves welcomed with the honour due to Christ himself. Columba died in the very year when another party of missionaries, led from Rome by Augustine, landed in Kent to begin the conversion of the English. The community on Iona, closed at the Reformation, has recently been re-founded as a place of hospitality and of rediscovery of the peculiar sweet wanderlust of Celtic spirituality.

PETROC (c.550). 4th June.
Our final Celtic saint is the Cornish abbot Petroc, who was buried at Bodmin, and revered as a healer and holy man.

Petroc's legend, too, is one of wanderings and exile. He arrived in Cornwall from Wales and on landing caused a miraculous spring to gush forth. His pilgrimages are said to have taken him as far as India, where he lived on an island and ate only fish. Back at Bodmin, he cured a dragon by removing a splinter from its eye, and lived with a tame stag as companion. The memory of the historic Petroc was cherished, for twenty-seven of the ancient churches of Cornwall are dedicated to him.

PART EIGHT. THE CONVERSION OF ENGLAND.

AUGUSTINE (605) 26th May.

How much did Pope Gregory the Great know about the state of the Irish church or about the work of David, Kentigern and Petroc? Probably very little; he was however aware that in contrast to the enthusiastically Christian Kings of the Franks, with whom he was in fruitful contact, the kings of the seven Saxon kingdoms of Britain remained cheerfully pagan, a situation he was determined to rectify.

In 594, he commissioned Augustine, a monk of Rome, to set out for Britain with a party of twelve followers, and win the Anglo-Saxons for Christ. Gregory's ordered mind already envisaged a properly organised new province of Christendom: his plan was to establish two archbishoprics at London and York, with twelve bishoprics under each. Things, naturally, did not run as smoothly as that.

Augustine was frankly terrified by his new vocation. Britain was beyond the edge of the civilised world. It took him three years to get to his goal; he tried to turn back halfway through France, and only the iron determination of the Pope kept him going. However, once arrived in Kent, things proved easier than he had expected. King Ethelbert of Kent had married a French princess, Bertha, who was a practising Christian. Although the King insisted on meeting Augustine in the open air (for some reason he believed that Christian magic was more powerful inside buildings) he was not unfriendly and even gave Augustine's party permission to rebuild and use an old Roman church dedicated to St Martin in Canterbury. As with Clovis in France, the combination of a pious wife and a bishop promising exotic contact with the still envied culture of Rome, undermined Ethelbert's resistance, and he and his nobles were baptised. Much to his surprise, Augustine found himself a success and the first Archbishop of Canterbury (the London plan was shelved as London was the capital of still pagan Essex).

Gregory took a keen interest in the mission and sent Augustine letters of advice and encouragement, including his famous advice to build on the Saxons' existing pagan religion, rather than seek to obliterate it. Churches should be built in places already regarded as holy, festivals celebrated in pagan holy seasons. Whether Gregory anticipated that the result of this policy would be that 1500 years later English Christians still name the days of the week in honour of their ancestral gods, is questionable.

Alas, Augustine's approach to the Celtic bishops, when he eventually made contact with them, was nothing like so tactful. His meeting with the Welsh bishops is one of the most tragic own goals in the history of mission. He greeted them seated on a throne, as a prince expecting homage from vassals, rather than rising to greet them as brothers and equals. The Welsh bishops retired bristling. On this showing, the conversion of the Saxons was not going to do much to heal the racial divide.

Augustine died and was buried in the abbey he had founded in Canterbury, a church now in ruins, but in its heyday as large and influential as the cathedral itself.

MELLITUS (624) 24th April.

Once the English mission was established, Gregory sent a second body of missionaries from Rome. Mellitus, who headed these reinforcements, crossed the Thames and entered the kingdom of Essex. He converted the King and was consecrated as the first Bishop of London. Unfortunately, on the king's death, the Essex mission suffered a set-back. The young princes, heirs to the throne, fell out with Mellitus for a curious reason. They were adamant in not wishing to be baptised, but they did wish, very strongly, to receive the 'white bread' of Holy Communion. Did they shrink from the full commitment of baptism while believing that they could appropriate some of the good magic of the new religion on their own terms? Not for the last time, members of the English upper class were infuriated by the pedantry of a priest who insisted on keeping the rules rather than giving them what they wanted. Mellitus was driven out of London, and retired to Kent, where he ended his days as third Archbishop of Canterbury. In his old age he was bedridden, but when a fire arose in Canterbury, he insisted on being carried out into the street to quench it by his prayers and his presence.

ST PAULINUS (644) 10th October.

King Ethelbert made a marriage alliance with King Edwin of Northumbria and sent his daughter Ethelburga north to be married. By the terms of the alliance, she was permitted to practise her faith and to take a chaplain with her. The chaplain's name was Paulinus. The familiar thin end of the wedge, a Christian queen, was being inserted into Northumbria.

Edwin was a fearsome monarch. Northumbria was the dominant kingdom of the day, though watched with envy by the Midlands kingdom of Mercia, and Edwin had made it stronger by uniting in his hands the two sceptres of Bernicia and Deira, the two realms of which Northumbria was made up. This he had done by the simple expedient of murdering the King of Deira, leaving his sons to go into exile in Scotland. These princes we shall meet again. Now he was not only marrying a Christian, but he had a guilty secret. In battle against the Mercians he had cried, like Clovis, to the God of the Christians for help, and had been victorious. He was not anxious to pay his debt.

A meeting was held of the Northumbrian nobility at which Paulinus expounded the faith he was bringing them. As the debate developed, one of the lords spoke in memorable words. Our life, he said, is like a sparrow which flies into a hall on a stormy night. For a moment it flashes in the light and warmth, then out it flies into the darkness and is gone. If Paulinus could tell them what lay in that darkness, could lift the veil of death, then he should be listened to. A pagan priest rose up and declared his disillusionment with the gods he had served so long. Taking his horse and a spear, he charged the statue of Thor and overthrew it. He was not struck down by a thunderbolt and this lack of a miracle had its effect on those who had venerated the broken statue.

The nobility were ready to convert, but the king hesitated. Could a faith based on love, fasting and the forgiveness of enemies really be suitable for the warrior overlord of England? While he sat thinking, Paulinus came up behind him and said softly, 'Do not forget your promise.' The King was thunderstruck. It seemed to him that Paulinus could only have known by supernatural means about his vow made in the heat of battle. His last resistance was overcome and he prepared for baptism.

On Easter Day 627, in a wooden church constructed for the purpose at York, Paulinus, newly consecrated first Bishop of York, baptised Edwin and many of his nobles.

If Edwin thought that by baptism he was gaining a lucky charm god to win his battles, he was disillusioned. A mere three years later the Christian king was slain in battle against his old enemy, the pagan Penda king of Mercia. Scandalously, Penda was helped by hordes of Christian Welshmen, for whom racial hatred meant more than religious brotherhood. The mission of Paulinus was in ruins. He escorted the widowed Queen Ethelburga and her small children back to Kent and accepted the less dangerous job of Bishop of Rochester. He was buried next to Augustine in Canterbury.

ETHELBURGA of LYMING (647) 4th April CDC.

Ethelburga is herself honoured as a saint, not merely for her role in bringing her husband to faith, but for her widowed career as abbess of Lyming. Anglo-Saxon royal women frequently became nuns when they were widowed; it was one of the few ways they were able to assert themselves independently of men; but that was not the whole story. In this precarious world, where one battle could plunge you from Queen to refugee, it made sense to everyone to seek first the kingdom of God and the heavenly riches.

JAMES THE DEACON (c.670) 11th October.

One other name must be remembered from the short-lived mission of Paulinus. When he fled south, he left the Christians of York in the charge of his deacon, James. Very little is known of this heroic man, who faced the full onslaught of the pagan Mercians, but he survived to attend the synod of Whitby thirty years later.

OSWALD (605-642) 5th August.

It will be remembered that King Edwin had gained his throne by murder. The true heir, the young prince Oswald, fled to Scotland. By a fateful chance, his chosen place of refuge was the island of Iona, where he lived for many years among Columba's monks. It was in

Iona that Oswald became a Christian. In 634, four years after the death of Edwin, he returned to Northumbria and defeated and drove out the Mercians. Installed as King, it was his fixed purpose to make his kingdom Christian. This was significant. In the end, Northumbria was to receive the gospel not from the south, from the papal-sponsored missionaries in Kent, but from the north, from the Irish Celtic monks who had formed the spirituality of the new King.

Oswald sent to Iona to request a team of Christian missionaries. The first group sent was not a success. Led by Corman, they found the Angles incurably addicted to worldly pleasures and to the violent, corsair life of their ancestors. The language barrier too was formidable. Corman withdrew in disgust, but as he reported his failure to the community at Iona, he was gently rebuked by another brother, Aidan. 'You should have given them the milk of the gospel first and when they were accustomed to that, weaned them onto strong meat.' It was decided that Aidan should lead a second group of monks and try again where Corman had failed. In 635 Aidan arrived in Northumbria.

AIDAN (died 651) 31st August.

Oswald welcomed his new missionary with delight and generosity. Aidan was granted any land he needed for a new monastic foundation, and he choose the island of Lindisfarne, off the coast from Bamburgh, the royal capital. Lindisfarne is a tidal island, connected by a causeway at low tide to the mainland, and its geography neatly symbolises the Celtic approach to mission, with its two pulls, away from the world into prayerful solitude, towards the world in preaching and service. On Lindisfarne, Aidan and his monks lived and prayed; from Lindisfarne they visited the royal court to assist Oswald in his christianisation of his kingdom, and also undertook preaching missions into the wild hills and fells of Northumbria, baptising ordinary people and building churches. The king gave Aidan every support, in the early days acting as interpreter himself; thanks to his years in exile on Iona, he was one of the few people fluent in both the Germanic and the Celtic tongue. He attempted to equip Aidan with a horse, as befitted a royal missionary, but this the saint steadily refused. He wanted to follow Christ in holy poverty, and to approach the country people as one of themselves, rather than as an emissary from on high.

The partnership of king and bishop was brought to an abrupt end by Penda, King of Mercia. Once again he invaded Northumbria; once again Oswald rallied his forces to defend his lands – but this time he was defeated. At Oswestry in 642 the Christian king was slain, and Northumbria was humbled, being divided again into its constituent principalities of Deira and Bernicia. Oswald's brother Oswy, who succeeded him, was eventually to defeat Penda and force him to admit missionaries into Mercia.

Aidan's work stood the test of King Oswald's death well. The collapse which followed the death of Edwin was not repeated. Aidan's clergy stuck to their posts, Lindisfarne remained a holy place, and there was no longer any serious danger that the Northumbrians would relapse into paganism. Aidan's relations with Oswy were good, until in 651 bishop heard that Oswy had forcibly reunited the kingdom by murdering his fellow king. Grief at this crime contributed to Aidan's death. He was buried on his beloved Lindisfarne.

CUTHBERT (640-687) 20th March.
In 651, an eleven year old boy was keeping sheep on the hills of Northumbria when he saw an amazing trail of light in the night sky. To the boy, the lights looked like angels. On the next day, he discovered that bishop Aidan had died, and he was convinced that what he had seen was the ascent of the saint into heaven. The shepherd boy received the vision as a sign, travelled to the abbey of Melrose and offered himself as a monk. He was to become the last of the great missionary saints working in the Celtic tradition, and perhaps the best loved of all of them.

Cuthbert lived through times of great change, as the Celtic church of Northumbria connected with and was challenged by the Roman traditions which linked the south of England with the churches of the continent, but these tumults seem scarcely to have touched him. He lived a charmed life, cocooned in miracle and in the love of the ordinary north country folk.

From Melrose, he was sent to the new abbey at Ripon as guest master – there he welcomed a traveller in the depths of winter, who vanished, leaving no tracks in the snow, but left freshly baked loaves of bread behind him. Cuthbert was entertaining angels unawares.

His life followed the familiar pattern of the Celtic missionary monk, trekking through the remote villages on foot, celebrating Communion on a portable altar and preaching as he went. He was often asked to pray for the sick, and miracles of healing are reported of him.

Even more than the other Celtic saints, one gets the impression that this life of active service was a sacrifice for him, offered to God out of love for his neighbour, when what he longed for was solitude and prayer. Cuthbert powered his missionary work by fearsome disciplines of prayer and fasting. On Wednesdays and Fridays he ate nothing until 4.00pm in honour of the Lord's passion, and where possible he spent whole nights in prayer, often walking into the sea and praying up to his neck in water, so that the cold would keep him awake. On a famous occasion, another monk followed him to the beach, to see what he got up to, and witnessed the shivering saint emerging from the sea at dawn. A pair of sea otters came from the water and wrapped themselves around Cuthbert's feet to warm them.

In old age, when the Celtic tradition very much felt itself on the defensive, Cuthbert was persuaded to become Bishop of Lindisfarne, to shepherd the community through difficult times. A terrible plague swept Northumbria, but Cuthbert remained steady. Craving solitude ever more urgently, Cuthbert's custom was to row himself over to Farne, a still more isolated island and to spend days alone there. In 687, he made what he knew would be his last voyage there. Terrible storms made access to Farne impossible for five days. When the monks finally managed to sail over, they found Cuthbert lying in his hermitage, clearly near death. When they asked him what he had been eating, the old man showed them five onions, only one of which had been nibbled, and said 'I have had plenty to eat.' After his death, he was buried on Lindisfarne, but during the Viking invasions, his body was taken to Durham for safekeeping where he still lies.

FELIX (647) 8th March.

The reason we know so much about the complex story of the conversion of Northumbria is that Bede, the first English historian, was a Northumbrian and had access to a rich collection of local material when composing his work. About the conversion of the remaining Anglo-Saxon kingdoms we know considerably less.

Felix, the apostle of East Anglia, was consecrated bishop in Burgundy and arrived in Dunwich in 631. With the help of King Sigebert of East Anglia, he worked successfully to plant the church for seventeen years, founding a school. His mission was supported by and loyally linked to the church of Canterbury. Dunwich has now been washed into the North Sea by coastal erosion, but the town of Felixstowe still preserves the bishop's memory.

BIRINUS (650) 4th September.

In 634, a similar mission was launched to the kingdom of Wessex, this time led by the Roman bishop Birinus. His original intention had been to work in Mercia, but on passing through Wessex, he found he had plenty to do. The king, Cynegils, was baptised in 635, Oswald of Northumbria stood godfather, and with the support of the two kings, Birinus set up his episcopal seat at Dorchester on Thames.

Thus by the middle of the seventh century, all the Anglo-Saxon kingdoms had been converted to Christ, except Mercia, still obdurately heathen under the formidable leadership of King Penda, and Sussex, among the poorest of the kingdoms, and cut off by the downs and by thick oak woods from regular contact with the more powerful realms.

In the next generation, the conversion of England would be completed and important decisions would be made about the sort of church the English would have. But before continuing the story, we must return briefly to the Eastern church and to the fortunes of the Roman, now Byzantine, empire.

PART NINE. THE EASTERN CHURCH.

HOLY CROSS DAY. 14th September.

The Eastern empire had survived relatively unscathed the era of barbarian invasions which had dismembered the western provinces. A Christian emperor still ruled in Constantinople, and Antioch, Jerusalem, Alexandria and the rest of the cities of the east still obeyed him. In 614, however, a newly aggressive Persia invaded the eastern provinces and captured the city of Jerusalem. The majestic churches founded by Helena and Constantine were looted and the relic of the true cross itself was captured. The Persians occupied imperial territory right up to the Bosphorus and the suburbs of Constantinople itself were burned. This disaster was reversed by the extraordinary military campaigns of the Emperor Heraclius, who by 627 had reoccupied all the invaded territories, and had won a mighty victory on the banks of the Tigris. In 629, Heraclius entered Jerusalem in triumph and there exhibited the True Cross, recaptured and restored to its rightful place. This victory was commemorated by a new feast, the Exaltation of the Cross, or Holy Cross Day, on 14th September. The victory is long forgotten, the relic long lost, but Holy Cross Day is still celebrated as a day for meditation on and thanksgiving for the victory Jesus won on the cross, a victory more enduring than any military triumph.

The celebrations of Heraclius were short-lived. Beneath a veneer of unity, the empire was hopelessly divided; most Egyptians and Syrians detested the theological agreements made at Chalcedon about the nature of Christ, and regarded their emperor as a persecuting heretic. The military and financial might of the Roman and Persian empires was utterly exhausted by these long and draining wars. Heraclius lived to see, a mere eight years after the first Holy Cross Day, the Arab followers of a new prophet, Mohammed, arrive on his frontiers. The provinces recaptured with such painful effort, fell like a house of cards before the invading Muslims, and the three great patriarchates of Antioch, Jerusalem and Alexandria, fell under the sway of a new, vigorous, non-Christian religion.

The Cross, however, is still a sign of victory, a victory this world does not understand.

JOHN DAMASCENE (657-749) 4th December.

After the Muslim invasions, Constantinople remained the eastern bulwark of Christendom, unconquered (except by her own Christian crusader allies) for eight hundred years; yet theological disagreement gradually severed the Greek and Latin churches, which remain divided to this day. In all the rich history of Byzantium and the Greek speaking churches, the English calendars only offer one more name to be commemorated, and we shall examine his life before returning to the story of Anglo-Saxon England.

The Muslims, after their conquests, did not actively persecute Christians and Jews in their dominions, regarding them as people of the book and true worshippers of Allah, even if imperfect in their refusal to recognise Mohammed as the supreme prophet. So long as Christians paid their taxes and did not attempt to convert Muslims, they were free to practise their religion. In fact, many, who would have been regarded as heretics by the clergy of Constantinople, found themselves enjoying more freedom under the Muslim Caliph than under the Christian emperor.

The father of John of Damascus was the Logothete, or official representative of the Christian community to the Caliph, and this office his son inherited. In 716, he had a conversion experience, gave up his post at court, and withdrew to the monastery of St Sabas, near Jerusalem, where he remained until his death. Virtually nothing is known of his life, but his writings have been more influential, and he is reckoned as the last of the Greek fathers.

His works took the form of vast, scholarly, syntheses of all the teaching of the early fathers, which he compiled and systematised with great skill. In his writings may be found excellent summaries of the doctrines of the Trinity and the incarnation. He was also devoted to the Virgin Mary and was one of the earliest to teach her immaculate conception, her birth free from original sin.

His ideal of the Christian life was built around the concept of 'theoria', a difficult word to translate – it means beholding, and expresses the conviction that we become like God by looking at him. This beholding is both intellectual, involving careful study of the doctrines of God, and spiritual, involving a prayerful gazing or meditation on the God whom theology unfolded. It was here that

John was fortunate to be one of the so-called oppressed Christians under Islamic rule.

The Byzantine empire was, at this time, split by the iconoclastic controversy. For centuries, Christians had used icons as a means of meditating on God and the saints. The disasters of the Muslim conquest caused profound heart searchings in Constantinople; for what sin could God be punishing his people? A puritan party emerged, convinced that a stricter interpretation of the second commandment, forbidding the worship of images, was called for. This commended itself to the consciences of many, especially as the conquering Muslims were conspicuous for their hatred of the visual arts in worship. The iconoclasts (breakers of icons) began a campaign of purification, dragging out and burning holy pictures and other church furnishings. For all their zeal, they were in a minority, but for a time the emperors supported their work.

From the safety of Muslim-held Jerusalem, John wrote a defence of icons, which remained the classic account of their legitimate use. Developing his concept of 'theoria', he explored how gazing on an icon representing Christ or one of the saints, far from being idolatrous adoration of an image, can draw the soul beyond the image to the reality the image portrays. The icon becomes as it were a window into heaven.

The iconoclasts finally lost their campaign, images were restored to the churches, and icons have ever since been central to the worship of the eastern churches.

In Western Christendom, John Damascene is best known for his hymns, especially his Easter hymns, 'The day of Resurrection'. and 'Come, ye faithful, raise the strain.'

Part Ten. Anglo-Saxon England.

BENEDICT BISCOP (628-689) 12th January.

In 653, two young Northumbrian noblemen set sail from Kent and began the long journey to Rome. Both had renounced great estates and high social status to seek the life of monastic perfection. Wilfrid had been a monk at Lindisfarne. Benedict Biscop had already founded two monasteries, at Jarrow and Wearmouth. He had travelled to Rome before; now at the request of the King of Kent, he was acting as guide to Wilfrid.

When we last visited Rome at the time of Gregory the Great, we were struck by the decay of the city, the shrunken population, the ruined aqueducts. Such would not have been the impression the city made on pilgrims from the newly Christian kingdom of Northumbria. They came from a land where luxury was a pig cooked on an open fire in a wooden hall with a thatched roof. They were confronted by marble churches hundreds of years old, mosaic floors, gorgeous purple and scarlet drapes, elaborate ritual involving incense, magnificent robes, the new fashionable Gregorian chant, and, above all, the libraries – hundreds of scrolls containing the wisdom of vanished cultures and the writings of all the most famous saints. Every church contained golden caskets of relics; the martyrs visibly poured their blessings on the vast city with its life of unimaginable sophistication. Benedict was in love with it all. He made four trips to Rome during his lifetime, and on each occasion returned to England followed by wagon-trains of booty, icons, relics, manuscripts, church furnishings, even the choir master from the Pope's chapel, treasures destined to adorn his monasteries, to transform their worship, to make them what he had seen in Rome, shrines in which could be glimpsed the beauty of heaven itself.

The work of Benedict Biscop brought the clash between Roman and Irish Christianity closer. It is important not to overstress the difference between the two traditions. All monks were dedicated to a life of fearsome personal austerity, fasting and keeping vigil to the very limits human nature could bear. Men like Wilfrid, enthralled by the glamour of the Roman way, drove themselves quite as hard as roving missionaries like Cuthbert or Aidan. Nevertheless, two visions of the church were meeting in Northumbria. Benedict Biscop and Wilfrid were cosmopolitan, enchanted by the rich culture and magnificence of Rome and the Mediterranean. The world where bishops refused to ride horses and trudged on foot from village to village was being eclipsed by something richer and more striking. The monks of Lindisfarne would naturally be anxious lest a precious simplicity, a stripped down quality of prayer, be lost as Benedict fastened his beautifully crafted statues of the twelve apostles across his chancel arch and supervised his new-fangled choir practices. In 664 the crunch came.

HILDA (614-68) 19th November.

Among the members of the Northumbrian royal family baptised by Paulinus was a princess named Hilda. Like many royal Saxon women, she entered religious life. If you did not mind the loss of family life, this was a shrewd move for a woman, looking to make a difference to society. A princess-nun was virtually certain to become an abbess, and as such would be an independent landowner with the social status of a bishop or earl, a woman visible in a masculine world.

Hilda's abbey was at Whitby, a double monastery for men and women, over all of which Hilda ruled. The monks and nuns worshipped together, but lived and worked separately. The men supplied chaplains for sacramental life, but the community's direction came from Hilda. She was called 'Mother' by everybody, and in her case this seems to have been more than the customary courtesy due to an abbess; she genuinely was the mother of the community, trusted and confided in by all.

Among her protégés was the poet Caedmon, who began life as a lay-brother, a cowherd working on the Whitby estates. When the harp went round after supper and people took it in turns to entertain the company, Caedmon, the legend says, would slip out to his cows, humiliated by his inability to sing. In a dream, an angel gave him words; he woke and recited his poetry to Hilda, who, impressed by the obvious gift of her illiterate farmhand, took the boy into the monastery and educated him. His poems are among the finest surviving works in Old English.

Whitby was so famous that it was chosen by King Oswy as the site for a synod summoned to determine the future orientation of the Northumbrian church. Should it follow Benedict Biscop and Wilfrid in enthusiastic submission to the customs of papal Rome, or remain loyal to the Irish Celtic traditions of Aidan and Cuthbert despite the resultant discord with the rest of Christendom? Ostensibly, the points at issue appear pedantic – Roman and Celtic monks tonsured their hair differently and different methods were used to calculate the date of Easter – but a whole church culture was being debated beneath these technical discussions.

Wilfrid made his name at the synod of Whitby. With the enthusiastic support of his friend Prince Alchfrid, he argued passionately for a full integration of Northumbria into the Roman communion. He won the day, apparently, by appealing to Christ's promise to St Peter 'I will give you the keys of heaven'. To king Oswy it seemed evidently prudent to keep in with the saint who controlled access to Paradise, and his decision was that Peter's church at Rome should henceforth be his church. The theology was crude but against the authority of the king there could be no appeal, and the monks of Lindisfarne and elsewhere were compelled to recut their hair and reorder their liturgical calendars. A party of hardliners went into an exile of protest in Ireland but the synod of Whitby is generally regarded as the moment when the two missionary streams of Anglo-Saxon England blended to form a united church.

CHAD (672) 2nd March.

Following the synod of Whitby, Wilfrid was the dominant personality in the English church, and at Prince Alchfrid's request, king Oswy appointed him Bishop of York. With his high regard for the church of the continent, and because the see of Canterbury was at that time vacant, Wilfrid departed for Gaul to seek his consecration there. But, as was not uncommon, he was delayed abroad for over two years, and during that time a conflict arose between Prince Alchfrid and his father. Both the causes and the course of this conflict are now obscure to us, but certain it is that Alchfrid disappeared, probably murdered. Wilfrid, his absent protégé, fell into disfavour, and Oswy appointed to the see of York a humble, gentle man named

Chad. Chad had been trained on Lindisfarne and had none of Wilfrid's scruples about accepting consecration from the Celtic bishops of the Irish tradition.

No sooner was Chad consecrated, than Wilfrid, having enjoying a splendid consecration in France, borne on a golden throne on the shoulders of twelve bishops, arrived home considering himself as rightful Bishop of York. Against the hostility of Oswy and Chad's occupation of his see, he could do nothing and he withdrew with as much grace as he could muster to the abbey he had founded at Ripon.

Chad's gentle nature was uneasy at this friction with a fellow Christian, but he was in any case not to keep his see long. The archbishopric of Canterbury was no longer vacant, and the man appointed to sit in Augustine's chair was one of the toughest and shrewdest administrators this land had ever known.

CEDD (664) 26th October.

Chad's brother Cedd is also revered as a saint. He was sent from Northumbria to Essex to reclaim the ground lost after Mellitus was forced to withdraw. His success was notable; he reclaimed Essex as a Christian kingdom and was consecrated Bishop of London. He maintained his links with the north, particularly with his home abbey of Lastingham, where he died shortly after the synod of Whitby.

THEODORE OF TARSUS (602-690) 19th September.

After the death of Archbishop Deusdedit of Canterbury in Whitby year (664), the two dominant Anglo-Saxon kings, Oswy of Northumbria and his colleague the King of Kent, sent a priest named Wigleard to Rome with the request that he be consecrated archbishop. Wigleard however had the misfortune to die of the plague shortly after arriving in Rome: the complications that ensued in England due to this prolonged vacancy in Canterbury have already been noted. In 668, Pope Vitalian consecrated his own choice for Canterbury, and many people must have wondered if the Pope knew what he was doing. The man chosen was a Greek monk aged 67, named Theodore. Theodore was born in Tarsus, in modern Turkey. He appears to have trained in Antioch, and left the east for Rome, presumably in flight before the Muslim invasions. Relations between

Rome and Constantinople continued to deteriorate, and Theodore brought his Greek scholarship to the help of the Pope in a vain attempt to end the Monothelite controversy. This was a refinement of the disputes over Christ's nature which the council of Chalcedon had attempted to settle: the Monothelites maintained that though Jesus had two natures, divine and human, he only had one will, because his human will was utterly absorbed in his divinity. The heresy was so subtle that anybody who attempts to speculate on what went on inside Jesus' head must sooner or later lapse into it, and it was not at first sight the sort of issue which was going to worry the average Anglo-Saxon nobleman; but Theodore proved to be an inspired choice, one of the archbishops who has done most to shape the English church.

At the time even the Pope seems to have had doubts about the wisdom of his own choice. He insisted that Theodore regrow his hair so that it could be tonsured in the Latin style, made him promise not to teach Greek heresies and gave him as companion a learned African abbot named Hadrian, whose secret brief was to prevent too much Greekery infesting the English church.

On arrival, Theodore discovered that only three bishops were actually alive and functioning in the whole of England, and he set about energetically reviving the church. His policy was that no diocese should exactly match the boundaries of a kingdom, to prevent kings from becoming too proprietorial over their bishops. He appointed bishops for the vacant sees of Rochester, Dunwich and Winchester, and created new dioceses in Worcester and Hereford. When he turned his attention to the disputed bishopric of York, he gave his backing to the Roman ordained Wilfrid and deposed Chad, whose Lindisfarne ordination appeared to him irregular. With characteristic humility Chad accepted this decision and was commissioned by Theodore as a missionary bishop to Mercia, which had, with the decline and death of Penda, finally opened its borders to Christian teachers. Chad thus ended his days as the first bishop of Lichfield. Wilfrid joyfully took possession at last of the diocese he considered his rightful property, but his joy was short-lived. Theodore proposed to divide Northumbria into three dioceses, Lindisfarne, York and Lindsey, and Wilfrid furiously resisted this clipping of his wings. But before pursuing the stormy career of Wilfrid further, we must meet another saint, a woman whose strange career raised up more enemies for this most tempestuous of bishops.

Theodore meanwhile consolidated his position by holding a synod at Hatfield at which his pet subject, monothelitism, was discussed and duly condemned: Wilfrid did *not* attend this synod. Theodore passed detailed legislation to give substance and permanence to his reforms and his dioceses were so shrewdly shaped that they have remained the principal contours of English church geography ever since.

Hadrian he installed as Abbot of Canterbury, and together the two men created a school of international renown. Having created a diocesan structure, Theodore filled it with learned priests, and a golden age began to dawn in Saxon England.

ETHELDREDA (Audrey) (678) 23rd June (17th October BCP)

The wife of Egfrith, who inherited the throne of Northumbria on the death of his father Oswy, was Etheldreda, a princess of East Anglia, who had early formed a determination to be a nun. Her first husband, from whom she received the Isle of Ely, accepted this and allowed her to separate from him - but dynastic considerations were brought to bear and against her conscience Etheldreda allowed herself to be married to King Egfrith. He adored her, their union lasted twelve years, but Etheldreda resolutely refused to allow the marriage to be consummated, saying that she was pledged to perpetual virginity. Egfrith's personal frustration was reinforced by anxiety over his inability to produce an heir – the scandal divided the court, some saying that the Queen should be obliged to fulfil her marriage vow, others honouring her as a living saint who preferred heavenly to earthly bliss. Wilfrid was foremost among those who supported Etheldreda; his encouragement of her in defying her husband was so blatant as to shock many. Thanks to his backing, Etheldreda was at last able to persuade the king to consent to a separation. She withdrew to her estates in the fens, where she founded the abbey, later cathedral, of Ely amidst the inaccessible marshes. There she ended her days, having at last found what she sought.

All heroic virgins become beautiful as their tales are retold, but Etheldreda really does seem to have been exceptionally beautiful, with a winning charm which made everyone, from her hapless husbands to the nuns of her community, adore her. In old age she was troubled by an abcess in her neck, which she accepted as penance for the delight she had taken in necklaces when a giddy young princess.

Wilfrid's part in her story earned him the hatred of King Egfrith, who already mistrusted him because he had been the favourite of his brother and rival Alchfrid. When Egfrith remarried the more compliantly connubial Erminburga, she too hated him because he was the supporter of her much-loved predecessor, in whose shadow she was not content to sit. When these royal hatreds were added to Theodore's attempts to bring order to the huge diocese of York and impose restraints on his flamboyant colleague, Wilfrid's position became precarious.

ETHELBURGA OF BARKING (675) 11th October.
Before pursuing the extraordinary adventures of St Wilfrid, we should attend to two other heroes of the religious life. St Ethelburga was the sister of Erconwald, whom St Theodore appointed as bishop of London once the missionary endeavours of Chad and Cedd had consolidated the Christian presence in Essex. Erconwald founded a nunnery at Barking, of which his sister became abbess. After the abbey was suppressed at the Reformation, the buildings were used to house a lunatic asylum – hence the expression 'Barking mad.'

ST BOTOLPH (680) 17th June CDC.
Another great abbot of this golden age was Botolph, whose monastery was at Boston in Lincolnshire. He was revered for his holiness and many miracles were said to have been done by him. Almost nothing is known of his life but he was greatly relied upon in the Middle Ages, and a remarkable number of English churches are dedicated to him.

WILFRID (633-709) 12th October.

While Etheldreda, Ethelburga and Botolph pursued holiness in the quietness of their several cloisters, Wilfrid's journey towards sanctity took an altogether more tortuous route. As we have followed his early career through the lives of his canonised contemporaries, it has became clear what a dominant personality of the age St Wilfrid was. We have seen him leading the Roman party at the synod of Whitby, contesting the see of York with St Chad, resenting the efficient interference of St Theodore, championing St Etheldreda against her husband. Modern writers have often suspected Wilfrid, seeing in him a precursor of the haughty medieval prince-bishops who would supplant the humbler. Celtic style of leadership associated with Aidan and Cuthbert. This is unjust; despite his exciting political career, Wilfrid expended much of his energy founding abbeys and leading missions into heathen territory and he certainly was as sincere in his desire for Christ and his kingdom as any other saint with less of a genius for making enemies.

As we have seen, Wilfrid bitterly resented Archbishop Theodore's decision to split the diocese of York into three, and his resistance played into the hands of his enemies at court. When Egfrith and Erminburga decreed Wilfrid's exile, Theodore did nothing to protect his colleague and acquiesced in his deposition. Perhaps he was moved by personal hostility to Wilfrid; perhaps he simply judged that, given the violent hatred of the Queen, the church in the north would have a better chance to flourish without its most talented bishop. Wilfrid believed, correctly, that he had been deposed contrary to canon law, and set off to appeal to the Pope in Rome. On his journey he found time to launch a mission to Frisia, and survived several assassination attempts by Northumbrian agents. He was sympathetically received by Pope Agatho, who asked him to give a keynote speech at yet another council opposing the Monothelite heresy.

Wilfrid returned to England in 680 with jubiliation, carrying with him a letter from the Pope entirely vindicating him and ordering his reinstatement in his diocese. So far was the Pope in the dark ages from being the autocratic ruler of Europe, that the king of

Northumbria simply ignored his decision and had Wilfrid thrown into prison.

These days of imprisonment were the bleakest of Wilfrid's life. He was severely maltreated, but his Christian character was proved by his ordeal. Like a New Testament apostle he passed the time in his dark cell singing psalms and his patience and joy in affliction had such an effect on those around him that his gaoler resigned his post, rather than collude in the punishment of a manifest saint.

His ordeal came to an end when Queen Erminburga fell dangerously ill, and believed that her illness was a judgement on her for her ill-treatment of a holy bishop. The king released Wilfrid, but although his wife duly recovered, all was not forgiven and he was once again obliged to leave the kingdom.

He went first to Wessex, but this kingdom, under the political domination of Northumbria, could not be a secure refuge for him, and he pushed on south into Sussex.

Sussex was a backwater, the last of the seven kingdoms to remain heathen, cut off from richer and more powerful neighbours by the south downs and the thick forests of the Weald. Although the king had accepted baptism as the condition of an alliance with Wessex (he received the Isle of Wight as a christening present) virtually none of his subjects had followed his example. They were moreover starving, due to a prolonged famine.

Wilfrid had been to Sussex once before. On that occasion he had been shipwrecked and the locals had attempted to murder him; the bishop's retinue fought manfully and got their lord off to sea again in one piece. Now he was to become the apostle of the South Saxons.

He won their gratitude by teaching them to fish, thus providing food and alleviating the famine. Then he set to work to preach. It is said that on the very day when the first baptisms took place, rain began to fall and the next harvest was assured. Wilfrid founded yet another monastery, at Selsey, as a permanent base for his mission.

From Sussex Wilfrid went to London where he was reconciled with the dying Archbishop Theodore. There he received news that his enemy King Egfrith was dead. Carrying with him letters from Theodore, Wilfrid returned home and was reinstated in his see and in his abbey of Ripon in 687.

He died twenty two years later, having had to endure another round of machinations, exile and appeals, for reasons which are now obscure to us. In the end the doughty old bishop wore out all his enemies and died peacefully at Oundle in the middle of that England whose Christian state he had done so much to consolidate.

THE VENERABLE BEDE (670-735) 25th May (27th May BCP)

We are able to know so much about the early saints of Northumbria, thanks to the genius of one man, the 'Father of English history,' Bede. Bede was born on an estate recently granted to Benedict Biscop for the maintenance of a monastery, and at the age of seven was given to the monastery of Wearmouth. This dedication of a young child to the monastic life appears shocking to us, but was extremely common in the early Middle Ages as a way of giving thanks to God. For Bede, at least, his parents' decision proved the gateway to a fulfilled life; as far as we know, he never questioned his monastic destiny and was entirely happy where he had been placed. Not surprisingly, the small boy hero-worshipped Benedict Biscop and became a firm advocate of the Roman customs Benedict and Wilfrid were introducing. He was still a child when he was chosen by Benedict as one of the monks sent from Wearmouth to found a new community at Jarrow, and here he remained for the rest of his life. The daily routine of a monastery became as natural to him as breathing; the daily mass, the seven offices of prayer built around the chanting of psalms, and above all the study. Bede was early recognised as a bright lad and was given every encouragement to develop his gifts. He was ordained deacon at 19, six years younger than the official minimum age, and was priested eleven years later. He read everything he could find and wrote impressively – sermons, commentaries, learned tomes on calculating the date of Easter, and of course, the 'History of the English church' for which he is famous. Much of his life was also spent in copying, for in a world without printing presses, every monk had a duty to build up the precious library by creating new copies of treasured works.

Bede's history is remarkable for its sense of structure, its judicious use of source materials and eye-witness accounts, and its readable style. Without him, we would know virtually nothing of how Christianity came to the Anglo-Saxons.

He died peacefully, having just dictated the last sentence of his translation of St John's Gospel.

ALDHELM (639-790) 25th May.

Among those who studied in Abbot Hadrian's school at Canterbury, founded by Archbishop Theodore, was Aldhelm, who around 680 was appointed abbot of Malmesbury and in 706 became the first bishop of Sherborne. The foundation of this diocese, covering modern Wiltshire, Somerset and Dorset, indicates how well established Christianity now was in Wessex. Although very little is known of Aldhelm's life, enough of his writings survive to show the sort of fruit which was being harvested from Theodore's campaign to educate the English clergy. From his letters we can tell that he was an enthusiastic supporter of Theodore's reforms, and from his devotional writing, both prose and verse, we see how the stories of the saints, and particularly those dedicated to virginity, were inspiring English Christians.

Aldhelm is said to have set his poetry to music and, by performing it in public places, to have attracted the west Saxons to the Christian faith in what was still very much a missionary diocese.

While the church was thus consolidating its position in England, new missionary endeavours were carrying the faith into the low countries and Germany, and English pioneers had an honourable part to play in this work of converting the lands from which the Anglo-Saxons had come.

PART ELEVEN. MISSION TO THE GERMANS.

LEGER (616-679) 2nd October CDC

The line of Clovis, king of the Franks, the Merovingian dynasty, was failing. Over the years since Clovis, his successors had allowed their position of leadership to be weakened until their kingship was one of mere symbolic and ritual significance. Under the so-called 'rois faineants' real political power was in the hands of the Mayors of the Palace, who attempted to centralise power in the name of the king, contending all the while with powerful nobles who were exploiting royal weakness to secure their own independence.

In 659, the Mayor of the Palace was one Ebroin, who, in the name of a succession of child kings, attempted to subvert the power of the nobles. Unfortunately, the means he used were violent and unscrupulous, and vulnerable heirs were exiled, dispossessed, even executed. A reaction to the Mayor's power was formed, and one of the leaders of the revolt was Leger, bishop of Autun, who had a formidable reputation as a just man and a monastic reformer. Things went badly for Leger, who managed to antagonise not only Ebroin but also the coalition of nobles who had originally been his allies. He was imprisoned by Ebroin, blinded, mutilated and finally executed. His fate shocked his contemporaries and it was not long before he was being venerated as a saint.

As we shall see, the early Middle Ages were susceptible to the 'Diana effect' whereby a prominent person meeting an untimely or tragic end was often regarded posthumously as a saint, even when the facts of their life manifested no particular holiness.

St.Leger has no connection with horse racing, the St.Leger cup being named after a noble English family and not the Burgundian bishop.

LAMBERT (633-701) 17th September BCP.

Another victim of the brutality of Ebroin was St Lambert, bishop of Maastrict. Lambert attempted to defend the rights of king Childeric, whose name Ebroin was using as a cloak for his activities, but in 674 was forced to abandon his diocese and retire out of the mayor's reach. However, in 681 Ebroin was finally assassinated by one of his victims, and his successor was Pippin d'Heristal, who was to be the founding father of the Carolingian dynasty. He recalled Lambert, and sponsored him in the missionary activities which were to be his chief claim to fame, working northwards into Frisia. This mission will be examined in more detail when we consider Lambert's English colleague, St. Willibrord.

Lambert's fruitful alliance with Pippin came to a tragic end when Pippin, who had been happily married for many years, suddenly took a mistress, Alpais. Lambert journeyed to the royal court at Liege to remonstrate with the Mayor, but Alpais, fearing his influence with her lover, caused her brother Dodo to assassinate Lambert as he was praying in the Chapel of St Cosmas and Damian. As with Leger, those shocked at this crime immediately began to venerate him as a saint.

The bastard son of Pippin and Alpais, Charles Martel, was eventually to succeed his father and become one of France's great warriors. He won a decisive victory against the Saracens in southern France, thus ensuring the Christian future of western Europe, and was the grandfather of the great Charlemagne, whom we shall meet again.

WILLIBRORD (647-739) 7th November.

The mission to Frisia, from which Lambert had been so abruptly removed, continued and flourished under an Englishman, St Willibrord.

Willibrord was a protégé of St Wilfrid, in whose monastery at Ripon he was educated and trained. Wilfrid inspired the young man with his own ideals, including a passionate commitment to unity with the Roman, continental church and a yearning for mission. When Wilfrid was forced into exile by King Egfrith and Queen Erminburga, Willibrord too left Northumbria, whether as an exile or as a gesture of solidarity with his master, it is now impossible to ascertain. His attention was drawn to Frisia, where Wilfrid had himself done some light missionary work. In 690, he presented himself before Pippin d'Heristal, and a firm alliance based on mutual respect was formed between the two men. Two years later, Pippin sent Willibrord to the Frisian mission field. In 695, he was consecrated in Rome as a missionary bishop, with authority to establish dioceses in the pagan low countries.

He based himself at Utrecht and later Echternach. Here, in a familiar pattern, he established monastic centres of worship, from which parties of missionaries went out into the surrounding country.

Pippin's support for Willibrord was not entirely disinterested. The new bishop was operating in a warzone, where Pippin was trying to subjugate Radbod King of Frisia. The Mayor saw conversion of the Frisians as a useful prelude to their political subjection.

Willibrord never succeeded in converting King Radbod, and ended up penetrating beyond his territory into Denmark, where he baptised thirty young men and brought them back by sea to France, to train them. Blown ashore in Radbod's territory, Willibrord deliberately defiled a pagan sacred spring by using it for baptisms. Radbod retaliated by martyring one of the missionaries, chosen by lot, but, struck by the courage of Willibrord and his companions, he sent the rest of the party safely home. It was only after Radbod's death in 719 that significant numbers of converts were made among the Frisians.

St Willibrord is patron saint of Luxemburg and Holland. His tomb at Echternach is still the site of a famous dancing pilgrimage every year, during which bishop, clergy and people dance in procession to the music of brass bands.

BONIFACE (675-754) 5th June.
The missionary work of Lambert and Willibrord was continued by the most famous of all those who brought the faith to Germany, the Englishman christened as Wynfrith. He is the patron saint of Germany.

As a young man, Wynfrith entered a monastery on Southampton Water, close enough to Wilfrid's foundation at Selsey for the lad from Devon to learn and be entranced by the stories of Wilfrid's missionary work in Frisia. His first attempt at joining this work, in 716, ended in failure, and he returned to England. But the longing to see the Germans, who shared a common ancestry with the Saxons, brought to Christ, never left him, and became the force which drove him for the rest of his life.

In 719 he went to Rome, where Pope Gregory II consecrated him bishop, gave him the new, Roman name of Boniface and despatched him northwards with the commission to establish and rule a diocese east of the Rhine among the heathen Germans

Like Wilfrid, Boniface thus began his work with Roman backing, firmly convinced of the need for all Christian churches to give obedience to the Pope. Like Willibrord, he received important backing from the French. In 714 Pippin d'Heristal had died and his son, the warrior Charles Martel, was vigorously expanding his power into Germany. His campaigning was bloody and effective. Between him and Boniface's missionaries, an uneasy alliance subsisted. At one level, Boniface welcomed the French mayor's support. Wherever French influence extended, he knew that lands would be generously granted to support new frontier monasteries, and his support for Charles was such that, when Charles finally induced the last Merovingian king to abdicate and enter a monastery, it was Boniface who presided at the coronation of Charles Martel, who now became the first Carolingian king of France. Nevertheless, Boniface could not condone the violent means by which the Germans were reduced and their lands opened for missionary work. Not for the last time, Christian missionaries found themselves open to the charge of colluding with an aggressive imperialist power as it advanced into heathen lands.

Boniface and his companions arrived in Germany in 722, and his first, most famous confrontation with pagans took place at Geismar. Here there was a huge oak tree where sacrifices were offered to Thor. Boniface took an axe and chopped it down. In this way he demonstrated to the watching Germans that Thor was powerless to protect himself against Christ; the early missionaries often 'took on' pagan Gods in this sort of public challenge. Legend relates that growing in the roots of the great oak, Boniface found a tiny fir tree. This he presented to the Germans as a symbol of their new faith; its evergreen leaves would symbolise for them the constant presence of Jesus in all times and seasons. This is supposed to be the first Christmas tree.

Boniface is better known to us than most early medieval people because his letters have been preserved. From them we get a vivid impression of an uncompromising idealist who was constantly prone to depression and anxiety as he pursued his huge mission. He was regarded with suspicion by the existing bishops and abbots whose territories fringed the area he was attempting to convert. Despite this he established new bishoprics and many new abbeys in Bavaria and the Rhineland, the most famous of which is at Fulda.

In his old age, he was diverted from his missionary work by the needs of the French church, which he was energetic in reforming. Backed by Charles Martel and his son, Pippin I, he held five great councils, at which demanding standards were set for the clergy. But his heart was in mission, and in 754 he set off on a final journey into Frisia. At the coastal village of Dokkum, his party was set upon by sea raiders and massacred. Boniface attempted to shield his head with the book he was reading; it has been preserved at Fulda, where the gashes of the sword and the stains of the martyr's blood can still be seen.

GILES (d710) 1st September.

While the church was thus expanding in northern Europe, it was also being consolidated in Provence. Here dwelt the legendary St Giles, who has given his name to a town near Arles where he founded a monastery.

What is now the south of France was than an independent monarchy, founded by the Visigoths. Giles arrived there from Athens and built himself a hermitage in the woods. His solitary life was so tranquil that he gained the trust of the wild creatures, particularly a hind, which fed from his hand. One day, Wamba king of the Visigoths was out hunting and pursued the hind, which took refuge with the saint. The huntsmen shot at it as it disappeared into a thicket and, on following it, discovered Giles, shot through the hand, embracing the trembling deer while the hounds crouched in reverence around. The incident made a profound impact on the king, who granted Giles lands to establish a monastery. The wound in Giles' hand never healed and he lost the use of his arm; he thus became patron saint of cripples, and also, presumably because of his love for animals, of horses. This explains why so many towns have churches dedicated to St Giles at their gates, for it was on the edge of towns that hospices for the sick and smithies for travellers' horses were often built.

Only a few years after Giles' death, Provence was over-run by Saracens from Spain. The Muslim invasion was finally checked by Charles Martel at Poitiers, but the Visigothic monarchy did not survive the liberation of the south by that energetic and ambitious king, who established a permanent, though often disputed, over-lordship over Aquitaine and Provence.

ALCUIN OF YORK (735-804) 20th May.
Charles Martel was succeeded by his son Pippin I, and then by his grandson Charles, known to history as Charles the Great, or Charlemagne.

Charlemagne continued his forebears' military success; his might extended the Frankish empire to the borders of Muslim Spain and over most of what is now Germany, Austria, Hungary and the northern Balkans. He and his paladins, led by Roland, or Orlando, subsequently became idealised perfect knights in the literature of the high Middle Ages, enjoying a reputation as high as Arthur's knights of the Round Table. But Charlemagne was much more than a military conqueror. He longed to give his dominions true Christian civilisation, and to that end made his court open to all the scholars of the age, whom he attracted by his wealth and power. Among those invited was an Englishman whom Charlemagne met at Parma in 781, Alcuin of York.

Alcuin was a noble Northumbrian distantly related to St Willibrord. He had served all his life in the monastery at York, where he had been ordained deacon. He seems to have accepted monastic life cheerfully enough, but the monk's quest for God in prayer was not central to his vocation. He was first and foremost a scholar, a lover of books and learning. By the time he died, his reputation was immense, and his service as Charlemagne's chief advisor on matters ecclesiastical and educational brought great prestige to that monarch.

Alcuin seems at first to have 'shuttled' between Charlemagne and his English responsibilities; he may have served as a diplomatic envoy between Charlemagne and Offa king of Mercia (builder of the famous dyke). In 796, he accepted, with reluctance, Charlemagne's offer of the abbacy of St Martin's, Tours, where he remained for the rest of his life.

It was here, early in 800, that Charlemagne visited him to discuss a bold idea, nothing less than the revival of the Roman Empire in the West. On Christmas Day 800, Charlemagne was crowned Holy Roman Emperor by the Pope in Rome, a development enthusiastically welcomed by Alcuin, who like most churchmen saw in a strong monarchy the best hopes of containing the violent anarchy of his times. Alcuin was less enthusiastic about Charlemagne's exploits in Germany, where whole armies of defeated Saxons were forcibly baptised at the sword's point; Alcuin wrote vigorously to oppose the notion that baptism could ever validly be given except at the free desire of the convert. His was, however, a minority view at the time.

Charlemagne desired to establish religious conformity in his empire, and to that end asked the Pope to send him a copy of the Roman rites, as revised by St Gregory the Great. It took about five years to winkle what was needed out of Rome, but the required volume eventually arrived and Alcuin, with other scholars, set about revising it. Not surprisingly, given the poor system of communications and the painful labour required to create books, there was little agreement in early medieval Europe over the structure and content of the church's services. Local churches adopted customs and rites which they happened across, or wrote their own material. Alcuin found that the Gregorian Sacramentary sent from Rome was in itself an incomplete resource, with no provision for much of the church's year. It is to his work of regularising and supplementing that we owe the current established structure of the liturgical year, with its Sundays after Epiphany, six weeks of Lent, Eastertide and then Sundays after Trinity (strictly, after Pentecost, for Trinity Sunday had not been established in Alcuin's day). Alcuin also created a book of supplementary material drawn from the existing traditions of the French church and including some of the best loved collects still in use in the Book of Common Prayer. Thanks to Charlemagne's reach over so much of Europe, the revised orders met with widespread acceptance and mark a major watershed in the history of liturgy.

PART TWELVE. THE VIKINGS.

EDMUND KING OF THE EAST ANGLES (840-869) 20th November.

In 793, there was brought to Alcuin in France tragic news. The Holy Island of Lindisfarne, the mother church which had nurtured the faith of Cuthbert and Wilfrid and had inspired the missions of Willibrord and Alcuin himself, had been sacked and pillaged by raiders from the sea. These were the Vikings, descending from Scandinavia in swift ships in search of easy booty. Before their onslaught, the wealthy Christian kingdoms of England crumbled. Northumbria lost for ever its dominance over English affairs. On the continent, the power of the successors of Charlemagne was undermined and the Holy Roman Empire shaken to its foundations. It seemed as though no Christian prince could defeat the pagan raiders from the sea.

In 856, a fifteen year old boy was crowned king of the East Angles. Edmund began his reign in turbulent times. The raids were rapidly becoming full-scale invasions. Every year larger Viking fleets crossed the North Sea and penetrated further inland. In 869, a large Viking host invaded East Anglia and took up winter quarters in Thetford. Edmund and his men went to oppose them, but they were defeated and the king was taken prisoner. The Viking leaders offered to spare him in return for a ransom and the abandonment of his Christian faith, but Edmund refused. He was put to torture, and his sufferings culminated in being tied to a tree, where the Vikings shot arrows at him. Finally he was beheaded. According to legend, the head was subsequently discovered in a thicket, guarded by a wolf, which followed the funeral procession and then departed. Edmund was buried at Bury St Edmunds, where a great monastic house grew around his relics.

Other kings attempted to oppose the Viking invasions but with similar lack of success. Saxon churchmen resigned themselves to what was seen as a divine punishment.

ANSKAR (800-865) 3rd February.

As the Viking menace intensified, it became more and more urgent to bring the Scandinavian lands within Christendom. The pioneer of this mission, which was not to bear fruit until two centuries after his death, was Anskar, known as the Apostle of the north. He trained as a monk at Corvey in Saxony, in the newly pacified and converted badlands at the frontier of Charlemagne's empire. In 826, Charlemagne's son Louis the Pious sent Anskar north to Denmark, where an opportunity for evangelism had opened up.

A Danish prince named Harald Klak had been forced into exile during dynastic quarrels, and during his six years sojourn in France he accepted baptism. He returned to Denmark a Christian and the protégé of the Emperor Louis, ready to welcome missionaries to his savage homeland. Harald's restoration was short-lived, but Anskar's mission survived his deposition and Anskar was even able to launch a mission into Sweden, where he converted a royal counsellor.

In 832, Pope Gregory IV consecrated Anskar Bishop of Hamburg with the grand brief of establishing churches throughout Scandinavia. For a few years, it looked as if the dreadful Vikings might actually succumb to the gospel, but in 845 the heathen hosts descended in a return to their old form. Hamburg was sacked, the Christian nobility of Sweden were expelled from their homeland and Scandinavia was closed to Christian influence.

Anskar built a new base for himself at Bremen, which was amalgamated with the ruins of the looted diocese of Hamburg. He continued to support missions into Denmark, but by his death he had failed to convert a single king or ruler. In worldly terms his life was a failure, but he is remembered as the pioneer, in whose footsteps others would follow and complete the work of converting the Vikings.

ALFRED THE GREAT (849-899) 26th October.

The missionaries had failed to tame the heathen, and Viking raids continued and intensified, destablising every community in western Europe which could be reached by coast or river. In England, the kingdom of Wessex found itself forced by events into a new prominence. Wessex had already established an over-lordship over the other southern kingdoms, Sussex, Kent and Essex. Now with the northern kingdoms Northumbria, Mercia and East Anglia entirely destroyed and over-run by Danish invaders, the king of Wessex found himself the only free Saxon monarch in England. From this circumstance, and from the greatness of King Alfred and his successors, the foundations of the modern British monarchy were laid.

Alfred's father was king Ethelwulf, who in 855 took his youngest son on pilgrimage to Rome. Like Benedict Biscop and Wilfrid before him, the young prince was amazed by what he saw in the eternal city. It brought home to him, how much Christian civilisation had been destroyed in his own land during the Viking wars, and began his lifelong love affair with learning. A famous story tells how Alfred's mother promised a beautiful book to the son who first learned to read it, and how Alfred, though the youngest, carried off the prize.

In 865, Ethelwulf died, and Alfred gave loyal support to his brother King Ethelred as he fought an increasingly desperate defensive campaign against an unprecedentedly huge Danish host moving westward from the dismemberment of Edmund's East Anglia. In 871, the royal brothers won a famous victory at Ashdown, but this was only followed by the arrival of Danish reinforcements and the death of Ethelred. Alfred inherited the throne when he had virtually nothing left to rule. He and the small band loyal to him took refuge in the marshes of Athelney, where may be placed the picturesque story of how the king lived incognito in a swineherd's hut, where he absent-mindedly allowed the cakes to burn on the hearth and was berated by the swineherd's wife, who little dreamed whom she was chastising. But in 878, the tide turned decisively. Alfred emerged from hiding, rallied the Saxons, won a victory and besieged the Danish army in its camp at Chippenham. The Danes surrendered and their king, Guthrum, accepted baptism, with Alfred standing as his godfather. Though far from beaten, the Danes got the message that the conquest of Wessex would not be a walkover, and diverted their attention to where the pickings would be easier. The status quo was formally recognised by the Treaty of Wedmore, by which England was divided into a Danelaw in the north and east, and a free Saxon Wessex in the south and west. In 888, Alfred re-conquered London, and fortified it; it now began to acquire the pre-eminence which would eventually make it the capital city. This campaign led to Alfred's being recognised as king and overlord by all the Anglo-Saxons.

Such military achievements are impressive enough, but it was the use he made of the peace which earned Alfred his title 'The Great'. His greatest desire was to restore the rule of law, re-establish education and learning, and rebuild the influence of the Christian church. The Danish invasions had had a catastrophic effect on the clergy, most of whom were illiterate and demoralised. Alfred did everything he could to train the clergy and restore their morale. He also sought to make the wealth of Latin Christian culture available to as many as possible, and to that end translated by his own hand St Gregory's 'Pastoral Rule' and other classic works into Old English. Despite chronic ill-health he worked hard; he is supposed to have invented the candle clock, measuring his time accurately so that each day he could give eight hours to his kingly duties, eight to study and prayer, and eight to rest.

He left behind him a kingdom strong and at peace, where Christianity was again flourishing and winning the hearts of the people. His warlike son and grandson re-conquered the Danelaw and for the first time made of England a united land owing allegiance to one king.

SWITHUN (d863) 15th July.

As an example of the ordinary life of the church of Wessex which Alfred sought to restore, we may take St Swithun, bishop of Winchester in the reigns of Alfred's father and brother. Winchester was an important city in Saxon England, for many years the seat of government, and Swithun is supposed to have tutored king Ethelwulf. Very little concrete fact remains about his life. He built a stone bridge for the city at East Gate and is supposed to have miraculously restored a basket of eggs dropped by a poor woman on the said bridge.

On his death, Swithun desired to be buried outside the cathedral where the feet of the worshippers could trample his dust, but on 15th July 971, his relics were translated to a gorgeous shrine within the church. The heavy rain which fell throughout the ceremony was interpreted as a sign of the saint's displeasure, and led to the superstition that if it rains on St Swithun's day, the following forty days will also be wet. Swithun's tomb was the site of many miracles of healing throughout the early middle ages.

CUTHMAN (870) 8th February CDC.
A humbler contemporary of King Alfred was the boy hermit Cuthman, who was led by God to leave his native Cornwall and travel east, pulling his aged mother in a cart. He vowed that wherever the straps of the cart snapped, he would stop travelling and build a church. This duly occurred in Sussex, in the village of Steyning, where Cuthman built his church and remained praying there for the rest of his life. Many such stories must have been lost over the centuries; this one reminds us that ordinary people too had their part to play in sustaining Christian England while the Danish hordes rampaged about them.

CYRIL (died 869) and METHODIUS (died 885) 14th February.
While Alfred was fighting back heathen Danes in Wessex, the Slav lands of central Europe were slowly succumbing to a more peaceful invasion, that of Christian missionaries. For the rulers of pagan Moravia (roughly, the modern Czech Republic and Slovakia) the question was not only whether they should adopt the Christian faith, but what sort of Christians they should become.

Since the coronation of Charlemagne as Holy Roman Emperor, the gulf between western Christendom and the Byzantine Empire, whose rulers traced an unbroken succession to the Roman emperors of classical times, had steadily widened. Although the breach was not yet official, the gap was already practically unbridgeable, and was reinforced by prejudices and cultural expectations on both sides. Eastern and Western Christians already found it easier to regard each other as heretics than as Christian brothers. The great missionaries to the Slavs, subjects of the Eastern emperor, were also to prove great builders of bridges and uniquely managed to operate, for a few years at least, with the blessing both of the Patriarch of Constantinople and of the Pope in Rome.

Methodius and his younger brother Constantine (later Cyril) were natives of Thessalonica. While Methodius forsook a promising legal career for monastic life, Constantine attracted the attention of Emperor Leo the Mathematician by his precocious gift for languages and served on several embassies to the Arabs and to the Khazars of Crimea.

The Byzantine empire relied on its prestige and its diplomatic skills to maintain its supremacy amidst constant pressure from Muslim and pagan neighbours. Methodius joined his brother on the embassy to the Khazars. Their intention was to convert them into Christians and client friends of the Christian emperor, but the Khazars ended up converting, uniquely for a pagan tribe, neither to Islam nor Christianity, but to Judaism. In 863, the Emperor Michael despatched the brothers on another missionary embassy, to what was to be the field of their life's work, Moravia, whose Prince, Ratislav, had asked the emperor to send him teachers of the Christian faith. The request was less naïve than it sounded, for Ratislav's dominions were already being surveyed by German, Latin-speaking missionaries from the West. The Prince regarded them with suspicion, for experience had shown that land-hungry German nobility followed German missions, and Ratislav hoped by allying himself to the Eastern church, to preserve his political independence.

Constantine and Methodius began immediately by translating the Bible and the liturgy into Moravian, using for the purpose an alphabet of their own devising by which the non-literate Slavic languages could be transliterated onto paper. This alphabet, the ancestry of the one now called the Cyrillic, proved a cornerstone of Slavic culture and made possible a written literature all over Eastern Europe and Russia. It is the lasting legacy of the brothers, but at the time was regarded with suspicious hostility by their German rivals, who believed that liturgy must be performed in Latin. In 867, Pope Nicholas the Great summoned them to Rome so that he might discover for himself the reality behind the accusations of heretical practice which had reached him. In Rome, Constantine died; it was on his deathbed that he took monastic vows and adopted the name Cyril by which he is now known. Methodius enormously impressed the Pope, who was won over by his arguments that the Moravians needed a liturgy in their own tongue, consecrated him bishop and sent him back to Moravia in 869 with full permission to continue his mission in his own way. Thus sponsored by both the Byzantine emperor and the Pope, Methodius' position should have been unassailable, but unfortunately he arrived in Moravia to discover that Prince Ratislav had been dethroned by a nephew who favoured the German churches in the complicated diplomatic struggles of the time. Methodius was put on trial at Regensburg as a dangerous innovator, and was imprisoned for four years until his release was secured by papal pressure. He continued his missionary work until his death, but his achievements were speedily dismantled by his opponents as soon as he was removed from the scene.

Their creation of the Slavic alphabet and their attempts to bring together east and west are the reasons why Cyril and Methodius are honoured as patrons of Europe. They are revered as saints by both orthodox and catholic Christians, although the average Anglican probably remains puzzled as to how they were allowed to take over St Valentine's Day.

WENCESLAS (907 - 929) 28th September CDC.
The Latin-sponsored bishops of Moravia persecuted the followers of St Methodius after his death, in the interest of re-establishing a more 'normal' form of western Christianity. Some of the missionaries fled westward into Bohemia, where the Christian faith soon began to be established.

At this period, Europe began to be beset by another wave of invaders, not only the Vikings from the north but the Magyars from the east. Under this pressure it was in the interests of frontier princes to seek the alliance and protection of the Holy Roman Emperors of Germany, the heirs of Charlemagne. So it was that the young and newly baptised Wenceslas, Duke of Bohemia, sought the patronage of Emperor Henry the Fowler for his newly build cathedral of St Vitus in Prague. The Emperor sent clergy and relics of St Vitus and Bohemia was firmly drawn into the German sphere of influence.

Wenceslas was murdered by his own brother, Boleslav, at the early age of nineteen. It used to be supposed that Boleslav was seeking to re-establish a patriotic Slavic government based on traditional pagan values, but in fact Boleslav continued the pro-German policy of Wenceslas and was certainly also a Christian – indeed, such was the popular fervour with which the murdered Wenceslas was hailed as a martyr, that the guilty brother was compelled to enshrine him in Prague and lead his people in venerating him. He remains the patron saint of the Czech people.

Sadly, the legend about Wenceslas which everybody knows from the carol was entirely fabricated by the hymn writer J.M Neale, and there is no evidence that he took any particular interest in bringing Christmas cheer to his peasants, whether resident by St Agnes' fountain or anywhere else.

DUNSTAN (94-988) 19th May.

Under the reigns of King Alfred's successors, the English people enjoyed about a century's respite from Danish invasions, and this was a second golden age for the Saxon church. In the reign of Athelstan, King Alfred's grandson, there came to prominence for the first time Dunstan, who was to do more to consolidate and reform the church than any other man of his generation.

As a young man, Dunstan was possessed of a faith so intemperately zealous as to verge on lunacy. He saw devils everywhere, was prone to visions, and scolded mercilessly all whom he saw falling into sinful ways. So unpopular did this odd boy become that he was asked to leave Athelstan's court, and as he departed was unceremoniously pushed into a ditch by resentful pages. He established himself in a hermitage at Glastonbury, where he took out his energies in mastering the craft of blacksmithing, meanwhile fighting long, vivid battles against Satan. A famous legend tells how the fiend appeared to tempt him in the form of a beautiful girl, only to be forced to reveal his cloven hooves when Dunstan clasped his nose with his smith's tongs.

In 939, King Edmund succeeded his brother and while hunting at Cheddar Gorge very nearly rode his horse over a cliff. For some reason, he believed he had been saved by the prayers of Dunstan and invited him back to court, making him Abbot of Glastonbury. This famous abbey now emerges into the daylight of history from its misty connections with Joseph of Arimathea and

King Arthur. Dunstan threw himself into the task of making it a model abbey, one which St Benedict would be proud of – though the monks were still kept awake by the noise of their abbot striking the walls of his cell with his staff to drive out devils. Edmund's brother Edred was an enthusiastic supporter of Dunstan's reforms.

In 955, however, the young Edwig succeeded to the throne and Dunstan at once made him his enemy. At the coronation, Edwig snubbed his important guests and left the feast to dally with his mistress Elfgifu and her mother. Sent to bring the king back, Dunstan expressed himself with such bitter anger that the king and the ladies all marked him down – his exile inevitably followed. He spent some years on the continent studying, but was recalled in 957 by Edwig's brother Edgar, reckoned as the first king of all England. Edgar was a fervent admirer of Dunstan and created him in rapid succession Bishop of Worcester, Bishop of London, and in 959 Archbishop of Canterbury. Dunstan's authority was established and the reforms so dear to his heart were pushed enthusiastically through. He encouraged monasteries and learning, insisted on high personal standards from the clergy, and continued to be unafraid to rebuke important people who were living immoral lives.

The ferocity of his youth had mellowed, though the passion for God remained, and he was remembered after his death as mild and gentle, more prone to tears than anger. Those who witnessed him saying mass were moved by the evident emotion which stirred him as he drew close to Christ's body and blood. He was an accomplished harpist and encouraged music in the churches. He is honoured as patron saint of blacksmiths and craftsmen.

OSWALD OF WORCESTER (died 992) 28th February CDC.
In his endeavours to reform the English church, Dunstan was fortunate that his own energy and talents were seconded by those of many other reforming churchmen, of whom St Oswald is the most prominent. As a young man he had been disgusted by the luxurious lifestyle of the married clergy of Winchester and had withdrawn to a French monastery at Fleury-sur-Loire. There he experienced the full power of Benedictine monasticism and, like Dunstan, was filled with desire to bring the churches of his native land fully into line with this

tradition. When Dunstan became archbishop of Canterbury, he used his influence with King Edgar to have Oswald appointed, in 961, to the vacant see of Worcester.

In Worcester, Oswald founded new monasteries, most notably at Romsey, and worked hard, though apparently with some cunning, to change the culture of his diocese, dissuading the clergy from marriage and encouraging monastic vocations. It was in this era that pressure on the clergy to accept celibacy as an indispensible part of their vocation began to build so irresistibly.

In 972 Edgar again used his personal influence to have Oswald installed as archbishop of York, and the following year the two archbishops, Dunstan and Oswald, presided at Edgar's coronation as King of all England and overlord of Great Britain. This was the famous occasion when Edgar was rowed on the Dee by six kings who acknowledged his lordship.

Little is known of Oswald's years at York. He died shortly after returning from the rededication of his abbey at Romsey.

EDWARD THE MARTYR (962-978) 18th March BCP.
The great King Edgar died in 975, leaving two young sons, Edward, aged 13, and Ethelred, aged no more than nine, the son of his second and surviving queen Elfthryth. There was as yet no law of primogeniture governing the succession to the throne, but Edward's claim was backed by archbishop Dunstan, who crowned him and proclaimed him king.

In 978, the young king visited his stepmother at her home in Corfe Castle, Dorset. Here a terrible crime was committed. Elfthryth met him at the gate with a cup of mead, and as the boy king drank to his hostess, he was seized and stabbed to death by her retainers. The crime was committed in order to secure the throne for Prince Ethelred. He was too young to be personally implicated and his succession was smooth. Dunstan pragmatically crowned him and the new king was an enthusiastic forwarder of the cult of his brother as a saint and martyr. He is known to history as Ethelred the Unready, and his reign saw the reappearance of the Danish menace and the overthrow of the great Saxon kingdom that Alfred and Edgar, Dunstan and Oswald, had struggled so hard to create.

THE TRANSLATION OF ST EDWARD 20th June BCP.

The Book of Common Prayer provides a second feast day for St Edward, commemorating the translation of his relics to a new shrine in Shaftesbury in 1001, where they were venerated throughout the Middle Ages. We see in this unfortunate prince and his swift canonisation by popular acclaim, another example of the 'Diana effect' by which celebrity and tragedy lead to sainthood in the minds of the people.

ALPHEGE (died 1012) 19th April.

The next saint we are to consider owed his popularity, like Edward the Martyr, to a tragic and violent end.

Alphege was another protégé of St Dunstan, who recommended Ethelred the Unready to appoint him Bishop of Winchester. Here he busied himself promoting the cult of St Swithun and rebuilding extensively the cathedral, introducing a fantastic new organ which was regarded as so loud that no one could listen to it without covering his ears. The Anglo-Saxons would have had difficulties with modern amplification systems.

In 1006, Alphege was appointed archbishop of Canterbury, second in succession to the great Dunstan. He sat in St Augustine's chair at an evil hour. The weak government of Ethelred had failed to contain, his malice had provoked, the Danish invaders, who now recommenced their raids and found no one to oppose their increasing demands for Danegeld, or ransom. In 1011, Canterbury was betrayed into their hands and archbishop Alphege was made prisoner.

Alphege bore his misfortune with courage, forbidding his ministers to attempt to collect the enormous ransom the Danes were demanding for his release. On 19th April 1012, the Danes lost patience. At a drunken feast furious anger erupted against the archbishop and he was pelted with ox-bones and finally done to death by a blow from an axe.

A later archbishop of Canterbury, St Anselm, argued that Alphege deserved to be venerated as a martyr though he had not strictly died for Christ. His refusal to allow ransom to be raised, out of pity for his suffering people, was a stand for truth and justice, both Christ-like qualities.

OLAVE King of Norway (995-1030) 30th July CDC.

The Viking invasions of England, in which St Alphege perished, ended the unsteady power of King Ethelred, whose death paved the way for a brief period of Danish rule under King Canute. This triumph of the Vikings was to prove at last the gate to the goal which Anskar and so many others had pursued so long and with such apparent lack of fruit – the conversion of Scandinavia. Canute, who as king of both of England and Denmark, dominated the Nordic world, was himself an ardent Christian and Christianity was in this era taken back to Norway and Sweden.

Olave Haroldson was a Norwegian prince who had led raids on England, in the process becoming fascinated by the Christian religion. On his election as King of Norway in 1016, he ended up fighting for Ethelred the Unready against the Danes! He began with great determination to plant the faith in his realm, building churches, demolishing pagan shrines, and inviting missionaries from England to train a native clergy. The Norse clans resented Olave's new faith and appealed for help to Canute. Political expediency triumphed over Christian solidarity in Canute's mind: he assisted the rebels, securing Olave's exile and his own election as King of Norway. In 1030, Olave returned to Norway but was defeated and killed at the battle of Stiklestend by his rebellious subjects. He was almost immediately venerated as a martyr, and with hindsight, the Norwegians regarded him as a national hero, championing their independence against the imperial pretensions of Denmark. The church established by Olave survived his fall and flourished, so that the descendants of the Norsemen who sacked Lindisfarne at last took their place within Christendom.

SIGFRID (d,.1045) 15th February.

Sweden was meanwhile also being won for the faith, although the details of the life St Sigfrid, the apostle of Sweden, are extremely obscure. He had been sent from York in the reign of Ethelred the Unready to Norway in about 995, but finding Norway unfruitful he went on into Sweden, where he succeeded in baptising the king and building a church at Vaxjo. Legend says that while he pressed on northwards into pagan lands, his established church was assailed by resentful pagans and his three nephews, whom he had ordained to lead the new church, were all killed. The King of Sweden attempted to force the killers to pay blood money to Sigfrid, but the saint refused to accept the money, offering instead full and free forgiveness. This action, in a society dominated by a revenge code and by the need to maintain one's own honour, made an immense impression, and many Swedes were baptised into a religion whose insistence on forgiveness transcended their traditional ethic. Sigfrid also worked in Denmark and by the time of his death the Christianisation of Scandinavia may be said to be irreversible.

HENRY II of GERMANY (973-1024) 13th July CDC.

The conversion of central Europe continued rapidly during this era, sponsored by a succession of powerful Holy Roman Emperors in Germany. We have already seen how Henry the Fowler fostered the growth of Christianity in Wenceslas's Bohemia. His heirs, the Ottonian dynasty, continued to resist the Magyar invasions by force of arms and to use Christian missionaries as a means of extending their influence among the Slavs. In 1002, the premature death of Otto III led to the election of his kinsman, Henry Duke of Bavaria as the new Emperor. Henry was consistent in using his power to further Christian mission. As Duke of Bavaria he married his sister Gisela to king Stephen of Hungary, the new kingdom carved out by the Magyar invaders on the banks of the Danube. Stephen went on to be a conspicuously Christian monarch, venerated as patron saint of Hungary. After his election, the Emperor Henry II sponsored the mission of St Bruno into Prussia and in 1012 founded the bishopric of Bamburg, as a centre of prayer and Christian culture from which the gospel might be spread into what is now eastern Germany.

His wife the Empress Cunegund is also venerated as a saint. She survived her husband by some years and was famed for her piety.

Part Thirteen. 1066.

EDWARD THE CONFESSOR (1002-1066) 13th October.
When Ethelred the Unready died, his widow Emma fled the power of Canute and took her young family abroad to Normandy, for she was a Norman princess. The young Prince Edward was therefore brought up under Norman influence. Queen Emma by contrast quickly returned to the English political scene, when she decided to accept the hand of King Canute and to resume her place as Queen. Her son by Canute, Harthacanute, was her favourite and she promoted his interests against those of her older son Edward. When Canute died in 1035, his two sons and the sons of Ethelred the Unready struggled for the crown. Edward and his brother Alfred landed near Southampton, but Alfred was captured by Earl Godwine of Wessex, who showed his loyalty to the Danish dynasty by handing him over to the king. The young prince was savagely blinded and died of his injuries. His death was to poison future relations between Edward and the powerful house of Godwine.

But by 1042, both the sons of Canute had died prematurely and Queen Emma and Earl Godwine, changing loyalty abruptly, brought about the succession of the thirty-eight year old Edward. He has traditionally been portrayed as too meek and otherworldly to be an effective ruler, but in fact he reigned for twenty-three years, and during that time built an effective power-base from weak and unpromising beginnings.

At first he appeared the protégé of Godwine. He married the earl's daughter Edith and the union appears to have been initially a happy one. Edward remained childless, though later legends that he took a vow of celibacy within marriage should be discounted. Edith's brothers, including the future King Harold, were promoted to positions of trust, and Godwine's family seemed unshakeable. Edward however retained a strong partiality for the Normans among whom he had grown up. He made a Norman archbishop of Canterbury and favoured his French relatives. Matters came to a head in 1051 when retainers of Edward's friend Eustace Count of Boulogne were attacked by local people as they waited to embark at Dover. Earl Godwine refused the king's orders to arrest those responsible and resentments long hidden burst into the open. Although Godwine was playing the patriotic card of Englishmen standing firm against overweening foreign favourites, the people rallied to the king and Godwine and his sons fled into exile. Edith was sent to a nunnery amidst rumours that a divorce was imminent. Edward was belatedly revenging himself for his brother Alfred's death.

By the autumn however all was patched up into an uneasy peace. Godwine retuned and was supported by the citizens of London. Edward pardoned him, took back his wife, and the Godwines were restored to favour. But the king had made it clear who was master.

In the second half of his reign, which was largely peaceful, Edward's reputation for holiness began to be established. The king was much loved by his people, who attributed miracles to him. He was said to have healed a woman with scrofula and this led to the tradition of 'touching for the king's evil' whereby the monarch laid hands on the afflicted who sought a cure – the tradition lasted until the accession of George I in 1714. Shakespeare uses the image of the holy king curing his people by his touch to throw into relief the villainy of Edward's contemporary Macbeth King of Scotland. Edward historically did intervene to overthrow Macbeth and replace him as King of Scots with Malcolm Canmore. Malcolm remained grateful for this assistance, as we shall see.

The most popular legend about Edward tells how he gave a ring from his own finger to a poor beggar. A few months later two English pilgrims in the Holy Land had a vision of St John the Evangelist, who gave them the ring, bidding them restore it to their king and tell him who it was he had unwittingly helped through his charity.

Edward's lasting monument is Westminster Abbey, which he founded and spent the last years of his reign enriching. He remains buried in a great tomb behind the High Altar.

His death in 1066, still childless, precipitated the famous struggle for power in which the Queen's brother Harold was elected king, only to face the double invasion of Harold Hardrada King of Norway and William Duke of Normandy. The latter conquered

England and was crowned in the Confessor's abbey as William I. Because Edward had favoured Normans, and was even said to have secretly promised his crown to Duke William, his reputation as an ideal king survived the conquest and for two centuries he was regarded as England's patron saint, until he was supplanted in the era of the crusades by the more dashing, though less English, St George.

MARGARET, QUEEN OF SCOTLAND (1093) 16th November.
Although William the Conqueror had slain Harold at the Battle of Hastings and was established as King of England, the Saxon royal family was not in fact extinct. Edward the Confessor had some young cousins, grandchildren of his brother Edmund Ironside, who had been born and brought up in distant Hungary, where their father had taken refuge during the reign of Canute. These young people, Edgar the Atheling and his sister Margaret, were brought back to England by Edward the Confessor, but being destitute of influence, were not considered serious candidates for the throne on the Confessor's death.

Edgar's and Margaret's world was changed for ever by the Norman conquest. When William I took the throne of England, the Saxon royal house was permanently disinherited and the Saxon people bowed to a new French-speaking ruling class. Edgar at first submitted to the conqueror, but later he was implicated in the northern rebellion against William, and when that rebellion was ruthlessly crushed, he and his sister fled north to Scotland.

We have seen how the King of Scots, Malcolm III, owed a debt of gratitude to Edward the Confessor, who had helped him recover his father's throne from the usurping Macbeth and he gave the royal exiles a warm welcome. This welcome soon became warmer, for Malcolm offered Margaret his hand and she became Queen of Scotland. This must have been a love match – despite Margaret's noble blood, she was penniless, with little realistic chance of recovering her lost position in England. Malcolm was certainly devoted to her, and when his advisers complained of the lavish alms Margaret was bestowing on the poor, he commented 'Let her alone. This generosity of hers will bring blessings on us all.'

Margaret became the exemplary queen, faultlessly carrying out her duties as wife and mother (three of her sons became kings of Scotland, and trained by their mother, were noted for their piety). But beyond these domestic duties, she acquired an influence of her own over the kingdom, powered entirely by her passionate Christian faith. She was worldly enough to value fine clothes and jewels and set about a reformation of etiquette and manners in the rather raucous Scottish court. More importantly, she gained the confidence of the Scottish clergy and was able to encourage greater devotion in the life of the church: more frequent communions, more careful observance of Sunday as a day of rest and Lent as a season of fasting. She obtained her husband's consent to remit the taxes charged on the ferry crossing the Firth of Forth (called Queensferry in her honour) in order to promote pilgrimage to the shrine of St Andrew, now rapidly becoming Scotland's patron saint. More personally, she lived a life of constant prayer and delighted to raise orphan children in the palace, whom she visited and fed with her own hands every morning.

Margaret died of grief and shock three days after hearing the news of the death of her beloved husband in a raid on Northumbria. Her daughter Matilda married King Henry I of England, son of William the Conqueror, and restored Saxon blood to the English royal family.

LANFRANC (c1010-1089) 28th May.

What became of the England from which St Margaret fled? In 1070, the Saxon archbishop Stigand was deposed by the Pope for irregularities both in his consecration and in his life. To fill his place, William the Conqueror summoned to England a Norman priest already highly regarded by the king, who for all his ruthlessness was genuinely pious. This priest was Lanfranc, the Benedictine abbot of Caen.

Lanfranc was an Italian born in Pavia and originally trained as a lawyer. He moved to France seeking learning and established a reputation as a teacher, but he was conscious of a deeper call. On a journey to Rouen he was set upon by robbers who left him stripped and blindfolded. He appealed to the countrymen who rescued him to be taken to the poorest monastery in the region: they took him to Bec, where Lanfranc found the abbot repairing with his own hands the monastery oven. Charmed by this simplicity, Lanfranc joined the community and gave himself ardently to the life of silence and prayer, even at one time considering becoming a hermit.

But whatever his hunger for prayer and solitude, Lanfranc's genius was for organisation and government, and this was recognised by his community, who elected him prior. In eighteen years Lanfranc transformed Bec from a poor, un-noticed community into one of the foremost monasteries in France, regarded as a model by the whole Benedictine order. He founded a monastery school, and scholars, both monastic and lay, flocked to Bec to obtain one of the best educations available. Lanfranc further distinguished himself by his controversy with Berengar of Tours over the Eucharist. Berengar, drawing on the authority of St Augustine, maintained that the Eucharistic elements remained bread and wine, becoming the body and blood of Christ only symbolically and spiritually. Lanfranc, drawing on the authority of St Ambrose, fought for the position which would later be refined into the doctrine of transubstantiation, the actual miraculous transformation of the elements into Christ's body and blood.

This eminent prior was head-hunted by William, Duke of Normandy, to be abbot of his new monastery at Caen, and when the Duke of Normandy became King of England, his most trusted priest was head-hunted again to be Archbishop of Canterbury.

William the Conqueror was determined to remould England into an efficient, tax-paying kingdom subservient to his will, and Lanfranc was an archbishop exactly matched to his king in temperament and gifts. Cool, rational, hard-working and clear-sighted, Lanfranc overhauled the English church in line with the best continental models. Dioceses were reshaped to make them more manageable. Four cathedrals situated in small villages were closed and the bishop's seats translated to more suitable cities – Sherborne to Salisbury, Selsey to Chichester, Lichfield to Chester, and Dorchester-on-Thames to Lincoln. Canterbury cathedral itself, which was in ruins after a fire, was demolished and rebuilt from scratch on the same design as Lanfranc's church in Caen. True to his monastic roots, Lanfranc encouraged the government of cathedrals by monastic communities rather than secular canons: new monasteries were founded at Rochester and Durham, and Lanfranc supported the (Saxon) monks of Winchester against their new (Norman) bishop, who wished to suppress them. For all his administrative skill, Lanfranc was never loved by the English people. He sustained a continuous feud with the monks of Canterbury, who resented his rationalisation of their liturgy and the way well-loved shrines to Saxon saints were omitted from the design of the new cathedral. Lanfranc purged the church calendar, striking out native saints whom he considered unworthy and substituting names from the Bible and from France and Italy. As a result many English churches were rededicated to more politically correct patron saints. Even St Alphege only kept his place thanks to the intervention of Lanfranc's pupil, the future Archbishop Anselm. On the other hand, Lanfranc sincerely revered the British proto-martyr Alban, and he did his best to serve the English church faithfully. He was a conquering Norman in an age of conquest and did more to shape Christianity in England than many archbishops who have been better loved.

OSMUND (died 1099) 16th July.
Typical of the new breed of bishops who came over with William and supported Lanfranc was St Osmund. He was one of the conqueror's domestic chaplains and served him as royal chancellor. During his term of office, he suppressed the use of Anglo-Saxon in official documents and regularised the use of Latin as the normal language of government. In 1078, he relinquished this post to become Bishop of Salisbury, a new title as the see had only recently been transferred from Sherborne. Osmund commenced the building of a new cathedral, but the present world-famous building owes nothing to him, as the first cathedral was built in the hill fortress of Old Sarum, and building on the present site did not begin until 1220. Osmund's administrative gifts led to his involvement in two other famous projects: the compiling of the Doomsday Book, and the collection and reform of liturgy which would coalesce into the 'Sarum use' the dominant liturgical tradition in medieval England, and one which was quarried by Archbishop Cranmer when he was writing the Book of Common Prayer.

Osmund was noted as exceptional among appointees from William's household for his chastity, lack of financial greed, and integrity in doing justice. Men like him were moulding the English church.

WULFSTAN (1009-1095) 19th January.

Only one Saxon bishop appointed before the conquest kept his place in the church of Lanfranc and William the Conqueror, and that was St Wulfstan, the monk-bishop of Worcester. Wulfstan was a pragmatist – he was one of the first Saxon notables to submit to the Conqueror, and while abbeys like Ely turned themselves into rebel headquarters, sheltering Hereward the Wake, Wulfstan co-operated fully with Lanfranc's reform programme, introducing the rule of St Benedict to the monks of Worcester on the most approved Norman, continental model. A charming legend tells that nevertheless Lanfranc wished to depose him and summoning him to Westminster, demanded his pastoral staff. Wulfstan replied 'I will surrender my staff only to him who gave it to me,' and laid the staff on the tomb of Edward the Confessor. Miraculously, no one could lift the staff except Wulfstan, to whom the saintly king thus showed that he was to remain Bishop of Worcester. In fact, however, Lanfranc thoroughly approved of Wulfstan. The Saxon bishop even demolished his cathedral and rebuilt it in the Norman style which was covering England with new churches: though it is recorded that he wept as he gave the order for the destruction of the place where his ancestors had worshipped.

Wulfstan was no mere time-server, however. He was a man of strong social conscience who went every year to Bristol at the far southwest of his diocese, to preach and work against the trade which shipped Anglo-Saxon slaves to Ireland. And while co-operating with the Normans, he worked tirelessly to preserve the Saxon culture of the English church. With his encouragement, the monks of Worcester continued to write their chronicles in Anglo-Saxon, thus almost single-handedly preserving English as a literary language. By the time he died, Wulfstan was revered as the grand old man of the church and his tomb was early a place of pilgrimage. Even bad King John particularly revered St Wulfstan, and desired to be buried next to him in Worcester Cathedral, where the royal tomb can be seen to this day.

PART FOURTEEN. CHRISTENDOM.

ANSELM (1033-1109) 21st April.

So far in our story, we have seen how natural in the early Middle Ages was the alliance of church and secular rulers. The support of a king like Edwin of Northumbria or Pippin of France could make or break a mission, and church leaders knew that their chances of reaching the population with their message depended on the patronage of rulers, who alone could endow monasteries and build parish churches. But in the twelfth century this alliance became strained. Lanfranc co-operated easily and naturally with William the Conqueror, but as the era of barbarian invasion came to an end and Europe began to experience stability and prosperity, the Pope and the most progressive bishops and abbots began striving for an independent church, which would truly be a visible sign of the kingdom of heaven, not accountable to any earthly power. This movement coalesced around the symbolic issue of investiture. The Pope was anxious to deny secular rulers the right to invest bishops with the symbols of their office. A bishop was more than a feudal magnate: he was an heir of the apostles and as such had a dignity which derived from no mere worldly authority. Thus in the next generation after the conquest, relations were far less cordial between the conqueror's son, William Rufus, and Lanfranc's heir, St Anselm.

Anselm's career followed that of Lanfranc with uncanny exactitude. Like Lanfranc, his family were minor nobility in northern Italy. Like Lanfranc, he crossed the Alps into France, restlessly seeking both knowledge and a direction in life. He came to Bec, established himself as one of the foremost scholars of that house, became prior in due course, and after Lanfranc's death, was elected to succeed his master as Archbishop of Canterbury. But with these external echoes, the likeness ends. Lanfranc was a man of action, a born administrator. Anselm was, above everything, a thinker, perhaps the most original mind in western Christendom since Augustine, and despite the many administrative duties to which he was called, his lack of any political instinct made him surprisingly ineffective as an archbishop.

During his years at Bec, Anselm developed, through long conversations with the brightest of his young monks, his distinctive way of doing theology – 'faith seeking understanding.' He wanted to find ways of justifying the faith which would depend entirely on reason and logic, and so begins his first great work, the 'Monologion', with the surprising statement that he will not refer to the Bible at all in his writing. Anselm was trying to escape the traditional use of scriptural and patristic texts to 'prove' points of doctrine by an appeal to an infallible authority. Surely, if Christianity were true, there must be reasons *why* it was true, and these reasons Anselm set himself to discover. He attempts to deduce from incontrovertible first principles all the doctrine of the Christian faith. Although he never quotes him directly, his work owes much to Augustine of Hippo: Anselm shared Augustine's interest in finding an image of the Trinity in the human personality. His writing is tightly logical, with every step carefully reasoned, and it has been widely acclaimed. But Anselm was not content. He wanted to find one argument for God's existence which would make all others unnecessary and, during vespers in the Abbey of Bec, in a flash of insight, he believed he had gained what he sought. In a sequel to the 'Monologion', the Proslogion,' he set forth what has come to be called the ontological argument. God, he said, may be defined as that than which nothing greater can be conceived. But to exist is greater than not to exist. Therefore, if God did not exist but the mind conceived of him existing, the mind would be conceiving something greater than God. Therefore God necessarily exists. The argument seems ridiculous on the surface, but its underlying probing of the nature of existence has intrigued philosophers ever since, with philosophers as great as Descartes producing their own versions of it, and philosophers as great as Kant refuting it.

From these congenial intellectual pursuits, Anselm was summoned to become archbishop of Canterbury. He was in England on business when King William II fell dangerously ill. William Rufus was not naturally pious, but on what he believed was his death-bed, he was in terror for his soul. His common practice was to delay appointing bishops to vacant sees, for during a vacancy the bishop's revenues went to the royal treasury. For this reason, the see of

Canterbury had lain vacant for many years, but the remorseful Rufus, hearing that so learned and holy a man as Anselm was in attendance, summoned him to his bedside, and supported by the tears and entreaties of his entourage, thrust the bishop's staff into Anselm's reluctant hands. Having thus appeased God, Rufus made a speedy recovery and lived to regret having chosen as archbishop a man of such inflexible righteousness, totally lacking in the political instinct which had made Lanfranc so successful a collaborator with the crown.

Despite the irregularity of his own appointment, Anselm conceived it to be his duty to defy the king and uphold the emerging papal orthodoxy that bishops must not receive their spiritual authority from laymen. To kings like Rufus and his brother Henry I, this stance was threatening. Bishops were landowners, suppliers of knights to feudal armies, and the king must maintain control over appointments to such key posts. Anselm was incapable of compromise and as a result spent long years of his episcopate in exile, trying to persuade the pope to support his position, which the pope, more keenly aware of the danger of alienating the powerful Norman kings, was in no hurry to do.

While in exile Anselm wrote the last book for which he is famous: 'Cur Deus Homo?' (Why did God become man). In it, with his customary unflinching logic, he addressed the question why God needed to become incarnate. After all, if God can do anything, surely he could forgive our sins without needing the atoning death of his Son in payment? Anselm's answer, conditioned by the feudal world in which he lived, was that God could not with justice allow his honour to be diminished, as mankind had diminished it by sinning. God's honour could only be restored by an equivalent compensation, which bankrupt mankind could never have paid, had not God, by assuming human form and dying, made recompense himself. This account of the crucifixion has had a long history - it is the ancestor of the classic Protestant doctrine of substitutionary atonement, in which Jesus is portrayed as bearing the punishment we deserve – but it can be used to sustain a deeply disturbing picture of God as a stern judge whose need to punish someone can only be assuaged by the sacrifice of the innocent Jesus. Like so much of Anselm's legacy to the church, it is an ambiguous gift.

Finally, reconciled to Henry I, Anselm was able to die in peace. He was particularly mourned by the monks of Canterbury, who treasured his wise efforts to retrieve their Saxon traditions after the trauma of the conquest years, but he left unsettled difficult issues of the relation of crown to church, which would trouble his successors for many years to come.

BERNARD OF CLAIRVAUX (1090-1153) 20th August.

The political campaign of the Popes to remove the church from the control of secular rulers had its spiritual counterpart in the intense series of reforms, often involving the foundation of new religious orders, which were to preoccupy many of the noblest souls in Christendom during the next two hundred years. The twelfth and thirteenth centuries seem to us one of the most glorious periods of Christian history when Europe, emerging from the dark ages, clothed itself with magnificent cathedrals and churches, and artists and poets laid the foundations for the triumphs of the Renaissance. But to those who lived in these creative times, it seemed as though the church was constantly threatened by corruption and worldly compromise, the fruits of its very success. Those whose lives we shall trace in the next part of our story were striving to escape from the institutional church and lead people back to something more nearly resembling the spirit of Jesus Christ, who during those years was revered less as the King reigning on high demanding the submission of monarchs, and more as the poor man of Nazareth, living without possessions and dying in a manner portrayed with increasing realism as horrific.

Bernard of Clairvaux was the son of a French nobleman and from his earliest years displayed a yearning for the heavenly city and for Jesus Christ, who alone can satisfy the longing of the human heart. His hymns, still frequently sung, express this wistful pining for the heavenly homeland – 'Jerusalem the golden', 'Jesus thou joy of loving hearts'. It was this unyielding devotion to Jesus, together with formidable talents as a preacher and organiser, that gave Bernard his extraordinary dominance over the Europe of his age.

Bernard found that he was quite unable to satisfy his longing through the conventional monastic life of his day. The Benedictine monasteries were enormously wealthy institutions, funded by vast estates: in them the choir monks who prayed and studied in privileged leisure were greatly outnumbered by the monastery servants. Moreover, the most 'up to date' monasteries had adopted the Cluniac reforms, a rich new tradition of worship in which an elaborate liturgy was celebrated with sumptuous music, ritual and church furnishings. Performing this liturgy took six or seven hours a day: it was the monk's full-time job. Bernard longed for simplicity, even harsh austerity, and he founded a new style of monastery. The rule of St Benedict was still the basis, but the Cistercians, as they became known, sought the wildest, remotest valleys for their foundations, where, with severe self-denial they worked manually to support themselves, worshipping in white-washed churches with none of the gorgeous pomp fashionable elsewhere.

The young Bernard was idealistic to the point of fanaticism, but his call to a harder way of living the gospel evoked an extraordinary response. Not only his own brothers but a whole generation of young aristocrats answered his call to abandon wealth and privilege and devote themselves to the Cistercian way. In the early days, Bernard imposed such rigorous fasts and so arduous a routine of work that many of his first disciples became dangerously ill, and many found that in practice the Cistercian way was too demanding, and sought to retreat into the relative comfort of the established abbeys. A high proportion of Bernard's surviving correspondence related to the problems created when monks wished to shift location in this way. As he grew older, Bernard dealt with individual cases with a growing compassion, but it is fair to say that generally he encouraged monks from 'laxer' traditions to transfer to Cistercian abbeys, while being much more hard-line in insisting that Benedictine abbots should return Cistercian 'runaways' to fulfil their vows in the new tradition. His influence was immense and such was his moral prestige that, especially after one of his pupils was elected as Pope, bishops and kings trembled when Bernard stirred himself about their affairs.

It is unfortunate for Bernard's reputation that in the two greatest campaigns of his life he took positions which a modern Christian would wish to repudiate. The great theological battle of his life was fought against Peter Abelard, famous for his illicit affair with the beautiful Heloise. There was much more to Abelard than one of history's great love affairs. An iconoclastic teacher in the new universities, he pushed on St.Anselm's project of seeking to find purely rational defences for Christian theological propositions. The trouble was that, with a maverick's delight in making the pompous squirm, Abelard enjoyed exposing the apparent contradictions in the corpus of traditional material which medieval scholars were taught to revere. His book 'Sic and Non' (Yes and No) marshalled quotations to show church fathers coming down on both sides of controversial questions; the book's none too subtle subtext was that appeals to authority and tradition could settle nothing, and everything needed to be rethought from first principles. Naturally Abelard's student fan club gleefully cheered him on, but Bernard was not amused. To him, this rationalist questioning of everything left no room for reverence or for faith, and turned Abelard into a monster combination of Arius, Pelagius and Nestorius. Where Bernard's reputation suffers is that, far from debating the issues fairly with Abelard, he used his European reputation as a giant defender of the faith to get Abelard condemned as a heretic and forbidden to preach. The Synod of Sens in 1140 obeyed Bernard and crushed Abelard without giving the younger man a chance to speak in his defence. Such tactics do not endear Bernard to a modern audience.

The other cause behind which Bernard threw all the weight of his reputation was the launching of the Second Crusade. In 1095 Europe had thrilled to the extraordinary success of the First Crusade. A company of western knights, braving unimaginable hardships and inflicting unimaginable cruelties, had wrested Jerusalem from Muslim control and founded four Christian states in the Holy Land. Crusade was launched as one of the highest and holiest causes, and the defence and recapture of the Holy Places haunted the dreams of Pope and kings. In 1144, news came through that Edessa, the most northern and vulnerable of the Crusader states, had fallen to the infidel. Bernard moved heaven and earth to launch a crusade for its recapture. King Louis VII of France and his wife Eleanor of Aquitaine, together with some of the greatest lords of Germany, France and Italy, took the cross and the largest feudal army yet seen, blessed by Bernard and assured of heaven's favour, departed for the Levant. Alas, the result was a fiasco. Quarrelling over their objectives and unable to work with the established crusader forces, Louis's army disintegrated and suffered ignominious defeat. Bernard blamed the sinfulness of the crusaders: Eleanor of Aquitaine had invented a dashing uniform for her ladies and had enjoyed a string of scandalous love affairs in the gorgeous palaces of the east.

The defeat of his dearest hopes turned Bernard all the more single-mindedly inward to seek the heavenly Jerusalem in his heart. His spirituality found an equivalent to the prevailing troubadour cult of love for a fair maiden in a passionate devotion to the Virgin Mary, who in this age began to be a focus for adoring prayer, and in a highly wrought allegorical interpretation of the Song of Solomon, whose erotic images were quarried by Bernard to express the intimate joy of the life of prayer. For all his flaws, he expresses the beauty and sheer joy of loving Jesus in ways that retained their power for generations.

AELRED OF RIEVAULX (1109-1167) 12th January.
King David of Scotland, son of St Margaret, had a steward named Aelred. The son and grandson of a priest, Aelred had been obliged to seek secular employment because of a new papal regulation, which made it illegal for the sons of the clergy to seek ordination; this was one of many small changes which were gradually establishing celibacy as normative for the clergy. One day in 1133 Aelred was returning from York, where he had been on business for his master – the King of Scots was a large holder of land in England. As they passed the valley leading to the Cistercian abbey of Rievaulx, Aelred's companions proposed a detour to view what was already a famous institution. The band of officials rode through the abbey lands, observing the prosperity which had been hewn from the rugged landscape by the labour of the brothers, the flocks of sheep for which Bernard's Cistercians were already renowned. As they entered the monastic enclosure Aelred underwent a sudden, cataclysmic religious

conversion. The party claimed monastic hospitality for the night, but next morning Aelred was unable to ride on to Scotland. He had been called, and he remained a Cistercian for the rest of his life, rising to become abbot of Rievaulx and so renowned for the beauty of his writing that he was known as 'the Bernard of the north.'

Aelred was altogether a gentler man than the great St Bernard. Although sincerely and, as far as we can tell, cheerfully celibate, it seems highly likely that he was gay. Even by the ornate standards of the time, his letters to trusted friends breathe passionate devotion, and contemporaries noted that as an old and ailing abbot, the monks chosen to tend to his needs were invariably young and beautiful. While fully committed to the austere Cistercian way, Aelred's monasticism was not of that chilly variety which seeks to mortify all natural human affection. His great book was 'On spiritual Friendship' and, while owing much to its classical prototype, Cicero's 'De Amicitia', the book is very much Aelred's own in its perceptive analysis of the delights and pitfalls of friendship as a way to God, and his certainty that a good friend is the best blessing God can give a man.

His last years were dogged by painful illness, to which he refused to concede comfort. He had a lean-to built for himself against the church wall, so that he could follow the church services from his bed, and died with exemplary patience.

GILBERT OF SEMPRINGHAM (1083-1189) 4th February.

Another monastic founder of this age of renewal in the church was Gilbert of Sempringham, who is less well-known because the order he founded, being purely confined to England, disappeared entirely when Henry VIII dissolved the monasteries.

Gilbert was the son of a Lincolnshire knight and, being deformed or crippled, was unable to ride a horse or go to war, and thus could not inherit the family estates. His father, who tenderly loved him, gave him a manor and made him the vicar of it – already the wealth of the church was providing convenient incomes for members of the upper classes who could not be expected to make their way in any suitably aristocratic sphere.

His father no doubt expected Gilbert to employ a curate to do the parish work and live comfortably off his tithes. But Gilbert was tougher than he looked. Despite his disability, he lived to be over a hundred years old, and this physical tenacity was matched by a spiritual determination.

The Gilbertine order began as a simple experiment. When Gilbert discovered that several of his female parishioners wished to live in perpetual virginity, he provided them with a house and wrote a rule of life for them. From this local, improvised beginning grew an order which numbered twenty-six houses, spread throughout the midlands. A peculiar feature of Gilbert's order as it took shape was that the houses were for men and women, living together but under different rules. The women lived enclosed lives as contemplative nuns; the men were expected to connect pastorally with their parishes, living as Augustinian canons and working as teachers and spiritual directors. Gilbert wished to associate his houses with the Cistercian order, but, uneasy at the presence of women in the Gilbertine houses, the Cistercians declined and he was left to develop his vision alone.

Throughout his long old age, Gilbert personally directed, visited and inspired the houses. Today his memory is preserved in Lincoln cathedral, where a shrine of modern, deliberately misshapen candlesticks commemorates a man who rose above his disability to be an inspiration to hundreds.

HILDEGARD OF BINGEN (1098-1179) 17th September.

Among those with whom St Bernard corresponded was a nun of the Rhineland, Hildegard, who, in the most constricted outer world it is possible to conceive, developed one of the most extraordinary and rich inner lives ever manifested.

Hildegard's childhood would nowadays be regarded as abusive. Vowed from infancy to the religious life, her parents gave her up, not just to be a nun, but to be an anchorite, that is a person literally walled in, to spend her whole life in prayer shut within one small house. From the age of five she was shut away in a sealed compound within a male monastery, to be the companion and disciple of an older anchorite named Jutta. Yet amazingly, within this tiny world, a few feet of space and one woman as friend and guide, Hildegard flourished and became holy. She owed her soul to Jutta's wisdom. Though outwardly restricted, her mind was original and fearsomely intelligent. After Jutta's death, she first gathered to her other women as partners in her work of prayer (it is not clear how they fitted into the tiny space allocated) and was eventually granted permission to leave the monastery, and found her own convent in more spacious grounds on the mountain above the modern town of Bingen.

In her spirituality, Hildegard celebrated life as a gift from God. Shocked contemporaries reported that within the privacy of the convent her nuns grew their hair long, wore beautiful and un-nun-like clothes and took part in singing, playing instruments and even acting plays. Certainly Hildegard's own musical compositions survive and have recently been revived in performance: and she wrote liturgical dramas for her nuns modelled on the comedies of Terence, the only classical playwright widely known in the Middle Ages. It is tempting to see the convent at Bingen as an early feminist community where women were free to explore for themselves the nature of God, without male dominance, in an atmosphere of creativity and supportive friendship.

There is inevitably another side to the story. Hildegard was as burdened as any of her contemporaries by the sinfulness of the world, and her concerts and plays, her essays on natural history and celebrations of female beauty, were staged within a context of rigorous fasting and prayer, pursued to the point of endangering her health, and resulting in a series of visions, which she recorded in her book 'Scivias.' Much of this visionary material consists of denunciations of sin and terrifying images of judgement and the end of all things. Hildegard's early humanism was lived within an awareness of divine anger as well as divine love – and it is this tension which gives her work and her life its creative bite.

ERIC, KING OF SWEDEN (d1170) 18th May CDC.
While Christianity in Western Europe was thus developing in cultural richness and spiritual depth, Scandinavia remained very much a frontier land, where the stark pessimism of traditional Viking

religion remained a real alternative to the new faith planted by Olave and Sigmund. Eric, the national hero of the Swedes, spent much of his reign establishing the church in Finland, by methods perhaps more kingly than apostolic. He was killed in battle against his rebellious subjects and, although a casualty of a struggle as much political as religious, was, like so many royal unfortunates before him, honoured as a martyr and venerated as one of the founders of Sweden.

THOMAS BECKET (1118-1170) 29th December.
Even to the enclosed world of Hildegard's convent came news of the crime which shocked Europe, the murder of an archbishop of Canterbury within his own cathedral, a murder which launched one of the greatest pilgrimage cults of the middle ages and made a saint out of the most unlikely material, proud, prickly Thomas Becket.

Becket was the son of a London merchant, destined for a clerical career and early prominent for his precocious intellect. He rose fast and when introduced to the new King of England, Henry II, he made an instant good impression by his charm and evident intelligence. Henry made him his Chancellor and the two men worked as a perfect team. Henry, restless, ambitious, contemptuous of pomp and dignity while acutely aware of how real power was gained and preserved, found Becket's eye for detail and administrative flair invaluable in fleshing out the reforms he was imposing on his empire, consisting not only of England and Normandy but also Aquitaine, which he had gained by his opportunistic marriage with Eleanor of Aquitaine. Louis VII had divorced her after her scandalous behaviour on the Second Crusade – her marriage to Henry Plantagenet transferred half France from her first husband to her second.

Becket revelled in the trappings of high office, and was famously teased for it by the King, who obliged him on one occasion to throw a rich fur cloak to a shivering beggar. It is usually assumed that Henry made Becket Archbishop of Canterbury in order to secure a reliable ally in a key post as he set about reforming the church. It is equally possible, however, that the promotion was an attempt to side-line Becket – he had masterminded a campaign to gain control of

Toulouse for Henry's empire, a campaign which came disastrously unstuck. Was the apparent golden gift of an archbishopric actually a way of removing from the sphere of action someone who had become a liability?[92] If that was how Becket perceived it, it would explain the antagonistic stance which the new archbishop immediately adopted towards his old friend and patron.

For Becket, as soon as he was enthroned, dramatically changed his ways. Gone were the flamboyance, the easy lordliness of manner, the conspicuous consumption. The new archbishop fasted, spoke little, set himself resolutely against the sins of the world. In particular, Becket stood obstinately for the liberties of the church and, in so doing, re-ignited the tension which had flared between William Rufus and Anselm.

William the Conqueror, with his unusually centralised version of the feudal system, had established a measure of control over the English church which was untypical of his age. Against this, the reforming ideals of twelfth century popes and saints had pulled: the church was not a department of state but an alternative society with its own government, hierarchy and courts of justice. The anomaly, whereby a churchman, accused of a crime, could appeal to the church courts and thus escape royal justice offended Henry II, whose life's work was to erode the jurisdiction of feudal and local courts and centralise the doing of justice in his own courts. When presented with the Constitutions of Clarendon, which subjected the traditional rights of the church to the demands of royal justice, Becket refused to sign. At the time he gained little sympathy by his stance. His own bishops regarding him as obstinate, unrealistic and exasperating and, when Becket fled the realm in disguise and appealed to the Pope for his support, he received only ambiguous encouragement. The aged Gilbert of Sempringham was compromised by this flight, and was briefly imprisoned on a charge of abetting the king's enemies. Long years of exile followed, in which Becket's cause became a bargaining counter in the power struggles between the Pope and the Kings of England and France. At last, however, a reconciliation was effected between Henry II and his archbishop, and Becket was free to return

---

[92] For more on this theory, see WL Warren 'Henry II'

to England. He came back to be welcomed as a living saint by the common people but his first action was deliberately provocative.

To ensure a smooth succession, Henry II desired that his oldest son, also called Henry, should be crowned in his father's lifetime and, in the absence of the archbishop of Canterbury, this ceremony had been performed by the archbishop of York and two other bishops, all old enemies of Becket since the controversy over the Constitutions of Clarendon. No soon had Becket returned than he excommunicated the three bishops for their usurpation of Canterbury's rights. The news was brought to Henry in Normandy by the affronted bishops and he, falling into a rage, uttered the notorious words, 'Who will rid me of this turbulent priest?'

Taking ship for England, four knights travelled to Canterbury where, three days after Christmas in 1170, they broke into the archbishop's palace and angrily taunted Becket with his disloyalty to the King. Becket remained undaunted by their threats and refused the urgent pleas of his staff to take measures for his own protection. The next day, 29th December, the knights returned and followed Becket into the cathedral, whither he had repaired for Vespers. As they broke in, the frightened monks scattered. The knights called angrily into the darkness 'Where is the traitor?' No answer came, but when the knights cried 'Where is the archbishop?' Thomas Becket spoke up. 'Here I am, no traitor but a faithful servant of God.' As his followers tried to pull him away, one of the knights aimed a blow, breaking the arm of Becket's cross-bearer and slicing off the top of the archbishop's head. An orgy of violence followed and Becket was left in a pool of blood while the murderers fled. The witnesses at once began to soak handkerchiefs in the sacred blood of the martyr, and within twenty four hours the first miracle of healing was being proclaimed. By his intemperate anger, Henry had transformed a stubborn, bitter man into a shining martyr of God. He could now never win his battle with Thomas Becket.

The king came to Canterbury, now the shrine of the blessed martyr, and did public penance, allowing every monk to whip his naked back and kneeling in prayer at Becket's tomb. All Europe rang with the scandal and Becket's name became powerful as people of all ranks vied to do him honour.

HUGH OF LINCOLN (1140-1200) 17th November.

As well as submitting to physical penance for the murder of Becket, Henry II undertook to perform works of reparation, as an expression of his contrition. Among these was the foundation of new religious houses in England, which were to be charterhouses, monasteries of the Carthusian order. This order, even more extreme than the Cistercian in its insistence on silence, solitude and voluntary poverty, had been founded by St Bruno in his great mountain fastness the Grande Chartreuse. To bring the Carthusian order to England, Henry invited from the Grande Chartreuse Hugh of Avallon, a man whose charm, integrity and evident holiness caused him to be hailed as a saint in his own lifetime.

Hugh pleased Henry II so much that he was in 1186, ten years after his arrival in England, offered the bishopric of Lincoln, then a huge diocese stretching from the Thames to the Trent. It cost Hugh much to accept this post and he only did so on condition that, as far as possible, he continue to live by his Carthusian rule. After an entire adult life spent in solitary prayer, Hugh was about to embark on the busy, public life of a medieval bishop.

His relationship with Henry II was a marked improvement on that of poor Becket. Hugh was genuinely compassionate and knew how to defuse a tricky situation with humour. On one occasion he had infuriated the king by excommunicating his chief forester. Henry summoned him to the court and then underlined his displeasure by pointedly setting off hunting without speaking to Hugh. The bishop followed him into the woods and caught up with the royal party in a clearing where Henry, still refusing to make eye contact, sat on a log sewing up a tear in his leather riding glove. Hugh sat and watched, then quietly said, 'How like your grandmother of Falaise you look.' The allusion was to William the Conqueror's mother, who was a tanner's daughter before the Duke of Normandy seduced her. The courtiers gasped, but Henry roared with laughter and Hugh was back in favour. Henry's sons Richard Coeur de Lion and even John had a similar respect for Hugh.

It was not just kings with whom Hugh was able to converse on equal terms. Wherever he went he treated people with a gentle courtesy which won their hearts. It was remarked of him that when he rode through villages and people ran out with their children to be confirmed, Hugh would always get off his horse before administering the sacrament – a story which throws an alarming light on the way less saintly bishops must have performed their duties to their humbler subjects. To outcasts especially Hugh was tender. Unusually in that intolerant age he protected the Jews, of whom there was a large, wealthy colony in Lincoln, and would not allow their persecution. And he made a practice of visiting leper colonies and tending the wounds of the sufferers with his own hands, a ministry which his entourage could hardly bear to watch, let alone share in.

One of Hugh's greatest achievements was the rebuilding of Lincoln Cathedral; much of his work is still visible in the present building. Many bishops of course promoted spectacular building projects in this golden age of church architecture, but Hugh again amazed contemporaries by the humble style of his work, for he would carry the stones with his own hands and reverence the ordinary masons as his Christian brothers.

He was an avid collector of relics and, on being offered the arm of Mary Magdalene to venerate, scandalised the monks of Vezelay by biting off a chunk to take away. 'Am I, who am permitted to receive in my mouth the whole body of my Saviour, forbidden the arm of Mary Magdalene?' he enquired innocently.

Such was the awe in which he was held that his canonisation followed swiftly on his death. The kings of England and Scotland carried the coffin at his funeral. His emblem in art is the pet swan which he tamed and taught to eat food from his hand.

DOMINIC (1170-1221) 8th August.
The nature of medieval society was changing. The great feudal estates still dominated Europe, with their villages of serfs centred on the parish churches, and the Benedictine and Cistercian abbeys forming centres of prayer and study in their rural fastnesses. But towns and cities were growing. The urban poor had needs different from those of villagers tied by immemorial custom to their lords and strip fields – while the urban rich, the new class of merchants and master craftsmen, had the education and curiosity to desire a more personal involvement in their faith. Enquiring minds asked awkward

questions and sometimes developed awkward answers. It was in the thirteenth century that the church began its unhealthy obsession with the eradication of heresy. But it was in the thirteenth century too that a new type of religious order emerged: the friars, the creation of two great and holy men, Dominic and Francis.

Dominic came from the fringes of Christendom, from Spain, now beginning to flex its muscles as the Muslim conquerors who had ruled it since the age of Charles Martel were finally driven out. Spanish Christianity has always been austere, uncompromising, even fanatical. Dominic was driven by a burning passion for truth and a desire to teach the faith more effectively.

In his day, southern France was consumed by the heresy of the Cathars. As usual, our information about these dissenters is largely filtered to us through reports by their enemies, but the Cathars seem to have been related to the ancient gnostics whom Ireaneus of Lyons had opposed. Like the Gnostics they despised the body and its works, seeing the physical world as the creation of an evil God and seeking release into a better world of pure spirit. The 'pure ones' who headed the sect forsook marriage and led an austere life with as little contact as possible with corrupt matter. More alarmingly, from the point of view of medieval popes and bishops, they derided the sacraments as meaningless and unnecessary and assured their followers that they needed no priest or church hierarchy to find salvation.

Dominic's conviction was that the Cathars could only be opposed by reasoned argument: people would only stay faithful to catholic Christianity if they understood it. Moreover, the faith must be taught by minsters whose lives gave credibility to their preaching. A church whose leaders conspicuously enjoyed enormous wealth while sitting light to the pastoral duties for the performance of which that wealth had been given, was not well equipped to speak against a movement stressing voluntary poverty and a humble return to New Testament ideals of brotherhood.

In 1204, Dominic was in Rome for the Lateran Council summoned by that grandest of Popes, Innocent III, for the reform of the church and the consolidation of papal power. The cause for which Anselm suffered and Becket died was now apparently triumphant, and the Pope was able to present himself as Christ's viceroy, the triple crowned king of kings, with power to dethrone the unworthy and give laws to Christendom. But Innocent III agreed with Dominic that the church must establish its rule in the minds and consciences of Christians, and he consented to the formation of a new order, the Friars Preachers or Dominicans, charged with teaching the faith and opposing heresy.

The Dominicans were not a conventional order. They did not remain cloistered within monasteries but travelled about, living lives of simplicity and prayer, and running missions, bringing the faith to any community threatened by ignorance or heresy. Dominic, severe to himself, was gentle and tender towards those to whom he preached, seeking to win the indifferent by reason, persuasion and love. It was unfortunate that his campaign of preaching in the Cathar heartlands coincided with the scandal of the Albigensian crusade. Innocent III, not trusting the power of preaching alone, turned the dreadful weapon of crusade for the first time against a Christian land. The beautiful civilisation of the south of France was eradicated, many ancient cities destroyed and their inhabitants, Cathar and catholic alike, were massacred. 'Kill them all,' a bishop accompanying the crusaders is said to have ordered. 'God will know who are his.' Dominic was not personally implicated in the crimes of this crusade, but Dominicans certainly accompanied the armies and organised heresy trials in the wake of the massacres. Dominicans too staffed the Holy Inquisition, the new and terrible weapon against heresy forged by the Popes in this era. It is hard to believe that Dominic would have approved the work to which his preachers were set: the modern Dominican order, humane, intelligent and attracting some of the finest minds in Catholicism, surely lives closer to his spirit.

Dominic is also credited with the invention of the Rosary, a form of meditation which was revealed to him in a vision by the Virgin Mary. The giving of the Rosary to Dominic is a favourite subject with painters, although the true origins of this devotion are more complex. The rosary encouraged the illiterate and those too poor to own Bibles, to live imaginatively within the events of Christ's life, death and resurrection, and its growth in popularity in the thirteenth century is an example of the way in which the human life of Jesus, in all its suffering and weakness, was becoming more central to the life of prayer.

FRANCIS OF ASSISI (1181-1226) 4th October.

At the Lateran Council, Dominic met a young Italian who, like himself, was in Rome to ask the Pope's blessing on a new order of friars. Dominic and Francis of Assisi were instantly attracted to each other, although they only met this once. Their visions were incompatible and each man pursued his own path. If the Dominicans represent the mind of catholic Christianity, the Franciscans surely represent its heart. Of all the saints, Francis speaks most clearly across the centuries, and the charm of his Christ-like simplicity still moves us today

The son of a wealthy cloth merchant, Francis had a golden, privileged youth, spending his father's money freely on fine clothes and leading the fashionable young men of Assisi in a life of horse races, late night concerts and revelry. He was always able to make people love him by his open spirit, generous sense of humour and infectious delight in beauty. His conversion came about when he was involved in a war with the neighbouring town of Perugia . He spent some months as a prisoner of war, and when he returned could find no satisfaction in his old life of cheerful self-indulgence. Sitting one day in the disused church of San Damiano, it seemed to Francis that the crucifix above the altar spoke to him. 'Francis, rebuild my church which is falling into ruin.' Francis first took this command quite literally and began to collect stones to restore San Damiano. Eventually he took the reckless course of selling some of his father's stock to raise funds for his building projects and, for Pietro Bernadone, who had watched his son's growing eccentricity with mounting concern, this was the last straw. He brought Francis before the bishop's court to seek restitution of the money he had lost. There followed a dramatic scene. Before the bishop and all the people, Francis stripped himself naked and returned his clothes to his father. 'I am no longer your son.' From now on he would forsake wealth and privilege and seek only poverty which, in the style of a troubadour, he called his lady.

Francis was first a laughing stock to Assisi as, in beggar's clothes, he tried to live according to the Sermon on the Mount, owning nothing, accepting no money but only scraps of food, and giving himself to prayer. But as other rich young men caught his vision and abandoned their families to become followers of Francis, laughter turned to distrust and hatred. In the first years, the Franciscans were outcasts, driven from respectable people's doors with curses. Yet Francis, living abjectly in the winter woods above the town, met all adversity with laughter, song and thanksgiving, convinced he was living the life of the apostles and would receive the blessing Christ pronounces on the poor, the hungry and the persecuted.

His spiritual worth was recognised and in time, especially after Pope Innocent approved the order, the people of Italy began to love the ministry of the Franciscans, arriving barefoot in their towns and villages, living by faith on gifts of food and preaching the gospel in vivid, homely terms. The order grew steadily as more and more men heard the call to give up everything for love of Christ and Lady Poverty.

It is easy to sentimentalise St Francis with his childlike joy in the beauty of nature and his love of theatrical gestures. He bought caged birds for the pleasure of setting them free, preached a sermon to the birds, tamed by gentleness a man-eating wolf, created the first Christmas crib with a real ox and ass, candlelit in a cave at midnight on Christmas Eve. Beneath the whimsy was an iron determination to win union with Christ, not just the sweet bambino of the stable, but the man of suffering who had first spoken to Francis from the cross. The record of fasting, tears, midnight vigils beyond what could be borne by poor 'Brother Ass', as he called his body, terrifies as much as the sunnier legend charms. But the asceticism of Francis always speaks of love. In earlier saints like Jerome, the call to celibacy and fasting sounds with accents of self-hatred and fear of sexuality. In Francis, as in Jesus himself, one feels that the renunciation of ordinary human happiness is driven by love, as willingly he divested himself of whatever might distract him from God.

Like all in his age, Francis was enthralled by the mystique of crusade, the holiest pilgrimage of all. But unlike his contemporaries, he saw the Saracens, not as God's enemies to be smitten, but as lost brothers to be reclaimed. He accompanied the Fifth Crusade to Egypt and made his way alone to the Sultan's court at Damietta to preach unarmed to the enemy. Legend says he offered to prove the truth of the gospel by walking through fire, but the Sultan would not permit such a trial and, moved by the simplicity of the friar, dismissed him with honour. Disillusioned by the savagery and debauchery of the crusaders, Francis returned to Europe to face his hardest test.

As the Franciscan order grew, questions about its organisation and purpose became more pressing. It could not remain for ever a loose group of beggars, united by devotion to Francis and by a willingness to live literally the Sermon on the Mount. Pressure was growing for the order to have buildings, books, a structure for carrying out its work. To the modernisers, such changes were only sensible. For Francis, the changes struck at the root of all he had tried to do. He never wanted just to found another religious order and, as the inevitability of change came home to him, he entered a period of profound depression. Isolated and withdrawn, he spent ever more time in prayer.

In 1224 on Mount La Verna, Francis experienced the climatic event of his life-long love affair with Jesus. The mountain had been given to the Franciscans by a sympathetic noblewoman as a place of retreat and prayer. Francis spent some weeks here with a few devoted friends, and it was here that he was given the mysterious gift of the stigmata, the wounds of Christ visible in his hands, feet and side. His union with the suffering Christ was now so perfect that it was manifested physically in his body. This terrifying gift of grace is a favourite subject in art; painters show the crucified six-winged seraph which appeared to Francis as the wounds opened in his body.

Francis lived only three years after this experience, in constant pain yet also in constant joy. His sufferings were exacerbated by the cruelties of medieval medicine, which he bore with heroic patience. His death was bizarre – aware that they were tending a living saint, whose relics would be of incalculable value, his companions competed to 'host' his death, different parties vying to win the prize of 'deathplace of St.Francis' which would guarantee a premier place on the pilgrimage trail. In the end, he was buried in his native Assisi, where a magnificent basilica, with frescos by Giotto, now covers his bones. His extraordinary Christ-like life at once inspired the finest Christians of the next generation to follow Jesus in the way of voluntary poverty, while his lasting impact on the church has been incalculable. In no other saint does the spirit of the gospels seem to shine with such unaffected, simple joy.

CLARE OF ASSISI (1219-1253) 11th August.
Among the followers of Francis, the most celebrated was Clare, the founder of the Second Franciscan Order, for women, as Francis was of the First Order, for men.

Clare was born, like Francis, in Assisi, and like him was a member of one of the powerful merchant families who by their wealth and prestige dominated the city's life. But as a woman, she could expect very little freedom in her life. While Francis rode and danced and roistered around the streets of Assisi in the cheerful independence of a rich young man, Clare, like every rich young woman, lived a cloistered life at home, only emerging to go to church and sheltered from all eyes outside her family. Her destiny would be an early marriage or an early entry into a religious house and her parents would make these decisions for her. It was Clare's spiritual genius to transcend this limited world and find for herself an inner freedom as wide as the outer freedom sought by Francis as he trudged the lanes of Italy in the service of Lady Poverty.

As Clare heard of the disgraceful breach of Francis with his family, and the extraordinary story of his early attempts to live the life of a beggar, her imagination was fired and she longed to share this life of utter self-denial. One night, Clare ran away from home. Somehow, she managed to unbolt the heavy street door without waking the household and, once out in the street, she fled to Francis. To him, she confided her conviction that God had called her too to the life of poverty.

Francis seems to have been perplexed by Clare. Even so radical a spirit as he hardly considered it possible for a woman to walk the streets and sleep out in the open. Yet Clare's vocation was undeniable. As a temporary expedient, he lodged Clare, and her sister, who had followed her, in a Benedictine convent. Clare's male relatives, who had come out in a posse to reclaim her, were convinced, after a stormy interview in the church, that there was no hope that Clare would return home to the marriage which had been arranged for her. But Clare was not content – the life of a Benedictine nun, as sheltered and secure as her childhood, had no appeal for her. She sought poverty and, even after she accepted that the life of a woman religious must be cloistered, she was determined that her convent should be un-endowed.

This was radical and dangerous. The convents of Europe, mostly Benedictine, were supported by vast estates, the gift of noble benefactors – from the produce of their estates the communities received their livelihood, and an individual monk or nun, though pledged personally to self-denial and poverty, lived in a community supported by considerable wealth. Founding a monastery was thus an extremely expensive undertaking and, as we have seen, was in the early Middle Ages mostly undertaken by kings, bishops and nobles, with all the privileges of the feudal system at their command. But Clare wanted her nuns to be poor, really poor. They would live strictly cloistered lives of prayer and self-offering, but their house would have no buffer zone of manors and farms to shield them from the hand to mouth sufferings of the real poor. Like the beggar friars, they would pray for and receive nothing but their daily bread in alms from the faithful.

Nobody thought this idea was realistic, but by the compelling power of her will and holiness, Clare got her way. She obtained the necessary licenses from Rome, she obtained the houses in which her sisters would live and she obtained vocations, as girls flocked to be part of the new movement. Even Hildegard had assumed that her nuns would be aristocrats, bringing large dowries with them to support the convent. Clare's order was open to all, and women from the emerging middle classes rejoiced to find that they too could give all for Christ.

The first Poor Clares really did nearly starve. They could not go out to beg for food as the Franciscans did. All they could do was pray and wait for someone to remember them. Clare held them together during these early days. Her determination and practical common-sense, together with her visible devotion to Christ, kept the little communities going. She was constantly ill because of her privations but she made no concessions and died at the age (very respectable for the Middle Ages) of sixty.

She is the patron saint, bizarrely, of television. She was chosen for this honour because of a legend which tells how one Christmas Eve, when she was too ill to go to church, she was granted a vision and experienced the whole service at her bedside.

BONAVENTURE (1218-1274) 15th July.

The divisions within the Franciscan movement, which had caused such pain to St Francis in his last years, grew steadily worse after the founder's death. The so-called 'spiritual' friars who attempted to hold to Francis's ideal of total poverty, owning nothing, became increasingly suspect to the church authorities, especially after they grouped themselves around Joachim of Fiore, whose luridly anti-papal prophecies of the end of the world made explicit the condemnation of the mainstream church and its worldliness always implicit in Francis' idealism. So bitter did the dispute become that it was actually declared a heresy to believe that Christ and the apostles had never owned property. But on the other hand, if the Franciscans distanced themselves from their founder's call to total poverty, what was to distinguish them from the Benedictines and all the other orders of cloistered monks, living off the income from their estates and endowments? The man who by solving this dilemma earned the right to be honoured as the Franciscans' second founder was Bonaventure.

Bonaventure, born in Bagnoregio in central Italy, was still a boy when the great St Francis died, but he grew up with a personal devotion to the saint because of his mother's conviction that Francis had miraculously healed him from a boyhood illness. It used to be thought that Francis had visited Bagnoregio and personally laid hands on the child, but a more likely interpretation is that Bonaventure's mother invoked the saint after his death. At all events, it was with a love for St Francis already in his heart that Bonaventure set off at the age of seventeen for the University of Paris.

Just as the Franciscans and Dominicans were preaching Christianity with a new edge in the new context of Europe's towns and cities with their merchant class, so the universities had been steadily replacing, as centres of intellectual life, the great rural monasteries which had nurtured men like Anselm, Bernard and Aelred. In their early days, universities were informal gatherings of scholars, who attracted students to their lectures and disputations, living on their fees and gradually developing the apparatus of statutes, colleges and endowed chairs by which they evolved into institutions resembling their modern counterparts. Student life was enormously exciting and emancipating, as bright young men travelled from all over Europe to Bologna, Paris and Oxford to sit at the feet of the great scholars of the day. Bonaventure spent twenty-five years in Paris and fell in love with learning. Medieval scholarship centred around the philosophy of Aristotle, whose works, interpreted through the disciplined arts of grammar, logic and rhetoric, demanded a concentration on clarity in thinking.

St Bonaventure's arrival in Paris coincided with a significant event in the history of the Franciscans, when one of the greatest masters of the university, Alexander of Hales, became a Franciscan and henceforth delivered his lectures from within the Franciscan convent, thus decisively uniting the new spirituality of Francis with the new learning of the university. Bonaventure himself became a Franciscan in 1243 and he did so convinced that his two great loves, academic learning and Franciscan devotion to Christ, could be fruitfully combined.

In 1257, the Pope asked Bonaventure to become Minister General of the Franciscans, with the specific brief of curbing the excesses of Joachim's 'spirituals.' Bonaventure was able to succeed in his task because of his outstanding personal holiness and simplicity, which commanded the respect of all his brothers. Under his guidance, the Franciscan movement developed the institutional forms it would need to flourish in the long term, while still holding true to the ideals of Francis. Franciscans were allowed houses, and owned books and other apparatus of study, but still lived off fees and alms rather than endowments. They continued Francis' mission to the poor, the lepers and the outcast, while developing a valuable role within the life of Europe's universities.

In his writings, Bonaventure displays the same happy marriage between intellectual rigour and a winning simplicity of devotion of Christ. His greatest work, 'The Soul's Journey to God' was developed during a retreat on Mount La Verna, where Francis had received the stigmata. Bonaventure used the image of the six-winged seraph which had appeared to Francis to give structure to an extended account of the six levels of meditation, two on the world of the senses, two on the human soul, two on God himself, by which a Christian may attain to contemplation of God. More accessible to a modern reader is his 'Tree of Life,' a set of meditations on the life of Jesus, part of a growing emphasis on the humanity of Jesus, and particularly his suffering, as the place where the heart is converted to love of God.

In 1273, Pope Gregory X appointed the Minister General a cardinal – tradition says that the officials who brought his hat to the convent had to wait until Bonaventure had finished the washing-up before he could speak to them. Thanks to his knowledge of eastern theology, he was of great assistance to the Pope in preparing for the Council of Lyons, whose great set-piece was to be the formal reconciliation of the Greek and Latin churches.

During the era of the expansion of Islam and of the crusades, the Byzantine Empire had been fatally weakened, losing virtually all its territory in Asia. At the same time, relations between eastern and western Christendom deteriorated, reaching a low point during the infamous Fourth Crusade in 1204 when an army of western knights actually sacked the city of Constantinople and ruled the Greek empire for seventy years. The second council of Lyons (1274) was an attempt by the Pope to reunite the church against the common threat of Islam, and formally it was a success, with representatives of the Greek church acknowledging the Pope's supremacy and agreements on the areas of theological difference being signed. In practice, the council changed nothing. The eastern delegates made their submissions in a desperate attempt to secure troops and money for the support of the Empire, but their signatures could do nothing to change the hostility of the Byzantine church towards the Pope, nor could the Pope's ecclesiastical success reanimate the moribund crusading spirit in the hearts of the western princes.

During this famous council, Bonaventure, who had worked so hard for its success, died. He was given the title of 'The Seraphic Doctor' in recognition of his worth as a teacher.

THOMAS AQUINAS (1225-1274) 28th January.

An exact contemporary of Bonaventure's at the University of Paris was the greatest theologian of the Middle Ages, recognised in his own day as the mirror image of the great Franciscan. Thomas Aquinas was a Dominican, given the soubriquet of the 'Cherubic Doctor' to parallel Bonaventure's 'Seraphic Doctor.' Perhaps no-one was ever more wholly given over to the life of scholarship and pure thought than this stocky, silent friar. In his early student days he was nicknamed the 'Dumb Ox' because of the taciturn way in which he chewed his way through lectures and reading lists. 'Do not mock him.' warned Albert the Great, his tutor, 'this dumb ox will amaze the world when he bellows.'

The life of Thomas Aquinas has little of interest: it is his thought that dominated him and commends him to us. Born in Italy, he studied first at Naples, where he joined the Dominican order, then in Cologne under Albert the Great, and arrived in Paris in 1252. He returned to Italy to fill various teaching posts in Dominican houses, then was back in Paris in 1268. He was on his way to join Bonaventure at the Second Council of Lyons in 1274 when he died. During all this time he read, thought, lectured and wrote.

Albert the Great trained Aquinas in the study which shaped his thought: the classical philosophy of Aristotle. Medieval scholars were fascinated by Aristotle, whose works had been becoming known in the west via Greek and Arabic sources, particularly the Arabic commentaries of Averroes and Avicenna. Aristotle's attempt to give a rational and comprehensive account of the nature of reality enthralled the twelfth and thirteenth centuries. We have seen how Anselm had set himself to think out a purely rational account of Christian faith, based on logic rather than on the quotation of authorities from scripture and the fathers. Aristotle's method seemed to give a priceless tool for the accomplishing of this task, and in

Aquinas' hands the tool was used to masterly effect. His two greatest works, vast both in volume and in scope, are the 'Summa contra Gentiles' and the 'Summa Theologia.' In the first, he attempts to demonstrate the truth of a Christian account of God from grounds which would be accepted by a pagan. In the second, which is unfinished, he probes with the same tool of Aristotelian logic the specifically Christian doctrines of Incarnation and Atonement, the church and the sacraments, the Last Judgement and the future life. In the course of this work, he achieves a magnificent synthesis of the theology of his time, leaving later theologians with little to do until the Reformation shook the whole basis of Thomist thought with new questions demanding new answers. His enduring influence on the Roman Catholic Church in particular was incalculable: until the second half of the twentieth century, the works and methods of Aquinas were the required basis of the training of all Roman clergy.

Amongst the achievements of Aquinas are the classic 'five ways' of demonstrating the existence of God, all variants of the quest for the origin of things. Aquinas traces movement and change back to the unchanging 'First Mover,' beauty and purpose back to the creator who is supreme beauty and who causes all things to exist. More esoterically, he was fascinated by the existence of angels and his attempts to tease out the nature of a bodiless intelligence's self-awareness and method of relating to God show that in another culture he would have made a good writer of science fiction – although sadly he never did actually attempt to discover how many angels could dance on a pin. His work on natural law has had immense influence on ethics. Thomas sought to establish the basis of morality as a rational understanding of human nature: for a human to act well was to act in accordance with the nature given by the creator. Thomas' account of what is 'natural' in matters of sexuality has formed (some would say, bedevilled) modern Catholic teaching about birth control, extra-marital sex and homosexuality. He formulated the theory of a 'just war' in an attempt to control and regulate the incessant violence of medieval life: his conditions – that a war have a just cause, be declared by a legitimate authority, have a right intention, have a probability of success and be proportionate to the wrong it attempts to redress (i.e the damage caused by the war must not be greater than the damage it was started to prevent) – are still worth consideration by statesmen today; indeed, many would argue that the devastating power of modern weaponry makes a just war by Aquinas' criteria impossible.

Interestingly, for a medieval thinker so concerned with obedience to the church's hierarchy, Aquinas also established the priority of conscience as the spring of action for a Christian. He examines with discrimination the problems caused by an ill-informed conscience or one whose perceptions have been twisted by sin or heresy, but he has no hesitation in declaring that faced with a choice between obeying the Pope or obeying conscience, a Christian must choose the latter. When he turns to the sacraments, Aquinas gave the classic account of Transubstantiation, the doctrine that the substance of the bread and wine is physically transformed at the altar into the Body and Blood of Christ. Aquinas' account only works if one takes for granted Aristotle's account of how things are what they are. Aristotle taught that every existing thing had a substance which made it what it was, and accidents which could change without affecting the essential nature. Thus, a human being is human because of its substantial humanity – accidents such as having two legs, being red-headed, or black, or male can differ without affecting the essential humanity of the person. The doctrine of Transubstantiation posits that, in the Mass, the substance, the essential being, of the bread is changed into the Body of Christ, while the accidents – being made of flour, taste, texture, appearance – remain those of bread. It is a highly technical account and attempts to make it work within a modern context rapidly become problematic – most modern philosophers and scientists would give very different answers to the question 'How is something what it is?' Nevertheless, Aquinas' doctrine remains the official doctrine of the Roman Catholic Church, and has enabled millions to experience by faith the real presence of Jesus in the Eucharist.

The examples just given will provide a sample of the breadth and depth of Aquinas' thought. It has to be said that of all the saints who have helped form the mind of Christendom, Thomas Aquinas is the least readable. One reason for this is his immersion in Aristotelian philosophy, which results in a highly technical vocabulary able to make and discuss exquisite distinctions in the quest for an ever finer logical description of reality. The language is impenetrable for anyone not trained in this philosophical tradition.

The second reason why Aquinas is hard to read derives from the way a medieval university functioned. In a world where books were rare and expensive, university life centred not on reading but on lectures and above all on debates. A student proved his worth not by writing an essay but by publicly defeating a rival in an oral dispute, conducted by strict rules of logic. The idea that the best way of finding out the truth is by setting up two experts to debate it in adversarial style has had an immense influence on, for example, our courts of law and the House of Commons, both institutions formed during the high medieval period when scholastic debate ruled the universities and thus shaped the way educated minds perceived reality. Aquinas, brought up in this world, constructs his books accordingly. The Summas are really a long succession of university debates, painstakingly piled one upon another. A question is posed, the arguments for and against are dispassionately arrayed, a magisterial decision is made and the arguments for the 'losing' position are carefully demolished. Often the point established by each of these mini-debates seems tiny, but step by step, logical positions are marked out, and by an accumulation of tiny points gained, a great truth is established. But following the long series of careful arguments is patient work, and it is easy to lose sight of the big philosophical positions for the sake of which the little debates are being hammered out. More than any other Christian thinker, Aquinas relies on interpreters and commentators for his influence to be felt.

Even the great man himself had his doubts in the end. We are told that in the last year of his life, Thomas had a direct experience of the presence of God so profound that he said 'Everything I have written seems like straw,' and after that he wrote no more. From this straw, though, succeeding generations continue to spin gold.

ELIZABETH OF HUNGARY (1207-1231) 18th November.
We can trace the influence of St Francis in the lives of his younger contemporaries. Nobles, churchmen and humbler people were all entranced by his vision of simple, Christ-like living, and for the many

who could not make the complete renunciation needed to become a Friar or a Poor Clare, Francis devised his Third Order, giving people living worldly lives a simple discipline to live by.

The young Princess Elizabeth of Hungary compressed into twenty-four short years a long life of experience. Her father, King Andrew II of Hungary, betrothed her as a child to the Landgrave of Thuringia, and from the age of five she was sent to the court of her future husband. When the young prince died, the engagement was simply transferred to his younger brother Ludwig. Already as a child, Elizabeth was noted for her grave piety, which made her unpopular with frivolous elements at court. The marriage was celebrated and consummated when Elizabeth was fourteen and it was an extremely happy one. Elizabeth bore three children and used her position generously to help the poor. A famous legend relates how Ludwig one day caught her smuggling a lapful of gain from his barns to distribute to the starving. He challenged her, demanding to know what she was carrying, and in the depths of winter Elizabeth implausibly cried out 'Roses!' When her husband pulled loose her gown, a shower of roses miraculously tumbled into the snow, which persuaded him to put no further bars on his wife's charity. It is certainly true that Ludwig revered his holy wife, and liked to hold her hands in his when she prayed, clinging by proxy to such reliable intercessions.

Elizabeth was only twenty, and in her third pregnancy, when news was brought to her that her husband had died of the plague on his way to take part in the crusades. The news prostrated her with grief.

Franciscans had been operating in Germany for five years and it was to them that the young widow turned in her despair. Her outward life was one of tragic deprivation; she was obliged to leave the Landgrave's castle, in circumstances now obscure, and her children were taken to be cared for by relatives. She longed to renounce the world and live in the spirit of St Francis. Unfortunately, she fell under the influence of one Conrad of Marburg, a man whose saintly self-denial masked a tyrannical, even sadistic, nature. He became Elizabeth's spiritual director and devoted himself to the work of tormenting her, all in the name of teaching her humility. Elizabeth entered the Franciscan Third Order, and lived a life of voluntary poverty under Conrad's guidance. He compelled her to dismiss the ladies who were her friends and substituted others who had secret orders to report to him everything their mistress did. He laid upon her a regime of rigorous fasting and humiliating penances. All this did not prevent Elizabeth from employing her fortune in the relief of the poor and in the foundation of a hospital, which she herself visited to act as a nurse. It took only three years of this life to kill her – her memory was revered by the poor whom she had championed and her tomb became one of the most popular pilgrim sites in Germany.

EDMUND RICH (1174 - 1240) 16th November.
As the culture of the Middle Ages reached its apogee, and with it the power of the church, earnest Christians found themselves caught in a dilemma. Francis and Dominic had attempted to pull the church back to its apostolic roots, with their call to simplicity, care for the poor and the preaching of good news, but the great Pope Innocent III who had sponsored their movements of renewal was at the same time engaged in a struggle for political pre-eminence, seeking to make the Pope ruler of Europe, with kings and princes bowing to Christ's vicar. Thirteenth century England saw a remarkable generation of bishops who tried to live their personal lives according to the rhythms of Francis and Dominic while living public lives in a world where bishops had enormous political responsibilities. In the struggle to rule by authentic Christian standards, the Pope was as often enemy as ally. This age was one where the Pope ceased to be revered as the holy leader of Christians and became suspected, or even despised, as the glittering world of power-broking and money-making in which he lived became the symbol of the corruption which was consuming the church from within.

Edmund Rich, who became Archbishop of Canterbury in 1231, was an austere scholar. His father died in his childhood, and his mother, Mabel of Abingdon, brought up her children on strict Christian principles, teaching them to fast and pray from their earliest years. Even when Edmund and his brother were students at Oxford, their mother, when she sent them parcels of linen, included hair-shirts for her boys, to remind them that penitence rather than roistering was the duty of a Christian scholar. Young Edmund was painfully earnest. He made a vow of chastity and, to confirm it, bought two rings, one of which he wore himself while placing the other on the stone finger of the Virgin Mary in his parish church.

Scholarship was always his first love, but he was drawn from the university to serve as Treasurer of Salisbury cathedral, then newly majestic from the grand building sponsored by Bishop Richard Poore. It is hard to imagine that Edmund made a good treasurer; he detested administration and his own finances were in permanent disarray due to the reckless generosity of his alms-giving.

He was at Salisbury, when he was elected Archbishop, and his seven years in that post were not the happiest of his life. While his chancellor and friend Richard of Wych showed himself a fine administrator, Archbishop Edmund could not avoid being drawn into controversy – with King Henry III over that indulgent monarch's attempts to enrich his favourites with church money; with the legal establishment over the perennial arguments about jurisdiction between church and common courts: with the monks of Canterbury, whose intrigues effectively ruined Edmund's plan to establish a collegiate church in Maidstone; and with the Pope. Ever since King John had yielded England as a papal fief, the successors of Innocent III had regarded the kingdom as a lucrative source of revenue. Edmund was appalled to be informed by the papal legate that his Holiness had ordered that the next three hundred English benefices to fall vacant should be presented to Italian absentees. He set out in 1240 for Rome, intending to remonstrate with Gregory IX and to complain of the behaviour of the Canterbury monks. He never arrived, but fell ill and died in France. He is buried at Pontigny, where the casket containing his remains stands above the high altar of that nobly proportioned church. Trying to be a saint within the realities of medieval church politics was not easy.

RICHARD OF CHICHESTER (1197-1253) 16th June (3rd April BCP).
Edmund's faithful chancellor, Richard of Wych, was profoundly shaken by his master's death, and his first desire was to turn his back on the world of affairs, which had contributed so much stress and

unhappiness to his friend's last years. He withdrew to Orleans and sought ordination in a Dominican convent, which he proposed to join. His hopes for a simple life of prayer and preaching were thwarted by his reputation as an able administrator. On the recommendation of Robert Grosseteste, the maverick reforming bishop of Lincoln, Archbishop Boniface nominated him as Bishop of Chichester in 1244. He was forced back into public life and into immediate conflict.

Henry III had already attempted to bestow the see of Chichester on a favourite of his own, one Robert Passelewe, and was furious at the archbishop's refusal to confirm this appointment. In an act of vengeful spite, he refused to release to the new bishop the temporalities of the see, held by the crown during the vacancy. Richard thus arrived in Sussex with no income and no home, even being forbidden to enter the city of Chichester. He found refuge with an old college friend who was rector of Tarring, a parish which, though in the heart of Sussex, was, by a typical medieval illogicality, part of the diocese of Canterbury. Until recently, visitors to Tarring would be shown the fig tree St Richard planted in the rectory garden. From this bolthole, the penniless bishop made gypsy visitations to his diocese, and this period of his misfortune was the time which won him the hearts of the people of Sussex. Here was a bishop without grandeur arriving by foot to confirm their children and preach in their churches. Henry III, lacking the strength of character to be a true tyrant, soon gave way to public opinion, and in 1246 Richard was allowed to take possession of his diocese. His reforming efficiency fulfilled the hopes of Bishop Grosseteste. He visited the churches of his diocese tirelessly, drawing up codes of conduct for the clergy, and expected them to comply. He insisted that monasteries which drew income from parishes should supply vicars to perform the pastoral duties, and should pay those vicars properly. He was loyal to the memory of his friend Edmund Rich, and played a leading role in that bishop's canonisation. It was while consecrating a chapel in Deal to St Edmund that he collapsed and died on Good Friday 1253. Among his dying words were the first sentence of the famous prayer 'Thanks be to thee, my Lord Jesus Christ, for all the benefits which thou hast won for me, for all the pains and insults thou hast borne for me.'

Sadly, the second, more popular part of the prayer cannot be attributed to St Richard, but the words effectively represent the spirit by which he lived and died. 'O most merciful Redeemer, friend and brother, may I know thee more clearly, love thee more dearly, and follow thee more nearly, day by day.'

ROBERT GROSSETESTE (1175-1253) 9th October.
Edmund Rich and Richard of Wych were both humble men, essentially conformists, who strove by their personal holiness and authority to reform the church while submitting to its existing structure. Their contemporary, Robert Grosseteste, the third of the great English bishops of Henry III's reign, was made of altogether more fiery stuff, and consequently has never been officially canonised by the Roman church.

Grosseteste came from a very humble Suffolk family and made his way entirely by his ability, which was prodigious. His early adult life was spent as a church administrator in Hereford diocese, and here his interest in science and philosophy matured. Thirteenth century Hereford was a centre for pioneer scientists; the Mappa Mundi, still displayed in the cathedral, is the most famous surviving evidence for this curiosity about the world. As we have seen, the high academic tradition, in which Thomas Aquinas worked, valued abstract reason and logic as the most vital tools for discovering truth. Grosseteste was naturally educated in this tradition, but he was fascinated by the world around him; experiment and investigation, the tools of the modern scientific mind, meant as much to him as the cerebral concentration on the inner and the spiritual which his culture told him was the royal road to truth. Naturally enough, his scientific bent manifested itself in works on astronomy, one of the four liberal arts taught in medieval universities, and on the calendar, essential practical knowledge in a church whose liturgical year was becoming ever more complex. But he also commented on Aristotle's 'Posterior Analytic,' a work about scientific methodology, and as far as we know, was the first person to study this work in depth. He taught himself Greek and Hebrew. It was only a matter of time before such a powerful intellect found its way to Oxford.

His public life began with his election, in 1235, to the see of Lincoln, then the largest diocese in England. The appointment marked the beginning of a passionate, increasingly angry campaign to impose the highest pastoral standards on his diocese. The church, by far the wealthiest institution in England, had long been quarried, by a series of gentleman's agreements, for funding for all sorts of necessary work: scholars at Oxford and Cambridge, civil servants in royal or papal service, chaplains and tutors in the houses of the nobility, all were paid by the gift of benefices, making them notionally responsible for the pastoral well-being of churches and parishes which they never visited. Popes and bishops had vested interests in the system, which they perpetuated by granting the necessary dispensations allowing non-residence, the holding of more than one benefice, and so on: their own income was greatly augmented by the fees paid for such permissions. A whole culture of scholarship, management, artistic patronage and clerical good living was thus enabled to exist, the only losers being ordinary parishioners who paid their tithes and dues for the privilege of being ministered to by a curate on starvation wages, when the incumbent got round to hiring one. This system Grosseteste took on. His visitations to the parishes, over a thousand, of his diocese spread terror around the midlands, as it became clear that the bishop would not complacently accept a share in the profits, and that he meant what he said when he insisted on well-paid priests living in their parishes and making the care of their parishioners their first priority. But the corruption went to the top. We have seen the despair of Edmund Rich when faced with demands from the Pope that three hundred English benefices be provided for Italian absentees in need of a steady income. Grosseteste was made of sterner stuff. He did not despair, he raged. He made two visits to the papal court at Lyons, during both of which he denounced, in the Pope's presence, the venal practices of the Curia, which poisoned the entire workings of the church. But popular resentment of the clergy, though growing, was not yet hot enough to provoke a reformation. Grosseteste, for all his fiery energy, could achieve little lasting change. At his death, pilgrimages began to his tomb, but attempts to have him canonised were firmly squashed by the hierarchy he had insulted. In later ages, he was remembered as one of the first Englishmen to protest against papal abuse of power, and also as a pioneer scientist.

MECHTILD OF MAGDEBURG (1210-1282) 19th November.

While in England statesmen bishops struggled to express Franciscan and Dominican ideals in the public life of church and nation, in Germany and the Low countries, groups of ordinary women were pushing on St Francis' ideal of Christian communities living in poverty and prayer. The Beguines took no vows as nuns and continued to live in the world, earning their keep by traditional women's work such as weaving and spinning. They lived together in simple communities, pooled their goods, gave generously to the poor, and tried to centre their lives on prayer. In one of these communities, in Magdeburg, from about 1240, lived one of the earliest and most original writers in the German language, Mechtild.

We know little of her family or background: her brother became a Dominican, and Mechtild chose a Dominican as her spiritual director. It was he who encouraged Mechtild to begin writing down her visions and spiritual experiences. The young woman had no Latin and wrote in her native tongue. In the seven books of her 'Flowing Light of the Godhead', she captured, in passionate prose and in lyrical verse, her intense, intimate relationship with Jesus. She uses traditional Christian images – light, flowing water, a presence in the dark, enlivened by tender motifs drawn from nature – birds in flight, gardens and trees. Much of her work is frankly erotic – Mechtild took very literally the relationship of love between a celibate woman and the Saviour Christ. At one point, she considers a standard topic for meditation – the worshipper imagines herself in the stable, nursing the infant Christ – but she rejects such a theme as beneath her: 'That is child's love, that one suckle or rock a baby. I am a full-grown bride. I want to go to my lover.'

Francis and Dominic had been shrewd enough to place their new orders under the protection of Pope Innocent III, but we have seen how even this had not prevented some developments within the Franciscan order being branded as heresy. After the horrors of the Albigensian crusade, church authorities became steadily more suspicious of groups of lay people developing 'alternative lifestyles,' no matter how innocuous their desire for simplicity and prayer might seem. The Beguines, groups of women living outside the authority either of husbands or of an enclosed religious order, were particularly suspect. In 1261, the diocese of Magdeburg ordered Beguines to go to their own parish priest for spiritual direction, and not to use friars or other outsiders. The experiments must be contained within legitimate structures. It may have seemed to Mechtild that life as a Beguine was too exposed for a visionary; she may have had concerns for her health, which was beginning to fail; she may have come under pressure or she may have seen a more withdrawn life as the necessary next step in her quest for union with her lover. At all events, in 1270 she left the Beguines and entered the Cistercian convent at Helfta, where she apparently never became a nun but was nursed and care for during her old age, dying blind and bedridden. She had an influence on the impressive group of nuns, led by Gertrude of Helfta, who continued to write in her visionary style. She is also believed to have influenced Dante, especially by her visions of Hell, and it has been speculated that she is the original of the mysterious damsel Matilda, who, in 'The Divine Comedy' meets Dante in the Garden of Eden and guides him to reunion with his beloved Beatrice.

LOUIS IX, KING OF FRANCE (1214-1270) 25th August CDC.
About 1238, a great banquet was held at Saumur in Anjou. The young king of France was there together with his mother, who had recently handed over to him the reins of government. Among the guests was the eighteen year old son of Elizabeth of Hungary, whose mother had met her tragically early death five or six years previously. The Queen made the young Landgrave of Thuringia sit near her and frequently kissed his forehead because, so she said, his mother must often have kissed that spot, and so her lips touched the lips of a saint.

The Queen was Blanche of Castile, whose marriage to the French dauphin forms one of the subplots of Shakespeare's 'King John.' And the young king, her son, was Louis IX, and the only French king to be canonised, regarded by his contemporaries as the model of a Christian King. The incident demonstrates both how quickly prominent holy persons were venerated after their deaths and how devout was the atmosphere at the French court.

Louis IX ascended the throne in 1226 at the age of twelve and, during his minority, his mother Queen Blanche governed as regent. It was a period of civil strife as noble factions defied the regent's authority and struggled for possession of the King's person. Louis possessed a remarkable integrity and on commencing his personal rule he gradually, by patience, force of character and his growing reputation for trustworthiness, reconciled to himself his quarrelsome nobility, and forged an impressive national unity. His greatest success was a treaty with the Count of Toulouse, which brought to an end the shameful Albigensian crusade in the course of which the noble civilisation of Languedoc had been irreparably damaged. Southern France has never since recovered its cultural supremacy over Paris and the north. Such was the king's reputation for justice that he was frequently asked to act as adjudicator in disputes between other rulers. He fought a skirmishing campaign against Henry III of England, who was overlord of Bordeaux and Gascony, but imposed and kept a peace, to the benefit of all the French. Nor were his poorer subjects forgotten; Louis devoted many hours a day to doing justice and frequently held court in his gardens or under an oak tree in his park, so that the humblest might have easy access.

Louis's piety was massive and expressed itself in thoroughly medieval ways. He was a devoted collector of relics and built the astoundingly beautiful Sainte Chapelle in Paris to house the cream of his collection, the very Crown of Thorns worn by Jesus on the cross. The chapel cost 60,000 livres to build, but the King paid more than double this sum, an astonishing 135,00 livres, to the Emperor of Constantinople for the relic. It can still be seen in Notre Dame.

For Louis' contemporaries, the crown of his greatness and holiness was his commitment to crusading, in an era when, for most rulers, the call to Jerusalem had become an ideal rather than a matter of practical policy. Louis led two crusades, the Seventh in 1248, and the Eighth in 1270, the last major attempt by a Western army to regain the glory of the First Crusade. The Seventh Crusade repeated the strategy of the Fifth which St Francis had accompanied, an invasion of Egypt in an attempt to de-stabilise the Sultan's rule close to his capital, and secure a town which could be exchanged for Jerusalem. Louis's first landing was successful; Damietta was captured almost without a fight, but as the French army attempted to ascend the Nile to Cairo (which they called Babylon), they were bogged down in a series of bloody battles where the canals and branches of the Nile were held against them. Louis himself was taken prisoner and only released for a massive ransom and a promise to quit the country. He visited the Holy Land and helped to fortify Acre and the coastal strip which remained in Christian hands.

The Eighth crusade, undertaken in old age, was a foolhardy attempt to divide Muslim power by capturing Tunis in North Africa. The campaign was a disaster and Louis himself died of dysentery in Africa, leaving behind him a beautiful set of instructions to his son on the art of ruling well, which was cherished as an heirloom by even the most dissolute or incompetent of French kings.

His reign may stand as the high point of medieval Christian culture, with its vision of secular lords ruling for the benefit of the church and with justice and peace for all (except, of course, the Saracens). Yet St Louis's success also lays bare one of the causes of medieval Christendom's decay – no pope in that era was revered as he was revered, and the example of a secular king living more virtuously and justly than Christ's vicars in Rome marked another stage in the disillusionment of many with the papal quest for universal dominion, a quest which was becoming increasingly bogged down in murky politics and finances.

PART FIFTEEN. SCANDAL AND VISION.

BRIDGET OF SWEDEN (1309-1373) 23rd July.

It was one of St Louis' successors, King Philip IV of France, who precipitated a major downward step in the history of the Papacy, when in 1309 he secured the election of the French Pope Clement V. Clement, wearied with Rome where the Popes were constantly buffeted by the local politics of Italian noble families, took the fateful decision to establish his court under French protection in his fief of Avignon. Here, the Popes remained for seventy years, a period later known as the 'Babylonish Captivity' of the church. Practically, the move made good sense. Avignon was close to the centre of Europe, and the Popes were better able to communicate with their clergy and lay rulers. Their palace at Avignon became the centre of a glitteringly wealthy and cultivated church. But spiritually, Avignon leached away from the Popes the immense prestige they possessed as heirs of St Peter. In Rome they had ruled from a city which was both the seat of the empire and the principal place of pilgrimage in Europe. Avignon, by contrast, never stood for anything more elevated than church law courts and immense financial transactions. Enthroned there, the Popes seemed more like chief executives of Church plc then shepherds of Christ's pilgrim people. Moreover, they were blatantly subject to the influence of the French king, as was shown when Clement V supinely acquiesced in Philip the Fair's destruction of the Knights Templar, arrested and tortured on trumped up charges, so that the wealth of their order might be confiscated. It became clear to thoughtful Christians that the spiritual standing of the papacy would be in jeopardy until the popes returned to Rome.

In far-off Sweden, in 1309, was born a woman who would have a great impact on these matters. Bridget's father was a nobleman and she was married at the age of thirteen to Ulf Gudmarrson, a courtier of the King of Sweden, by whom she had eight children; one of them, Christina, was herself destined to become a saint. Bridget was widowed in 1344 but even before this event she had realised that prayer, rather than domesticity, was to be the centre of her life. She experienced visions and heard Christ speaking to her. Her devotion concentrated on the sufferings of

Christ, over which she pondered in almost grotesquely intimate detail. When her husband died, she used her wealth and social standing to found a new religious order, the Brigittines, and became first abbess of the mother house at Vadstena. But she had the true Scandinavian love of travel. She and her husband had already made the pilgrimage to St James in Compostella – Ulf had died of a disease picked up on the return journey – and now, only five years after her widowhood, she left her newly founded convent to make the great pilgrimage to Rome. She never returned.

Bridget was profoundly shocked by the state of the great city, like herself widowed, deserted by her lawful husband, the Pope. She fell in love with the place, haunted the shrines of the apostles and martyrs, distributed her wealth to the poor and lived a life of holy poverty and prayer – but not, however, of seclusion from the world. She soon became one of the sights of the city, a living saint whose cell was an important stop on the itinerary of pilgrims and tourists and whose visionary intimacy with Jesus drew many to seek her counsel. She used this influence to campaign vigorously for the return of the Pope, bombarding Avignon with petitions, prayers and messages from Christ to his vicar. She did not live to see her quest succeed, for she died five years before Pope Gregory XI finally returned to the Vatican, splitting the papacy and Christendom in the process.

Bridget's greatest influence in succeeding centuries was as a source of devotional material. From her visions she derived the curious information that Christ had suffered exactly 5,480 wounds during his passion. Bridget wished to do honour to every single one of those saving gashes and she devised a series of fifteen prayers, each focusing on a different aspect of the passion. Known as the fifteen 'O's of St Bridget, a person who recited the fifteen prayers every day for a year would succeed in honouring Christ's wounds with one prayer each – and this became a popular devotion. In an era of Black Death, war and political instability, Christians were drawn increasingly to love and reverence the suffering Christ, who shared their vulnerability and weakness.

CATHERINE OF SIENA (1347-1380) 29th April.

The woman who was to be instrumental in bringing to pass St Bridget's vision of a papacy restored to Rome, was Italian, of humble stock and had so extraordinary an impact on the church of her day that she was the first woman to be named a doctor of the church.

Catherine Benincasa was the twenty-third and youngest child of Giacome, a prosperous dyer, and his wife Lapa. From her childhood, there was something unusual about this girl. At the age of seven, she was returning home with her brother when she stopped dead in the street and refused to move. For her, the clouds and sunset had taken on the form of Jesus, appearing to her visibly. It was the first of many apparitions and from this early age she consecrated her virginity to her heavenly lover. Nowadays, the young Catherine would be regarded as clinically depressed. She refused all her mother's efforts to arrange a marriage for her. For three years, from the age of sixteen to nineteen, she refused to leave her room except to go to church. She was unwashed and unkempt even by medieval standards. She tried obsessively to avoid eating and sleeping and made herself sick if she thought she had eaten too much. She self-harmed. The Benincasas were as worried by their daughter as any modern parent would be. But the tree is judged by its fruit. What made Catherine unusual was her ability to use all the distress and self-loathing of unhappy adolescence in her quest for God, so that He was able to make her a saint. At the age of nineteen, she had the formative experience she called her spiritual marriage. The Virgin Mary and Christ appeared in her room and Christ betrothed her to himself, placing on her finger a ring which was invisible to everyone else but remained objectively real to Catherine for the rest of her life.

Shortly afterwards, Christ commanded her to leave her solitude and begin to care for the sick and the poor. Catherine joined the Dominicans as a tertiary and gradually gained a reputation around Siena, visiting, nursing, patiently loving. When plague struck the city, she healed miraculously priests who displayed plague symptoms. In these years, she gathered about her a band of disciples, her 'family,' who supported her and travelled with her for the rest of her life – other women, priests, male religious, and her own mother, finally accepting that this crazy, astonishing child of her was never going to settle down and make a conventional match. Catherine remained convinced that the active service of others could always legitimately interrupt devotion and prayer, and she was frequently exasperated by priests and hermits who used their prayer life as an excuse for avoiding the arduous work to which she summoned them.

Her life was powered by an extravagant inner love for Jesus, expressed in many hours of fasting and silent prayer. She experienced the gift of the stigmata, though again only she could see the wounds, and believed that her incessant headaches were a gift from Christ, a sharing of his crown of thorns. Her union with Christ gave her an astonishing self-assurance, expressed in forthright letters to popes, kings and anybody else who needed reminding of their Christian duty.

Her great opportunity came in 1376 when, after a period of war in Italy, the city of Florence employed her as an ambassador to the Pope in Avignon. The political objective failed but, once introduced to Pope Gregory XI, she constituted herself his principal adviser, begging him for peace for Italy, for freedom from taxation for the poor, and above all for a return to Rome. Her reverence for the Pope as symbol of Christ's rule (she called him 'Christ on earth') was matched by the uncompromising severity of her judgements upon any individual who sat in Peter's chair. Thanks to her, Gregory made the traumatic decision to leave Avignon and return to Rome. There he promptly died and plunged the medieval church into its worst crisis.

The cardinals elected Urban VI as Gregory's successor, but he appears to have been driven mad by the authority entrusted to him. Hot-tempered, violent, and obsessed by his own importance, he had in a matter of months alienated most of the cardinals who elected him. Six of them returned to Avignon, declared the election invalid, and chose as Pope Clement VII, a cardinal who had made his reputation in butcher-like wars in northern Italy. Now Christendom was divided, with two Popes, each claiming to be God's anointed, each threatening damnation to those who refused obedience, each unscrupulously using the machinery of medieval government to wring money from the clergy and people. France, Sicily and Scotland supported Clement; England, Germany and most of Italy,

Urban. In neither Pope were Christ-like qualities apparent. The great schism, as it was called, took fifty years to heal and by the end of it the papacy was fatally devalued. Catherine of Siena believed the Pope to be God's appointed means of reform in the church. In future generations those who longed for reform would see the Pope as obstacle, not opportunity.

The last years of Catherine's life were spent heroically rallying Christendom in support of Urban, though she could not be blind to his faults. She died in Rome, radiantly receiving the sacrament and all the clergy in the city attended her funeral.

Apart from her astonishing letters, her best known work is the 'Dialogue' in which her soul questions God the Father and he replies, explaining the mystery of salvation. The image around which the book is constructed has become a favourite of evangelistic preaching ever since. Catherine portrays Christ as a bridge spanning the gulf between God and sinners, making possible a return to the Father. The book is vividly personal, containing some of the most terrifying imaginative reconstructions of the state of the damned ever penned – few Christian writers have described so acutely what it might feel like to go to Hell – and summoning believers to a union with Christ, both exquisitely painful and supremely joyful. Onto the image of the bridge Catherine superimposes to surreal effect the picture of a three step climb up the crucified body of Jesus, embracing his feet through desire, hiding in his side through love, finally achieving union by kissing his mouth. As a record of a soul's love affair with Christ, the 'Dialogue' is unsurpassed.

SERGIUS OF RADONEZH (1314-1392) 25th September.
St Sergius was a contemporary of St Catherine and, like her, lived a life devoted to prayer, but otherwise might have been on a different planet.

Far from the beauties, intricacies and cruelties of early Renaissance Italy, the Russian people lived on the frontiers of Christendom, hundreds of miles beyond the ken of all but the most adventurous westerners. The Russians had been Christians for centuries, owing loyalty to Constantinople and the eastern church, but for a hundred years they had borne the brunt of the Tartar invasions.

Genghis Khan and his Golden Horde had established sovereignty over the steppes and had also been converted to Islam. Christian Russians were the oppressed underdogs, but the Princes of Moscow were beginning to dare resistance to their overlords.

The father of Sergius was a victim of the Golden Horde. His family lands near Moscow were devastated by Tartar raiders, and the family reduced to destitution. In these circumstances, a fortuitous meeting with a wandering monk easily persuaded the ten year old Sergius that this world had little to offer and that he would be better advised to seek the eternal riches. Like John the Baptist, the boy determined to live alone in the wilderness and to seek God.

In the deep birch forests near Zagorsk, Sergius built himself a house which he dedicated to the Trinity and there he lived, feeding himself by the labour of his own hands, his only companion a bear cub which he had found and tamed. Inevitably, reports of his holiness attracted others and by 1340 he had a dozen disciples, living in abject poverty even by the standards of Russian serfs, and giving themselves to prayer. The gentle, kindly spirit of Sergius profoundly affected all who met him. He was said to be illuminated by ineffable joy and he had the sort of unpretentious humility which was genuinely happy to potter about doing little acts of kindness. His main recreation was whittling toys as gifts for visiting children.

This simple man found himself used for the good of his country. The Russian nobility was distracted by hereditary feuds: its weakness was the Tartar's strength. Sergius was able to act as go-between, his contempt for riches securing him from any suspicion of self-interest. In 1385, he reconciled Prince Oleg of Riazan with the Grand Prince Dmitri of Moscow, leader of the Russians, and together these princes were able to turn the corner in the struggle for national freedom. Dmitri had stood in awe of Sergius ever since his famous victory at the Battle of Kulikovo, which he believed had been won thanks to the prayers of Sergius and his monks.

By the time Sergius died Russian freedom was assured and the gentle monk was a national hero, his monastery of the Trinity a place of national pilgrimage. The Orthodox Church remained until the twentieth century one of the chief badges of Russian identity.

WILLIAM OF OCKHAM (1285-1347) 10th April.

Despite the very different worlds in which they lived, Catherine of Siena and St Sergius would have found they had much in common – a burning desire for solitude held in tension with a calling to serve others for the love of Christ. But in Western Europe, the ancient Christian consensus that in monastic life and the self-dedication of vowed celibacy the highest life was to be found, was coming increasingly under attack. The 'Babylonish captivity' of the Avignon Popes and the great schism which followed it brought many Christians to despair of the church as institution, and during the fourteenth and fifteenth centuries, the monasteries, entangled in wealth which so glaringly contradicted the ascetic ideals of the monastic founders, came to be seen as part of the problem rather than the solution.

As our story returns to England, we shall see, first, how two Oxford theologians began asking questions which undermined the medieval church's self-image and ultimately led to the Reformation; and, second, in the lives of four mystics, how people of very different temperaments came to prefer the solitude of the hermitage to the common life of the monastery and were tempted to claim priority for their own direct experience of God over the established teaching of the church. In the twelfth and thirteenth centuries, saints founded religious orders and served the institutional church as bishops and abbots. In the fourteenth and fifteenth centuries, those remembered as saints are found more often among the ranks of the mavericks, the outsiders, those whose personal vision put them at odds with popes and bishops.

William of Ockham died in the year Catherine of Siena was born. Like her, the course of his life was shaped by the Avignon papacy though he shared neither her profound reverence for the Pope nor her prophetic ability to bring about change in papal circles.

William was born in the Surrey village of Ockham and at the young age of fourteen joined the Franciscan order, receiving his education at their London house. It was not long before his intellectual gifts were recognised and he was sent to Oxford, where he delivered his lectures on the 'Sentences' of Peter Lombard, the customary first step in the long syllabus which led a man to become

'Master of Arts.' Ockham's prowess in the medieval university's show-piece debates earned him the nickname of the 'Invincible Franciscan'. His great work was a 'Summa Logicae,' a huge textbook on logic, that foundation stone of all medieval thinking.

Ockham's thought challenged received wisdom in two main ways. Firstly, he tried to simplify the enormously complex accounts of how reality is real which commentators on Aristotle from Aquinas onwards had developed. A long tradition of Christian thought, stretching back through Augustine and Aristotle to Plato, took it for granted that general 'forms' were more real than individual objects; that is, a good person was good through her participation in a quality of goodness which existed eternally in the mind of God. Ockham's conviction, with which the modern world concurs, was that actual objects and persons in the world of sense are the primary real things and that abstractions like 'goodness', 'reason' and so on have no independent existence but are convenient mental short-hands to explain something which two people have in common: A is rational and B is rational, but their common display of reason does not make 'reason' an entity which exists independent of A & B. In general, Ockham disapproved of the introduction of unnecessary concepts to complicate an account of reality – hence his famous 'razor' which states that entities must not be multiplied without reason. If you can give an account of how something happens without recourse to angels or to philosophical abstractions, then there is no excuse for intruding such beings into your account. This way of looking at reality had alarming implications for the doctrine of transubstantiation, as formulated by Aquinas. If things have their own reality without participating in a substance 'more real' than themselves, it is harder to make sense of the idea of bread 'becoming' Christ's body by a change of substance while remaining, to all observation, bread.

More generally, Ockham pulled away from the conviction of older theologians like Anselm and Aquinas that human reason could make discoveries about God by logical argument from first principles. For Ockham, the medieval quest for a rational basis for faith undermined God's sovereignty. God is free to do what He likes and cannot be bound by any human system of ideas about what he 'must' logically do. In this insistence on God's absolute right to do as he pleased beyond the scope of human wisdom to challenge, Ockham was a true precursor of the Protestant reformers such as Calvin, who were deeply distrustful of human reason as a guide to God.

In 1324, Ockham's views caused him to be summoned to Avignon: his writings were to be examined for heresy. An old Oxford rival, John Lutterell, discovered fifty-six heretical propositions in Ockham's 'Sentences' commentary. But during his stay at the papal court, Ockham had fallen in with the 'spirituals' of his order, still, despite the mediating work of St Bonaventure, locked in controversy with Pope over the Franciscans' right to live in absolute poverty. In 1328, just as Ockham was being acquitted of the charges against him, he, in a magnificently arrogant turning of the tables, declared that it was Pope John XXII who was the heretic, and that by condemning the view that Christ had lived in poverty, he had forfeited his right to teach the church. Not surprisingly, an order was issued for Ockham's arrest, but he escaped to Genoa and put himself under the protection of the Holy Roman Emperor, Ludwig IV, who had his own reasons for opposing papal pretensions. For the rest of his life, Ockham lived at the imperial court, working with Marsilius of Padua on the political and theological dilemmas which arose when a Pope was found to be in error. Ockham's solution was a General Council of the church, harking back to the glory days of Nicaea and Chalcedon: a gathering of the whole church would have the authority to rebuke the Pope and instigate reform. In fact, long after Ockham's death, it was in fact a General Council which finally ended the scandal of the great schism and brought back unity to the Papacy.

The Invincible Franciscan died at Munich, still an exile, still opposing papal corruption.

JOHN WYCLIFFE (1330-1384) 31st December.
In 1377, just as the great schism was about to break out, Archbishop Sudbury of Canterbury attempted to bring to trial a suspected heretic. Master John Wyclif of Oxford University had brought himself to public notice by his book 'De Civili Dominio' – 'About the rule of the State.' Wyclif was a prickly, disappointed man. He had lived

most of his adult live in Oxford, had for a short time been Master of Balliol, but had somehow never achieved the preferment he hoped for. Now he was at least to achieve notoriety. 'De Civili Dominio' reflected on the perennial medieval problem: in a world of hierarchies and inherited privilege, what could be done with those who had a right to rule but were manifestly unfit to do so? Wyclif's answer was radical. He suggested that if God was the giver of lordship, bestowing it and its attendant material goods on whom he saw fit, then no human being could claim an inalienable right to power and goods in perpetuity. On the contrary, if a person lived an ungodly life, he forfeited his civil rights and could be justly deprived of his offices and income, which could be bestowed on someone who would rule after God's heart. The book was a scholarly treatise by an unworldly, if angry man. Nowhere was any guidance given as to how the ungodly could be identified or who had the right to strip them so ruthlessly of their livelihood. But 'De Civili Dominio' attracted the attention of John of Gaunt, ruling England as regent for his nephew the boy King Richard II. As applied to the church, John of Gaunt saw how Wyclif's ideas could be very useful to him. In the aftermath of the Black Death and locked into the last inglorious phase of the Hundred Years War with France, the government was chronically short of money, while the church was by far the richest institution in the land, and protected from most taxation to boot. If unjust rulers could be justly deprived of their lands, what did that say about monasteries which collected tithes but failed to provide parish priests for their estates, or canons who grew fat on the profits from illegal pluralities? What did it say about the Avignon Popes, widely perceived as lackeys of the King of France, England's great enemy, and as widely resented for the way they milked the English church to reward with benefices absentee favourites in the Curia? Not surprisingly, Gaunt used Wyclif's writings to put pressure on the church and extract money, promises of reform, or both. No surprise either that the church authorities responded with accusations of heresy. The resulting confrontation at St Paul's cathedral was a scandal. Archbishop Sudbury, with Bishop Courtney of London and the judges, awaited Wyclif, as did a large crowd of Londoners, drawn by curiosity and the fame of the controversial preacher. Wyclif was escorted to his trial by John of Gaunt, Lord Henry Percy and a large body of men-at-arms, a delicate hint that the critic of unjust lordship was not going to be choked by the trivialities of a court of justice. The presence of Gaunt, who was extremely unpopular, threw the citizens into a ferment: a riot was only just averted and continuing the trial was impossible. Wyclif returned to Oxford the protégé of the most powerful man in England. But when he was again attacked, in 1382, he found himself less well protected. This time, the accusation was that he had denied the doctrine of Transubstantiation, but in the meantime, the Peasants' Revolt had taken place. Archbishop Sudbury had been lynched by the mob: John of Gaunt's palace at the Savoy had been burned to the ground: suddenly the governing classes were less amused by preachers who explored the possibility of bringing down unjust lords and redistributing their property. Gaunt did not abandon his man – there was no stake for Wyclif – but he was obliged to leave Oxford and retire to his country parish of Lutterworth. There, bitter and disappointed, he set himself to revise his writings but, in 1384, as he attended mass after Christmas, he suffered a massive stroke and died on New Year's Eve without recovering the power of speech.

Soon after his death, Wyclif became the figure-head of the Lollard movement, the underground network of Christians who preached against the established church, denied the Eucharistic sacrifice and distributed copies of the scriptures in English. Although Wyclif had certainly championed these causes, it is unclear how far he had gone beyond the academic, Latin-speaking world of the university and tried to make his ideas accessible to ordinary people. And although the earliest English Bible was issued in his name, there is no evidence how much, if any, of the translation comes from his hand. Nevertheless, somehow the unhappy maverick loner became transformed in popular memory into the 'Morning Star of the Reformation,' the earliest prophet raised up by God to speak against the corruption of the church. Archbishop Sudbury, whose murder was similar to that of Thomas Becket, received no martyr's honours. His adversary, John Wyclif, was widely revered as a saint. Popular sentiment was slipping away from the established church and siding with its critics.

RICHARD ROLLE (1300-1349) 20th January.

The calling to a hermit's life was as old as St Anthony of Egypt, older even than Christianity if we return to John the Baptist in the wilderness, but in the fourteenth century, as anger at the corruption and materialism of the church's hierarchy grew, more and more of the most devout Christians were drawn, not to the organised piety of the religious orders but to the solitary prayer of a hermitage. Medieval life was crowded, noisy and intensely public: small wonder that so many sought peace in a withdrawal from the world.

Richard Rolle was at Oxford University some years before Wyclif, sponsored by the archdeacon of Durham, but he appears to have suffered some adolescent crisis, dropped out without taking his degree, and returned to his home in Thornton, Yorkshire, a troubled and troubling nineteen-year old. Here, he began his career as hermit, not by seeking a license from his bishop, but by a typical piece of flamboyance. He asked his sister to meet him in a wood, bringing with her her grey and white gowns and their father's rain-hood. Cutting these garments up, he constructed a hermit's habit for himself and promptly ran away from home. He was discovered in Pickering church the next evening, rapt in prayer in the lady of the manor's pew – so impressed was she by his piety that she forbade her servants to move him when she arrived for vespers. The next day, Rolle preached a sermon which amazed the hearers by its passion and eloquence, and a hermit was born.

Rolle seems to have had the knack of fascinating and annoying in equal measure. He never lacked patrons and followers, but was always on the move, usually after a quarrel with those who sheltered him. His life was dominated by an intense love for God, which drove him to seek solitude and prayer. When he felt closest to God, he experienced a great heat, which at times made him feel that he was physically on fire. This experience furnished the name for his most famous book 'The Fire of Love.' Passionately, Rolle describes his love affair with God and calls his readers to join him in abandoning the world and giving themselves to prayer.

Rolle could be as harsh as Catherine of Siena or Wyclif in denouncing the religious orders and the parish clergy, but unlike them he does so, not as a reformer but as an outsider. In the last analysis, it seems that other people did not matter to him very much; the centre of life for him always lay in solitude, questing for the heat and sweetness and music of Paradise, to which only prayer gave access. He spent his last years as spiritual director of the nuns of Hampole, and is thought to have died in the Black Death.

WALTER HILTON (1343-1396) 24th March.
We know little of the life of another great English mystic, Walter Hilton, who in the generation after Rolle produced one of the great books on the spiritual life, the 'Scale of Perfection.' Hilton may have lived as a hermit himself and he certainly wrote his book for a female anchorite to advise her on her chosen life of solitary prayer, but he spent most of his life at Thurgarton, as an Augustinian canon. These canons followed a rule of life based on that devised by St Augustine of Hippo for his household. They were neither monks nor friars, but priests living a collegiate life and trying to balance prayer, study and pastoral work in their surrounding neighbourhood.

Hilton may well have been involved on the side of the authorities in the clampdown following Wyclif's disgrace. He certainly writes with distaste about the excesses of heresy and its encouragement of a false individualism. For all their common commitment to prayer as the centre of life, one senses that Hilton would have had little sympathy with Richard Rolle and his flamboyant self-absorption. For Hilton, the keys to the life of prayer are found in a life lived with others – no progress can be made unless a person is growing in humility and in love. To these virtues, he returns again and again. His desire for humility in particular makes him welcome misfortune as a gift from God: there is nothing like discomfort and disappointment for revealing pride and self-will in the heart and driving a Christian back to humble reliance on Jesus.

Hilton takes sin seriously and has none of Rolle's certainty that a love manifested in experiences and emotions will carry a person beyond its clutches. The image of sin, formed within the heart by the seven deadly sins, must be demolished by a steady repentance, so that the true image of God seen in Christ may be printed on the soul.

The unknown woman who received this treatise must have been greatly helped by the measured, realistic and humane advice of this wise man of prayer.

JULIAN OF NORWICH (1343-1417) 8th May.

If we know nothing of the woman for whom Walter Hilton wrote his book, we know little more about her contemporary and fellow anchorite, Julian of Norwich, who was the first woman we know of ever to have written a book in English, and one of the most remarkable mystical writers in any language. We do not even know her name, for the name 'Julian' properly belongs to the patron saint of the church to which her cell was attached.

It is possible to romanticise the hermit life of Richard Rolle, striding about the Yorkshire dales, free and uncommitted, settling to pray where the spirit led. Much harder for most moderns to comprehend is the calling of the anchorite, who was literally sealed in to live the whole of her life in prayer in one place. The life an anchorite chose was not quite as extreme as Gothic fantasists portray: she was not walled into an airless tomb. Most anchorites lived in a three-roomed house, with a little garden. A servant did shopping and helped with domestic work. One window opened into the church, against whose wall the little house was built, so that the anchorite could hear services and receive communion. Another opened on the street, so that she could receive visitors and offer help and guidance. But there was no door. The anchorite entered her home intending to stay there with God for ever. This takes St Benedict's emphasis on stability to extremes.

On 8th May 1373, the year St Bridget of Sweden died, Julian nearly died too. She was thirty years old and as a young woman had made a recklessly dangerous prayer – that she might see the Passion of Christ bodily, that she might experience the pain of death before her actual death, and that she might receive three inner wounds, of sorrow for sin, compassion for sinners, and love for God. On 8th May, her prayers were answered. She was thought to be dying and her parish priest was sent for, bringing a crucifix to comfort her in her last agony. As Julian lay helpless, unable to speak, the figure on the cross grew and moved, and for five hours she experienced a series of fifteen 'showings' as the full reality of the Passion was unfolded for her. She recovered and lived another forty years, which she spent in the anchorite's cell attached to St Julian's church in Norwich. For twenty years she prayed and reflected upon what she had seen, and then she was ready to write her book, a profound exploration of life, when its meaning is centred on the Passion of Jesus.

Like so many late medieval writers, Julian's focus on the physical sufferings of Christ is obsessive and almost frightening. She describes the beads of blood like herring scales, the strips of flesh peeling away from the gashes made by the crown of thorns, the discoloration of the face as the blood drains away, Unlike, say, Catherine of Siena or Bridget of Sweden, she does not move from contemplation of the suffering for sin to denunciation of the sin. There are no angry rants about corrupt Popes and venal clergy, only a luminous concentration on the joy with which God thus gives himself for love. When Christ has harrowed her with the vivid scenes of torture he asks. 'Are you content? If you are content, I am content.' Christ, says Julian, would have died a hundred times if he could, so deep is his desire to spend himself for his beloved. Julian sees the whole of reality as a hazelnut held in God's hand, yet this tiny thing is passionately loved by God, who holds and guides every human being towards a consummation which will mean bliss for all. 'All shall be well, and all shall be well, and all manner of thing shall be well.'

Julian herself, as a good medieval Christian, was troubled by the serene optimism of her showings. Why no tour of hell? she asked God, puzzled at the omission of this essential part of a visionary's itinerary. She received the answer that 'sin is nought.' There was nothing to show, because sin is the unreal place where a person hides who has not yet seen God in Christ. The devil does appear in her book, but as a frustrated buffoon, constantly heaping humanity with pains and temptations, only to see God joyously turning every trial and failure into a new opportunity for love and holiness. Julian sees a servant fall in the mud, yet all the staining cannot stop his Lord loving and pitying him – nor can Julian in the end say whether the servant is Adam the sinner or Jesus the Saviour, gladly taking on himself the pain of falling, the stains of sin.

Julian's writing fell into obscurity after the Reformation, but has been rediscovered in the twentieth century, and she is now the best-loved and most popular English mystical writer. This is perhaps because of her lack of any sense of God as wrathful and condemnatory, certainly because of the way she explores feminine imagery, calling Jesus 'our mother' and bequeathing us a different vision from that of traditional patriarchy. But her greatest appeal surely springs from her total trust in a God who loves her and has promised to bring all things to good. Rarely has that vision been so beautifully captured as in this strange little book written by a wise woman in a room with no door in Norwich.

MARGERY KEMPE (1373-1440) 9th November.

Among the many people who visited Julian in her cell at Norwich was a middle-aged housewife, mother of fourteen children, who had come to consult the anchoress about her inability to stop crying. Any mention of the passion of Christ, the sight of a crucifix, a purple passage in a sermon, was enough to set her off, loud, prolonged, anti-social weeping. Julian was able to reassure her from her own experience that tears were a gift from God by which the Holy Spirit provoked a person to contrition for sin and compassion for the suffering Saviour. She was sent on her way comforted.

This woman was Margery Kempe of Lynn, the daughter and wife of merchants in the town, whose spiritual biography, dictated to her parish priest and rediscovered in 1934, is a compellingly vivid portrayal of daily life in the late Middle Ages.

Margery was married to John Kempe at the age of twenty. The birth of her first child threw her into a dangerous fit of mental illness – she self-harmed and was kept locked in a dark room for six months. At the end of this time, she experienced a vision of Christ coming to her and telling her she was healed. She asked her husband for the key to her pantry, made herself some food and found she was capable to living a normal life. But she remained mentally and emotionally unstable and her story is really a heroic account of a quest for a holy, Christ-centred life mediated through a passionately erratic personality.

During the early years of her marriage, Margery outwardly lived the worldly life of a prosperous merchant's wife, enjoying fine clothes and social success and endangering her husband's profits by her taste for luxury and good living. Inwardly she was experiencing a series of devotional visions which eventually drove her to seek her husband's permission to live under a vow of chastity and to travel continuously on pilgrimage in England and abroad. She reached both Rome and Jerusalem, and visited most of the cathedrals and shrines of England. Her sense of Christ's presence was almost physical; she imagined him lying next to her in bed and placed herself in spirit within vividly realised meditations on his life, helping to wrap the baby Jesus in his swaddling clothes, or offering to make the Virgin Mary a hot drink as she returned shattered from the crucifixion. And to all of this intense inner experience she responded with loud, ugly weeping. Again and again she was rejected by her fellow-Christians, embarrassed or exasperated by her antics. Angry congregations turned her out of sermons; the pilgrim party which she accompanied to the Holy Land cut her dress short and treated her as their fool, before finally abandoning her in Venice. She was outspoken and confident in a way that was unacceptable for a married woman, with neither noble birth nor a nun's habit to cushion her eccentricities. She simply did not fit into her society; people did not know what to make of her. And yet, wherever she went, she also made friends and brought healing and a new start to many. A monk to whom she revealed his secret sins of lechery repented and went on to be prior of his order. A man whom she met in church praying in tears for his wife, who, like Margery herself, was suffering violent post natal depression, took her home where she calmed the woman, prayed for her, and brought her back to sanity. To many people she spoke prophetic words which challenged and changed them.

All of this, the weeping, the confident speech on theological topics, the ministry of prophetic healing, made her an object of intense suspicion to the church authorities. Since the trial of Wyclif and the Peasants' Revolt, the higher clergy was hardening into an attitude of fear of heresy and distrust of any desire by lay-people to read the Bible or discuss matters of religion. Margery was summoned before both archbishops on suspicion of being a Lollard, a follower of Wyclif. On each occasion, she defended herself with wit and unabashed loyalty to what Jesus had shown her, earning grudging respect and declarations of her innocence. The fearsome archbishop Arundel, the burner of heretics and persecutor of the English Bible, even took her for a walk around his garden and asked her to pray for him.

Margery did not spend all her life on the road; the care of her family was a duty she took seriously even though it pulled her away from the life of devotional prayer for which she longed. In the late 1420's, her husband John fell downstairs in the night and sustained serious head injuries which resulted in brain damage. Margery nursed him for the rest of his life and describes with cheerful lack of self-pity his confusion and incontinence which 'added to her labour, what with the washing and wringing of clothes.' She was distressed that this work of care kept her away from church, but was reassured by Christ that when she cared for her husband, she was caring for him and that he received this service as joyfully as any time spent in prayer. We see here one of the earliest statements of a theme which was to become dominant in the ensuing centuries of Reformation; that God can be served as well in the home and the workplace as in the cloister, and that holiness can be attained by ordinary people living in the world as well as by extraordinary people who forsake the world. For all the pain and confusion of her life, Margery Kempe's book is a unique witness to the way ordinary Christians, outside the charmed ranks of the religious orders, were seeking and finding a living relationship of faith with Christ.

JOAN OF ARC (1412-1431) 30th May.
Our final saint from the fifteenth century, like Margery Kempe and Julian of Norwich, received extraordinary visions from God, but, even more markedly, these visions led her way beyond what was considered godly or even possible behaviour for a woman, behaviour which led in the short term to her condemnation by the church she revered, and in the long term to her becoming the most famous female saint of all time, except for the Virgin Mary.

As Joan of Arc spent her childhood in rural Lorraine, the daughter of a prosperous peasant farmer, the kingdom of France was close to destruction. Henry V of England revived the English claim to the French crown and with it the Hundred Years War. Joan was three when Henry won his famous victory at Agincourt, which he followed up by securing the Treaty of Troyes, by which he was adopted as the French king's heir, the existing Dauphin Charles being disinherited. Only his own premature death, which left his infant son King of England and France, prevented Henry consolidating his audacious triumph. As it was, even without Henry, the English kept the upper hand militarily, thanks largely to their alliance with the Duke of Burgundy, alienated from the French king by the dynastic murder of his father. The Dauphin Charles, without money or support, eked out a miserable existence at Chinon. He was unable even to be crowned, as Rheims, scene of every coronation since St Remigius crowned Clovis, was well within the territory controlled by the English.

Joan's life could not have seemed more distant from these matters of high politics. She sat and span with her mother, she led her father's sheep out to pasture, she said her prayers in the little village church of Domremy, and she played with the other village children around their fairy tree. But from the age of thirteen she began to see visions and hear voices. St Catherine of Alexandria, St Margaret of Antioch and the archangel Michael appeared to her and told her to go to the Dauphin and save France. Joan tried to ignore these voices, but at last was compelled to obey. She overcome the objections of her own father, who threatened to drown her if she went off with the soldiers, and of her Lord of the Manor, Robert de Baudricourt, whom she persuaded by sheer persistence and force of personality to give her a horse and a set of boy's clothes and send her to the Dauphin. She was only seventeen. By the age of nineteen she would be dead.

The Dauphin was naturally cautious when confronted by a peasant girl claiming that God had sent her to lead his armies to victory, but after Joan had miraculously picked him out from a crowd of courtiers and hailed him as king, he began to be impressed. Her naïve reverence for him must have been refreshing after the contempt with which he was treated by his own lords; moreover Joan was able to reveal to him a secret known only to himself. It is likely that this secret concerned the persistent rumours that he was illegitimate, the son of one of his mother's many lovers. However that may be, Joan put fresh heart into him and he sent her to join his troops, which were to dislodge the English army besieging Orleans.

So began Joan's year of glory. By pure audacity, the young girl, dressed in white armour and carrying a banner of the Virgin Mary, broke into Orleans and drove back the English besiegers. After that, she was adored by her troops, who followed her lead to win four victories over the previously unconquerable English. The climax of the campaign was the coronation of Charles VII at Rheims. Joan stood beside him throughout the day in her armour, a living saint, worshipped as the saviour of France.

Her luck did not last. At the battle of Compiegne, she was dragged from her horse and made prisoner by the Burgundians, who sold her to the English. In English-held Rouen, she was tried by the church as a heretic and a witch. The account of her trial, and of the simple direct answers she made to the never-ending series of questions about every aspect of her short life, makes moving reading. She persisted in refusing to confess that her voices were demonic and she was condemned to be burned. A soldier made a cross for her to hold at the stake, and she died with the name of Jesus on her lips.

The French court, which had done nothing to save her, succeeded in having the sentence of heresy revoked twenty-five years later, but it was not until 1920 that Joan was finally officially canonised and supplanted St Denys as patron saint of France. With her unquestioning faith in the Blessed Sacrament and the saints whose statues filled Domremy church, she seems a quintessentially medieval figure, but George Bernard Shaw, in his famous play 'Saint Joan', suggests mischievously that, in her defiant choice to obey her own conscience rather than the ecclesiastical authorities, she was in fact the first Protestant.

PART SIXTEEN. REFORMATION.

BARTOLOME DE LAS CASAS (1484-1566) 20th July.

Sixty years after the burning of Joan of Arc, occurred an event which was to change for ever the way Christendom perceived the world, and, though the process was stained by cruelty and genocide, was the first step in establishing Christianity as a worldwide religion. In 1492, Christopher Columbus crossed the Atlantic in three small ships and discovered the island he named Hispaniola, now divided between Haiti and the Dominican Republic. A year later, a small boy of nine was in the crowd in Seville to watch the astonishing victory parade of Columbus, displaying to the people of Spain seven live natives ('Indians' as Columbus, convinced he had reached Asia, dubbed them), together with gorgeous parrots, bizarre native artefacts and, biggest lure of all, objects fashioned from solid gold. It was the gold that sealed the fate of the unhappy Hispaniolans. Within a lifetime, not only their island but the whole of central and southern America, including the great Mexican empire of the Aztecs, had been subdued by the Spanish conquistadores.

The nine-year old who watched these marvels, innocent of what they portended, was Bartolome de las Casas. Almost at once, America took over his life. His father and uncle both joined Columbus' second voyage to his 'Indies,' and made enough money to train Bartolome as a lawyer. In 1502, de las Casas himself went west, serving in a Spanish army which subdued unconquered portions of Hispaniola, and being rewarded for his pains by the grant of a 'hacienda' or farm, and becoming an important citizen of New Spain. In 1510, he was ordained priest, at first apparently unperturbed by the conflict between his calling to spread the gospel in these new lands, and his complicity in what was a rapacious drive to grab the riches of a continent by enslaving and ultimately destroying its inhabitants. Within a generation, the entire native population of Hispaniola had perished, killed by a combination of overwork in Spanish goldmines and plantations, trauma at the destruction of their civilisation and, worst of all, smallpox, brought by the conquerors and to which they had no immunity.

Two incidents transformed las Casas from a beneficiary from all this cruelty into its harshest critic. The first was a sermon preached in 1511 by the Dominican Antonio de Montesinos, in which he denounced the exploitation of the Indians; the second was the participation of las Casas in the burning at the stake of a rebel chief, Hatuey. When las Casas, like a good missionary, pressed baptism on the unhappy man, promising that after his torments he would enter Paradise, Hatuey asked whether there would be white men in heaven. On las Casas' saying that there would be, 'Then,' said the Indian, 'I die unbaptized, for I have no desire to go anywhere where there are men as cruel as the Spanish.' The mirror held up to him and his colleagues appalled las Casas. After two years of agonised soul-searching, he released his slaves, renounced his estate, joined the Dominican order and dedicated the rest of his life to seeking justice for the Indians.

He was not alone. Throughout America, thoughtful Christians, particularly in the missionary orders, were shocked at the abuses to which the native peoples were subjected. Their preferred solution, admittedly paternalistic, was to gather the Indians into communes run by the religious orders, where they would participate in the profit of their labours, learn the Christian faith, and be civilised by gentle arts rather than coercion. Conditions on the church estates were certainly idyllic compared with what most people were suffering at the hands of more materialistic Spanish settlers, and the Indians loved their clergy, whom they saw as their only protectors, and many of whom, like las Casas, were enlightened enough to value and try to conserve the native cultures. Las Casas' own early attempt at planting such a commune was however a failure, overwhelmed by hostility from the surrounding planters. His genius was that of a campaigner and a publicist. Innumerable times, he crossed the Atlantic in the tiny ships of the day, trying to win over public opinion in Spain to his cause. In this, he was highly successful. He enjoyed the consistent support of the Spanish monarchs, Ferdinand and Isabella, who, while not averse to the glory and treasure making its way towards them from their new empire, had a genuine desire for the welfare and conversion of the Indians. The statesman Cardinal Ximenez was likewise a faithful patron of las Casas. Bartolome's books, exposing what was happening in America, shocked devout Spaniards and his 1552 'Brief Report on the Destruction of the Indians' became a best seller.

On the other hand, most Spaniards who lived in the American empire saw las Casas as a mischievous trouble-maker and attempts were made on his life, so that when he was made Bishop of Chiapas in Guatemala he had to be attended by an armed guard. He was a hot-headed, angry man who made many tactical and strategic errors, alienating moderate planters who could have become allies. His worst strategic mistake was to recommend that, to release the Indians from their sufferings, planters should obtain workers from the physically tougher races of Africa. Las Casas seems naively to have assumed that Africans would travel to America voluntarily and would have protection under some sort of indenture system: by the time he dissociated himself from what was actually happening, the horrors of the slave trade were already established, a trade which would poison relations between three continents for three centuries.

Nevertheless, the single-minded campaign of las Casas had its successes. In 1537, Pope Paul III issued the Bull 'Sublimis Deus,' which confirmed that the American Indians had rational souls and property rights, which it was sinful to infringe, and six years later the king of Spain decreed his 'New Laws,' guaranteeing his American subjects freedom from slavery and equality under the law, and proposing penalties for those who killed, dispossessed or exploited them. Both of these milestones were achieved through the lobbying of las Casas. The great campaigner himself continued to fight for the implementation of these paper rights in the badlands of Mexico. He finally retired to a Spanish monastery where he died.

MARTIN LUTHER (1483-1546) 31st October.

As the Spanish conquest of South America continued with unstoppable impetus, it must have seemed to the Renaissance Papacy that the Christendom over which they ruled was set to expand to the world's end. Sadly, the sixteenth century dawned on a Christendom greatly weakened much nearer to home than Brazil and Mexico. Turkish power seemed to be conquering Europe as rapidly as Spain took over the Americas. In 1453, while Western princes continued to wrangle in the death throes of the Hundred Years War, Constantinople, the great imperial capital of the Eastern church, was conquered by the Turks; in 1529 they were besieging Vienna and south east Europe was under a Muslim dominance which would last until the nineteenth century. Meanwhile, in Germany, a storm was brewing which would split the unity of the medieval church for ever, and, in a quest for reform and truth, subject Europe to a century and a half of violence and cruelty in the name of Jesus.

Renaissance Popes enjoyed life, seizing with both hands the opportunity for sumptuous living which the growing wealth and sophistication of southern Europe made possible. They glittered as princely patrons of all that was new, exciting and cultured – sponsoring the humanist scholars who were rediscovering the riches of ancient literature, commissioning marvellous statues and pictures from Michaelangelo and Raphael, re-inventing the ruin-dominated city of Rome as a place worthy of its imperial past with sumptuous churches, palaces, fountains and triumphant arches, posing as connoisseurs of fine literature, fine jewels, fine wine and fine women. None of this splendour had much obvious connection with the mission of Jesus of Nazareth, and all of it was paid for by the depressingly familiar means which had been denounced by church reformers ever since Catherine of Sienna and William of Ockham: taxes on the profits of church courts, simoniacal fees received from every priest entering on possession of a new benefice, exemptions granted (for cash) to noble clergymen permitting everything from under-age ordination to plurality of benefices. Above all, the Pope, as dispenser of sacramental grace and holder of St Peter's keys, was at the head of the indulgence system.

Pope Leo X was set on rebuilding St Peter's Basilica, a project which was to produce one of Europe's finest buildings. The money was to be raised by a special sale of indulgences. Those who contributed to the building fund would receive, as a reward for their piety, guarantees from the Pope that they and their loved ones would pass quickly through Purgatory, their penances commuted, into the joys of Paradise. In the hands of a salesman, like the Dominican Tetzel, this theologically dubious development of the age-old doctrine of penance was turned into an offensive piece of profiteering, coining money from the credulity and superstitious fears of Christian people. As Tetzel campaigned around Saxony, a young lecturer at Wittenberg University, Martin Luther, decided that enough was enough. On 31st October 1517, he nailed to the door of Wittenberg castle an announcement of his intention to debate the morality of indulgences in ninety-five theses. This action has been seen symbolically as the start of the Reformation.

We have seen that there was nothing new about calls, often angry and determined, for reform of the church. What was new about Luther was that he lost patience with the papacy entirely. For him, papal rule over the church was not a flawed institution in need of reform in order to do the job God intended. The Pope was a usurper, his rule abominable, and Luther denounced him as the Anti-Christ, the false prophet who Jesus warned would delude and mislead the church.

Martin Luther had become an Augustinian at the age of twenty-one as the result of a vow made to God in the terror of a thunderstorm. Although an exemplary religious, he had caused a storm at Wittenberg university by his attempts to over-turn the traditional syllabus. Luther distrusted the church's marriage with Aristotelian philosophy and wanted his students to read the biblical texts with clear eyes, not squinting through the elaborate system of interpretation built up by the medieval scholarly tradition. His ideas spread rapidly, thanks to the newly invented printing press. Wittenberg had its own press and startled readers throughout Germany were thus able rapidly and cheaply to read Luther's ideas.

Central to Luther's thought was the doctrine of justification by faith. For years, Luther had feared the righteousness of God, which appeared to him as an inhuman perfection, condemning him and all sinners. A new reading of the letter to the Romans revealed to him that God's righteousness was an active principle, the merciful work of God in imputing his righteousness to others. This righteousness was imputed to sinners through the sacrificial death of Christ, and it was received by faith. Salvation was a simple matter of trusting God to keep his promise and justify the ungodly.

As he began to live in the freedom of this new faith, Luther's anger intensified against the system under which he had been brought up. The clergy, it seemed to him, had stolen the freedom which was a Christian's birth-right. With their vows of celibacy and monastic rules, they had set up a false holiness and barred ordinary Christians from entering it. With their monopoly over the sacraments and idolatrous Masses, they presumed to control access to the grace of Christ, access which any person of faith could secure by a simple prayer for God's mercy, without the paraphernalia of the church and its money-making. As the controversy grew, as Luther debated his views with increasingly eminent churchmen and published his stormy, passionate calls for reform, 'An address to the Christian Nobility of Germany,' 'The Babylonian Captivity of the Church,' 'The Freedom of a Christian,' so more and more people became excited by the new vision of Christian faith Luther offered. Holiness was being relocated. Christ was to be sought not in the cloister or the hermit's cell, but in the faithful living of secular lives, in the markets, the shop, the home and in marriage. The role of the ordained clergy was reduced to teaching and leading public prayer. Luther had rediscovered the biblical doctrine of the 'priesthood of all believers.'

Matters came to a head in 1521 at the Diet of Worms where the Holy Roman Emperor, Charles V, brought Luther to trial on charges of heresy. Even if the defiant ex-monk did not actually say, 'Here I stand. I can do no other,' his position was clear. He was no longer prepared to compromise with the old order and his condemnation duly followed.

Luther's patron, the Duke of Saxony, came to his rescue and staged a kidnap of the reformer, carrying him beyond the church's reach and imprisoning him for his own safety in the Wartburg, a remote ducal castle. Here, in less than a year, Luther completed his great translation of the Bible into German. The printing press did the rest. Now, all over Germany, educated people could discus Luther's ideas and study the New Testament texts to which he appealed without the intervention of the clergy.

The turmoil caused by Luther's ideas, when combined with economic and social grievances, erupted into violence. In Wittenberg, extremists began to loot the churches, destroying 'idolatrous' pictures and statues and mocking the rituals of the services. Throughout Germany, a great Peasants Revolt began, as tenant farmers took the law into their own hands and refused to pay tithes and rents to the monasteries and bishops, who they now learned were servants of Antichrist. The Duke brought Luther back to restore order. Luther was shocked by what was being done. Despite his anger at the church, he had a deep reverence for the sacraments and taught a doctrine of consubstantiation – the bread and wine, while remaining themselves, were infused with Christ's presence, as a red-hot poker is infused with fire. Nor did Luther wish to see sacred art vandalised, provided no superstitious reverence was paid to images. Under his guidance, the Lutheran church which was beginning to form maintained a decorous, beautiful liturgy in which Protestant extremism was discouraged. In his least glorious hour, Luther also denounced in savage terms those who were rebelling against their natural lords, and encouraged the ruling classes in their brutal reassertion of order.

Luther remained at Wittenberg for the rest of his life, marrying an ex-nun and earning the love of his disciples by his unpretentious hospitality. He was a stocky, earthy man, full of laughter, occasionally vulgar, always passionate, with his heart leading his head. His teaching split the Holy Roman Empire, as the different dukes, counts, and free cities each made their decision: to declare for the Reformation and break with Rome, or to remain loyal to Catholicism. By the time of his death, most of northern German and Scandinavia was Lutheran. The unity of Christendom was broken, but a new generation of Christians had been set free to read and interpret the Bible for themselves.

JOHN FISHER (1469-1535) 6th July.
The response of one Christian king, Henry VIII of England, to Luther's assault on the church was immediate: he wrote a book against Luther, the 'Defence of the Seven Sacraments,' a book which earned him the title of 'Defender of the Faith,' a gift from the Pope which still adorns British coinage. In his theological endeavours, Henry VIII was ably seconded by John Fisher, Bishop of Rochester, and the foremost English theologian of his day. Fisher wrote carefully and at length against Luther, and his works were long

treasured by Catholic writers as a source of telling quotes from the church fathers.

Fisher had been early head-hunted by the king's grandmother, the scholarly Lady Margaret Beaufort, who made him her spiritual director. By her patronage, he became the first Professor of Theology to occupy the chair she had newly founded at Cambridge, and went on to become in 1504 Bishop of Rochester and Chancellor of Cambridge University. As Lady Margaret's trusted ally, he was instrumental in the founding of St John's College, and even persuaded the notoriously thrifty King Henry VII, Lady Margaret's son, to pay for the completion of King's College Chapel. He laid down that no languages should be spoken at St John's but the scholarly tongues of Hebrew, Greek and Latin, and was instrumental in inviting the great humanist Erasmus to Cambridge.

As Bishop of Rochester, he was much more 'hands on' than most late medieval bishops, performing most of his ordinations personally and spending much time in residence in the diocese. Such was his prestige at the time of his writings against Luther, that Henry VIII was often seen with a kingly arm around the bishop's shoulders. It must have been a bony experience, for Fisher was strictly ascetic.

All Fisher's earnestness and scholarship could not prevent Lutheranism from penetrating England. Many of his fellow-countrymen were determined to study the ideas of the great German and, fatally for Fisher, his royal master was about to discover the disadvantages of loyalty to the Pope.

WILLIAM TYNDALE (1494-1536) 6th October.
In 1523, the Bishop of London, Cuthbert Tunstall, received a visitor. The young man, a scholar from Cambridge, brought with him a translation of an oration of Isocrates as a gift and a testimonial of his scholarship. The young scholar's request was to be taken into the Bishop's household and be sponsored while he completed a translation of the New Testament into English. Tunstall was a scholar himself and a friend of Erasmus and Thomas More, the celebrated humanist lawyer whose house in Chelsea was a sanctuary for the learned and cultured. Nevertheless, the young man from Cambridge was quickly made aware that his project found no favour

with the Bishop. Shortly afterwards, he went to Germany, carrying with him his working manuscripts. William Tyndale was never again to visit his native land: perpetual exile was the price he paid for his life's vocation, to provide the English people with the scriptures in their own language.

The hostility of Tunstall, no natural bigot, reveals how entrenched in its views the English church establishment had become since Wyclif's days. The education of the laity and in particular the making available to them of scripture had come to seem so dangerous that a desire to read the Bible in English was itself a declaration of heresy.

Tyndale was a man with a passion and to that passion he gladly sacrificed his life. He travelled about the great cities of Germany – Cologne, Worms, Hamburg, finally settling in Antwerp. Nowhere could be safe; everywhere he was pursued by agents of Henry VIII and the English bishops, using every diplomatic weapon to induce the local rulers to arrest Tyndale and destroy his work. In Cologne, the first twenty-two chapters of Matthew were set up and printed, before a warning that arrest was imminent sent Tyndale and his accomplice scurrying to Worms. Here, a complete New Testament was finally produced and the dangerous work of smuggling the book into England began. Inevitably, Tyndale's German travels increased his devotion to Martin Luther, and much of Luther's biblical interpretation was published as commentary in Tyndale's text. The Lutheran association whipped up the English establishment to even greater loathing. Tyndale's Testament was publicly burned, and before long those found guilty of selling or reading it were being burned too. At the king's instigation, the urbane Sir Thomas More began a deeply unedifying pamphlet war against Tyndale – the great scholar and author of Utopia descended to page after page of spiteful, scatological invective, so great was his hatred and dread of heresy.

Tyndale meanwhile had taught himself Hebrew and by the time of his untimely end had completed the translation of the Old Testament books Genesis to 2 Kings. He had also produced volumes of prolix and passionate Protestant theology, his great opus being 'The Obedience of a Christian Man,' a work which promoted Martin

Luther's idea of 'two kingdoms.' The church, teacher of spiritual doctrine, ought never to have grasped at temporal power, the temptation which had reduced the Popes to antichrists and spoilers of Christendom. Secular power ought to be wielded by godly rulers, to whom Christians truly owed the obedience unjustly usurped by the Papacy. By one of the great ironies of history, this book came into the hands of Henry VIII, Tyndale and Luther's great enemy, who approved of it with the words 'This is a book for me and all kings to read.' Henry had been give 'The Obedience' by the delectable Anne Boleyn, a young lady with distinctly Protestant leanings and other qualities which were about to change the history of the English church.

Tyndale's translations were masterly, rendering the biblical texts into plain, simple English whose memorable phrases and speech-rhythms have shaped English prose style ever since. The translators of the Authorised Version used and adapted Tyndale, so that through them his English has been the most read of any writer over the centuries. To read Tyndale's assured prose and to reflect on the fear, hurry and secrecy with which the work was done is to be in the presence of a wonder.

Anne Boleyn's patronage could not save Tyndale's life, for her advancing favour with the king, culminating in his divorce of Queen Katherine of Aragon and marriage to Anne in 1533, created an unbridgeable gulf between Henry and the Emperor Charles V, Katherine's nephew. And it was Charles who was ruler of Antwerp, where Tyndale was sheltering, claiming the diplomatic privilege of the colony of English wool merchants in that city, and benefitting from the city council's willingness to turn a blind eye to Lutheran activity. But when he was lured by a false friend into a trap, arrested and smuggled away to Brussels, the reforming party in England could not save him from Imperial justice. Tyndale was burned at the stake as a Lutheran heretic in 1536. His last words were, 'Lord, open the King of England's eyes.'

THOMAS MORE (1478-1535) 6th July.
By the time Tyndale was burned, his great enemy, Sir Thomas More, had been dead a year, both men victims of the battle between

traditional Catholicism and reform which raged in the tyrannical breast of Henry VIII. More and Fisher had both been loved by the King, but both were destroyed without mercy when they dared to obstruct the royal will.

It has become fashionable to sneer at Thomas More, until recently eulogised as a wit, a man of letters, a civilised and loving family man, a martyr to conscience, a 'man for all seasons.' In most recent biographies and novels, the other side of More has been emphasised – the bigoted hater of heretics, prepared to countenance torture, perhaps even administering it personally, spectacularly denying to others the freedom of conscience he claimed for himself. It is certainly true that if Luther was a monk who could only find peace by breaking out of the cloister and reclaiming the holiness of marriage and secular work, Thomas More was a married man and successful professional, who never ceased secretly to yearn for the life of a monk. The witty, gracious host whom Erasmus and his humanist friends met at Chelsea concealed within a deep shame that his love of sex and need for worldly success had turned him aside from the ascetic self-denial of such men as the saintly Bishop Fisher. More's spiteful, obsessive crusade against heresy probably derived its force from the self-hatred generated by his own failure to live up to the holiness he admired and yet dreaded.

He must have been ambitious despite his air of cultured detachment from power politics. Why else, when the King's great minister Cardinal Wolsey fell, would he have accepted the post of Lord Chancellor, putting himself at the centre of public life just as it was becoming clear that Henry's desires were leading him to a place where More could never conscientiously follow?

For Henry VIII, the hater of Luther and Defender of the Faith, was also a man divided against himself. Genuinely pious, Henry was nevertheless one of those people who manage to convince themselves that if they want something badly enough, it must be God's will they should have it And what Henry wanted was a son. To get one he was prepared to divorce his ageing wife Queen Katherine and marry his vivacious mistress, Tyndale's admirer, Anne Boleyn. When it became clear that the Pope was not going to grant dispensations for this to happen, Henry was prepared to restructure radically the church in his dominions.

It is a mark of the authority of the Tudor monarchs that so few Englishmen were prepared to stand against the royal will. The bishops, threatened with a corporate charge of high treason under the statute 'Praemunire,' which forbade appeals to the Court of Rome without royal approval, supinely surrendered and signed the declaration which acknowledged the king as head of the English church, against whom no appeal was possible. By one legislative act, Henry VIII had abolished the Pope's power in England and separated the Church of England from catholic Christendom. Only one bishop resisted, John Fisher, who had stood by Katherine of Aragon during the divorce proceedings, had defended her in court and was now committed to the Tower for treason.

For a long time, Thomas More kept his head down. He promoted Henry's new marriage arrangements in parliament as it was his duty to do as Lord Chancellor, and held his tongue. He seems to have believed that Henry had promised not to compel him to act against his conscience provided he did not speak against the new arrangements. Perhaps he hoped that his position of power would enable him discreetly to put the brakes on the dismantling of the church he loved. His position speedily became untenable. The new archbishop of Canterbury, Thomas Cranmer, lost no time in pronouncing the King's marriage to Katherine of Aragon invalid and the marriage and coronation of Queen Anne followed speedily. Thomas More resigned and withdrew to poverty in Chelsea. He still believed the king's affection would secure him against attack, but the silence of so famous a man spoke eloquently and as the birth of Anne Boleyn's child (surely the longed for Prince?) drew near, Henry became ever more grimly determined to ensure nothing could overshadow his son's legitimacy. A new Act of Parliament made it treason to question the king's headship of the church or the legality of his marriage, and when Thomas More, for all his silence, refused to sign it, he joined Fisher in the Tower.

The final tragedy was precipitated by Pope Paul III, who in an act of futile defiance, appointed Bishop Fisher a cardinal. A furious Henry VIII declared that Fisher would not have a head to put his new hat on, and sure enough the old bishop, pitifully thin from fasting, was dragged out to Tower Hill and beheaded before a horrified crowd.

It was obvious that it could only be a matter of time before More followed him. He had endured months of imprisonment, ceaselessly interrogated and using all his lawyer's skill to baffle attempts at making a charge stick. His books were taken away and his family only allowed to see him on their promising to make him sign the Act. In the end, a statement by Sir Richard Rich, probably perjured, gave the jury the legal excuse they needed to bring in the verdict the king required. Thomas More was beheaded on 6th July 1535. His beloved daughter Margaret Roper broke through the crowd to embrace him for the last time as he was led to his death. At the last, he passed beyond fear and his remarks on the scaffold show his urbane wit and self-possession. He thanked a man who helped him up the steps 'but for my coming down, let me shift for myself.' He asked the executioner to be sure not to sever his beard, 'for it is no traitor.' In his speech to the crowd he declared 'I die the king's good servant, but God's first.' Thus courageously he died, and his 'Dialogue of Comfort,' composed in prison, indicates that this complex, contradictory man found peace at the last.

THOMAS CRANMER (1489-1556) 21st March.
The executions of More and Fisher were followed by a series of spectacular falls from grace, as the architects of the English Reformation fell foul of the king who had never really wanted the church to change, only to do as he told it. Anne Boleyn, for whose love the king had gambled everything, failed to produce the longed-for son, and was beheaded on trumped up charges of adultery. Thomas Cromwell, the all-powerful secretary who master-minded the dissolution of the monasteries, also ended on the scaffold. The great survivor of the reign was the gentle archbishop of Canterbury, the least politically astute of all the glamorous figures which filled the court, yet loved by Henry for his very meekness, Thomas Cranmer, despised by some as a cowardly time-server, yet indisputably by his discreet, unyielding stance for reform and by his mastery of liturgical prose, the architect of the reformed Church of England.

Cranmer had risen fast from obscurity to the highest spiritual office in the land. He caught Henry VIII's eye when the divorce crisis was at its height, by his suggestion that the universities of Europe might be appealed to for verdicts on the legality of the king's marriage to Queen Katherine. Henry's affection for, and trust, in Cranmer remained constant so that Cromwell once enviously observed, 'You were born in a happy hour, I suppose, for do or say what you will the King will always take it well at your hand.'

Cranmer was abroad in Germany on a mission for the king when his elevation to Canterbury was announced. He must have been taken by surprise, for he had just acted with uncharacteristic recklessness and, like Luther, broken his priestly vow of celibacy by marrying Margaret, niece of the reformer Osiander. What might have been overlooked in a humble priest was impermissible for the archbishop of Canterbury and poor Mrs Cranmer was obliged to remain hidden for the rest of Henry VIII's reign, although there is unfortunately no truth in the oft repeated catholic slander that Cranmer made a special box to carry her in as he journeyed around the kingdom.

Although the break with Rome was virtually inevitable at the time of his appointment, Cranmer dutifully observed all the medieval protocol, receiving his pallium, his stole of office, from the Pope and a blessing from Rome. He must have had his fingers crossed as he submitted to what he privately considered an unscriptural proceeding, but his action was subsequently important. It meant that uniquely among the reformed churches of northern Europe, the Church of England maintained an unbroken link to the pre-reformation hierarchy, and was able to claim that its ministry still derived its authority from the apostolic succession.

Cranmer had studied Luther and was a much more convinced reformer than Henry VIII. He pushed for reform as far as he dared. Just a year after Tyndale's martyrdom, English Bibles were placed in every parish church, with the king ostentatiously displayed on the frontispiece dispensing truth to his subjects. Cranmer was unable to persuade Henry to allow an English liturgy; he was however allowed to publish a Litany in English, and even to insist on its use in all processional rites.

As he got older, Henry VIII veered back to a conservative position and in 1539 passed the Act of Six Articles, making it heresy to deny transubstantiation and maintaining Communion in one kind only, clerical celibacy and confession to a priest. Cranmer was thus forced onto the defensive, but his enemies went too far in attempting to ruin him personally. A petition was delivered to the king denouncing the archbishop's views, now heresy under the Six Articles, but Henry, while travelling on the Thames in the royal barge, handed the denunciations to Cranmer saying jocosely 'Ah my chaplain, I know now who is the greatest heretic in Kent,' and promptly appointed Cranmer to chair the commission investigating his own misconduct. A few days later, Cranmer was summoned before the royal council, who ritually humiliated him by making him wait outside the council chamber 'among the foot-boys.' When he was eventually admitted, the conservatives attacked him furiously, but he meekly produced King Henry's ring, given him as a guarantee of his safety. The council, realising they had gone too far, panicked and were treated to a royal tirade by the king, who arrived on cue to take advantage of their confusion. The incident is dramatized in Shakespeare's 'Henry VIII.' Cranmer retained the king's affection to the end and Henry died clasping his archbishop's hand.

His successor was the boy king Edward VI, a convinced Protestant, and now Cranmer's reforming desires, tactfully moderated during Henry's reign, emerged and flowered. English parish churches were transformed. They were stripped of their statues and candle stands, the walls were whitewashed to erase the colourful medieval paintings, and the chantry chapels, endowed to pray for the souls of the dead, were closed. In 1549, Cranmer at last achieved his greatest desire, the provision of a liturgy in English. The Book of Common Prayer was largely his own work and was a masterly piece of editing and collecting. The aim was not simply to translate the services from Latin into English, but to create forms of worship which would be authentically biblical and protestant, and to simplify the ornate and complex medieval liturgy so as to render it accessible to lay people. Cranmer was a literary genius who valued enough of the past to make the resulting book both beautiful and a thoroughly diplomatic transition from old to new for a population much more religiously conservative than the elite at King Edward's court. Cranmer reduced the traditional monastic offices from seven to two, Morning and Evening Prayer, and while retaining the age-old recitation of the psalms and canticles, placed at the centre of these offices two long readings from the Old and New Testaments. The Eucharist was drastically simplified and restructured, cutting out all material which might encourage veneration of the elements of bread and wine, and introducing extensive penitential material; the result is a memorable meditation on sin and forgiveness, centred on the cross. Cranmer's book was revised in 1552, becoming more uncompromisingly protestant. Remaining devotions to the Virgin Mary and prayers for the dead were removed and the Communion rite further sharpened to prevent any ghost of transubstantiation from appearing. This Book of Common Prayer was his lasting legacy to the Church of England and the English language, and the majestic rhythm of its prose has never been surpassed. At the time, it was hated as all new liturgy is hated, and armed rebellion took place in Cornwall in protest at its universal imposition as the form of public prayer throughout the realm.

The Protestant Reformation in England looked secure, but in reality it depended on the slender lifeline of the sickly boy king Edward VI. His death at the age of sixteen sent Cranmer and the Protestant party into a panic, for the rightful heir was Edward's half sister Mary, the daughter of Katharine of Aragon and a staunch Catholic. Forced to choose between his two most heartfelt loyalties, legitimate monarchy and reformed religion, Cranmer chose his faith and backed an attempt to secure the throne for Edward's cousin, Lady Jane Grey. When Jane's nine day reign was over-whelmed by the popular support for Mary, it seemed clear that both the Protestant cause, and Cranmer himself, were doomed.

HUGH LATIMER (1485-1555) 16th October.
Among those who, like Cranmer, were to suffer for their faith under the new regime, Hugh Latimer was prominent. His reputation had been built on his preaching, which was fiery, compulsive and very long. Court officials had to hint to him that Henry VIII liked his sermons to last less than an hour and a half. Edward VI had more

stamina, and at his court Latimer often preached for more than four hours.

Latimer, like so many English reformers, got his education at Cambridge and was part of the 'Little Germany' group which met to discuss Lutheran ideas at the White Horse. In 1536, as the break with Rome became inevitable, he was appointed Bishop of Worcester, where he gave an enthusiastic lead in implementing the dissolution of the monasteries. The great religious houses, nurse of so many of the great saints of former ages, had shrunk to a shadow of their former selves. If not the nurseries of vice that Cromwell's propaganda made them out to be, they were smaller and no longer at the forefront of Christian civilisation. The universities had taken over their role as promoters of learning, and Renaissance scholarship and spirituality made much traditional monastic piety seem gloomy and superstitious. Many monasteries were in effect religious gentlemen's clubs, where elderly celibates lived comfortably on endowments which had grown over the centuries and pottered harmlessly through a ritual day which had lost its power to challenge or inspire. Latimer, a thorough reformer, was zealous in exposing the hypocrisies and closing the houses of a system he no longer believed capable of promoting Christ's kingdom. In particular, he attacked superstitious relics and images. The great statue of Our Lady of Worcester was burned outside the cathedral, and Latimer exhibited publicly the fraud which had sustained the Holy Blood of Hailes: a supposedly miraculous phial of Christ's blood was in fact regularly topped up with fresh duck's blood. A central theme of Latimer's preaching was the Lutheran insight that Christians might live holy lives as fruitfully within the married home and the workshop as in the cloister – more so, indeed, for the monk's labour was sterile, while the Christian in the world built up the prosperity of the realm.

On the question of prosperity, however, the Bishop of Worcester soon found himself in conflict with the King. Of humble background himself, Latimer had a deep sympathy for the poor, and naively assumed that the vast wealth confiscated from the dissolved monasteries would be reinvested in godly projects – schools, hospitals, alms-houses and the support of a preaching clergy. It soon became clear that the majority of the spoils would go to the Treasury or be paid out to buy the support of the nobility and gentry, the less scrupulous of whom made fortunes in a land transfer which changed the English landscape for ever. The Act of Six Articles was the last straw for Latimer, who resigned his bishopric and spent the last years of Henry VIII's reign in retirement and under constant suspicion of heresy.

Edward VI's reign was his time of glory, when his preaching dominated the reforming court. His style was fiery and uncompromising, delivered in a homely manner with much colloquial wit and a telling use of anecdotes. The subject matter is oddly disappointing. Latimer made little of the great Lutheran doctrines of grace, faith and justification. His sermons are moralistic and usually very angry, better at denouncing the follies of popery and the evils of the get-rich-quick culture of the court, then at sketching a positive evangelical alternative. In an age when the poor were vulnerable because of rapid inflation, the enclosure of common lands and the replacement of charitable monastic landlord by grasping secular squire, Latimer's voice cried for justice and pity. By the time of Lady Jane Grey's failed coup and Catholic Mary's succession, he was an old man, and, like Archbishop Cranmer, marked for vengeance by the new regime.

NICHOLAS RIDLEY (1500-1555) 16th October.

Nicholas Ridley, whose name is for ever linked to Latimer and Cranmer by the tragedy which was about to unfold, was a younger and sharper man, and no less dedicated to the work of reform. Again, this North country boy made his name at Cambridge, becoming Fellow of Pembroke in 1524 and Professor of Greek in 1535. He became a protégé of Cranmer, who appointed him one of his Six Preachers. This institution, which still survives, was an attempt by Cranmer to gain reforming benefit from the dissolution of the monastery at Canterbury; out of monastic estates he was able to fund lectureships attached to the cathedral and bestow them on men like Ridley who had the ability and conviction to preach the new religion. But Canterbury Cathedral chapter was still dominated by ex-monks, and under their conservative rule Ridley was eclipsed. The death of Henry VIII ensured his rise – to Bishop of Rochester in 1547 and

Bishop of London in 1550. In the capital he supported Cranmer's liturgical reforms, energetically remodelling church interiors to be fit receptacles for the new rite. The old stone altars were ripped out and the east end sanctuaries in which they had stood were no longer used as the focal point of worship. The new Book of Common Prayer Communion was to be celebrated in the middle of the nave (still usually uncluttered by pews) with the people gathered around a wooden table on which common bread and wine were set forth. The new setting stripped the rite of mystery and magic ('Hocus pocus' as the Protestants contemptuously garbled the sacred words 'Hoc est corpus - This is my body.') and redesigned it as a memorial meal of disciples gathered round a supper table. Ridley, less patient than the ever diplomatic Cranmer, opposed his senior when he felt the archbishop did not press reform hard enough. He disapproved of Cranmer's decision to encourage people still to receive Communion kneeling and bare-headed, and there was a celebrated row over the installation of Bishop Hooper of Gloucester, who refused to wear traditional bishop's robes, but was over-ruled by Cranmer. Where possible, Cranmer wanted to woo traditionalists by retaining harmless forms from the past; Ridley wanted reform, plain and simple.

And Queen Mary, on her accession, proved to be plain and simple too in her desire to un-do the work of the last two reigns and return her country to papal obedience

Latimer, Ridley and Cranmer, deposed from their sees, were imprisoned for two years in the city prison at Oxford, before being brought out to be tried as heretics. The three martyrs behaved characteristically. Ridley defended himself with quick wit and determination. Old 'Father Latimer,' weakened by his long imprisonment, adopted the helpless posture of a simple Christian who had forgotten all his Latin and Greek. Cranmer, who believed as genuinely in the divine right of kings as in reformed Christianity, crumpled under the inquisitor's pressure and signed six recantations of his Protestant beliefs. But in the end the two weaker men made the gestures which have caught the imagination of history. It was poor old Latimer who, as they tied him to the stake, cried out 'Be of good cheer, Master Ridley, and play the man. We shall this day by God's grace light such a candle in England, as shall never be put out.' As for Cranmer, when his turn to suffer came six months later, the inquisitors pushed him too far. As they pressed for yet another public renunciation of the reformation, the old man found his courage, recanted his recantations and at the stake thrust into the flames the 'wicked right hand' which had signed his acts of cowardice, so that it might burn first.

RICHARD WOODMAN and COMPANIONS (1555) 19th October CDC.

Not only bishops and eminent persons perished in the fires of Mary's persecutions. The Queen had begun her reign with the best of intentions, inspired by the wave of popular support which had swept her to the throne and destroyed the hapless Lady Jane Grey. At first, her restoration of communion with Rome met with broad acquiescence – the Reformation had yet to grasp the hearts of the conservative majority of the population, although it was quite clear that the church would never regain the monastic estates which had enriched the new aristocracy in the reigns of Henry and Edward. But Mary's popularity suffered badly after her marriage to Philip II, King of Spain: English people (rightly) assumed that the marriage was an attempt by Philip to secure England as part of the Hapsburg Empire. As opposition stiffened and the queen's personal life grew unhappier, her determination to root out Protestantism grew colder and harder. In the last three years of her life, over three hundred people were burned for their beliefs. The story of their sufferings entered national folklore, and Mary scored a spectacular own goal. Her short reign changed public perception of Roman Catholicism for three hundred years. Instead of being 'the good old religion of our grandparents' English people henceforth saw the church of Rome as bigoted and cruel, less a religion than a conspiracy run by cruel Spaniards and plotting priests.

Among the ordinary victims of 'Bloody Mary' the memory is liveliest of the martyrs of Lewes, who suffered in 1557. Prominent among them was Richard Woodman, a prosperous iron maker, employing one hundred people in the parish of Warbleton. Woodman first came to the attention of the authorities in 1554 when he denounced his vicar for papistical practices. He was arrested on a charge of interrupting a lawful minster in the performance of his duties, but was able to escape by claiming that as the vicar of Warbleton was married, he was not, in the eyes of the restored Roman hierarchy, a lawful minister – an intriguing example of how lines of loyalty and practice were being blurred between reformers and traditionalists. Woodman had met many advanced Protestants during his time in prison and emerged more radical than he had gone in. He began a new career as a lay preacher and his re-arrest and condemnation as a heretic were inevitable. On 22nd June 1557, he and nine others were publicly burned at Lewes. Their memory is kept alive by a Martyrs Memorial on the hill above the town, and by the spectacular annual celebration of Guy Fawkes Day in Lewes, where the local bonfire societies still manifest a robustly anti-papal spirit.

PHILIP HOWARD (1557-1595) 19th October. CDC.

The reign of Mary was cut short by her death from stomach cancer in 1558, and her half-sister Elizabeth, daughter of Anne Boleyn, ascended the throne. While by no means so enthusiastic a Protestant as her brother Edward, Elizabeth had no hesitation in repudiating her sister's Catholic Acts. She sought a form of religion capable of uniting her kingdom after twenty years of religious strife, and her Acts of Settlement and Uniformity, passed soon after her accession, established the Church of England as Catholic and reformed, repudiating Rome and basing its worshipping life on a moderate revision of Cranmer's Book of Common Prayer. For the majority of English people the new order quickly became the national Christianity, but two bodies of people were increasingly alienated from the Church of England as Elizabeth's reign progressed. One were the Puritans, the most radical reformed Christians, for whom the Prayer Book and the ceremonial and music associated with it retained dangerous vestiges of popery and the Antichrist. The other were Roman Catholics, who, while outwardly conforming to the state church, maintained the old ways, harboured priests and heard mass in secret. The stage was set for new martyrs.

Philip Howard was the son of the fourth Duke of Norfolk, the godson of Philip II of Spain. As such, he was heir to the premier dukedom of England, and his wealth was increased by his marriage in 1571 at the age of fourteen to his father's ward Anne Dacre. In the year of his marriage, Philip's world changed when his father was implicated in a plot against Elizabeth: he had proposed marriage to Mary, Queen of Scots, and planned to seize the English throne in her right. Norfolk's execution as a traitor barred his son from inheriting his title, but he was Earl of Arundel, a title inherited through his mother, and for some years lived the ruinously expensive life of a courtier – vying for the Queen's favour by lavish tournaments, masques and hunting parties. In 1582, his wife Anne became a Roman Catholic and in 1584 he followed her into the old church. Public opinion was hardening against the church of Rome. The various conspiracies to put Mary, Queen of Scots, on the throne and above all Pope Paul V's provocative condemnation of Elizabeth as a heretic (1570), which absolved her catholic subjects from their allegiance and implied that her assassination would be a meritorious act – all this made Roman Catholics seem sinister traitors, and measures against them increased. Roman priests could not legally enter England, and many of the heroic men who did come were captured and executed by the cruel traitor's death of hanging, drawing and quartering. The conversion of a prominent nobleman with a family history of treason would not be overlooked. Philip decided to flee abroad, but his ship was intercepted and in 1585 he was sent to the Tower of London. Three years later he was alleged to have asked for masses to be said for the success of the Spanish Armada and was condemned to death. The sentence was never carried out but Philip Howard remained a prisoner for the rest of his life, writing books of devotion in his cell and earning a reputation for saintly piety. His Latin carving can still be seen in the Tower: 'The more affliction we endure for Christ in this world, the more glory we shall obtain with Christ in the next.'

The diocese of Chichester commemorates Richard Woodman and Philip Howard on the same day: a nobleman and a commoner, a Protestant and a Catholic, both men of Sussex, both martyrs for their loyalty to Christ as they conceived it.

ENGLISH SAINTS AND MARTYRS OF THE REFORMATION ERA. 4th May.

Enough has been said about the course of the Reformation in England to make it clear what a divided nation sixteenth century England was. On both sides of the religious divide, protestants and catholics were prepared to risk death to bear witness to the truth as they saw it. We acknowledge their heroism, but from our perspective it is impossible to sympathise with their willingness to inflict death on others. We take religious pluralism for granted, and it is hard to think one's way back into a world where it was inconceivable that a subject might differ from the official religion of his country and still be a loyal patriot. The Pope still called catholics to acknowledge his claim to secular lordship over Christendom. Henry VIII and Elizabeth regarded the religion they established as both symbol and test of their subjects' loyalty to their regime. In an age where religious differences were debated with passionate conviction, all sides saw toleration of heretical beliefs as acquiescence in the certain damnation of those who refused the truth. In the next part of our story, we shall see, first how the Puritan pressure for more thorough-going reform exploded into civil war and regicide; and then how slowly and painfully England felt its way to an acceptance of religious difference as something that need not threaten national unity.

JOHN CALVIN (1509-1564) 26th May.

What was it that powered the reformers, made them so certain that they were doing God's work by dismantling the medieval church and rebuilding from first principles, gave them the courage to endure fire and torture in the firm conviction that heaven awaited them?

Luther's initial challenge to the vested interests of the church had echoed around Europe, but his direct influence in shaping reformed churches was largely limited to Scandinavia and his native Germany. In France, Switzerland, the Low Countries and the British Isles, reformers looked for inspiration to a Frenchman who nearly became a Catholic priest and whose logical, careful mind produced writing which redefined Christianity for a new world.

Jean Calvin was a bourgeois, educated at Paris and destined by his family for a career in the church, where a comfortable canonry had been reserved for him. We know very little about the circumstances in which this good catholic boy became a convert to evangelical Protestantism, but in 1535 Calvin fled from Paris, where the catholic authorities were stamping down on reform and took up residence in Geneva, the Swiss city state which was to be his home for most of the rest of his life. Here, in 1536, he published the first version of 'Institutes of the Christian Religion,' the book which made his reputation. He continued to expand and revise this book for twenty years, and the final version, published in 1559, is a huge, comprehensive guide to Reformation theology. Calvin was obsessively hard-working, rising at four every morning to get to his desk, and finally undermining his health by his refusal to give himself any rest.

The 'Institutes' made an immediate impact and Calvin was head-hunted by the reformer William Farel, who invited him to share his visionary task: to transform the city of Geneva into heaven on earth, a model Christian community formed on biblical principles and biblical norms. The city council had already expelled the Catholic bishop and stripped the churches of the trappings of popish idolatry. Now Farel and Calvin built a new church in their place. Their demands were too extreme for the people of Geneva, who threw them out in 1538, but three years later Calvin was invited to return, and from them on his influence and authority in Geneva were unchallengeable.

Calvin's church rejected bishops and all the medieval hierarchy of celibate priests and monks. Instead, a council of ministers were elected by the people and governed the church with the help of lay deacons and elders. The Presbyterian system had been born.

The City Council kept its own authority, separate from Calvin and the ministers, but city and church worked together to create a system of moral surveillance and discipline which they believed would create a truly godly community. There was no distinction between church and state, nor between private and public life. The minsters intervened to investigate, and the council to punish, every conceivable form of vice and folly – adultery, gossip and slander, domestic quarrels, most addictive or wasteful pleasures. Geneva gained a Europe-wide reputation for solid, serious, uncompromising gospel living, and reformers visited the city and were impressed, carrying Calvin's vision back to their homelands.

To open the 'Institutes' is to enter a different world from the complex, technical Aristotelian analysis of Thomas Aquinas, or the intensely subjective meditations on prayer of the medieval mystics, and immediately makes it clear why Calvinism spread so successfully among the intellectuals of northern and western Europe. Apart from a profound veneration for Augustine and a sneaking fondness for Bernard of Clairvaux, Calvin has little use for the traditional authorities. Instead, he bases his whole thought on Scripture, which he reads and interprets literally, dissecting verses and books with a clear rationality which foreshadows the scientific thought which formed modern Europe. Calvin, one feels, would not have opposed Galileo, and his style, accurate, spare and expressing a wholly logical theology is far more readable than the rambling anger which powers many reformation divines.

It is Calvin's thought, rather than his style, which is likely to shock most modern Christians. It is a stark account of reality which refuses to evade or soften any of the harder, harsher verses of the Bible. For Calvin, the God who hardened Pharaoh's heart to lead him to certain destruction in the Red Sea, and commanded the massacre of Amalekite women and children, was absolutely the same as the Father revealed in Jesus Christ; the medieval allegorical readings, which allow the reader to soften Old Testament cruelty, are dismissed as 'frivolous' (a favourite Calvin term of abuse). The distinctive doctrines of Calvinism have often been summed up in the mnemonic TULIP: Total depravity; Unconditional election; Limited atonement; Irresistible grace; Perseverance of the Saints.

By Total depravity is meant, not that human beings are totally evil, but that there is no part of human nature untouched by the Fall. Reason as well as emotion, logical choices as well as passionate desires, all are corrupted and alienated from God, so that human beings have no power whatever to contribute to their own salvation. Unconditional election means that God has already chosen which souls he has elected to be saved, and in this choice of God, human merit plays no part. God is free, for his own unfathomable reasons, to bring some to heaven, others to hell. Limited atonement is the terrifying but logical development of this strong doctrine of predestination. If God has already chosen who is to be saved, then it is nonsense to say that Jesus died for the sins of the whole world – his saving work is limited to those for whom God wishes its benefits to be available. Irresistible grace proclaims the sovereignty of God in another way: no human being can save himself, and similarly no human being can prevent God saving when he chooses to put forward his grace. And the Perseverance of saints promises that through every temptation and trial God will give his elect the power to win through victorious.

For Calvin, every event in life, large or small, must be accepted as the direct action of God. Nothing happens without his choosing it to happen. He illustrates predestination by reflecting on how, from birth, one child will be born to a mother with full breasts, another to a dry-breasted woman, ensuring that it will grow malnourished. In Calvin's universe, there is no room for misfortune or unhappy accidents. God has actively willed and providentially created the situation of both these babies, the healthy and the sickly.

It is hard at first for a modern reader to understand how this harsh creed had such a profound effect on so many people, empowering the Dutch to rise against their Spanish oppressors; drawing one sixth of the population of France into reformed churches, despite the ever present threat of persecution; inspiring the Scots to banish their Catholic Queen Mary and to build their own Presbyterian kirk; and driving the English Puritans to fight against and execute their King; not to mention the heroic endurance of Puritans like the Pilgrim Fathers who crossed the Atlantic in an attempt to found cities more purely Christian even than Geneva.

First, the 'Institutes' bear powerful testimony to the deep anxiety produced in people of certain temperaments by medieval Christianity. If forgiveness came by confession of sins, how could you be sure that your confession had been full enough, accurate enough to merit salvation? If the stain of sin must be cleansed by penances, pilgrimages and indulgences, how could you ever be certain that you had done enough to earn God's friendship? Christians tormented by such scruples reacted with relief and joy to the message that in Christ God had done everything and nothing could be added or taken away by human effort.

Then, in a dangerous world, where child mortality, plague, famine and war were never far away, it was an unspeakable comfort to know that every event, no matter how cruel it seemed, was part of the master work of a God who promised that all would work for good for those who were to be saved. Certainly, a peculiar anxiety developed among people desperately trying to work out what divine Providence was doing in their experience of tragedy and grief, but on the whole, a belief in God's direct, unchallengeable action in the world helped many to deal with chaos and random disorder.

Then, the egalitarianism of Calvinism was exciting for the new bourgeois classes, eager for success and resentful of the assumptions of aristocratic hierarchy; to see how entrenched hierarchy was, one has only to reflect on the way words like 'noble' and 'villainous,' which originally described social classes, have become loaded with moral assumptions. Against the medieval belief in merit by birth, Calvinists could set a world where no one, rich or poor, noble or bourgeois, had any merit except by God's gracious election, and where a shoe-maker or housewife, inspired by the Holy Spirit, might rebuke a bishop or a king. All sorts of energies were unloosed by this re-evaluation of who mattered in society.

Finally, Calvin, like all the reformers, relocated the centre of godly living. The saints lived, not in celibate monasteries, nor even in churches – Calvin was curiously relaxed about Sabbath day observance, correctly distinguishing that Jewish Sabbath laws applied to Saturday and had no direct relevance to Christian Sunday worship – but in the home, the workshop, the law-court and the library. Ordinary Christians who became Calvinists found a new dignity and worth in labour which aristocratic clergy dismissed as 'servile works.' The 'Protestant Work Ethic', paradoxically, enriched and empowered people who believed that works were of no avail to propitiate a holy God.

Later in our story we shall see something of the spiritual quality of those who were trained by Calvinist theology. Our next step, however, is to survey the movement known as the 'Counter-Reformation.' Not all reformers believed the Pope to be Antichrist nor wished to sever their links with the past. But the saints who remained in communion with Rome transformed medieval Catholicism just as surely as those who felt called by God to reject that communion.

PART SEVENTEEN. COUNTER-REFORMATION.

IGNATIUS LOYOLA (1491-1556) 31st July.
In those same fertile 1530s, while Henry VIII removed his kingdom from papal obedience and John Calvin laboured over his 'Institutes,' a group of young idealists at the University of Paris took a vow to travel together to the Holy Land, there to live as hermits in perfect imitation of Christ. Their leader was a noble Spaniard, Inigo or Ignatius Loyola, destined to found one of the most famous and controversial of all the catholic orders.

Ignatius was always an idealist. Reared on the Spanish traditions of chivalry, honour and holy war, his desire was to excel as a soldier and gallant courtier. In 1521, he commanded the Spanish garrison of Pampeluna, then being besieged by the French. Ignatius led his men with dash and bravado, until his leg was broken by a cannon-ball. The garrison surrendered, and the French, impressed by his panache, took him to his home castle to recuperate. There he endured agonising operations on his leg, which left him with a permanent limp, and a long, dull convalescence. He asked for books of chivalry, but there were none in the castle. Desperate with boredom, he began to read what was available; lives of Christ and the saints, and gradually he became gripped. By the time he was well enough to leave the castle, his dreams had changed. He no longer yearned for military glory, but to outdo all the saints in penance and prayer.

Loyola wandered for the next few years; it took time for him to focus what his new vision was calling him to. He went on pilgrimage to the shrine of Our Lady of Montserrat and left his armour and sword there, a sign of his determination to use only Christ's weapons, humility, obedience, acceptance of suffering. He withdrew to the cave of Manresa, where for eight months he lived a solitary life of prayer. Here, he discovered how to use his vivid romantic daydreams in spiritual formation, a form of meditation which became his distinctive contribution to Christian spirituality. Building on the work of medieval Franciscans like Bonaventure, Ignatius developed his Spiritual Exercises. By a concentrated effort of the imagination, the worshipper constructs an incident from

Christ's life, dwelling on each detail, applying the five senses – what did the stable, the fishing boat, Mary Magdalene's jar of ointment, smell like? Over time, the object of the exercises is to let Christ's life become so real that not only the emotions but the will and reason are converted to a Christ-like perspective. The Exercises, dummy-run by Ignatius in his cave, were to have a great future in the formation of the Jesuit character.

After abortive attempts at teaching (he was arrested by the Spanish Inquisition) and pilgrimage (he was forbidden to travel to Jerusalem, for fear of the Turks) Ignatius arrived in Paris in 1528 where he studied theology. Here he made the friendships which were to be so central to his mission. He shared a room with a young Navarrese nobleman, Francis Xavier, who, by odd coincidence, was the brother of two of the captains at Pampeluna who had been responsible for laming Loyola. Xavier disliked Loyola on sight – poor, dirty, ageing, limping and with a distasteful addiction to prayer, he was not a suitable friend for a gallant man about town with a fortune to make. Yet over the months they lived together, Ignatius won Xavier's respect and eventually his devoted discipleship. He was among the six who took the vow to travel together to the Holy Land.

The companions got no further than Venice, where they discovered that hostilities with the Turks were at such a pitch that no boats could be had. They gravitated to Rome where Ignatius Loyola was ordained and celebrated his first mass in 1539. Rome was to be Ignatius Loyola's base for the rest of his life. In 1540 he finally found the great work for which he had been searching – with papal encouragement he founded the Society of Jesus, the Jesuits.

Ignatius had tried to be a knight errant, a teacher, a contemplative hermit and a crusader: his order combined elements of all those vocations. It was radically different from the medieval orders which preceded it. Jesuits had no distinctive habit or dress; they were under no obligation to recite the lengthy offices which formed the spiritual cornerstone of the older orders; they were to live in the world, not separated in convents. All of this was designed to free them to be a missionary order, going out into a Europe split by the Protestant Reformation, and into the world beyond Europe where the majority of the human race still knew nothing of Jesus. The Jesuits were not subject to the authority of diocesan bishops but reported directly to the Pope. They became the storm-troopers of the counter-Reformation. By the end of Ignatius' life, thousands of men had vowed themselves to this new way of serving Christ, and Jesuits were working in every continent of the world. They quickly acquired a reputation as educators, and Jesuit schools were sought after by Catholic aristocrats and gentry. Their bold willingness to face danger led to their infiltrating countries such as England where Roman Catholicism was outlawed; many of the mission priests who risked death to keep the old religion alive were Jesuits.

Ignatius himself proved to be a formidable organiser, building up a central administration for the order at Rome and devoting himself to directing his strange new empire – hundreds of his letters survive, addressed to every part of the world on every conceivable topic. He insisted on rigorous obedience, could be harsh when his decisions were questioned, but remained very much a father to the order, commanding affection and personal loyalty as well as respect.

The efficiency, rapid spread and single-mindedness of the Jesuits, have aroused suspicion and dislike at every period of their history – both from Protestants, who had lurid tales to tell of their misuse of the confessional and their involvement in political assassinations; and from fellow Catholics, jealous of their move into educational and missionary fields regarded as the preserve of older orders. But that the Roman Catholic church emerged in the sixteenth and seventeenth centuries from the medieval corruption and domination by vested interest which had defeated the best efforts of great Popes and saints, was due in large part to Ignatius Loyola. No less radically than Luther, he called the church back to a vision of holiness and a dedication to Christ.

FRANCIS XAVIER (1506-1552) 3rd December.
The Jesuit order was less than a year old when Ignatius Loyola and Francis Xavier, those most faithful of friends, were separated for ever. In 1541, the Portuguese ambassador was leaving Rome for his native land and asked the Pope to supply missionaries for the King of Portugal's expanding overseas dominions. The Pope consulted

Loyola and Francis Xavier was sent. He left Lisbon on a voyage round Africa to India which took over a year, and never returned to Europe.

We have seen how in the wake of Christopher Columbus the Spanish had conquered, colonised and converted South America, and the appalling suffering of the natives which ensued. In this same Age of Discovery, Spain's great rival Portugal, while establishing a presence in Brazil, was exploring in the opposite direction. Portuguese navigators rounded the Cape of Good Hope, built trading posts in Mozambique and Angola, and founded a sea route to India. In Portuguese Goa, with its brutal mix of fortune hunters, slave-traders, drunks, pirates and pioneers, Francis Xavier landed, with a simple unambitious aim, to convert the people of India to Christianity.

There was, in fact, an indigenous Christian church in south-west India, for centuries totally isolated from the west, and claiming descent from the apostolic mission of St Thomas. Xavier sought to rebuild morale amongst these poor people, despised by their Hindu compatriots and savagely exploited by the Portuguese. His tactics were simple in the extreme; he would arrive in a village, display pictures of Christ and the Virgin Mary, give a simple explanation via an interpreter, teach the children the Lord's Prayer and Creed by heart, and baptise hundreds who responded to his call. He realised too well that this sketchy beginning to faith would need long-term support to grow to maturity, and founded a college at Goa to train Indian priests, but his priority remained to cover as much ground as he could and introduce as many people as possible to the basics of Christian faith. He lived simply, commanding respect from people whose Hindu holy men also lived ascetically; sleeping on the ground, barefoot and underfed, his reputation for holiness was his greatest evangelistic asset.

After three years, he moved on to Malaya and the Dutch East Indies. The years he spent there he regarded as his happiest, despite constant danger and appalling physical conditions. He was shipwrecked, attacked by the natives, lived off rice and water, and spent long months up country in Borneo among cannibals and head-hunters. It took three years for a letter to come through from Ignatius in Rome. Then, in 1549, Xavier set off for Japan.

He had prepared carefully for this next stage in his missionary journey, interviewing Japanese students and attempting to learn a Japanese version of St Matthew's gospel by heart. But he found Japan a much harder mission-field to crack. He admired the Samurai rulers of the islands – their warrior code had much in common with the knightly ethos which had formed him and Ignatius Loyola – but the ragged cassock, the bare feet and beggar's diet which had commanded reverence in India, invited merely ridicule and embarrassment in Japan. Xavier rethought his strategy, and reinvented himself as the well-dressed ambassador of the King of Portugal, waiting on the local ruler and presenting him with the wonders of western technology, a clock and a pair of spectacles. Now secure of upper-class patronage, Xavier began to make converts. The meeting of the two cultures proved challenging to both parties. Xavier was shaken by the distress of his converts, when, steeped as they were in Japanese reverence for their ancestors, they were informed that all those revered names, because they had died unbaptized, were certainly burning in Hell. Some discreet tinkering took place, enabling the cult of ancestor-worship and catholic veneration of the saints to cross-fertilise in ways calculated to offend purists on both sides. But Xavier's extraordinary restlessness drove him ever on to new projects, and the Japanese church was only two years old when he left to prepare for an assault on the greatest and most alien civilisation in all Asia. India and Japan were not enough: Francis Xavier wanted China.

The Chinese empire was almost entirely sealed off from the outside world and not all Xavier's persistence and adroitness could procure him a passport. For months he camped out on an island opposite Canton, gazing longingly across at the vast forbidden land. At last he bribed a Chinese ship to take him across illegally. During the difficult voyage it became clear that he was dangerously ill, and he landed in China only to die on the beach, attended by his oriental servants. With great fidelity, these men preserved his body and carried it back to Goa, where he was buried. In ten years of ceaseless travel and unquenchable energy, he had established the Christian church in three great Asian civilisations and died trying to enter a fourth.

MARTYRS OF JAPAN 1597. 6th February.

Before returning to Europe, we may look forward a generation at the tragic yet heroic fate which befell the church in Japan. The seeds planted by St Francis Xavier bore spectacular fruit. Japanese people came forward for baptism in their hundreds, and as contacts between Japan and Europe intensified, scores of missionaries, Jesuit, Dominican and Franciscan, arrived in the country to further the work; nor was it long before native Japanese were ordained to the priesthood. All was going well until the Shogun Hideyoshi underwent a dramatic change of policy towards the west. He feared that the newcomers were destroying the essential Japanese way of life, and he put increasing barriers in the way of foreigners landing or doing business in Japan. Christianity, as one of the principal carriers of alien ideas into Japan, was suspect and, before long, fiercely persecuted. In 1597, at Nagasaki, twenty-six priests and friars, including several Japanese, were crucified in fierce mockery of their holy pictures. Eye-witness relate the courage and joy with which the martyrs met their fate, praying, praising God and exhorting the people from their crosses, until finally, to the accompaniment of groans from the crowd, the soldiers ended their sufferings with bamboo lances. But the persecution now unleashed was organised and determined. Clergy and leaders were martyred and the baptised were forced to renounce their faith publicly by spitting on crucifixes or by trampling underfoot specially made ceramic tiles painted with the Virgin and Child. Meanwhile the ports were closed and contact with the mother churches in Europe and India severed. The strain was too much for a new church to bear. The Japanese persecution is one of the few in church history which succeeded in virtually destroying a flourishing church. When Japan finally re-opened its ports to foreigners in the late nineteenth century, only tiny pockets of Christian believers remained in the country. One of the great might-have-beens of history is how Asian history would have played out had Japan become as Christian as, say, the Philippines.

CHARLES BORROMEO (1538-1584) 4th November CDC.
The foundation of the Jesuit order heralded the beginning of what is often called the Counter-Reformation, a movement of spiritual renewal within the Roman Catholic church, which reformed the old medieval structure as radically as the Protestant reformers did in their separated churches. The late sixteenth and early seventeenth century saw a remarkable number of men and women of great gifts and heroic sanctity, who transformed the Roman church from within. Had people of this calibre arisen a hundred years earlier, would the radical protests of Luther and Calvin have been needed? We shall examine three pairs and a trio of saints whose lives encapsulate the Counter-Reformation, first in Italy, then in Spain, the New World, and finally in France.

The young Charles Borromeo looks at first sight like an example of all that was wrong with the Renaissance church. Born of a noble family in Milan, related by marriage to the powerful Medici family, he was the second son and therefore destined from childhood for a career in the church. At the age of twelve he was made Abbot of Arona. There was no expectation that he should reside in his monastery or contribute anything to the life of the monks; every expectation that he should spend the abbot's annual income of £13,000. Then, when Charles was twenty-two, his Medici uncle was elected to the Papacy and immediately made his favourite nephew a cardinal, administrator of the huge archdiocese of Milan and bearer of a sheaf of other important portfolios, including supervision of the church in the Spanish Netherlands, Portugal and Switzerland, and responsibility for the Franciscan and Carmelite Orders and the Knights of Malta. All this was handed to a young man fresh from university, not even yet ordained to the priesthood. Had Luther been Italian, the pamphlets would have written themselves.

Yet all was not as it appeared. Though nepotism had made Charles Borromeo's fortune, the young man had the organisational talent to make full use of the opportunities that had been given him. Moreover, from boyhood, he had been marked by a deep moral earnestness. Throughout his college days he had refused to spend one penny of his abbot's revenues on himself, giving it all to the poor and often going hungry, when his father, quite understandably, declined to give him another income to supplement the princely one family influence had already obtained for him.

Ever since 1534, the Renaissance Popes had been making sporadic attempts at church reform through the Council of Trent, which reconvened for its final sessions in 1562. The young Cardinal Borromeo attended and helped to shape the Tridentine decrees. Inevitably, in that age of religious hatred, much of the council's energy was devoted to staking out catholic positions against Lutheran and Calvinist heretics. Catholic doctrine on the relationship of good works to saving faith and the nature of the Eucharist was reformulated in an aggressively, anti-Protestant manner. Protestant monarchs were excommunicated and those who had hoped that the council would help heal the divisions of Christendom were disappointed. But the Council also gave much time to pastoral matters, looking at the training, lifestyle and duties of the clergy. Enforcing the new programme would take up much of Charles' energies during his time as Archbishop of Milan. Everywhere the clergy were called back to their duties and to stricter ways of life. Monasteries and convents, which had become boarding houses for the gentry, found their luxuries stripped away, regulations about worldly visitors enforced, new regimes of prayer and fasting imposed. Parish clergy were required to be celibate, to live in their parishes, to be educated, to train to hear confessions and preach sermons. Charles opened some of the earliest ever Sunday schools, and gave great energy to establishing schools, seminaries and hospitals. There was plenty of money for such projects, once wealthy benefices and sinecures had been pruned. Inevitably vast vested interests were disgruntled by this determined assault on their privileges and in 1567 an aggrieved lay brother, from an order firmly recalled to its foundation vows of poverty, went so far as to disguise himself as a servant, enter the archbishop's house, and shoot him in the back as he knelt at Evening Prayer. Fortunately, the bullet did not penetrate his thick clothing.

However hated by the church's elite, the common people of Milan loved their archbishop and hailed him as a living saint. When plague struck the city in 1572, the archbishop made his will and refused to leave town with the rest of the rich. He stayed with his people throughout the affliction, visiting the sick, organising food supplies and hospital services, praying and inspiring. By the time he died, his reforms were irreversible, morale had been restored to a clergy newly dedicated to service and self-denial and many ordinary people were rediscovering living Christian faith.

PHILIP NERI (1515-1595) 26th May.

In 1578 Charles Borromeo sent a letter to Rome to his lifelong friend Philip Neri, a simple priest, asking him to send some of his brothers to found an Oratory in Milan. Philip Neri refused – he did not believe it was the right time – and the incident caused a coolness between the two. Deeply though they loved each other, the two men could not have been more different. Philip Neri, a middle-class boy with no family fortune to back him, was a stranger to the world of aristocratic prestige and power where Borromeo moved as a native, and where Charles devoted his life to administrative reform, Philip Neri remained by choice outside the official structures of the church. Nevertheless, his influence was so great that before his death he was hailed as the Apostle of Rome.

Philip Neri was born in Florence. As a small boy he narrowly escaped death in a bizarre accident, when a donkey fell through a trap-door into the cellar where he was playing. With hindsight, his friends saw his preservation as providential. He was sixteen when, sponsored by a wealthy uncle, he arrived in Rome to study. Shortly after his arrival Philip, who was a remarkably pretty lad, was propositioned by a group of older students. Philip, not content with rebuffing their advances, so spoke that the group finished by spending the night in prayer together. All his life, Philip Neri remained acutely sensitive to sexual sin; he said that he could smell un-confessed unchastity and those who came to him for confession were frequently confounded by the supernatural way in which he put his finger on their concealed sins, although given that much of his work was with Italian boys aged fourteen to nineteen, preoccupation with sex was probably not that hard to diagnose.

It was not only the sexual promiscuity of Rome which shocked Philip, but its blatant juxtaposition of religion and debauchery. Everyone, from the Pope to the Guild of Prostitutes, took part in elaborate, theatrical religious ceremonies, and then relaxed in outrageous parties adorned by all the wealth and artistic resources of the high Renaissance. Blasphemy added a fashionable frisson to revels which saw the Pope dress as Satan at midnight feasts in the catacombs, and the mistresses of cardinals drinking toasts in the Communion plate. Philip's reaction to all this was to withdraw into a self-chosen discipline of poverty, prayer and simple living. He was persuaded, very reluctantly, to accept ordination but, in a city overstaffed with priests, never held a regular beneficed post. Instead, he haunted the great churches of Rome, spending long hours in prayer, and assisting when asked with the sacraments. His devotion to the Blessed Sacrament was so great that he could never celebrate without weeping; at the end of his life the tears had worn grooves in his cheeks.

Philip Neri's great gift was his charm. He could talk frankly and winningly to anybody: everyone was his friend. His special gift was for getting alongside young men and he soon had a devoted band of followers attempting to share his way of life. He refused to organise anything that might resemble a religious order, but despite the lack of formality, or perhaps because of it, his reputation spread. He was given the use of a church, and there his daily sermons drew huge crowds, many of whom stayed to benefit from his great gifts as a spiritual director. He acquired a reputation as a miracle-worker; those he prayed for got better. In the end, pressure of numbers forced organisation upon him and he founded the Oratory, a loose company of priests who continued to live and minster in the world, but encouraged each other by a shared rule of life and by frequent meetings together. Like many Puritans (Calvin and Oliver Cromwell are two other examples) the only art which Philip Neri really delighted in was music, and the Oratory gradually developed a unique form of musical meditation, where a sacred story was given an extensive presentation by a chorus, orchestra and soloists. The new form took its name from the place where it was presented, and the Oratorio was born.

Under Philip's guidance, the people of Rome rediscovered earnestness in their religion and priests with a serious longing for holiness and a concern for mission, especially to the poor, began to reshape Christianity in the holy city.

TERESA OF AVILA (1515-1582) 15th October.

The same quest for renewal and holiness was being conducted in Spain, a very different place to Rome. In the sixteenth century Spain was the wealthiest country in Europe, its kings enriched by the fabulous treasures brought across the Atlantic from their American possessions. By dynastic marriage and conquest, Spain also ruled Sicily, Naples, Milan and the Netherlands, and the Kings of Spain were cousins of the Holy Roman Emperors. Yet Spain, proud, punctilious, dominated by a code of honour, was also a place ruled by shame and fear. First the Moors, descendants of the Muslim conquerors, were expelled, then the Jews too were exiled; and the many who had Moorish or Jewish blood in their families lived under constant suspicion of not being true Spaniards or true Christians. The Spanish Inquisition was already infamous, and the knee-jerk reaction of the inquisitors was to regard any unusual piety or enthusiasm as suspicious, evidence of private judgement which could lead to heresy or Protestantism.

Teresa of Avila was born into a family which, because of Jewish ancestry, had to try extra hard to demonstrate their impeccable, loyal Catholicism. Religion was the atmosphere in which the children lived, as were the tales of knight errantry which so entranced the young Ignatius Loyola. At the age of seven, Teresa persuaded her older brother Rodrigo to run away with her. Their plan was to travel to Africa and be martyred by the Moors, thus gaining the golden city promised by Christ to his faithful. Fortunately, the children were intercepted outside the city gates and brought home by their uncle. Teresa grew up to be a high-spirited, talkative, intelligent and determined girl, in a society where these qualities were not necessarily regarded as virtues in young women. She certainly seems to have frightened herself by her appetite for life, for in her late teens she offered herself as a nun in the strict Carmelite order, although, as she herself later confessed, 'I was most hostile to the life of a nun.' During her early adult years, Teresa lived in a state of constant tension. She found the routine of convent life boring, was frequently depressed, yet was constantly drawn back to the frustrating, incomprehensible work of contemplative prayer. Her physical health was dreadful – she suffered from an unending series of fevers and migraines and was often physically unable to work. Oddest of all were the visions and spiritual experiences which came to her against her will. She tried her hardest to repress and hide them, for they disturbed and frightened her, and her confessors, unable to make sense of these phenomena, confused her further with bad advice. She describes these experiences carefully in her writings and struggles to articulate principles for interpreting them: are they gifts from God, delusions of the devil or tricks of an over-heated imagination? Many saints have had odd experiences in prayer; few have been so level-headed in evaluating them as Teresa. Her most famous experience was of being pierced by a spear of desire which made her swoon with pain – an incident immortalised by Bernini's sculpture. Her oddest experience, which is attested by unimpeachable eye-witnesses, was frequent levitation. She was physically lifted off the ground in prayer, a phenomenon which exasperated her, as it made her a sideshow and prevented her getting on with her work.

All of this intense inner life was being lived out in the ladylike context of a convent where few of the nuns had any genuine vocation to the life of prayer and where most were only too glad to take advantage of the traditional exemptions from poverty, fasting and solitude, which had gradually crept in. Nuns had their own little flats, tastefully furnished, where suppers to their own taste were brought them by their personal servants, and where visitors of both sexes brought them the gossip of the town. Teresa and a few others were increasingly disturbed by this genteel, undemanding version of monasticism, and finally, in 1567, she and some companions broke away to form a new convent, strict, unreformed, 'uncalced' or shoeless. Poverty, silence, prayers, austerity, were once again to be taken seriously, as in the days of Benedict and Bernard.

In her breakaway convent at Avila, San Jose, Teresa found peace; at last her ardent nature could repose upon Christ, whom she honoured as her king – he is most frequently referred to in her writings as 'His Majesty.' But in her fifties, after an adult life entirely spent in an enclosed convent, she broke out into an astonishing whirl of creative activity. As news of her reformed Carmelite community spread through Spain, she received requests from nuns everywhere to help them escape from the stultifying triviality of their life and to re-conquer the spiritual heights. Teresa founded thirteen more reformed convents, and this work kept her constantly travelling, under the harsh Spanish sun, over mountain tracks and across parched plains. She and her nuns attempted to maintain their enclosure by travelling in closed wagons; they must have been stifling. Teresa remained fiery, even in her relationship with God. On one occasion, a mule bolted and Teresa was tipped into a ditch. 'God!' she is said to have cried, as she emerged from the thorns and nettles and shook her fist at heaven, 'If this is how you treat your friends, no wonder you have so few of them.' At the same time, Teresa was requested by her spiritual director to write an account of her inner life and so to her demanding administrative and pastoral work was added a huge labour of writing. Her great books, the 'Way of Perfection' and 'The Interior Castle' show every sign of being written in haste, in moments snatched from other duties. At times the writing is almost 'stream of consciousness' as Teresa tells us about her headaches, the sudden calls away from her desk, which impede the flow of her thought. The books strike a modern reader as strange, with the oddly hierarchical arrangement of states of prayer, each carefully differentiated by its symptoms. But it is impossible to deny that when we read Teresa we keep company with someone who knew what she was talking about, with the wisdom and experience to distinguish emotionalism and self-deception from the true work of grace in the soul.

For all her uncompromising devotion to the hard Carmelite way of self-denial, Teresa remained warm-hearted, a lover of life, and loved as well as feared by her nuns. She scolded them unmercifully, but then spent evenings with them playing the guitar and singing. She forsook luxury, living on a sparse vegetarian diet, but writes with childlike pleasure to friends outside the order when a Christmas treat of fruit or sweets arrives. In ten years she burnt herself out. At the age of sixty-seven she was sent for urgently by her friend the Duchess of Alba, to pray at the bedside of her daughter-in-law, who was in difficult labour. Although very ill, and crippled by a broken arm which refused to heal, Teresa set off and travelled fast. She arrived to hear that the baby had been safely delivered. 'Thank God, she said. 'This saint will no longer be needed.' She was put firmly to bed – 'It is twenty years since I went to bed so early' – and died a few days later. Her writings on prayer are so theologically significant that she is one of a tiny handful of women to have been declared a 'Doctor of the church' by the Roman Catholic hierarchy.

JOHN OF THE CROSS (1542-1591) 14th December.

In 1567, just as Teresa was entering the most fruitful period of her life, she met a young priest, newly ordained, who had come to Medina to celebrate his first mass. The spiritual antennae of the ardent elderly woman twitched as she spoke to this young man, so pitifully small and thin, whose deep, dark eyes indicated that he lived in the same world as she did. She invited him to join her entourage and the following year they travelled together to Valladolid. John was learning from a mistress of the spiritual life how to found and sustain a discalced Carmelite community. One of history's great spiritual friendships had begun.

John of the Cross, as he was later known, was the son of a silk weaver. His father died when he was two, and his mother brought up her three sons in genteel poverty. John's intelligence was spotted when he attended a small charity school, and a benefactor, Don Alonso Alvarez, sponsored him as a pupil of the Jesuit academy of Medina. Don Alonso was also impressed by young John's unusual leisure-time activity, helping out as a volunteer at the local hospital where he displayed remarkable tenderness, tact and resilience in his handling of the sick.

When he completed his school years, John was offered a good chaplaincy by Don Alonso, and his Jesuit tutors were also keen to enlist him in their order. John turned his back on both and, 21 years old, entered the Carmelite order. He was sent to study theology at Salamanca University, but for all his academic brilliance he knew that scholarship was not his true calling. After the meeting with St Teresa he was left in no doubt as to what his vocation was: if there had been doubt, that imperious lady speedily removed it. He was to do for men's convents what she was beginning to do for women's: reform the Carmelite order.

Initially John acted as spiritual director of the community at Avila. This included hearing the confessions of the great Teresa herself. Teresa was delighted; at last she had found a priest who understood her mystical life and could give her useful guidance. Meanwhile, resentment of the reformers was growing and those who did not dare attack Teresa found John more vulnerable. He was at the centre of a complex political wrangle over licenses, areas of jurisdiction and rights to officiate. When the papal nuncio, who protected John, died in 1577, his enemies pounced. He was found guilty of a technical breach of discipline and handed over to the superiors of his order for punishment.

It is difficult to credit the vindictiveness with which John was treated by the unreformed friars of his own Carmelite order. In the middle of a winter's night, a group of soldiers broke into his quarters, handcuffed and blindfolded him, and took him away to the monastery in Toledo. Here he was kept in solitary confinement in a dark cellar, with no light or heat. He was not allowed to change his clothes, was fed on bread and water, and was brought out each day to be flogged in front of the community. Teresa was desperately pulling strings to get him released, but he remained in this tiny room for nine months, until finally he managed to escape by slowly loosening the screws on his door lock. One night he was able to knock the door open, and let himself down the convent walls on a rope made from strips of blanket. He hid in a nearby convent of Teresa's nuns, and then lived secretly in a local hospital. Eventually he was appointed by his friends to a remote reformed convent in the mountains of Andalusia, where he was relatively safe from re-arrest.

John kept himself sane during this terrible ordeal by writing poetry in his head. When he was able to do so, he wrote down his compositions and they are among the classics of Spanish literature. Writing in traditional ballad forms (his poems were intended to be sung) John used the imagery of Spanish love poetry to create an intense, highly emotional description of his affair with God. The poems breathe Spain: hot nights, scented gardens, rugged mountains over which goatherds wander, desert streams delighting the senses by their cool refreshment, in the midst of which the beloved ardently seeks her spouse. The most obvious biblical source of inspiration is the Song of Solomon, but John decisively reimagines the ancient Hebrew eroticism and makes it his own.

In 1579, Philip II King of Spain intervened to heal the breach between the two Carmelite orders. The discalced acquired a provincial of their own, who was sympathetic to what they were trying to achieve. The danger of persecution receded. John was able to do what he loved best. He founded monasteries, acted as spiritual director to a host of seekers, lay and clerical, prayed, and wrote. His prose works are largely commentaries on the poems, interpreting them line by line in accordance with an austere theology of self-denial and renunciation of the senses. The phrase always associated with St John of the Cross is 'the dark night of the soul.' By this, John was describing something more than the experience of depression or alienation from self. His version of Christianity was one in which Jesus deliberately withdrew himself from the perception of his lovers, taking with him all joy and certainty. This was a process of purgation, in which the soul, forced to face its own nothingness, grew in love through the experience of waiting helplessly for God. The true saint learns to love God for himself, not for any happiness or gifts God may give.

John's gentle, forgiving spirit won the love of most who met him, but there must have been something in that malnourished body, those big pleading eyes and that total refusal to fight back that awakened the inner bully in some men. In his last illness he was again treated with rigid harshness by the prior of the convent where he was staying. After terrible sufferings, he called on the day of his death for the cruel prior and humbly asked his forgiveness for the trouble he had caused. The other man, reduced to tears, became a changed character, but it was too late to save John, who died the death he had prayed for, isolated, dishonoured, alone with Jesus.

MARTIN DE PORRES (1579-1639) 3rd November.

In the hundred years or so which had passed since Christopher Columbus made his voyage across the Atlantic, Spain's hold on South America had consolidated. Although the brutality and genocidal violence of the conquest had subsided, Spanish America was still a brash, get-rich quick, frontier-land, in which little pity was shown to those who fell behind in the race for self-aggrandisement. On the surface, the imposition of Spanish culture was total. Spanish was the dominant language, Catholic Christianity the dominant religion. Yet South America was a continent of deep racial divisions. The Indians, original inhabitants of the land, lived in servitude to the Spanish ruling class, and below them again were the thousands of blacks, slave and free, brought over from Africa to do the heavy work on plantations and mines which killed the native Indians. Despite the witness of Bartolome de las Casas and others, the church was infected with the racism of the society it helped to shape. The Dominican order in Peru refused to accept as members anyone who had a black or Indian parent. In living memory debates had been held to determine whether non-Europeans had souls.

In the 1570s, a Spanish hidalgo disgraced himself by not only taking a black mistress but also fathering two children on her, Martin and Joanna. Juan de Porres took no responsibility for his illegitimate family but left them in Lima, Peru, while he went off to a new post in Ecuador. Martin and his sister were brought up in poverty. He seems to have been an enchanting child, with a smile which won hearts and a remarkably gentle, loving spirit. From early childhood he could not resist giving things away, so that his mother sometimes beat him in exasperation, when her limited resources were given to people even poorer than themselves and the generous little boy condemned his own family to hunger.

When he was eight and Joanna six, the children were unexpectedly taken away by their father to Ecuador, but Senor de Porres seems to have wearied of his embarrassingly dark children, for three years later they were back in Lima. The boy Martin was apprenticed to a barber-surgeon, where his gifts as a nurse became apparent. His heart was set on God – at the age of eleven his landlady surprised him in an all-night prayer vigil, his arms outstretched in imitation of the crucified. He longed to be a Dominican, but because of the racist rules of the order, could only be accepted as a house-servant, lower than the lay-brothers, virtually a slave. He was daily cursed and abused as a 'mulatto dog' by the friars of pure Spanish blood, but persisted in his own course of cheerful acceptance. He began to collect waifs and strays, greedily pocketing scraps of food and small sums of money to give to beggars who crowded the monastery gates. His sister, now married, grew resigned to visits from her brother with yet another small child, rescued from the streets, to be housed until Martin could find a permanent home for it. His gentleness extended to animals. Stray cats and dogs loved him, and a favourite anecdote relates how Martin was once discovered feeding a dog, a cat and a mouse from the same dish; so great was the animals' trust in Martin that their mutual hostility was suspended. When the Prior ordered him to clear the monastery of dogs, Martin took his menagerie to the long-suffering Joanna's house, where his persuasion of them not to soil the house but to go out to the street was regarded as a miracle. Equally charming, though less plausible, is the tale of how he persuaded the mice who infested the sacristy to go and live outside where, in return for their not spoiling the church linen, Martin fed and protected them.

Gradually his reputation for holiness spread. Novices puzzled by their lessons found that the son of a slave was wise enough to help them unpick Thomas Aquinas. Sick friars who abused their nurse with racist insults, grew ashamed when their harshness was repaid by gentleness, smiles, and occasionally miraculous cures. The climax came when a Spanish nobleman, seeking to gain holiness by association, asked Martin to adopt him. Even the gentle Martin could not resist a little bitterness at this request. 'Why' he asked, 'would you want a Mulatto dog as your father?'

By the time Martin died he was regarded a saint. The coffin of the black outcast was carried by the viceroy of Peru, the Bishop of Cuzco, the archbishop of Mexico and a royal judge. After the funeral mass, the crowds in the church went mad, virtually stripping the body as they snipped off fragments of clothing for relics. By the sheer force of forgiving love, Martin de Porres had won veneration from a whole city. He is now patron saint of race relations.

ROSE OF LIMA (1586-1617) 23rd August. CDC.
A contemporary of Martin de Porres in the same city of Lima won equal popular acclaim for her supposed sanctity, although her chosen path to God will strike modern Christians as strange, even disgusting.

Isabel de Flores y del Oliva was born into a large, relatively prosperous Spanish family, and from an early age was called 'Rose' because of the beauty of her complexion. She grew up to be an unhappy, haunted creature who hated and feared her own beauty, anxious lest it lead herself or others into sin. So extreme was this feeling that she rubbed chilli peppers into her cheeks in an attempt to spoil her skin and make herself ugly. She modelled her life on Catherine of Siena, imitating her by joining the Dominican Third Order, by taking a vow of celibacy, and by separating herself within the family home. She built a hermitage in the grounds and there she lived, tormenting herself with unimaginable austerities. She trained herself to eat virtually nothing, drank only water which had had a foul-smelling weed soaked in it, wore a metal crown of thorns, the points of which were disguised with flowers, whipped herself three times a day, and even constructed a hideous bed for herself, with the mattress replaced by a layer of broken glass and sharp stones, a contraption which she admitted filled her with terror as bedtime approached.

Had you asked Rose why she chose such a life, her answer would have been that she was offering her sufferings for the salvation of her country. At one level she was taking to extremes the element of physical penance which had been part of Christian devotion since the days of St Anthony and St Jerome; a self-hatred sharpened by catholic misogyny and its association of the female body with sin. At another, she was acting out the distress of colonial Peru, that society built on genocide and racial hatred, where conquerors and dispossessed alike fed on Christian images of crucifixion and martyrdom to assuage their guilt. Rose's behaviour undoubtedly connects with that of any unhappy adolescent, self-harming or acting out her grief in eating disorders, but because she was somehow able to connect with the love of Jesus through her self-abuse, extraordinary spiritual fruits emerged from her unhappiness. Though dreading her own beauty, she was able to create beauty outside herself, making exquisite lace and filling her garden with flowers; these she sold and used the proceeds to help the poor. She gave unstintingly to the many destitute around her, earning their love – it was they who hailed her as a saint. Her early death was self-inflicted, but her memory was venerated. She was the first person born in the New World to be officially canonised, and she is patron saint of America, and, more disturbingly, given the ambiguous role model she offers, of teenagers.

FRANCIS DE SALES (1567-1622) 24th January.
In France, the Counter Reformation had rather a different flavour than it had in elegant Italy, fierce Spain, or the tormented, fanatical lands of Spain's colonial empire. The persecution of Protestants which had driven John Calvin to leave his native land had developed into a bitter religious war, in which atrocities had been committed on both sides. These wars had now been brought to an end by Henry IV, the Protestant King of Navarre turned Catholic King of France ('Paris is worth a mass'). Under this pragmatic and powerful monarch, it was not likely that extremism of the Spanish type would find favour. The three French saints whom we are now to consider were characterised by a faith which charmed by its gentleness and challenged by its humane devotion to the poor. Though true children of the Counter Reformation, still much preoccupied with fasting, meditation and self-denial, their concern was not so much with monastic withdrawal, as with finding ways by which men and women living worldly lives might yet manifest the glory of God.

Francis de Sales was born in Savoy, high in the French Alps. He was the cherished son of a noble family who expected great things of him. A great deal of money was spent on his education in Paris, and he returned home to a father ready to share the administration of his estates with his beloved son and to an arranged marriage with an heiress. So great was the weight of parental expectation that Francis did not dare to tell his father that for years he had felt a call to the priesthood. Matters were resolved by Francis' cousin, himself a priest, who spoke privately to the Bishop, and procured from him a papal bull nominating Francis as the Provost of the see of Geneva. This administrative post would give Francis rank in the diocese second only to the bishop himself. Faced with this fait accompli, and unable to incur the dishonour to the family which a refusal would bring, Francis' father consented with bad grace to his son's ordination.

The administration of the diocese of Geneva could not be regarded as an enviable job in 1593. The diocese was in disarray. The nominal cathedral city was in the hands of Calvin's heirs, and no Roman Catholic priest could set foot in it. The Bishop had made a home for himself in the beautiful but remote city of Annecy, nestling between mountains and a clear blue lake. The rural hinterland of the diocese, politically part of the duchy of Savoy, consisted entirely of alpine villages, in most of which, demoralised by the conflict between Catholics and Calvinists, Christian worship of any sort had ceased.

Basing himself at Thonon, a town on the south shore of Lake Geneva, Francis de Sales set about reconverting the whole region to Catholicism. This he did with the gentleness of manner and kindness to individuals which marked his whole life. He re-opened the catholic church for worship and at first preached to empty walls. When he attempted to revive the custom of placing ash crosses on the foreheads of penitents at the beginning of Lent, the people rioted and Francis was obliged to flee the scene. But children loved him and flocked around him: their parents gradually began to talk and to listen; the elderly found him tirelessly patient; his personal charm made roads for his doctrine. Soul by soul, people began to come back. After two years, de Sales had a congregation of two hundred. After four years a great act of devotion known at the 'Forty Hours' was celebrated, beginning with a Procession of the Blessed Sacrament from Thonon to Annemasse, along the lakeside, and continuing with mystery plays, solemn masses, and at the heart of it all, forty hours of continuous prayer before the Blessed Sacrament. The occasion was a catalyst. Teams of priests worked throughout the festivities, hearing confessions, reconciling wanderers to the Church, presenting them in batches to the Bishop for confirmation. Without force or any sort of legislative back-up, by sheer force of personality, Francis de Sales had converted a region. He even made a visit, in plain clothes, to Geneva itself, where he had long talks with the great

Calvinist leader Theodore Beza. The two men parted with great mutual respect, though neither could shift the other ideologically.

In 1599, Francis became in name what he had been for five years in fact, Bishop of Geneva, a post he held for the rest of his life. On a visit to Paris, he so impressed Henry IV that the king hinted at promotion to a richer, more influential see. 'Sire,' de Sales replied. 'I am married to a poor wife. Would you have me leave her for a rich one?'

For poor his diocese undoubtedly was, and de Sales threw himself into the work of reconstructing an all but derelict organisation. Patiently he waded through swamps of law and custom to enable him to secure the funds held by decaying religious houses and re-deploy them for the founding and repair of parishes. Indefatigably he travelled up and down the wild alpine passes, preaching in hilltop villages and towns, reinvigorating the clergy, training them, finding money to pay them. He was not a natural mountaineer. On one occasion one of his assistants, having waited for him at the top of a pass, exclaimed 'How slowly you ride, Father.' The Bishop smiled gently and replied 'Ah Father, we jog along, we jog along as best we can.'

While developing this active ministry, de Sales was kept busy with a parallel ministry of spiritual direction, keeping in touch by letter with gentlemen and ladies anxious for his advice. For one of these ladies he wrote the book which enables us to overhear his legendary charm at work, 'Introduction to the Devout Life.' The book is a short, readable guide to the art of living with total devotion to Jesus amidst worldly duties and cares. Francis begins by stating his conviction that there is no way of life, courtier, tradesman, soldier or housewife, where it is impossible to live with devotion, and he proceeds to demand the highest standards, yet applying his advice with realism, gentleness and a shrewd psychological insight. The book is peppered with homely illustrations: in one passage, the busy Christian is encouraged to be like a toddler picking blackberries, holding his father's hand tight with one hand while with the other he reaches out for the fruit.

Though many saints have written more profoundly or lived more heroically than Francis de Sales, few can have been so loved, and by people of all classes from kings and cardinals to servant girls and shepherd children. He longed for retirement and for space to pray, but was drawn back again and again to his active duties by his love for his people. He died while returning from a journey to Avignon. With an old man's stubbornness he insisted on lodging in what was little more than a garden shed in the grounds of a convent and refused to let anyone see how ill he was. In fact he was almost loved to death, tortured by the terrible medical treatments of the time, blisterings and cauterizings with red hot irons, and unable to rest because of the endless procession of well-wishers and relic-hunters, wanting the dying man to bless rosaries and prayer books. Even so patient a man as de Sales had his limits. When an eager abbess pressed him for a final thought, a word of wisdom on his deathbed, he snatched a piece of paper and scrawled on it the one word 'humility.' It was indeed his watchword.

JANE FRANCES DE CHANTAL (1572-1641) 18th August CDC.
In 1604, Francis de Sales had business in Dijon. In his prayers at Annecy, before he set off, he became convinced that God wanted him to found a new religious order for women, and as he prayed, he was given a picture of a tall young woman in widow's weeds. Once arrived in Dijon, he agreed to preach a series of Lent sermons, and as he did so became aware that a woman was listening with marked earnestness. She seemed to de Sales to be the woman of his vision, and he asked to be introduced to her. They talked for a long time and agreed to meet again at the pilgrim town of Sainte Claude. A great spiritual friendship had begun.

For Jane Frances de Chantal her meeting with Francis de Sales was the turning-point of her life. She had been a charming, wayward young girl, who tamed wild starlings with sugar-lumps. At the age of twenty-one, she married Christophe de Chantal, a young baron much given to hunting and duelling. He wife became the love of his life, tamed him, forced him to get up for church by waving her candle across his face until he woke up, and bore him six children in their eight years of marriage. But this happiness was cut short. Out hunting, Christophe was accidentally shot by a friend who thought he was a deer. He was carried back to his chateau in agony and died nine days later. Jane Frances was utterly distraught by this calamity which caused a massive upheaval in her hitherto sunny and unquestioning faith. Even five years after her meeting with Francis de Sales she was still unable to forgive her husband's hapless killer or even endure being in the same room as him. She plunged into a depression which was exacerbated by two cruel men. One was a priest who was her disastrous choice as spiritual director. A control freak of the worst sort, he obliged her to vow to obey him absolutely, to keep their relationship a secret, and never to change her director. He then proceeded to load her with a regime of mechanical prayers, fasts and penances which did nothing to release the young widow from the hole she was digging. The second man was her father-in-law, who invited her to make a home for herself and her children with him. She did so only to find that he was half senile, prone to cruel rages, and conducting an affair with his housekeeper, who subjected Jane Frances and the children to countless petty humiliations.

Friendship with Francis de Sales lifted Mme de Chantal out of this pit of grief and unhealthy dependancy, and gave her back a healthy, life-enhancing relationship with God. Gently but firmly, he quieted her scruples about her rash vow, and encouraged her to break her link to her spiritual director. Bishop and widow were soul-mates; from their first meeting they understood each other and moved without prompting to mutual acts of love and guidance. Their friendship was largely sustained by letter, for Francis de Sales was always busy and always conscientious. This friendship, which sustained both of them for the rest of their lives, is one the loveliest examples of non-sexual love between a man and a woman which history affords.

In 1607, Francis and Jane were together in Annecy. Together they made two momentous decisions. They arranged a marriage between Jane's fourteen year old daughter Marie-Aimee and Francis' twenty-four year old brother Bernard. At the time Jane saw this marriage as a sacrifice, since her daughter would have to leave Burgundy and live in Savoy, but as she and Francis talked further, she saw the hand of God in the arrangement. For Francis de Sales now asked his friend to form a new sort of religious order. The dream says much of Francis' humane realism about human nature. As the Catholic church responded to the challenge of the reformers by putting its house in order, saints like Teresa and John of the Cross had worked to restore the spirit of monastic houses, making them more austere, more demanding, more physically gruelling places to live, for people who were ardent about losing themselves for love of God. But Francis de Sales realised that such harsh environments could not accommodate many women who, gently brought up, suffering the trauma of early widowhood, in poor health after years of child-bearing, nevertheless longed to be of use to God in a world where secular professions were barred to women. The order Jane de Chantal founded with his help, which became known as the Visitandines, worked differently from the Carmelites so fiercely reformed by Teresa. It recruited older women, not the child vocations so common in more traditional orders. The members were given a moderate rule of daily prayer, silent and communal, and fasting. But instead of an emphasis on solitude and self-discipline, the sisters of the Visitation were sent out to visit, calling at the homes of the sick and poor and offering practical help. Jane eagerly embraced Francis' vision, but she was anxious about her children, all of whom were aghast at the thought of their mother becoming a nun. The marriage of Marie-Aimee and Bernard de Sales made everything easier. The younger Chantal girls lived with their sister, within easy walk of the Visitation, where they were educated, becoming great pets of the community. Jane's son, the fifteen-year old Celse-Benigne, was inconsolable however. When she finally left home for Thorens, in 1610, he threw himself on the floor before her, crying, 'Mother, I am too weak to be able to stop you leaving, but to go you must trample on your son at your feet.' Weeping uncontrollably, Jane de Chantal stepped over her boy and mounted her horse. The boy went into the army, died in Richelieu's wars against the English, and left a daughter who was to become the famous woman of belles-lettres, Mme de Sevigny.

Under the guidance of Jane de Chantal, the new order grew rapidly – in the France of the Thirty Years War there was no lack of gentlewomen widowed young who wanted to do something useful with the rest of their lives. Jane finished her life in Paris as mother superior of a successful order. She had outlived all but one of her children, and Francis de Sales as well. As an old woman she taught her nuns simply to say to everything, 'Vive Jesus.'

VINCENT DE PAUL (1581-1660) 27th September.
In 1619, Francis de Sales and Jane de Chantal were in Paris, seeing to the foundation of the Visitation convent there. On this visit they met a young priest of peasant stock, short, stocky, with an ugly face irradiated by a huge smile. Vincent de Paul got on instantly with the two older saints, and Francis invited him to become chaplain of the Paris Visitation. This duty he performed for the rest of his life, later becoming Jane de Chantal's spiritual director. But this spiritual work, important though it was, was only a small fraction of the work of the man who ranged over the whole of French society and became known as the Apostle of Charity.

France of the early seventeenth century, refracted as it is for us through the lens of nineteenth century romanticism, has an air of dashing glamour. D'Artagnan and Cyrano de Bergerac swagger lace-bedecked, and girt with rapiers, through a Paris full of zest, intrigue, duels and impossibly romantic affairs of honour and the heart. Beneath the panache of the upper classes, however, lay misery for many. The wars of religion, formally ended by Henry IV, had left a nation divided by sectarian bitterness, with Protestants almost as much hated and discriminated against, as were Catholics in contemporary England. Many had been ruined by fighting which laid waste villages and provinces, and the streets of Paris teemed with crime, poverty and degradation. St Vincent de Paul's achievement was to rouse the conscience of a whole nation to awareness of the plight of the poor.

Like d'Artagnan, Vincent was a Gascon, reared by peasant parents in the foothills of the Pyrenees. His exceptional piety and intelligence were early recognised by his family, who made great sacrifices to pay for his education. He was ordained priest at the age of twenty.

In 1606, he began a terrible adventure. While on a sea voyage to Marseilles, his ship was attacked by Barbary pirates. Vincent was made prisoner and sold as a slave in the markets of Tunis. For two years he served first a fisherman and then an apothecary, before being sold to a renegade Frenchman, who had converted to Islam and worked a farm on the African coast. The patience and piety of Vincent awakened the conscience of his master, and the two of them made their escape across the Mediterranean to Avignon, where Vincent's master was tearfully readmitted to the Catholic church. This extraordinary episode confirmed in Vincent an acute sensitivity to the needs and feelings of the poor and deprived.

Vincent travelled to Paris, where at first he lived as so many other clergy lived, attending on the court, competing for the favour of those who had livings to bestow. A converting experience occurred when he met a fellow-priest who had been crippled for years by depression and doubt. Vincent in prayer offered himself to Christ for this sufferer, begging to take on himself the other's depression. Astonishingly, his prayers appear to have been answered, for the other priest was relieved of his burden, while Vincent entered a prolonged period of darkness. This ended when he made a sacrifice of himself to God, vowing to be for ever the servant of the poor and the sick. He remained for the rest of his life cheerful, prayerful and focussed with iron will on doing what God gave him to do. He was a formidable organiser and so hard a worker that it is difficult to believe that one man achieved all that he achieved.

Vincent became parish priest of Clichy, a post he held for less than a year, but that was long enough for him to effect a dramatic improvement in the morale of the people. This pattern repeated itself throughout his life; a short, concentrated time spent in a particular place or on a particular project, which he used to inspire, train and set up structures which worked a lasting transformation. He was head-hunted from Clichy by the wealthy and devout de Gondi family, who wanted a tutor for their sons, and their contacts and financial support made possible much of his most significant work. He systematically worked through the churches on the Gondi estates, holding missions in each and effecting the same transformation as had been seen at Clichy. We can only summarise briefly the other achievements of St Vincent.

M de Gondi appointed him chaplain to the royal galleys, where hundreds of criminals worked as oarsmen in conditions of near slavery. Vincent did much to give hope to these most hopeless of men, and used his influence to ameliorate their conditions. A charming legend, surely apocryphal, relates that Vincent once took the place of one of these condemned men so that he could return home to visit his sick family – surely not a deal the authorities would have countenanced.

Vincent became deeply involved in the training of the clergy; he was much in demand as a preacher for ordination retreats and for missions. As a network of clergy inspired by him developed, he founded the Congregation of the Mission, inspired by Philip Neri's Oratory. The Congregation was a loose alliance of working clergy committed to revival in parishes and the service of the poor. As many aristocratic women were moved by Vincent's missions and desired to be of practical use, he devised for them the order of Ladies of Charity, organising volunteers into teams to visit hospitals and the homes of the poor. The quality of service proved to be patchy; as the novelty thrill of being charitable wore off, some ladies found their social diaries were squeezing out their turns on the rota, while others took to sending their maids in their stead. With the help of Louise de Marillac, a married woman of profound spiritual gifts, Vincent launched the Daughters of Charity, an altogether humbler and more focused partnership with the parish clergy. Increasingly, despite his contacts and influence at court and in polite society, Vincent was drawn to make the poor his priority. Any form of distress claimed his attention and his formidable powers of organisation – the foundling children abandoned on the streets of Paris, agricultural workers struggling on farmlands ruined by years of civil war, soldiers in need of chaplains, refugees from the areas devastated by the Thirty Years War. His disciples were taught to put service of the poor above everything else, for Jesus was to be found primarily in the neighbour in need. 'If you leave your prayers to attend to someone who needs your help,' said Vincent, 'You leave God to attend to God.'

At the age of eighty, Vincent was refusing to slow down or make concessions to his own physical exhaustion. His friends compelled him to stop walking and travel by coach, but he was still up every morning at four o'clock to pray. He died in his chair, because he was too tired to go to bed.

PART EIGHTEEN. THE GOLDEN AGE OF ANGLICANISM.

RICHARD HOOKER (1554-1600) 3rd November.
In tracing the development of the Counter-Reformation and its influence on the catholic nations of Europe, we have run ahead of ourselves. We must now return to the Church of England and see how it developed when the age of martyrdom was over. The early seventeenth century has been called the 'Golden Age of Anglicanism,' witnessing as it did the lives and writings of a host of England's finest preachers and poets.

Elizabeth I, by her Acts of Settlement and Uniformity, attempted to draw a line under the havoc caused in the English church by her father, brother and sister. The Church of England she helped to bring into existence was designed to unify the nation, to be a spiritual home for a broad spectrum of theological beliefs. Yet it could never satisfy the whole nation. The Church of England defined itself against the Church of Rome as Protestant, and its thirty-nine articles laid out a broadly Calvinist, reformed approach to the controversies of the day. Roman Catholics were regarded as traitors and obliged to conform to the church or face heavy penalties. But in its liturgy, in its bishops and ordained clergy, in its retention of saints' days, clerical vestments, ceremonies such as signing baptised children with the cross and administering communion to a kneeling congregation, much of the pre-Reformation tradition of church life was continued, too much for many thoughtful Christians. The Puritans as they were mockingly called, regarded the English Reformation as incomplete and the English church as still tainted with Popery. The Golden Age of Anglicanism was also an age of bitter controversy over the shape of the national church. The Puritans wished every aspect of church life to be grounded in the will of God expressed in scripture: any tradition or convention which had no explicit command in scripture, they regarded as malign.

Richard Hooker, a man of humble Exeter parentage educated at Corpus Christi College, Oxford, came to be regarded as the Father of Anglicanism, beginning that tradition of balance which seeks to sustain the Church of England as Catholic, yet not Roman; Reformed, yet not Protestant. His outward career was not particularly distinguished: it is his writings for which he is remembered.

In 1586 Hooker became Master of the Temple, the London church of the Inns of Court, attended by barristers and lawyers, among whom were then numbered many of the smart men about town. Hooker's preaching was careful and intellectual, his manner understated to the point of dullness, but those who attended to his matter found a powerful defence of historic Christian truths and a pastoral awareness of the anxieties generated by a Calvinist doctrine of faith alone. By this preaching ministry, Hooker was drawn against his will into controversy, for the Temple church had attached to it a lectureship, whose trustees awarded it to a puritan named Walter Travers. Every Sunday afternoon, in his lecture, Travers attacked the positions taken up by Hooker in the morning, and the ensuing war of the pulpits afforded great entertainment to the clever, erudite congregation; until it was stopped as unseemly by the Bishop of London, who compelled Travers to resign. Hooker disliked the bitterness of controversy. He was a mild man who took care to speak of his opponents with gentleness and respect and even, remarkably for the time, believed that Roman Catholics might go to heaven, because, despite the idolatry and superstition which disfigured the old church, they had a devotion to Jesus which might be accepted by a merciful God as saving faith.

It was becoming clear that Hooker's gifts were principally literary and in 1591 he accepted the country living of Boscombe, in order to have more leisure for writing. It is in this period of his life that he produced his great work 'The Laws of Ecclesiastical Polity.'

Hooker's aim was to place the controversies of his day in the context of an understanding of the nature of law in God's providence. He examines natural law and the law of conscience, from which all particular human laws derive their validity. He pays particular attention to the role of reason, without which neither writers nor interpreters of Scripture could operate. Scripture reveals everything necessary to salvation, but it does not contain all truth about every subject, and where scripture gives no clear guidance Christians have liberty to develop their own laws of church governance, which need not always be the same. National churches have their own traditions, and so long as these serve to build up a godly people, a specific scriptural warranty is not necessary. The Roman Catholic Church uses many godly customs, and these need not be abandoned by a reformed church simply because they are Roman. Everything should be judged on its merits, with due regard to legitimate authority, in the Church of England's case the Queen and Bishops.

Hooker's prose has been praised as among the finest in English, although modern readers may find it convoluted and Latinate. The ideal it expresses of a church built on the triple pillars of scripture, tradition and reason, and grown-up enough to speak politely to those with whom it disagrees, remains normative for Anglican identity.

LANCELOT ANDREWES (1555-1626) 25th September.

A near contemporary of Richard Hooker, Lancelot Andrewes was the foremost preacher of his day. He was above everything a scholar, fluent in the learned languages, Hebrew, Greek and Latin, and deeply read in the church fathers and in more recent theology. His eloquence brought him fame in the last years of Elizabeth I, before whom he preached frequently, but it was James I who gave him preferment, making him successively Bishop of Chichester, Ely and Winchester.

James VI of Scotland inherited the English throne of his childless cousin Elizabeth and continued her policy of maintaining national unity via the established church. He was opposed by the Roman Catholics, most famously in the Gunpowder Conspiracy of Guy Fawkes, which consolidated the national myth of the papist as treacherous, cruel and foreign: and by the Puritans, who longed to see the Church of England shake off its bishops and ceremonial and become a Presbyterian church on the model of Calvin's Geneva. James had heard enough such clamours during his years on the Scottish throne, and had so far managed to maintain a balance between the elected presbyteries of the Kirk and the Scottish bishops, who still exercised leadership in the church. He was not pleased to find his new southern realm convulsed by similar struggles. In 1604, James organised the Hampton Court Conference, bringing together the leading Puritan and Episcopal thinkers in a quest for unity.

Lancelot Andrewes was prominent among the speakers at this conference, which predictably achieved little except to entrench all parties in their existing opinions. The conference did have one lasting fruit: James' decision to publish an authorised version of the Bible, a translation reliable and untainted by sectarian bias in the translation. Andrewes headed one of the six teams of scholars to whom this work was confided and he is responsible for about one third of the text of the Old Testament. The Authorised, or King James' Version, was a conservative revision, using Tyndale's translation as its basis, and its majestic language was already consciously archaic at the time of its publication. Its beauty and universality gave it an importance almost impossible to exaggerate. The spirituality of every English speaker we shall meet for the rest of this book was formed by the cadences and memorable phrases of the Authorised Version, which simply was the Bible in English for the three hundred years when England made its greatest contribution to world history.

Although he attempted to take his diocesan responsibilities seriously, the daily routine of Bishop Andrewes remained scholarly and monastic to a degree many modern bishops would envy. His chapel and study were the focus of most of his waking hours. He was up and reading at first light, and anyone attempting to drag him from his books to discuss worldly matters before four in the afternoon met with his serious displeasure. The fruits of his learning were the extraordinary series of sermons preached to James I and his court. Andrewes' mind was fine and fond of ornate turns, both of language and of thought. He typically dissects a phrase, mining it for every possible association, wrapping it in cross-references and clever wordplay, before applying it to the daily conduct of his hearers. Yet his style is colloquial, almost chatty – you can imagine him leaning over the pulpit to bring a point home. These would have been difficult sermons to fall asleep in.

Andrewes lived to preach to the young Charles I, but by the time he died the alliance of divinely appointed king and bishop, which seemed so natural and providential to him, was beginning to unravel before the demands of Puritans, who were increasingly able to take the moral high-ground from the courtiers who delighted in

Andrewes' elaborately worked sermons. Chief among his modern admirers is T.S.Eliot, who famously reworked his great Epiphany sermon to form the opening lines of 'The Coming of the Magi.'

Lancelot Andrewes is buried in Southwark Cathedral, which was then one of the principal churches of his diocese of Winchester. Winchester extended to the Thames until the nineteenth century.

JOHN DONNE (1571-1631) 31st March.
The London in which Richard Hooker and Lancelot Andrewes preached, the London of Elizabeth I's old age and James I's reign, was an exciting place to be alive. England was experiencing a new prosperity and a new self-confidence, after triumphantly defying the might of Catholic Spain. As Spain's colonial empire began to decay, the seeds of Britain's were being sown by intrepid merchants, adventurers and colonists, who filled London's docklands with tales of marvels. On the South Bank, Shakespeare's plays were being given their first performances, the pinnacle of an amazing literary achievement by English poets and dramatists. An audience capable of appreciating these master-works was growing up among the middle-classes, as the lawyers of the Inns of Court and the sons of city merchants vied to charm or buy their way into the aristocratic world of the Court at Whitehall. Those who had money spent flamboyantly on architecture, art and music, together with less durable status symbols, masques, processions, tournaments and banquets. The age had its savagery, the bear-baiting pits, the fiendish ingenuity of public executions, the filth and lack of privacy of a medieval city growing at a far faster rate than its infrastructure, the ever-present threat of plague. But to a young man with talent, social connections, or a reasonable amount of family money, early seventeenth-century London was a playground full of marvels. Calvinist orthodoxy called people to turn their backs on worldly vanity and prepare for the grave, but even the devout found it hard to heed such sombre calls. The young men whose careers we next examine, all persons of great talent and charm, were strongly drawn by the delights of this teeming, energetic world, all achieved some success within it, but all discovered in the end that they could only find peace by withdrawing and searching for the city of God.

John Donne was brought up in the thick of the Catholic resistance to Elizabeth's religious settlement. His uncle was a Jesuit, banished from England as a traitor; his brother died in prison awaiting trial for sheltering a Popish priest; his mother remained a staunch Catholic until her dying day. As a young man, Donne cut himself off from his family by conforming to the established church, although nothing could be less conformist than his lifestyle. A member of Lincoln's Inn, Donne sat lightly to his legal studies, privately resolved never to practice as a courtroom lawyer. Instead he lived as a wit and a womaniser, a man of easy charm with a wide circle of friends, moving with raffish cheerfulness among the playhouses, taverns and brothels of London. His poetry, written for circulation to his friends and never intended for publication, forms an artful and shameless defence of a promiscuous lifestyle. – Donne celebrates the transient yet intense joys of his illicit love affairs with polished charm. The poems also betray his formidable intelligence. If Donne spent evenings drinking and nights in beds where he had no business to be, he was also up early to pursue his other great passion, reading. His poetry, sometimes called 'metaphysical,' plays with elaborate conceits and extended metaphors and rejoices in dexterous verbal trickery. A flea had drawn blood both from Donne and from the lady he is pursuing – their blood is already mingled within the insect – would sex really effect anything very different?

As secretary to the Keeper of the Seal, one of England's foremost legal officers, Donne was getting a reputation as a useful, intelligent and discreet agent, marked for promotion to better things. In 1601, his life changed forever when he made a secret marriage to a teenage girl ten years his junior, Ann More of Loseley Park. The marriage caused a minor scandal, earned Donne the furious enmity of his new father-in-law, a famously short-tempered country squire, and more seriously estranged him from his employer and patron Lord Egerton, who promptly sacked him. Donne's promising career at court was over. He had married for love – some of his most poignant verse was written for Ann – but his love was to be tested by the hardships of his married life. Ann's father grudgingly gave then a small, cold house in the country and a small, cold income to live off, but Donne felt acutely how cut off he was from the busy, stimulating, culturally rich world of his bachelor days, and had to battle hard against depression. We know nothing of Ann's point of view, but in his correspondence, Donne veers between affirming his continuing devotion to his wife, resenting the demands of his noisy children, regretting the life he could hope to live no longer, and blaming himself for failing to make Ann happy. At least twice he escaped on long foreign tours, leaving Ann to cope on her own for months at a time. They had twelve children, of which seven survived. Legend says that Donne chalked grimly on his kitchen door as the implications of his runaway marriage became clear. 'John Donne, Ann Donne, Undone.'

Donne scraped a living by writing eulogies and verses for aristocratic patrons, including the Duke of Buckingham, James I's infamous favourite, whose assassination is related in 'The Three Musketeers.' Highly placed persons suggested ordination to Donne, but he shrank from it, partly out of shame for his well-publicised immoral past, partly because such a step would confirm the failure of his efforts to win worldly success. In 1617, he accepted ordination, surely one of history's most reluctant vocations, and in the same year his wife died in childbirth. In every sense Donne was beginning the world again.

He threw himself with great earnestness into his new work and preferment came quickly. In 1621, thanks to Buckingham's patronage, he became Dean of St Paul's, the great cathedral which would henceforth be the stage for his amazing career as a preacher. His sermons, lasting from one to two hours, electrified the hearers and drew vast crowds. All Donne's formidable intelligence, his learning, his satirical wit, his poet's ability to draw together ideas and make them illuminate each other, his sheer gift of language, were poured into these remarkable performances. Two recurring themes were the unity of the human family – 'No man is an island, entire and in itself,' is his most famous line – and the inevitability of death, for which Christians must earnestly prepare themselves. So pervasive is the theme of death that many have found Donne's sermons morbid, gloomy, guilt ridden. One thing they are not is pessimistic. Donne forces us to attend to death so that we may be freed from vain attachment to this life, but he does so in the firm conviction that in

Jesus God will raise his faithful to a life in eternity which death will be powerless to challenge. 'Death, thou shalt die,' finishes one of his holy sonnets.

As death approached him, he had himself painted tied up in his shroud and asked that the painting serve as model for his funeral monument. The monument can still be seen, the only tomb from Old St Paul's to survive the Great Fire of London.

GEORGE HERBERT (1593-1633) 27th February.

In 1625, the year of James I's death, plague struck London. John Donne took refuge, during the height of the infection, with his old friend Lady Magdalen Danvers, in her house in the pleasant village of Chelsea. Lady Magdalen had been first married to a kinsman of the Earl of Pembroke, and was one of the titled ladies whose patronage meant so much to Donne in his lean years. He was riding into Wales to the country seat of her son, Sir Edward Herbert, when he wrote one of his greatest religious poems 'On Good Friday, riding westward.' Now, at Chelsea, he spent some days in the company of Magdalen's younger son, George. No record remains of any conversation between them, which is a pity, since George Herbert was, like Donne, one of England's foremost poets, and like the older man, had recently quit the uncertain world of court politics for a career in the priesthood. It would be fascinating to know what advice the Dean of St Paul's had to give the aristocratic cadet.

Magdalen Herbert lost her first husband when her son George was four, and brought up her ten children with a mixture of tenderness, determination and unshakeable Christian principle. The family lived in Charing Cross, whence the child George went to church at St Martin's (still then actually in the fields) and was educated at Westminster School while Lancelot Andrewes was dean. He had a successful career at Cambridge University where in 1619 he became public Orator. The office requires the making of elaborate Latin speeches in honour of visiting dignitaries, and was a good stepping-stone into public life. Herbert became MP for his family seat, Montgomery in Wales, but in the same year he entered Parliament he took orders as a deacon. Judging by the poetry he wrote at Cambridge, his faith had always meant more to him than politics. He was given a canonry at Lincoln Cathedral, an office which required no heavier duty than a yearly sermon, and continued to live a gentlemanly life in his mother's house. He seems to have been undecided how best to order his life.

He finally took decisive steps in 1629 when he married Jane Danvers, a cousin of his stepfather, and the following year became Rector of Bemerton, near Salisbury. The parish contained Wilton House, the seat of the Earls of Pembroke, and it was their influence which secured Herbert's preferment. Here he wrote his charming little book 'The Priest to the Temple,' an idealised portrayal of parish ministry in the Church of England's golden age. The country parson, as portrayed by Herbert, celebrates the services of the Prayer Book with simple dignity, catechizes the children and visits his parishioners in their homes, questioning them carefully about their prayers and morals. His wife attends to their illnesses, and the parsonage is an open house, offering hospitality to great and small alike. The picture of settled, blameless routine is so alluring that it comes as a shock to find that Herbert lived this idyll for only three years before his premature death. He was a great lover of music and used to walk into Salisbury twice a week to hear Evensong sung in the cathedral.

He leaves behind him his poems. Compared to his great contemporary Donne, Herbert seems a milder, happier man, though no less artful in the composition of his lyrics. Where Donne presents his relationship with God as a war, with his sinful heart battered into submission and held in check by the fear of death, Herbert's experience is more like a love affair – even when he presents himself as rebellious (as, for example, in 'The Collar') it is the tender love of Jesus which calls him home. It is no surprise that many of his poems have been used as hymns, 'Teach me, my God and King,' 'Let all the world in every corner sing,' and 'King of glory, King of peace' being the best-loved.

NICHOLAS FERRAR (1592-1637) 4th December.
Late in the 1620's, George Herbert travelled into Huntingdonshire to visit the benefice which belonged to him by right of his Lincoln canonry. His journey took him near Little Gidding, which he took the

opportunity to visit. This was the home of Herbert's close friend, Nicholas Ferrar, who with his extended family was conducting a remarkable experiment in community living.

Like Donne and Herbert, Nicholas Ferrar turned to ordination after a colourful series of attempts to make his mark in the secular world. His father was a prosperous London merchant. Ferrar, the sixth of seven children, was a sickly child and at Cambridge a preciously serious teenager. With family money to back him, he had no urgent need to earn a living, and when he left Cambridge, he decided to travel. He set out in 1613, as part of the entourage of James I's daughter Elizabeth, who was going to be married to the Elector Palatine of the Rhine. Ferrar soon left the royal party and struck out on his own, spending the next four years wandering around Europe observing life and manners. He was both attracted and repelled by what he saw of Counter-Reformation Catholicism in Italy, France and Spain. Like many student back-packers since, Ferrar's money ran out, leaving him stranded in Spain. He was obliged to walk from Madrid to the coast and beg a passage home on an English ship.

Once back in London, Ferrar followed his father into business, and served on the Board of the Virginia Company. This body, the brainchild of Sir Walter Raleigh, was one of the earliest attempts by England to rival the wealth and prestige of Spain by founding colonies in the New World. Alas, Virginia had no mines of gold and silver to exploit, and its tobacco plantations were not able to repay investors – though Ferrar himself was recommended by his doctor to take up smoking as a cure for insomnia. The Company foundered amidst accusations of incompetence and corruption. Ferrar became MP for Lymington in 1624 and used his year in Parliament principally to move the impeachment of the Earl of Middlesex, one of those blamed for the failure of the Virginia Company.

But Ferrar's mind was already turning from the vanities of this world. In 1625, he bought the decayed and uninhabited manor of Little Gidding, and the following year he moved up there with his mother, his brother and sister and their families, and a large troop of servants. Before leaving for Huntingdonshire, Ferrar was ordained deacon by William Laud, the recently consecrated Bishop of Bath and Wells, and a firm favourite of the new King, Charles I. He was offered various pieces of preferment but declined them all. He was not looking for advancement, but for a new way of living.

At Little Gidding, the family lived a communal life built around prayer. They met for the Prayer Book offices of Morning and Evening Prayer in the parish church (restored at the expense of old Mrs Ferrar) and had besides four meetings for prayer daily in the house, together with a night vigil, which family members took it in turns to maintain. The psalter was recited daily and the rest of scripture read through in a regular cycle. Resources were shared and the family met daily for a sort of chapter. They earned money from book binding, and Nicholas Ferrar himself wrote voluminously, although he continued to endure poor health. To visitors like George Herbert, Little Gidding seemed a miracle, a creation of heaven on earth, combing the domestic joy of family life with the ordered holiness of a monastery.

But that was also exactly how it appeared to more hostile observers. Beyond the secluded world of Little Gidding, the church was becoming ever more tormented by its internal divisions. The party of the Puritans, which dreaded the Book of Common Prayer as a relic of popery, and hated the bishops because of their association with the claimed divine right of James I and Charles I, this party grew ever stronger. Ferrar's experiment, conducted by a man who had spent years prowling around the idolatrous shrines of Europe, seemed only too clearly an attempt to smuggle Romish practices into the national church. By the time the Civil War actually broke out, Ferrar himself was dead, and his family could not maintain their eccentric community against the spirit of the times. Little Gidding was ransacked by Roundheads. Ferrar's writings were burned, and his attempt to reinvent the Christian community appeared to have failed. The memory of Little Gidding lived on, however, and Nicholas Ferrar became a hero to those in the late nineteenth and early twentieth century who again sought fruitful ways of combining community and family life. T.S Eliot called one of his Four Quartets 'Little Gidding' and famously described Ferrar's church in the words 'You are standing where prayer has been valid.'

WILLIAM LAUD (1573-1645) 10th January.

In 1627, John Donne preached at Whitehall before King Charles I. For reasons impossible to deduce from the blameless version of his sermon which Donne wrote up after the event, something he said infuriated the King. William Laud, the same Bishop of Bath and Wells who ordained Nicholas Ferrar, was sent to obtain a copy of the sermon and make sure the preacher was suitably chastened. Donne was thrown into a panic by his interview with Laud, and never did really understand what had been so offensive in his sermon. But the incident underlines the ascendancy of Laud. A firm friend of Charles' favourite, the Duke of Buckingham, he was promoted rapidly in the early years of Charles' reign – Bishop of London in 1628, Archbishop of Canterbury in 1633. In the King's eyes he could do no wrong, a fact which would not in the end work in his favour.

William Laud was an easy man to laugh at: he was short, fat and red-faced, with a fussy, pompous, prickly manner. He also had a genius for making enemies: he was outspoken in giving his opinions, hot-tempered in defending them, and jumpily thin-skinned in dealing with the consequences. He saw plots by his enemies everywhere, and filled his private diaries with accounts of his dreams about them and his speculations about what God might be trying to tell him. But he was a truly scholarly man; his happiest days were probably those spent at his beloved Oxford, first as President of St John's and then as Chancellor of the University. He greatly enriched the Bodleian Library and founded a Chair of Arabic. His reputation was made when he was asked (unsuccessfully as it turned out) to prevent the conversion of the Duke of Buckingham's mother to Catholicism by debating with her Jesuit adviser, Fisher. The Duke's gratitude was boundless: Laud's rapid promotion was ensured.

Laud was already a marked man by the Puritans. As Dean of Gloucester, he had courted controversy by moving the altar, which Cranmer's rubrics placed in the centre of the cathedral, back to its traditional place against the eastern wall, where he surrounded it by rails and commanded worshippers to bow to it. To Laud, this was a matter of restoring order, seemliness and dignity to the Communion Service; to the Puritans it was only one step away from restoring the

Mass in all its Baalite obscenity. Nor were they mollified by Laud's uncompromising defence of bishops as a divinely ordained order set apart to govern the true church. Laud implied, if he did not actually say, that sister Protestant churches in Germany and Switzerland were no true churches, as they lacked bishops. He strongly implied, if he did not actually say, that the Roman Catholic hierarchy merited more respect than the presbyters and elders of Reformed congregations. The elevation of such a man to the highest office in the land made it daily more difficult to see how the Church of England could continue to be a spiritual home for all English Christians.

Laud's early years as Archbishop coincided with the years of Charles I's Personal Rule, the King's attempt to demonstrate that a divinely appointed monarch could rule his people justly without the assistance of Parliament. High Anglican divines had always revered the doctrine of the divine right of Kings. Thomas Cranmer believed that Henry VIII was God's anointed servant to lead the nation out of popish slavery. Andrewes and Donne preached the duties of obedience every year on the anniversary of the Gunpowder Conspiracy. Laud went further, and regarded insult to the King as a kind of blasphemy; the King was a walking icon, a living sacrament. The religious cause of bishops was being ever more closely identified in the public mind with the political cause of tyranny.

In one of those moments which fix the reputation of a public figure for ever, Laud, presiding in the Court of Star Chamber, commanded three writers who had criticised him to be placed in the pillory, their ears cropped and the letters S.L (seditious libeller) branded on their faces. The public decided that S.L. stood for 'Stigmata Laudis' – the brand of Laud. One of the branded, Prynne, went on to be a Member of Parliament and one of King Charles' bitterest critics.

For Charles could not do without Parliament for ever. His strategy of ruling alone could only work if he exercised economy enough to be able to do without the grants of tax money which only Parliament could bestow. Ironically, it was Laud, detested since the Prynne affair, who precipitated the disaster which was to make the summoning of Parliament inevitable. In Charles' northern kingdom of Scotland, the Presbyterian challenge to the bishops was intensifying: Charles lacked his father's shrewdness in maintaining the balance of power in the Kirk. To Laud and the High church party, this was intolerable. The King needed no persuasion to attempt to stamp his authority on Scotland. In 1636, he ordered that the Book of Common Prayer be used throughout his northern realm. Rational debate about the merits of the Prayer Book was by now impossible. It had become a symbol, an idolatrous mass book foisted on the elect, godly people of Scotland by Charles' popish queen and the disguised Jesuit Laud. A riot took place in Edinburgh Cathedral at the first reading of the new liturgy, and within two years the King was at war with Scotland. Charles' aggressive policy had achieved exactly what he most wanted to avoid, the end of episcopacy in the Church of Scotland. Moreover wars cost money and in 1640 the Long Parliament was summoned to assist the King in his difficulties. The new Parliament was dominated by Puritans, and it was immediately clear that assisting the King was the last thing on its agenda.

Laud was by now one of the most hated men in the kingdom. Even the King's jester ventured a satirical pun, telling his master, 'Give great praise to God, and little Laud to the devil.' One of the first moves of Parliament was to accuse the Archbishop of high treason and to lodge him in the Tower. Here he blessed the king's most trusted minster Wentworth, Earl of Strafford, as he went to the block, a victim of Parliamentary attainder. For Charles, the *real politik* decision to sign his friend's death warrant provoked a sense of guilt which never left him; for Laud, the sight of a trusted colleague being led to death was so distressing that he fainted. Thereafter he remained in prison, a helpless spectator of the early days of the English Civil War, as trust between King and Parliament broke down irretrievably, the King left London in disgust to call his loyal subjects to arms, and the dreadful tug of loyalty between Charles and his Commons divided families and communities in every county.

By 1644, Laud's trial was bogged down and all attempts to secure his condemnation were failing. The charge of treason rested on the conviction that Laud had been plotting to sell the nation to the Pope, and for this there was no evidence at all, not surprisingly as the real Laud, not the bogeyman he had become, was as resolute against popery as any of his opponents. The prosecution attempted to claim that various minor faults proved against Laud amounted cumulatively to High Treason, but this claim was rightly mocked by the archbishop's defenders: 'I never understood before this time that two hundred couple of black rabbits would make a black horse.' In the end, disgracefully, Parliament passed a Bill of Attainder, over-riding the courts. Irrespective of any evidence, Laud would die because Parliament wanted him dead.

On 10th January 1645, the old man, bewildered and dishevelled, was led out to Tower Hill. He managed to make a moving last speech. ('This is an uncomfortable place to preach in.') defending his conduct and his opinions and declaring himself willing to suffer with Christ and for Christ. As the axe severed his head, the legend of Laud the martyr was born.

Laud remains a controversial figure, blamed by many historians for provoking by his intransigence the very Puritan extremism he was trying to put down, He is not easy to love. But for Anglicans reflecting on his story with hindsight after the sufferings inflicted by Oliver Cromwell, Laud's uncompromising stand for the Book of Common Prayer made him a martyr for true English reformed Christianity. His death was certainly unjust and the way he met it, noble.

CHARLES I (1600-1649) 29th January.

By the time Laud was finally brought to the block, his old master and friend King Charles I was in no position to help him. For three years the King had not been able to enter his capital. The royal court, camping in romantic discomfort around the quads and cloisters of Oxford, was a military headquarters. The King was at war with his Parliament and throughout the three nations of England, Scotland and Ireland loyalties split and small battles and sieges disfigured landscapes and divided neighbours.

This book is not the place to attempt a detailed account of the causes and course of the English Civil War. We have already seen that one powerful motor of the division which led to war, was difference of religious ideology. Laud, drawing on the high church tradition of the great Jacobean preachers, wanted a church of

England, certainly truly reformed, but with a beauty and stateliness in its forms of worship, and a sacramental depth in its spirituality, which drew on the wisdom of the patristic period. The Puritans wanted a church where plain men drew plain messages from the plain reading of scripture. Their Calvinist vision of the church rejected bishops as unscriptural and popish, and longed for a pure church, governed by a presbytery of elders after the model of Geneva and the Scots. As the war bred extremism, yet more radical Christian voices began to be heard, the Independents, who experienced the direct prophetic force of the Holy Spirit and rejected all forms of government and discipline larger than the local congregation. Cromwell's New Model Army, the decisive military factor in the war, was also nurse of the god-fearing Independents, men from labouring classes who, finding God gave them power to bring down Kings and bishops, were disinclined to respect the man-made dignities of Members of Parliament and Presbyterian elders.

What should become of the King when the war was finally over? Charles I was an odd, formal, private man who engendered passionate loyalty and indiscriminate hatred both in his own lifetime and ever since. Never bred to be king, his boyhood was overshadowed by his glamorous older brother Henry, whose early death propelled Charles to the throne. He was fastidious, proud, reserved, and secretly terrified of being seen to be weak. He was devoted to his wife and children, one of the few Kings of England to be entirely faithful to the marriage bed. He spent a fortune on art and architecture, processions and masques, yet lacked the common touch of Elizabeth I, so that the glory and glamour never made him a way into his people's hearts. He was fiercely loyal to his friends, yet weakly betrayed them when put under pressure. He had a punctilious code of personal honour, yet used every dirty trick in the book when negotiating with his enemies. His years of Personal Rule were represented as text-book tyranny, a trampling on the birth-rights of his subjects, yet his Parliamentary opponents subverted the constitution and the common law with far more deadly effect in their opportunistic experiments in wielding power. This was the man with whom all the parties who had helped to bring him down must nervously negotiate as the Civil War stuttered to a resolution.

After the Battle of Naseby, where Cromwell's psalm-singing troopers destroyed Prince Rupert's cavalier forces, it was clear that Charles could not hope for military victory in war. But the name and person of the King could still lend legitimacy to any successor regime and the squabbling began. Fearful of the New Model Army and its extremists, to whom he was the 'Man of Blood,' Charles left Oxford and surrendered himself to the Scots. On his journey northward he visited Little Gidding and was duly impressed by the sober, seemly Anglicanism of the community, but the price of a deal with the Scottish army was, he very well knew, an agreement to abolish episcopacy and introduce Presbyterian church government into England. Charles played for time, but it was clear that such a change disgusted him and his prevarications and double-dealing convinced the Scots commissioners that they could achieve no lasting settlement in partnership with the King. Early in 1647 they sold the King to his English parliament for £100,000. But Parliament, notionally commanding the army which had beaten the King, was losing its grip. The Army was agitated, electing its own officers and refusing to disband at the orders of Parliament. Cornet Joyce appeared with a troop of horse at the country house where Parliament was lodging Charles and asked the King to accompany him. 'Where are your instructions?' asked Charles. 'They are there, Sir,' replied the cornet, pointing to the waiting cavalry. 'Your instructions are in fair character,' said the King. 'legible without spelling.'

Now in the hands of the army, Charles was offered a very modern-sounding solution to the religious quarrel: complete liberty of conscience for everyone (except of course Roman Catholics). Could he have save his life and reign had he accepted? Charles was by now so used to double-dealing and procrastination that he let the opportunity slip and instead, with incredible folly, escaped from the Army, fled to the Isle of Wight and summoned his subjects to rally and re-open the war. The result could not be in doubt. By the end of the year, Carisbrooke castle had become the King's prison, not his headquarters. The Army's leaders were alienated from Charles and only one solution to the problems he posed seemed possible.

During his stay at Carisbrooke, the myth of the Royal Martyr began to gather strength. Active, Charles was a liability. Passive and a prisoner, he was the focus of increasing romantic loyalty. Various faithful servants and gentry made repeated efforts to rescue the King. Dashing and impractical arrangements were made with boats, disguises and even phials of nitric acid to dissolve the iron window bars of Charles' room. Inevitably the authorities got wind of these antics and the King was taken to London, there to stand trial for high treason.

On 20th January 1649, the trial of Charles Stuart began. The judges appointed all refused to serve and Parliament in embarrassment had to appoint others. The King wore his hat throughout, refusing to acknowledge the court's authority: for him a king tried for high treason was a contradiction in terms. When sentence was pronounced 'in the name of the people of England,' a masked woman, Lady Fairfax, whose husband had led armies against Charles, cried from the gallery 'Not half the people of England, not a quarter of them. Oliver Cromwell is a traitor.' Charles spent his last night in Whitehall Palace; he was permitted to say farewell to his younger children – his adult sons, the future Kings Charles II and James II, were safe in exile. The bitter weeping of the little girl and boy, who adored their father, distressed the King and brought tears even to the eyes of his guards. On 30th January, the King dressed in two shirts, lest he should shiver and be supposed to be afraid. He received Communion and read with his chaplain the Passion of Christ from Matthew's Gospel. He was led through the first-floor window onto the scaffold which had been erected in Whitehall. There he was beheaded. The watching crowd gave a great whispered groan and by nightfall handkerchiefs soaked in the blood of the royal martyr were on sale. The execution of the King appalled many and contemporaries at once began to describe Charles as a saint and a martyr. His was the only name added to the Anglican calendar between 1540 and 1980; the anniversary of his death was marked by a special service of national penitence and churches were dedicated to him. As so often before, the misfortunes of a morally imperfect royal elevated him to saintly status in popular eyes.

PART NINETEEN. RESTORATION AND DISSENT.

JEREMY TAYLOR (1613-1667) 13th August.

The execution of Charles I meant the threat of extinction for the Church of England. Oliver Cromwell personally had remarkably enlightened views on liberty of conscience – he allowed Jews to settle in England for the first time since the reign of Edward I – but he drew the line at popery, and for most of those who had fought the King, Prayer Book Anglicanism was a papist wolf in a Protestant fleece. Bishops were abolished, the church disestablished, and all who would not consent to Presbyterian government were deprived of their livings. Thus the downfall of Charles I meant suffering and hardship for many ordinary clergymen.

Jeremy Taylor gives us a typical example of what a royalist, Church of England man might undergo in these years. An attractive young man, with blond hair and an engaging pulpit manner, he was educated at Caius College, Cambridge. Early in his career, he was invited to preach at St Paul's cathedral, where he caught the eye of Archbishop Laud. Laud's patronage won him a fellowship at All Souls, Oxford, the rectorship of Uppingham, and the post of Chaplain to Charles I. This promising little career was cut short by the outbreak of war. Taylor spent much of the war in Oxford with his king, in increasing poverty, for Parliament had sequestered his living at Uppingham and given it to a Presbyterian minister. As the royalist position weakened, Taylor withdrew to Wales, where he was besieged with the royalist garrison in Cardigan Castle, and taken prisoner by the Roundheads. He was set free fairly speedily, but found himself without income or prospects in an England where the rules about church had drastically changed.

At this point Taylor was fortunate in finding a patron in the Earl of Carbury, who welcomed the destitute priest into his home in Carmarthenshire, the quaintly named Golden Grove. Here, living in retirement, Taylor wrote the works which have established his reputation, 'Holy Living' and 'Holy Dying.'

These works reveal how Taylor, in common with many Anglican clergy, was withdrawing from the battle-lines which had defined churchmanship during the Reformation era. The Calvinists had argued for a strong doctrine of predestination, against the so-called Arminians, who championed freewill, and for a Presbyterian church government, against traditionalists who held by the Elizabethan settlement and the catholic orders of ministry. It seemed that these disputes about doctrine had brought nothing but misery, division and warfare upon church and country: theological argument had not brought about the kingdom of Heaven. Taylor was not alone in seeking to redirect his readers' attention to the plain, down-to-earth call to live a holy life. His two great books centred Christian discipleship on the practical duties of sobriety, righteousness and godliness. Under these three headings Taylor discussed the moral virtues which commend a person to God. Mainstream English Christianity has always maintained this pragmatic approach to religion, fighting shy of doctrine and concerning itself with teaching people how to be good. For two centuries after his death, Taylor's books remained best-sellers, and if his style, loaded with the finest seventeenth-century rhetoric, has repelled modern readers, he is still an important witness to the popular, ethical strand in Anglicanism.

On a trip to London, Taylor made a new friend in Viscount Conway, who in 1658 offered him a benefice on his Irish estates. In Ireland, Taylor was reported to the authorities for using the sign of the cross in baptism, but his trial was aborted by astonishing news from England. Following the death of Oliver Cromwell, Parliament had voted for the restoration of the exiled king, Charles II.

RICHARD BAXTER (1615-1691) 14th June.
The return of Charles II, initially to great national rejoicing, meant a reversal in church policy. Now the episcopal party would find favour and the Presbyterians persecution. Charles was personally eager for tolerance, but his supporters wanted revenge.

Among those who suffered under the new regime was the wise and moderate Puritan divine Richard Baxter. A Shropshire lad, he never had the chance of a university education but was self-taught to a high level, having a voracious taste for reading.

In 1641, he was offered a lectureship at Kidderminster Church, under rather curious circumstances. The vicar, Charles Dance, was man of easy morals and indifferent as a preacher. His more serious parishioners were preparing to denounce him and have him removed as unfit, when he bought time by agreeing to the endowment of a lectureship, which might provide sermons more to his critics' taste. Baxter, the new lecturer, was blamed for inciting the anti-vicar party in the town, and hissed in the streets as a Roundhead. As the war closed in, he felt it prudent to leave Kidderminster for Coventry, where there was a Parliamentary garrison. For a time he served in the Parliamentary forces, as chaplain to Whalley's Troop; his first-hand experience of the brutality and misery of war sickened him. In 1657 his health obliged him to retire from active ministry, and it was during these years of retirement that he wrote the book for which he is famous, 'The Saint's Everlasting Rest.' The book is a series of meditations on Heaven, which Baxter wrote convinced that Christians would only find the courage they needed to live joyful lives, if they had a clear vision of the glory ahead of them. The book is a beautiful example of the best of Puritan spirituality, with a demanding vision of holiness tempered by compassionate realism about human nature.

Shortly after its publication, Baxter returned to Kidderminster, this time as vicar. The Presbyterians had ousted Charles Dance, whom Baxter treated with conspicuous forbearance, allowing him to live in the Vicarage while Baxter himself took lodgings. Now began his glory days. His reputation as a preacher soared; five galleries had to be added to Kidderminster church to accommodate the crowds who came to listen. When he went as guest preacher to St Laurence, Jewry, in London, the church was so full that the vicar sat in the pulpit, the only space left, with Baxter preaching standing between his legs. He continued to write voluminously – over 150 titles flowed from his pen, also many poems and hymns, of which 'Ye holy angels bright,' is the best known. He attempted to serve all his parishioners, continuing to provide Prayer Book services for those who wanted them alongside the freer Puritan devotions and sermons. He was moderate in politics, deploring the execution of Charles I and deeply distrusting the increasingly dictatorial attempts of Cromwell to govern the country. But none of this was to help him at the Restoration of Charles II, after which he never knew ease or security again.

Charles wanted a settlement that would promote religious unity, and his first moves tended to reconciliation. The deprived Cavalier clergy were restored; Jeremy Taylor was made Bishop of Down, and Connor, a promotion which made the last six years of his life a misery, as he battled at the hopeless task of imposing Prayer Book Anglicanism on a diocese of Roman Catholics and Presbyterians. But moderate Puritans were courted. Baxter was appointed a royal chaplain and offered the diocese of Hereford, but he declined it. Although prepared to work with Anglicans, he was too much a Presbyterian to compromise his integrity by accepting an office which, if not illicit, he regarded as optional and controversial. In 1661, he spoke for the Puritans at the Savoy House Conference, which tried to bring together the supporters and opponents of episcopacy, but in 1662 the so-called Cavalier Parliament passed acts which made Baxter's position impossible.

The Book of Common Prayer was re-imposed as the only legal form of prayer in English churches. In the century of its existence, it had moved from being a defiant iconoclastic statement of reformed Protestantism, to becoming the badge of loyalty for royalists, reactionaries and traditionalists. Unlike Elizabeth I, Charles II found it impossible to build even a semblance of unity around the Prayer Book. Perhaps as much as a third of the parish clergy were ejected or resigned their livings because they would not swear to use the Book. Baxter was one who left. Although not personally averse to the Prayer Book, he would not swear away the liberty of pastors to use what forms of prayer they judged fittest to help their parishioners. For the rest of his life he lived a precarious existence just on the wrong side of the law, preaching at private services in his home and writing always. He was twice imprisoned for illegal religious activity and in his old age was tried and harangued by the infamous bully Judge Jefferies. These trials enhanced the respect in which the old man was held. People were shocked to see a man whose life was marked by moderation, serene wisdom and transparent holiness, being railed at as a common criminal. By the time Baxter died, it was clear that, whatever the law said, dissenting churches were here to stay, and that dissenting churches were capable of producing saints.

Baxter's 'Everlasting Rest' was for two centuries one of the most widely read books in English, although it is little known today. It suffered by association with Puritanism. In the nineteenth century, Eliot's Mrs Glegg in 'The Mill on the Floss' asserts the righteousness of her vixenish temper by ostentatiously reading 'Everlasting Rest.' The association is unfair. The book is a gem and still gives us glimpses of the sheer lovable nature of its author.

JOHN BUNYAN (1629-1688) 30th August.
The persecuted Anglican Jeremy Taylor, the persecuted Puritan Richard Baxter: they are joined by a third persecuted figure, more radical than either and the writer of a book more popular than either 'Holy Living' or 'Everlasting Rest,' a book still regarded as one of the classics of English literature.

John Bunyan was the son of a travelling tinker, given only the most rudimentary education, and following his father's trade. His autobiography 'Grace Abounding' gives a fascinating insight into how the upheavals of the age of Cromwell and Charles II were affecting those at the bottom of the social scale. While Taylor dined at the tables of his aristocratic patrons, and Baxter buried himself in omnivorous reading in his study, John Bunyan and thousands of working people like him were hewing out for themselves a passionate, personal faith, based on nothing but the Bible and an earnest desire for salvation. While Calvinism had empowered ordinary people, encouraging them to read the Bible and debate the issues they discovered without the mediation of the clergy, it also created and sustained a profound anxiety in believers. The struggle against popery meant that all external signs of salvation must be discarded as worthless – no sacrament, no minster, no liturgy, could be a guarantee of Christ's saving presence. The emphasis was on the personal regeneration of a sinner's heart – your salvation was assured by a highly subjective spiritual experience of personal conversion. The classical Reformed emphasis on predestination created extra anxiety. If God had predestined you to damnation, might not he give you a false sense of conversion and acceptance, the more effectively to accomplish your doom? Was the inner voice, so earnestly sought, divine, diabolical or the product of human self-deception? We have seen St Teresa agonising over similar dilemmas from her very different Spanish Catholic perspective. Bunyan's writings are suffused with an ever-present anxiety about the possibility of damnation, although, perhaps for that very reason, few Christians have written so movingly of the sheer joy of being found by Jesus the Saviour.

Bunyan regarded his teenage years as an appalling sink of depravity. He certainly had a deserved reputation as a heavy drinker and a heavy swearer, although we may judge him less harshly than he judged himself when we find that among his worst sins were bell-ringing and an enjoyment of sports and games on a Sunday afternoon. He married at the age of twenty-one Mary, a girl as poor as he, whose great treasures were two books of devotion left her by her father. John and Mary read together and John worried about the discrepancy between the holiness he read of and the self-indulgence in which he lived. His first call to conversion came during a Sabbath-profaning game of Tip-Cat (a game resembling golf) when he suddenly heard a voice say 'Wilt thou leave thy sins and go to heaven, or have thy sins and go to hell?' This experience was far from being a conversion to a peaceful, calm Christian faith; rather it initiated a long period of anguish, in which Bunyan eagerly read his Bible for signs of God's favour, while often convinced that he was irretrievably damned. For a while he was convinced he had committed the mysterious 'sin against the Holy Ghost' for which Christ declares there is no forgiveness. Eventually these agonies subsided and Bunyan's faith matured, under the guidance of John Gifford, the Baptist minister of Bedford. The Baptists kept themselves apart from other Christians, convinced that infant baptism was invalid and that to be saved one must undergo 'believers'' or adult baptism. Bunyan was re-baptised as an adult and in 1655 began a career as a Baptist preacher, although his own children were all baptised in infancy, an intriguing comment on the fluidity between denominations which prevailed in this era.

Like all members of dissenting churches, Bunyan was persecuted following Charles II's restoration. In 1661 he was arrested for illegal preaching. The magistrates were inclined to be lenient, and Mrs Bunyan used what influence she had to press for clemency, but Bunyan's intransigent attitude ('if you release me today, I shall preach tomorrow') made conviction inevitable. He remained in prison for the next eleven years, earning respect from fellow-believers and opponents alike for his cheerful and prayerful endurance of hardship.

Charles II, always more personally inclined to tolerance than his minsters, issued a Declaration of Indulgence in 1672, under which Bunyan and other dissenters were released. For three years Bunyan worked hard, converting a barn in Bedford into a Baptist church; a chapel named in his honour still stands on the site. But Charles was obliged by Anglican pressure to withdraw his indulgence in 1675 and Bunyan returned to prison. Such was his reputation for holiness by now, however, that six months later he received a pardon, and he spent the last years of his life unmolested. He died in London, having caught a severe chill on a winter journey to bring about a reconciliation between an estranged father and son.

While he was in prison, Bunyan wrote the book for which he is famous, 'The Pilgrim's Progress,' for long the most read book in English after the Bible. It is an allegorical tale, relating the journey of Christian from the City of Destruction to the Eternal City. On his journey Christian meets adventures and trials, being caught in the Slough of Despond, captured by Giant Despair and persecuted by the frivolous inhabitants of Vanity Fair. He converses with engagingly drawn types, such as the hypocrite Mr Worldly Wiseman, and acquires allies, Faithful and Hopeful being the chief. The style is deceptively simple, almost like a folk-tale, with the beautiful cadences of the Authorised Version laid alongside the everyday colloquialism of the streets of Bedford – Bunyan's allegories talk like real people. The book was such a success that Bunyan wrote a sequel, detailing the adventures of Christian's wife Christiana and her stalwart helpers Mr Greatheart and Mr Valiant-for-truth. Bunyan being Bunyan, he experienced agonies of conscience over whether it could be right to commend God's truth by the use of fiction – but the verdict of posterity has vindicated his decision to publish. 'Pilgrim's Progress' was read everywhere – even so worldly a family as E.Nesbitt's Bastable children played at 'Pilgrim's Progress' on wet afternoons, and for many children from god-fearing families, the story was one of the few reliefs from the tedium of Sabbath observance.

GEORGE FOX (1624-1691) 13th January.

Although the age of martyrdoms, of burnings at the stake and beheadings on Tower Green, was over, the later seventeenth century remained, as we have seen, an age of intense religious intolerance. The Anglican Jeremy Taylor, the Presbyterian Richard Baxter, the Independent John Bunyan, all experienced persecution for their beliefs. And there was one group of Christians whom all right thinking people united in condemning – the Society of Friends, or, as they were jeeringly called, the Quakers. While the process by which various radical Christian groups coalesced to form the Friends, is too complex to rest on one individual, there could have been no Quakers without the eccentric genius of George Fox.

Like Bunyan, Fox was an unhappy youth, whose restless quest for peace was hindered rather than helped by the orthodox Reformed religion which Puritan England offered him. As a teenager he left his home in Leicester and spent some years wandering aimlessly about the country, never sticking at a job for long, scouring his Bible for guidance, pathologically anxious about his salvation. He consulted various clergymen, but they had no comfort to give to a boy who, beneath the self-dramatising attention seeking, was in real spiritual pain. One advised him to sing psalms, another to soothe his nerves by taking up smoking, while his own parish priest, after initially trying to be sympathetic, at last concluded he was mad. The ultimate misunderstood teenager, Fox at last found peace thanks to the guidance of the Puritan Nathaniel Stephens, and in 1647 he began the highly individual career of preaching, which was to be his life.

Fox developed his own version of Christianity, centred on his conviction that an Inner Light was made available to anybody who genuinely sought it. He carried to its logical extreme the Protestant suspicion of outward means to salvation. Not only did he reject as unnecessary churches and their hierarchies and traditions; he considered the sacraments superstitious and even denied that the Bible was binding on a believer who was truly guided by the Spirit within. Fox turned his back on the 'steeple-houses', and the ordained clergy who had been so useless in his time of need and sought no other authority than his own illuminated conscience. In a famous vision on Pendle Hill in 1652, he heard God promise to give him the land if he would but preach faithfully. As people began to listen and a group formed about him, an original way of being Christian developed, which was hated and feared by all with a stake in more traditional ways of following Christ.

The Society of Friends got its nickname, 'The Quakers,' from a scornful magistrate who mocked the way they shuddered with holy dread as they prayed together. Some Quaker customs were merely quaint – they rejected the traditional names for the days of the week, which are of course named after pagan gods, preferring the biblical usage 'First Day,' 'Second Day' and so on. They retained the singular 'thou' in addressing each other; this usage was becoming archaic, but the Quakers mistrusted the reason driving the change, which was that the plural 'You' was felt to be more polite outside the family circle, as 'vous' is preferred to 'tu' in formal speech in French. The Quakers disliked 'You' as they disliked all formal courtesy and honours conceded to social status. They refused to use titles such as 'Mr' and 'Mrs', kept their hats on in the presence of their social superiors, eschewed bowing and curtseying and all false forms of gentility. But the Church was threatened when they rejected baptism and the Eucharist and refused to pay tithes, and the state was threatened when they refused to swear oaths in law courts or to serve in public office. Some of the positions they took up were truly radical. The Quakers were the first Christians since the earliest church to maintain a totally pacifist position, denying the validity of any violence in a Christian's life. And they were the first English Christians ever to take seriously the role and gifts of women in church leadership.

Fox's own wife, Margaret Fell, whom he married in 1669, was a pioneer of women's ministry. Theirs was very much a marriage of minds. Fox remained as undomesticated as when he was a wandering teenager, and he appears to have had little need for emotional intimacy or sexual fulfilment. But he treated Margaret seriously as his equal in his work and encouraged her and other female Quakers to preach, prophesy and lead congregations in prayer.

This of course only made the movement more suspect to conventionally-minded people. The Quakers were viciously persecuted both by Cromwell's government and by that of Charles II. Cromwell himself met Fox and had a long talk with him, which he found profoundly moving, but society was not yet ready for the Quakers' uncompromising egalitarianism.

Fox himself experienced the difficulties common to charismatic, prophetic reformers. It is all very well to reject man-made authority and rely on the direct guidance of the Holy Spirit; but what happens when the Holy Spirit gives other people guidance which is unacceptable to you? The movement was split by disagreements between Fox and a convert called James Nayler, who had once ridden though Bristol on a donkey re-enacting Palm Sunday, as a sign that the end was nigh. When the two men met, Fox expected Nayler to kiss his hand as an acknowledgement of his authority. When Nayler refused, Fox responded by bidding him kiss his foot instead. The power-struggle poisoned early Quaker life, with each leader accusing the other of working with an ungodly spirit.

Ever restless, Fox travelled widely, visiting the American colonies in 1671, where he preached to the black slaves and was disappointed not to be able to reach Red Indian country. Fox's message was perceived as particularly threatening by the plantation owners, but Fox was at pains to deny attempting to end slavery; he hated slavery but held by his pacifist convictions and refused to countenance rebellion. His labours in Europe bore great fruit, and by the time he died there were Quaker communities in Holland, Germany and other countries.

Fox remains a controversial figure, stormy and dis-satisfied, a breaker down of authority who spent much energy trying to stamp his own authority on his followers. The Quaker movement has remained theologically and politically radical, but has lost its association with charismatic happenings; waiting on the Spirit at a modern meeting is usually a far more peaceful experience than it was in the days when George Fox and Margaret Fell presided.

THOMAS TRATHERNE (1636-1674) 10th October.

As we survey the turbulent religion of the Commonweath and the Restoration, one name stands apart from the noisy struggle. Thomas Traherne lived an undistinguished life, proceeding from Brasenose College, Oxford to a country parish in Credenhill, Herefordshire, and finishing his life as chaplain to the household of Sir Orlando Bridgeman, a cavalier politician. He took no part in the stormy events of his era, and would be utterly unknown were it not for a chance discovery.

In 1896, one W.T.Brooke bought from a book barrow in London a tatty old manuscript, which turned out to be the only copy of unpublished poems and prose meditations by Traherne. The scholarly detective work of Bertram Dobell rescued and presented to the world two and a half centuries after his death, the lost and forgotten voice of a beautiful Christian. Other works of Traherne have continued to be discovered; one manuscript was taken singed from a burning rubbish tip in Manchester.

When we read Traherne's 'Centuries of Meditations' we are taken to a different place. In these singular writings there is none of the tormented anxiety about hellfire, predestination and personal salvation which drove men like Bunyan and Fox. Instead we keep company with a man of golden optimism, who believed that each person possessed the universe within his own soul, and that a poor man who had learned to receive each day's experience as a gift from God would be richer than a king, plagued with the torments of ambition and the need to possess. Traherne vividly remembered his early childhood when a field of corn or a view of the road through a garden gate could be a vision of Paradise. He believed that if we could relearn a child's acceptance of things and lack of need to own and control, we would be happy. He sought God in the countryside and in natural beauty and his writing, though often artful in the tradition of Donne, has an innocence and simplicity lacking in that more complex, self-tormenting soul.

Since his work was rediscovered, Traherne has earned his place as a witness to God's goodness whose voice must be listened to by anyone who wants fully to understand 17th century Christianity.

THOMAS KEN (1637-1711) 8th June.

During the early years of Charles II's reign, his minsters considered the Puritans, who had been responsible for his father's execution, to be the chief religious enemies of the state. By the end of his reign, his subjects were far more worried by the perceived threat of a reviving Roman Catholicism. Charles had no legitimate children and his heir was his brother, James, Duke of York, an open convert to Catholicism, who made no secret of his desire to return England to Romish allegiance. Lacking his brother's cynical charm or his father's romantic ability to inspire loyalty, James had no lovable features to mask his Stuart arrogance. His accession in 1685 made inevitable a second national rebellion against his house. Anglican clergy were this time prominent among those who opposed the king, and the most celebrated of these opponents was the newly elected Bishop of Bath and Wells, Thomas Ken.

Ken was a man of sweet and forgiving nature, which veiled a stiff, unyielding conscience. After the early loss of his father, he was brought up by his sister Ann and her husband Isaak Walton, the author of the minor classic 'The Compleat Angler.' Educated at Winchester and New College, Oxford, Ken spent his early ordained life in various posts in and around Winchester Cathedral, before being appointed in 1679 chaplain to Princess Mary, the Duke of York's daughter, who was living in Holland with her husband William, Prince of Orange. The appointment was not a success. While charmed, like everyone who knew her, by the amiable Princess Mary, Ken could not like the surly Prince, and he incurred William's displeasure by conducting, without his consent, the marriage of one of Mary's ladies-in-waiting. After a few months he was back in Winchester. Here, his conscience led him to risk the displeasure of Charles II. The Merry Monarch was visiting Winchester and Ken was asked to lend his house to the royal mistress Nell Gwynne. This, on moral grounds, he refused to do, which the affable Charles chose to find endearing rather than insulting.

In 1683, Ken saw further royal service as chaplain to a naval delegation to Tangier, a town Charles had received from the Portuguese as a dowry when he married Catherine of Braganza, but which the British government now desired to evacuate. On this voyage Ken made firm friends with the diarist and naval commissioner Samuel Pepys, and together they tackled the commander of Tangier, one Kirke, who was notorious for his foul mouth and loose morals. Ken was rewarded for this service by being offered the bishopric of Bath and Wells. Charles II is said to have remarked 'Odds fish! Who shall have Bath and Wells if not the little fellow who would not give poor Nelly a night's lodging?' A few months after Ken's consecration, Charles died and the new bishop attended his deathbed.

The Catholicism of the new King James II caused consternation among his subjects, whose folk memory of the old religion was largely dominated by Bloody Mary and Guy Fawkes. Within months of his accession, his nephew the Duke of Monmouth, illegitimate son of Charles II, had started a rebellion in the West Country, but this was easily put down. Ken prayed with Monmouth on the night before his execution and accompanied him to the scaffold. He then departed for his diocese, which had been the heartland of the rebellion, and was now being ruled under martial law by his old enemy, Kirke, abetted by the infamous Judge Jefferies. Ken was able to save some lives by his intervention, although hundreds of people tainted by association with Monmouth were summarily executed.

Back in London, Ken preached uncompromisingly against Roman Catholicism, among his hearers being the King's own daughter Princess Anne. In 1688 James issued a Declaration of Indulgence, revoking the legal penalties on Catholics and Dissenters: this he ordered to be read in every parish church. The Archbishop of Canterbury, six other bishops and a large number of the clergy refused to obey. Ken was one of the Seven Bishops, whom James in fury committed to the Tower. For a month London was in uproar awaiting news of the bishops' fate, and when the judges ruled that they had been right in defying an unconstitutional command, the capital erupted in joy. Scores of boats accompanied the bishops up the Thames in what became a triumphal procession from the Tower, and every window was illuminated. Shortly afterwards, James II panicked, fled the country, and abandoned his throne to his Protestant daughter Mary and her husband who, in the 'Glorious Revolution', took power in a bloodless coup.

This development placed Ken and other Anglicans with delicate consciences in a dilemma. They had opposed James when he behaved, as they thought, illegally, but he was nevertheless their anointed King to whom they had sworn allegiance, and ever since the days of Henry VIII, Anglicans had taken their duty to God's anointed king with the utmost seriousness. After agonising over their position, Thomas Ken and many others decided that they could not conscientiously swear fresh oaths of allegiance to a man who, however well-intentioned, was a usurper. The non-jurors, as they became known, resigned their offices and considered themselves out of communion with the Church of England. Ken spent the rest of his life living quietly on an annuity at Longleat, the home of his friend Viscount Weymouth.

The non-juror schism was a tragedy for the Church of England, as such divisions over secondary issues always are. Many of the holiest and most inspirational leaders quit the church and the ensuing bitterness took half a century to heal. Some non-jurors were angry and attempted to perpetuate an alternative, 'pure' Church of England, but Ken refused to participate in such manoeuvres, using all his influence as an ex-bishop to heal the divisions and bring people together.

Apart from his record as a man of integrity in a corrupt age, he is remembered for his hymns 'Awake my soul,' and 'Glory to thee, my God this night.'

ISAAC WATTS (1674-1748) 25th November.
By the reign of William and Mary it had become clear that the future of Christianity in England was pluralist. The dream that the Church of England could ever be the religion of the entire English people was dead, and the dissenting churches were accepted in practice if not ideologically. The various legal discriminations against non-Anglicans remained on the statue book, but their practical force was dissipated by the Toleration Act, which made the establishment of non-conformist places of worship legally possible. Theological writers might wax violent in print, but the days of burnings at the

stake, of violent revolutions in the name of religion and of imprisonment of religious minorities were over. Slowly, Christians of different denominations began to learn to live with others as members of a common civil society.

This is not to say that discrimination against dissenters ceased. They were still barred from most forms of public office and from being educated at the Anglican universities of Oxford and Cambridge. No-one could take a degree there who would not also take the sacrament according to the rites of the Church of England.

So it was that when a clever boy like Isaac Watts, the son of an Independent deacon in Southampton, sought further education, he went to a Dissenting Academy in Stoke Newington, where he arguably received a better education than he could have gained at the universities, with their increasingly fossilised syllabuses. Watts was a precociously able wordsmith. His father began teaching him Latin at the age of four, and as a student he already had a reputation for facility both in verse and prose. After a spell as a private tutor, he became assistant minister at Mark Lane Dissenting Chapel in London, and following the retirement of the minister, was ordained as minister in 1702. He proved a good preacher and conscientious pastor, building up the congregation, but at enormous personal cost. His health was frail; he was obliged to take prolonged 'time off' to regain his energy at Bath; and in 1713 he suffered a complete nervous breakdown and was obliged to retire. It was clear that, however gifted, he had not the stamina or temperament for church work. He was rescued by a hospitable landowner, Sir Thomas Abney, who invited him to stay for a week and ended up effectively giving him a home for life. As permanent house-guest of the Abneys, Watts was able to do what he did best, which was to write. His hymns are justly famous, the best-loved being 'When I survey the wondrous cross,' a classic expression of devotion to the crucified Jesus. He was a man of wide interests and wrote much about the education of children, as well as verse for children to read. Modern readers might find much of his output moralising and sentimental, but in its day a verse like 'How doth the little busy bee' became a classic learned by heart by generations of children, and still well enough known in the 1860's for Lewis Carroll to parody it in 'Alice in Wonderland.'

Part Twenty. Enlightenment.

THOMAS BRAY (1656-1730) 15th February.

A new interest in education was not confined to non-conformists. Isaac Watts' contemporary, the impeccably Anglican Thomas Bray, devoted his life to promoting Christian education.

Bray was a farmer's son from Shropshire, was educated at All Souls, Oxford, ordained in 1681 and eventually became Rector of the Warwickshire parish of Sheldon, a place where, according to the custom of his day, he did not feel obliged to reside. He was married twice; his first wife Elenor died in childbirth three years after her wedding. His second marriage, to Agnes Sayer, lasted longer although the couple had to endure the early death of all their children.

Bray made his fortune and reputation in the early years of William III's reign. The Archbishop of Canterbury made an appeal to parish clergy to take seriously their duty of catechising, that is, teaching the faith both to adults and children. Bray's response was to publish his 'Catechetical Lectures,' a book which sold out and earned him £700. He had found his vocation.

As a newly celebrated author, Bray was contacted by Francis Nicolson, the governor of the American colony of Maryland. After a period of turbulence, Nicolson was keen to establish an Anglican church in his colony, which had originally been founded by Roman Catholics. He invited Bray to come and help him organise theological education and a parish system. Bray was keen to go but was dissuaded by friends in the government because the political situation in Maryland was so uncertain. In fact it was five years after the initial contact before he finally set sail, but those five years were not years of idleness. In 1695, he began to campaign for the establishment of libraries in America, for the use of Anglican clergy, who were commonly too poor to buy books of their own. After an initial campaign to secure government funding for his project failed, Bray founded a charity to raise funds for his libraries. This was the Society for the Promotion of Christian Knowledge (SPCK). It proved an enormous success, and so-called Bray libraries were established both in America and in England. Libraries became something of an obsession for Bray. When he finally made the long voyage to Maryland, his conversations with the crew of his ship revealed that they too lacked Christian education, and he founded Seafarers Libraries in the principal ports of the West Country. His time in America gave him a new passion for mission and for enabling the church in the New World to grow. On his return to London he campaigned vigorously for the establishment of American bishoprics, and founded his second great charity, the Society for the Propagation of the Gospel (SPG).

In 1706, he was instituted into a London living, St Botolph's, and from here he directed his educational work with unabated vigour until his death. His work bore lasting fruit, and English dioceses continue to use Bray libraries to this day.

WILLIAM LAW (1686-1761) 10th April.
In 1714, the death of Queen Anne, the second daughter of James II to reign and die childless precipitated a second round of the non-juror schism. Anne's heir by Act of Parliament was her second cousin George, Elector of Hanover, but many Britons, including many clergy, could not overlook the claims of her younger brother James Stuart, barred from the succession because of his Roman Catholicism, but rightful King in the eyes of many. He and his son, Bonnie Prince Charlie, were to disturb British politics for half a century, and at George I's accession a fresh wave of clergy unable conscientiously to swear allegiance to the new King, were deprived of their livings.

Among those scrupulous objectors was a young man for whom a promising career had beckoned in university and church. William Law resigned both his living and his university fellowship, and for some years lived a hand-to-mouth existence, starving for conscience' sake. He was rescued, like Thomas Ken and Isaac Watts, by a generous patron, in Law's case by Mr Edward Gibbon, who took Law into his house and made him tutor to his son. This boy would eventually be the father of Gibbon the historian. William Law's friendship with the Gibbon family lasted for the rest of his life. While under their roof, he wrote the works which were to make him famous, the most influential of which was 'A Serious Call to a Devout and Holy Life.' The book's title is an accurate summary of its content. Law set out to challenge the prevailing culture of early Georgian England, where people, nominally Christian, paid lip-service to their faith with pious platitudes and a little light church-going, but in fact lived worldly lives, seeking wealth and social prestige. In simple, direct prose, Law exposes the hypocrisy and folly of those who claim to believe the gospel, but give not a tenth so much effort to preparing for Heaven, as they do to cosseting their health and advancing their careers. Law sets his readers the highest standards, condemning as an irrational and impious waste of time theatre-going, parties, concern for dress, and dancing. The book is enlivened by the famous 'characters', satirical portraits of typical figures, to illustrate the various virtues and vices: Calidus, the businessman obsessed with making money; Flavia, the woman of the world who believes she is charitable because once in half a year she tosses half a crown to some poor person who takes her fancy; Miranda, the personification of true charity who regards herself as 'only one of a certain number of poor people that are relived out of her fortune.' A true son of the enlightenment, Law appeals throughout to reason as the guide to escaping the follies of self-indulgence, and commends Christian self-denial as enlightened self-interest. If the soul is to live for ever, it is simple common sense to devote most of one's energy to its care.

'A Serious Call' had an immense influence, shaping in many minds the outline of what a true Christian life should be. Among readers deeply moved by it were Dr Johnson and John and Charles Wesley, and even Edward Gibbon, no friend to the Christian church, conceded that 'had not (Law's) vigorous mind been clouded by enthusiasm, he might be ranked with the most agreeable and ingenious writers of the times.'

Law earned enough by his writing to live in modest comfort and in his late years joined with two female friends, Mrs Hutcheson and Hester Gibbon, the sister of his pupil, to build at King's Cliffe, Northamptonshire, an attempt at a perfect Christian community. True to his principles, he lived simply, eschewed expensive pleasures, and gave away the bulk of his income in alms. In old age, he was increasingly drawn to mysticism, treasuring the writings of Jacob Boehme and spending long hours in prayer. This quest for authentic, personal religious experience, just as much as his rational insistence on a sober, god-fearing lifestyle, made Law a prophet of the coming religious revival which was to make Evangelicalism the faith of most earnest English people by the end of the century.

JOSEPH BUTLER (1692-1752) 16th June.

The eighteenth century, upon which we now embark, is often called the 'Age of Enlightenment,' the age in which scientific thought and a regard for reason as the measure of truth, replace the zealotry and bigotry of the age of faith to which it succeeded. It is certainly true that to many educated minds the classic Christian controversies, Catholicism versus Protestantism, Calvinism versus Arminianism, had discredited Christianity itself. Quarrels, often upon abstract points of doctrine, had too often led to persecution, cruelty and civil war but now the fires of doctrinal zeal had burned themselves out, and to a mind which prided itself on philosophical indifference, both parties too often appeared equally ridiculous. The eighteenth century was the first in which respectable people could operate as atheists, and even where things were not carried that far, many thinking people espoused deism, a system where the miracles and revelation of Christianity were purged away, leaving a bloodless belief in an abstract and distant deity, whose only effect on the world he had created was a call for his creatures to live by rational benevolence.

This is not to say that eighteenth century religion lacked passion. But just as the literature of the time was concerned, not with the fall of princes but with domestic themes, the trials of a virtuous servant girl or the wanderings of a disinherited foundling, so those in earnest about their faith sought for an authentic, personal relationship with God, which, although undergirded by classical theology, was centred, not on understanding the Trinity or plumbing the depths of predestination, but on the quest of the self for salvation. 'What must I do to be saved?' was the intensely personal question which drove the spirituality and ethics of the early modern era.

What characterises eighteenth century piety, when compared with the seventeenth century, is its optimism. There is a new sense that the world is good, made for our enjoyment by a benevolent creator and that human nature is capable of a rational, good response to this good God. One writer who certainly began from this starting point was Joseph Butler. Brought up in a dissenting family, he early made the decision to conform to the Church of England, and was thus eligible for an Oxford education at Oriel. He was ordained and in 1726 published 'Fifteen sermons,' which established his reputation as a heavyweight thinker. He caught the attention of Queen Caroline, wife of George II, who appointed him a clerk of her closet. His principal duties appear to have been attending the Queen's evening parties and making stimulating conversation with the intellectuals she loved to patronise. At this time he published his most famous work 'The Analogy of Religion, natural and revealed, to the Constitution and Course of Nature.' With his reputation as a serious theologian established, Butler was preferred, first to the see of Bristol, then to that of Durham, in Horace Walpole's famous phrase 'wafted to that see in a cloud of metaphysics.' Butler was a sober, reserved man who never married and whose writings give little clue to his personality. He was a bad manager of money, which he spent mostly on building projects and on generous gifts to charities and to the poor. His study was the centre of his life. There is little indication that, either as parish priest or as bishop, he spent much time on pastoral work, although he was loved and admired for his mildness and integrity of character.

'The Analogy of Religion' makes clear its objective by its title. Butler wrote to convince sceptics that Christianity, far from being superstitious or incredible, was entirely compatible with the nature of things, as these could be discovered by human reason. He drew what was becoming a conventional distinction between 'natural' and 'revealed' religion 'Natural' religion was what the human mind, unaided, could discover by examining the world: that the world was created, that its order, beauty and goodness testified to the goodness, wisdom and power of its creator, that this creator required moral behaviour from his human creatures and had given them conscience as a guide. 'Revealed' religion dealt with doctrines which could not have been known had they not been supernaturally revealed through scripture: the Trinity, the Incarnation, the existence of Heaven and Hell. Butler's contention is that, far from being embarrassing medieval relics, which an enlightened deist can afford to ignore, these revealed truths are entirely consistent with a rational account of God and form one harmonious system which alone can satisfy the hunger of a human heart which knows itself incomplete without God. Butler's writing is rational, abstract, serious and concerned with establishing a philosophical basis for true moral living. It had a great effect on serious-minded readers and was still regarded as a model defence of the faith in the mid-nineteenth century. Modern readers are less likely to be convinced by Butler's starting point, that the world is self-evidently ordered and benevolent, but his exploration of how concepts like duty and conscience affect our conduct, is still valued by students of ethics.

SAMUEL JOHNSON (1709-1784) 13th December.
If any one person were to be chosen to represent eighteenth century England, it would be Dr Johnson. Only two fictional characters, Falstaff and Mr Pickwick, can rival his image as the quintessential hearty clubbable Englishman, and only Oscar Wilde has had his one-liners more frequently quoted: 'The man who is tired of London, is tired of life,' 'The noblest prospect which a Scotsman ever sees is the high road which leads him to England.' 'Depend upon it, when a man is to be hanged in half an hour, it concentrates the mind wonderfully.' We see Johnson through the eyes of his biographer Boswell, who has given us an unforgettable portrait of the great man holding court in the taverns of Fleet Street, capping witticisms with the wits and rascals of the age.

It may seem surprising to find this apparently worldly figure included in a list of saints, but there was much more to Samuel Johnson than a club-man and trader of smart remarks. Throughout his life he was dogged by depression, self-disgust, loneliness and regret, and it is the spirit in which he lived through these negative experiences that makes him an exemplar and a spiritual as well as a literary giant.

Johnson's father was a book-seller and book-binder in Lichfield, a man who was as good a craftsman as he was a poor businessman. Young Samuel was ungainly and clumsy, with poor sight and defective hearing; like many clever, ugly boys he soon learned how to use humour to win pre-eminence over handsomer, more athletic classmates. He had all his life something uncouth about him, never managing to escape an atmosphere of dirt and squalor, and notorious for the appalling way he mangled books as he read them. He compensated for his clumsiness by a delight in physical exertion which was often eccentrically expressed; all his life he loved walking, and even in his fifties would vault over a gate, roll down a hill or strip off to swim in a river as the fancy took him.

His very great intelligence and phenomenal memory were early recognised, and he was sent to Oxford, but money troubles meant he was unable to take his degree. Staying with a friend in Birmingham, he made his controversial choice of wife; he was twenty-five, Tetty Porter was a plump widow of forty-five with a daughter Johnson's age. She had money, cynics noted, but it appears to have been a love-match. It was not on the surface a happy union. Johnson used his wife's money to open a school, which was a failure, never attracting more than half a dozen pupils. Penniless again, Johnson left his wife in the midlands and walked to London determined to succeed as a writer. With him went his prize pupil, destined to be a lifelong friend, David Garrick, who would be the greatest actor of his age. As soon as he could afford to do so, Johnson sent for Tetty, but she was never happy with their hand-to-mouth existence and soon became an alcoholic, spending much of each day in bed lamenting her unhappy lot. Johnson spent much of his time away from home, even renting a separate apartment to have somewhere solitary to write. Nevertheless, when Tetty died, Johnson was devastated, whether from guilt, whether from real love, whether from loneliness. He kept the anniversary of her death as a day of mourning and seems to have missed her more the older he got.

He was earning uncertainly as the writer of moral essays for periodicals; his fortunes changed when he bought out his famous 'Dictionary,' an amazing single-handed attempt to define the English language. His reputation as a learned man was made, and his money worries were ended when the government offered him a pension. He later brought out a critical edition of Shakespeare and a set of 'Lives of English Poets.' He did not admire Donne, whom he found over-subtle – 'the reader, though he sometimes admires, is seldom pleased.'

His public success and his pose as a man so independent and outspoken as often to verge on rudeness covered a private humility and a deep charity. He constantly berated himself for his laziness, self-indulgence and lack of order. He was not, actually, despite his image, given to pleasures of the flesh. Though addicted to tea and, later, to opium as a sleeping-draught, he drank very little alcohol and he fought manfully, from Christian principles, against sexual temptation – he once famously remarked to Garrick, 'I'll come no more behind your scenes, David, for the silk stockings and white bosoms of your actresses do make my genitals to quiver.' He was quietly benevolent, dropping pennies into the laps of homeless children as they slept, and welcoming into his home an increasing number of unfortunate, aged and sick dependents. His lifelong servant was the black ex-slave Samuel Barber, whom he educated and made his heir.

To lay the pompous certainty of his public writing alongside the ruthless honesty of his journals and letters is to gain an unforgettable impression of a man who knew great pain, spiritual and physical, was often tempted to behave below his own high standards, yet never despaired, prayed often and loved loyally. Gordon Mursell comments memorably 'His faith always trembled on the edge of terrible doubt. And that is exactly why he matters.'[93]

JOHN WESLEY (1703-1791) CHARLES WESLEY (1707 – 1788)
Doubt is not a word one associates with John Wesley, although the conscience of this passionate, uncompromising man gave him perhaps as much unhappiness as anything Dr Johnson experienced.

In 1739, when Joseph Butler was Bishop of Bristol, a disturbing phenomenon was reported to him. A young clergyman, with no parish of his own, was holding large meetings in fields and yards, preaching without licence to crowds of the poorest inhabitants of Bristol. Butler investigated and, in words as memorable as they are apocryphal, rebuked the ardent John Wesley: 'Sir, the pretending to extraordinary revelations and gifts of the Holy Ghost is a horrid thing, a very horrid thing.'

---

[93] Gordon Mursell 'English Spirituality' Vol.2, p.110

Wesley was not deflected from his course by Bishop Butler's doubts, despite his great reverence for the 'Analogy.' It would be surprising if he had been, for he had only reached his position of notoriety as preacher to the nation after great heart-searchings. No-one was ever more anxious to be certain that what he did was pleasing to God, nor more obstinate in holding firm once that certainty was obtained.

John Wesley and his brother Charles were two of the ten children of Samuel and Suzanna Wesley. His father was a parish clergyman, but it was his mother who dominated the boys' childhood. Suzanna united a strong personal faith with convictions about child-rearing which bordered on cruelty. A child, born in original sin, must have its will broken and be taught obedience to be fit for the kingdom of heaven. The young Wesleys were not allowed to play with any other children and such pastimes as they did have were punctuated by regular prayers and regular beatings. When John was five years old the Rectory caught fire and the little boy was trapped in an upper room. Neighbours came to the rescue and just managed to pull him out of a window before the roof collapsed. His mother referred to him, in scriptural phrase, as 'a brand plucked from the burning,' and the boy grew up with a sense that God had preserved his life for a reason.

John went up to Christ Church, Oxford, where his brother Charles followed him. Together the Wesley brothers, pursuing the vision of William Law, set out to become perfect Christians. They and their group of friends sought to regulate every minute of their lives, to make sure that no moment was wasted in idleness but that each day would be filled with activities that could stand examination on the Day of Judgement – prayer, meditation, study, visits to the poor and to prisoners, and exhortations to the heedless and sinful. In an Oxford where most students devoted themselves to drinking, gaming and wenching, the 'Holy Club' became notorious – here the brothers were first mocked with the name of 'Methodists.'

John Wesley was not however happy. Nothing he did could satisfy his relentless conscience; no good conduct could convince him he was secure in Christ. After ordination he and Charles set off to America, longing to do God's work by converting the heathen. On the voyage, they were impressed by the courage in stormy weather of a party of Moravians – their faith, with its Quaker-like emphasis on quiet waiting on God for inner illumination, had a lasting impact on Wesley.

The mission to Georgia was a disaster; no heathen were converted and John Wesley got into hot water through his emotional immaturity. He fell in love, dithered about whether his duty called him to celibacy, gave mixed signals which confused the girl and reduced her to tears, and when she married another man, convinced himself it was his duty to bar her from Communion. He left the colony under a cloud with a reputation tainted by scandal.

Back in London, in 1738, he had his famous conversion at a Christian meeting in Aldersgate Street. A Moravian elder was reading Luther's preface to the Romans, and as Wesley listened he felt a weight lifted from him. 'I felt my heart strangely warmed. I felt I did trust in Christ, Christ alone, for salvation.' The experience of faith as a free gift of grace, irrespective of his arduous searchings for man-made holiness, was formative.

In 1739, the course of Wesley's distinctive ministry began to open before him, when an old Oxford friend, George Whitefield, invited him to visit him in Bristol. Whitefield was a phenomenally popular preacher, who had recently begun to hold open-air meetings in the poor areas of his parish, speaking to miners and to others who would never venture through the respectable doorway of a church. While there, Wesley took his courage in his hands and delivered his own first open-air sermon. The response was astonishing. People were moved to tears and surged forward to claim the offer of grace. For the rest of his life, Wesley was to be a travelling preacher, riding the length and breadth of the country and preaching, often eight or ten times a week to huge crowds of poor people, many of whom had never heard the Christian gospel before.

It is as hard to reconstruct the effect of a great preacher as it is to reconstruct the effect of a great actor. The printed versions of Wesley's sermons which have come down to us are not obvious crowd-pleasers. There are no funny stories, no 'human interest' anecdotes, any appeals to the emotions are restrained and careful. We are given carefully reasoned, biblical argument, expounding the key Christian doctrines. It was the intense earnestness with which these tracts were delivered that brought them home to uneducated listeners. People felt the Spirit move as John Wesley spoke, and they responded with charismatic outbursts, some weeping, some laughing, some falling senseless, some giving in to paroxysms of shrieking which were interpreted as the struggles of the devil against grace. Charles Wesley joined his brother and he too became a travelling preacher.

Just as the enthusiasm was great, so was the opposition aroused by the Wesleyan mission. Wesley and his disciples were pelted with rubbish and stones; attempts were made to lynch them; on occasion the houses of Wesleyan sympathisers were trashed or even burnt to the ground. Behind this mob attack lay the hostility of more respectable people. Bishop Butler was not the only one to be unsettled by the anarchic forces the revival was releasing. Technically in breach of canon law, because he preached outside his own parish, Wesley was excluded by many of his brother clergy who barred him from their pulpits, locked their churches against him and even preached in opposition to his message.

This was a tragedy, because the Wesleys never saw their work as setting up a new church; they sought to revive the Church of England and reconnect it to the people. Wesley was aware of the transience and dangers of an emotional response and formed his converts into classes, small groups who would meet to pray and to encourage each other to persevere in gospel living. These groups would one day become Methodist churches. But the expectation was that Methodists would continue to attend public worship in their parish churches; classes were not allowed to meet at service times. It was the obduracy of conservative Anglicans as much as the radicalism of Wesley which forced Methodism to become a new denomination.

Wesley was never afraid of controversy when his conscience led him into it. He became bitterly divided from his brother revivalist Whitefield because of his rejection of the reformed doctrine of predestination. Calvin's doctrine that God had foreordained some to salvation and others to damnation had, as we have seen, been a cornerstone of Reformation teaching, bringing comfort and disquiet perhaps in equal measure to thoughtful Christians. John Wesley was the first major figure to sound the very modern note of horrified revulsion from this central belief: 'It represents the most holy God as worse than the Devil, as both more false, more cruel, and more unjust.'[94] In taking this position, Wesley escaped from the dilemma which had perplexed the Reformed church ever since Luther first taught justification by faith. If all the work of salvation is done by God and none by the justified sinner, is there any visible sign by which we may know who is saved? Is the gift of salvation the arbitrary act of an inscrutable God? Following his heart, Wesley was briskly certain that this was a non-issue. God desires all to be saved and has made the means of salvation available in his Son. When Christ is preached, all who hear have the power to make a response of faith, and therefore all have personal responsibility for their own salvation. This new emphasis on the importance of personal response makes Wesley the father of the Evangelical movement. From his time onwards, holiness movements within the church followed a pattern which modern Evangelicals can easily recognise and own. A loving God offers salvation, which is appropriated by a personal response, and salvation is testified to by a subjective experience of 'being saved' which matters far more than objective marks such as baptism or church membership. By making the essence of salvation an experience, rather than a doctrine or a sacrament, Wesley was carving out a way of being Christian which would fit neatly the individualism of the modern era.

Not that Wesley let his followers off lightly with an assurance that once you had given your life to Jesus you were safe. He was one of the few Christians who have taken literally St John's statement that no-one who truly knows Christ can possibly sin.[95] Wesley's doctrine of holiness proposed that a spirit-filled Christian ought to expect to live a sinless life. It is a doctrine in its way as terrifying as predestination and explains the awe-inspiring earnestness of late eighteenth and early nineteenth century evangelicals. They aimed at perfection and nothing less would satisfy.

---

[94] sermon preached 1739, quoted Tomkins, 'John Wesley', p.78.
[95] 1 John 3.9.

Wesley's personal life was less edifying than his doctrine; his weak point continued to be women. In 1748, he fell in love with a widow named Grace Murray. Charles Wesley, for reasons it is now hard to discern, was horrified at the thought of his brother marrying and did everything in his power to break off the engagement – successfully, for Grace eventually married another man. Within a year of the wedding, John Wesley (surely on the rebound) had engaged himself to Molly Vazeille, whom he married in 1751. The marriage was catastrophically unhappy. Wesley refused to compromise his travelling evangelist lifestyle and Molly detested the discomfort when she accompanied him and was furiously jealous of his female converts when she did not. By mutual agreement they spent most of their time apart.

Charles's opposition to John's marrying is the more inexplicable given that he himself was very happily married and had several children. Domesticity had its inevitable effect. While the unhappily married Wesley continued to travel and preach to his dying day, the happily married Wesley settled down into a more conventional parish ministry. Charles' lasting contribution to the church was the wonderful series of hymns he wrote, including such classics as 'Hark, the herald angels sing,' 'Guide me, O thou great Redeemer,' 'And can it be?' 'Love divine, all loves excelling,' and 'Jesus Christ is risen today.' Hymn-singing was virtually unknown within the Church of England in the early eighteenth century – thanks to the experience and example of the Methodists, it was universal by the end of the nineteenth.

The split between Methodism and the Church of England finally occurred when Wesley once more turned his attention to America. The colonies there suffered from a dearth of ordained clergy, largely due to the failure of the English bishops to find a legal way of creating an American episcopate. After long prayer, John Wesley, to the horror of Charles, decided that as a priest he was entitled to ordain other priests and send them to America with power to ordain others on their arrival. As with predestination, his pastoral heart had over-ruled theological correctness, but the decisive break with the historic orders of ministry made schism inevitable and Methodists soon ceased to regard themselves as Anglicans.

But the evangelical movement, unleashed by the preaching of Whitefield and the Wesleys, spread across all denominations and formed the souls of a heroic generation. In the next part of our story we shall see how Evangelicals transformed the church, in preaching and parish ministry, in foreign mission, and above all in a rediscovery of the church's social mission.

SAMUEL SEABURY (1729-1796) 14th November.
The problem of how to provide clergy for the American colonies was not solved by the Wesleyan schism. Indeed, with the War of American Independence, it became intractable. In 1776, the colonies declared themselves independent of the British crown and formed themselves into the republican United States of America. Most American clergy remained loyal to King George III and many left the States for Canada or the mother country. Once again, the link of loyalty between crown and church so firmly forged by Henry VIII and Cranmer, was provoking an identity crisis among Anglican clergy.

The Episcopal Church in the new nation was left with no means of perpetuating its ministry, as there was still no bishop resident in America. In 1783, ten Episcopalian clergy in Connecticut met to elect a bishop. The man chosen was Samuel Seabury, who had been ordained in England, had been imprisoned during the war for his loyalty to Great Britain, but had now reconciled himself to being a citizen of the United States. Seabury was sent to England to seek episcopal consecration, but this was denied him. The English bishops could not see how an Anglican bishop could validly be created without taking the customary oath of loyalty to the Crown, and Seabury was a citizen of a republic. Seabury therefore crossed the border to Scotland. Here, the established church was Presbyterian, and it was the non-conformist minority which had retained the historic catholic episcopate. The Episcopal Church of Scotland owed its existence to resisting not just Presbyterianism but also the Hanoverian succession; it had links with the English non-jurors. In 1784, Samuel Seabury was consecrated in Aberdeen and returned to Connecticut, where he proceeded to ordain America's first home-bred priests and deacons. He also, out of loyalty to his

Scots allies, pressed for the reform of the American Prayer Book in line with the Scottish, which has a higher doctrine of the Eucharist than the English Book of Common Prayer.

Alarmed by the spread of an episcopate potentially loyal to the memory of Bonnie Prince Charlie and the Stuarts, the British government finally managed to frame and pass an Act enabling the consecration of bishops for the colonies. Had it done so earlier, Wesley's break with the Church of England might have been avoided. The new Act made it possible for the Church of England to keep up as the British Empire grew inexorably through the next century. Thus Samuel Seabury's visit to Scotland was the catalyst making possible the creation of the Anglican Communion, now a worldwide family of episcopal churches in communion with the Archbishop of Canterbury.

PART TWENTY-ONE. THE EVANGELICALS.

JOHN VENN (1750-1813) 1ˢᵗ July.

The preachers and congregations of Methodism were mocked and reviled by many in the established church but the changes wrought by the Wesleys were not confined to their own movement. Their insistence on personal conversion, practical holiness and effective pastoral care set new standards to which thoughtful Christians of all denominations could not fail to respond. A typical straw to show which way the wind was blowing was John Venn, who became Rector of Clapham in 1792.

Venn knew Clapham well, as he had been brought up in that charming Surrey village; his father, himself a notable preacher, had been curate there. After a Cambridge education, Venn was ordained and for ten years served as rector of Little Dunham, Norfolk. He was the first rector to reside in the parish for seventy-five years. As we have seen, even such exemplary priests as George Herbert and Joseph Butler saw no disgrace in receiving stipends from parishes they seldom visited, paying curates to do the actual work. Venn's generation was the first to question this ancient practice – it was becoming axiomatic that a priest should live among his people, or to put it another way, that a man paid to do certain work, should do it. John Venn's wife, Catherine King, gave him seven children, one of whom, Henry, we shall meet again. These children were strictly brought up: no dancing, no card games, careful vetting of whom they were allowed to play with. The shape of the devout family was forming itself against eighteenth century laxity. As Rector of Clapham, John Venn found himself in a position of considerable influence. Clapham was then pleasantly rural, and as it was within easy reach of London, it was a sought after location for members of Parliament and other wealthy men who had business in town but wished to live in the country. Many of these influential men were members of Clapham church, nicknamed the 'Clapham sect' as their work for social reform, driven by their Christian faith, began to make an impact. The rector led the way in founding a village society, whose members distributed help to the poor and organised medical treatment. Venn's most famous parishioner, William Wilberforce, was a leading figure in the campaign to abolish slavery. Venn himself, with the Cambridge preacher Charles Simeon, was one of the founders of the Church Missionary Society (C.M.S)

Conscientious parish work, gospel preaching, a strictly moral home life and uncompromising campaigns against injustice and poverty: four of the hallmarks of a Victorian Evangelical. Yet John Venn disliked the word and refused to call himself 'Evangelical.' Like the word 'fundamentalist' today, the world 'evangelical' in popular usage perhaps meant 'someone who is more extreme in religion than I and my friends.' But the very fact that a man who rejected the word lived so whole-heartedly in the spirit of the movement, in itself demonstrates its dominance.

CHARLES SIMEON (1759-1836) 13th November.

Charles Simeon, who worked with Venn to found the CMS, was another evangelical who achieved national influence. This was due to a lifetime of faithful preaching at the heart of the city and university of Cambridge.

Charles Simeon belonged to the charmed circle of upper-class Englishmen who all knew each other and together ran Great Britain and her steadily growing empire. Educated at Eton, his arrival at Cambridge was a matter of course. As soon as he arrived at King's College, he was thrown into perplexity by being informed that all members of college would be expected to receive Communion at Easter. To many undergraduates this was a mere matter of form: in Simeon it provoked a crisis which would shape his whole life. Acutely aware of how unworthy he was to receive the sacrament, he plunged into a course of devout reading and was deeply moved when he realised that Christ, the sacrificial lamb, had borne his sins for him. The Easter Communion marked his conversion; from now on, to please Christ and preach Christ was all his business.

On his return home at the next vacation, with his father's agreement and his older brother's approval, he introduced that staple of the devout Victorian household, family prayers – wife, children and servants gathered together while the paterfamilias read the Bible and suitable devotions. The spread of this custom was perhaps as responsible as any changes in the church for the growth of earnestness among the Victorians.

Back at Cambridge, Simeon's early attempts at living for Christ were marred by that common undergraduate folly, drunkenness. Disgusted by his failure, the young man became a lifelong teetotaller; in late life his tea-parties were to be a defining part of his image. In 1783, at the youngest possible age, he was ordained priest and at once became friends with other serious evangelical clergymen: John Venn was to be a lifelong friend. Some young Christians agonise over what God wants them to do. Charles Simeon had no such anxieties. A few months before his ordination a job had fallen vacant. It was a job Simeon wanted, knew he was fit for and determinedly secured. His father shamelessly used his influence with the Bishop of Ely to win preferment for his son, and the newly ordained Simeon became vicar of Holy Trinity, Cambridge, a post he held for the rest of his life. He knew that from this parish at the heart of the University, he would be able to have an influence around the world.

His early years were difficult, to put it mildly. The churchwardens and settled congregation of Holy Trinity were affronted at having an untried boy appointed as their vicar; many reacted by locking the pews which they rented (thus providing the church's income) and staying away. When others came to hear the young Evangelical, Simeon put out benches for them, but the churchwardens threw the benches out.

Simeon was therefore in the ludicrous position of preaching to empty, locked pews while the aisles were crowded with a standing congregation. The atmosphere was not helped by the presence of distinctly un-evangelical undergraduates who came to heckle, sneer and disrupt. Simeon's reaction to all this was not always a model of saintly restraint. He was very young and, good upper class boy as he was, loved his horses as much as his books. He spent a lot of his leisure time in the stables. He also had a fiery temper and did not respond diplomatically to his opponents, either in the pulpit or out of it. But Simeon was nothing if not determined. For ten years he fought a double battle, externally with those who opposed his message, internally with his own rebellious nature. In both battles he was victorious. For thirty years his church was a power-house of biblical preaching, crowded with students, many of whom went on to be ordained or to hold eminent positions in society. With hours of prayer and iron self-discipline, the self-willed young man was transformed into a gentle, patient elder who gave tirelessly his time to help troubled souls and guide young men in search of a vocation. He never married and rarely left Cambridge, but over the years his sermons ranged virtually the whole Bible, so that the published twenty-one volumes of sermon outlines formed a commentary on scripture which proved invaluable to later generations of preachers. One copy of this work was presented to the Prince Regent; it is hard to believe that he kept it by his bedside, as he did the novels of Jane Austen.

A great preacher himself, Simeon was determined to teach others to preach. There was then no specialist training for those seeking ordination. An Oxbridge degree was qualification enough. Simeon began preaching classes for undergraduates, coaching them not only in content and structure but in voice projection and techniques of delivery. He was also anxious to secure livings for men he could trust to preach the Evangelical gospel. In those days the right to present a clergyman to a living could still be bought and sold, and such rights were not infrequently auctioned. Simeon used his personal wealth to buy advowsons (as they were called) and founded the Simeon Trust to exercise the patronage. The Trust still exists and provides Evangelical minsters for scores of Anglican parishes.

In his old age, Simeon was an institution. He was never greatly loved by the university beyond his own disciples, but he was undoubtedly respected. At his death, he was buried in King's College Chapel under a simple stone, at his own request.

HENRY MARTYN (1781-1812) 19th October.
Though his most important work was the revitalisation of the English church, Charles Simeon also cared passionately about world mission. As we have seen, he and John Venn were among the founders of the Church Missionary Society, and he maintained a correspondence

with many clergymen who were serving as missionaries in the increasingly far-flung outposts of the British Empire.

For these were years when English people began to be proud and excited about their worldwide colonies, 'acquired,' in a famous phrase 'in a fit of absence of mind.' The long wars against Napoleon had tested and confirmed the superiority of the Royal Navy and in every continent competition for influence between France and Great Britain was being decided in British favour. Already the East India Company ruled directly over about a quarter of India while exercising a more or less blatant indirect power over many other states ruled by native Princes. Of all the overseas colonies, India fascinated the English Evangelicals most. Its ancient culture, exotic allure and rich religious traditions (aka benighted idolatry to English readers) excited, shocked and challenged those who were called to win the world for Christ.

There came to Cambridge in 1800 a shy, delicate, fearsomely intelligent young Cornishman named Henry Martyn. From the first, he was a disciple of Simeon, and listened entranced as the older man read out descriptions of India and of the pioneer missionary work being done there. Henry Martyn longed to be a missionary, although after his ordination in 1803, he continued to live in Cambridge, working at Holy Trinity as Simeon's curate. At home in Cornwall, he fell in love with a devout Evangelical, Lydia Grenfell, and it was the abiding grief of his life that he was unable to persuade her to go with him to India.

He finally set off in 1806, having secured a post as chaplain to the East India Company. The long voyage ended in disappointment, for the Company, ever anxious about unrest among the natives, forbade its employees to do any missionary work among Indians. The chaplains were expected to provide religious consolation for English residents only, and even that was nervously censored: the Magnificat, with its stirring promises that God would put down the mighty and exalt the humble and meek, was banned from Evensong in Calcutta, lest it give the natives ideas.

Martyn corresponded with fellow evangelicals in India and back at home: he started some reasonably successful schools: he struggled with his melancholy, self-doubting temperament: he learned a lot about Indian culture and religion in his conversations in the bazaars and along the riverbanks. Two things became clear: one, that he was not going to convert many Indians to Christianity, and two, that his real genius was for languages. In the four years he spent in India, he learned Arabic, Persian and Urdu, and largely completed translations of the Bible into these languages. All the time he was suffering from tuberculosis, and it was apparent he would not live long.

In 1810, despairing of the restrictions which the East India Company placed on his work, Martyn resigned his post and set out to travel home overland. He enjoyed some months in Persia, where he completed his Persian Bible and debated the merits of Christianity, Islam and Zoroastrianism with local scholars. But hopes of seeing Lydia again before he died drew him westward. The journey proved too much for his failing strength, and he expired on 16th October 1812 in an obscure Turkish town. He was buried in the local Armenian Christian graveyard. He was thirty-one years old.

Martyn considered himself a failure, but from the moment he knew he was ill he was determined to give everything for Christ, accepting an early death as the price he was prepared to pay. His translations were his legacy. Charles Simeon and other influential sympathisers arranged for their publication and distribution and his Urdu Bible and Arabic New Testament remained widely read in India until the end of the nineteenth century.

WILLIAM WILBERFORCE (1759-1833) OLAUDAH EQUIANO (1745 – 1797) THOMAS CLARKSON (1760 – 1846) 30th July.

In 1807, the year after Martyn sailed for India, occurred a momentous event in the history of the British Empire. After two decades of prevarication, the Houses of Parliament finally passed into law an Act which abolished the slave trade throughout Britain's colonies. For two centuries this iniquitous traffic, shipping captive black Africans across the Atlantic to work in the Caribbean plantations, had made fortunes for British investors and colonial pioneers. Because slavery was so profitable, because no-one could imagine how the plantations would function without slave-labour, most people preferred to avert their eyes and not to know the cost in human degradation of the national fortune-making. As we have seen, even consciences as finely-tuned as George Fox and John Wesley shrank from confronting the evil directly, although on their visits to America, they attempted to preach to and make contact with the black slaves. It was the Evangelical movement which brought into the open the collective guilty conscience of the nation and, through tireless campaigning, brought the evil to an end. Among those who fought this campaign, the foremost name is that of William Wilberforce.

Almost an exact contemporary of Charles Simeon, Wilberforce was the son of a wealthy Hull merchant. He was educated at Cambridge and in his early twenties decided to enter Parliament. He was elected as a member for his home town, and began his political career already firm friends with the future Prime Minister, William Pitt. Despite their warm attachment, Wilberforce never held office under Pitt. His work could best be done as an independent backbencher.

William Wilberforce was a short, slight man possessed of considerable personal charm. He lived the ordinary life of a gentleman about town, drinking heavily, keeping late hours and gambling. He was a man who was always loved wherever he went, affable, kind, genuinely interested in other people and remembering to do small kindnesses when he promised to do so. He had a great sense of humour, reducing his friends to helpless laughter with his gift for mimicry, and also had a beautiful singing voice. In 1785, he was converted to Evangelicalism after a course of serious reading and reflection on the idleness of his life. For the rest of his life, he was ardent in pursuing the Evangelical vision of personal holiness, like many in the early nineteenth century keeping a diary to record his good resolutions and many lapses from them. In one diary entry occurs a detail which reveals much about the levels of self-indulgence in the society from which he was converted: the newly Christian Wilberforce resolved never to drink more than six glasses of wine with a meal – and this was an attempt at moderation!

Wilberforce was not only keen to improve himself; he wanted to help others too, and during his first years as an M.P, he was casting around for a cause to which he might devote his energies. In 1788, he was visited by Thomas Clarkson, a young man already committed to the abolition of slavery, and a few months later Clarkson asked him to become the parliamentary leader of the campaign. This Wilberforce agreed to do, noting 'God Almighty has set before me two great objects, the suppression of the slave trade and the reformation of manners.'

On 12th May 1789, Wilberforce made his first speech on slavery. It lasted three and a half hours, and drove home with carefully researched detail the full horror of the trade. His stand incurred the hostility of the many MPs whose families or the boroughs they represented had made a fortune through slavery. The long struggle had begun.

Most British people were in denial about slavery. Few had any first-hand experience of the system, and most preferred to believe that slaves were humanely treated, that their living conditions were superior to their savage huts at home in Africa, that by crossing the Atlantic they had the opportunity to hear the gospel, and in short that nothing could be more fortunate for the average African than being taken to work in a civilised country. Turning round public opinion involved the abolitionists in the first modern-style publicity campaign in history. Thomas Clarkson assembled a fearsome collection of West Indian torture implements, with which he toured the country explaining the savage cruelty which was visited on slaves. Wilberforce employed researchers to interview slavers and men who had worked on the plantations, building up an irrefutable dossier of evidence to confute those who wished to remain ignorant. The most powerful book in the campaigners' library was the autobiography of Olaudah Equiano, who had himself been a slave. Equiano was kidnapped as a boy in West Africa and carried to the Indies to be sold. His book describes in harrowing detail the dreadful things that were done to Africans and the terrible effect they had on a loving and sensitive boy. Brought to England by his master, Equiano eventually achieved freedom, was baptised at St.Margaret's, Westminster, became a Methodist and married an Englishwoman. His book became a best-seller, but he never lived to see the abolition of the trade. He died as he was preparing to return to West Africa, where

Wilberforce had persuaded him to take part in the establishment of a free country for ex-slaves in Sierra Leone.

As the campaign intensified, well-wishers boycotted shops selling sugar produced by slave labour, and wore medals designed to highlight the issue, such as Josiah Wedgewood's famous bas-relief of a slave, with the slogan 'Am not I a man and a brother?' But all the energy and imagination of the campaign was needed, as the hostility of vested interests and the apathy of the majority defeated again and again the Bills which Wilberforce brought into Parliament year by year.

He received great support from his wife Barbara, his dearly loved children and his evangelical friends: he worshipped at Clapham with John Venn's 'Clapham sect' and used his network of friends to lobby unceasingly. As well as the slavery campaign, Wilberforce wrote a book 'A practical view of….. Real Christianity,' in which he exposed the socially acceptable mores of the upper classes and called for practical Christian living. He was mocked by those who knew him only by reputation, but loved by those who knew him personally. For all his earnest striving after order, he was hopelessly disorganised and lived in a welter of unanswered letters and a chaos of projects half-finished; he never learned to say no. Most of his servants were too old to be useful and were kept on out of love, and the house was often full of bewildered guests, who had been impulsively asked to dinner, only to find that their host had forgotten about them and gone off to see someone else.

Gradually the opposition was argued down and after ten years of campaigning the slave trade was abolished. It took a further 26 years before slavery itself was outlawed in the British Empire. On 26th July 1833, the Bill to abolish slavery was passed by the Commons. William Wilberforce died three months later. His life had been given to the cause.

ELIZABETH FRY (1780-1845) 12th October.
William Cobbett, the social campaigner, famously attacked Wilberforce, the man of West End dinner parties and aristocratic connections, because, while his heart bled for black slaves on the other side of the world, his social conservatism blinded him to the

miseries of the English poor, as the industrial revolution took hold. But as the nineteenth century advanced, there would be scarcely any area of misery or vice, scarcely any abuse of power or corrupt system, which would not be researched, denounced and changed by Christian reformers. As an institution, the Church found it hard to keep up with an unprecedented rate of social change. Britain was ceasing to be a rural and becoming an urban nation. Industrialisation was degrading the poor while making fortunes for the rich. The railways were creating a communications revolution and migration to the cities was creating an under-class of rootless people. The response to this by many Christians was a heroic resolve to do something and a phenomenal energy and conscientiousness in doing it. Elizabeth Fry, the Quaker, may be taken as a precursor of things to come.

Since the heady days of George Fox, the Quaker movement had steadied, and now possessed the quietly moderate tone of today's Friends Meeting Houses, rather than the ranting revolutionary energy of the seventeenth century. The Friends still retained their peculiar customs, their quaint clothing, plain speech, non-liturgical worship and unusual welcome for the spiritual gifts of women. Where industry and thrift were encouraged, worldly success followed, and Elizabeth Gurney was born into one of the wealthiest merchant families in England. The Gurneys were 'gay Quakers,' who permitted themselves indulgences in matters of fashionable dress and dancing, games and music. These were frowned on by the 'plain Quakers', who held rigidly to the good old ways. Elizabeth, high-spirited, impetuous, quick-tempered, and a little spoiled, surprised everybody by marrying in 1800 Joseph Fry, a 'plain Quaker' and apparently shyer and more serious than his bride. The marriage was a blissfully happy one, and the couple had eleven children, only one of whom died in childhood. But Elizabeth found her married life had its trials; her new relatives disapproved her extravagance, her slapdash approach to housekeeping and her indulgent ways with her children: she would not have them beaten, insisted on breast-feeding them herself, and bought them far too many treats. When she became a recording minister of the Quakers and had to sit among the leaders at the front of the meeting, she suffered agonies as she watched the misbehaviour of her children fidgeting their way through the long silences, while other families sat as good as gold.

In 1813, Elizabeth Fry began the work for which she is remembered. A friend of her youth, Fowell Buxton, was attempting to reform the condition of English prisons, and his sister Anna proposed to Elizabeth a visit to Newgate. Elizabeth was horrified by what she saw. The prison was a network of open rooms, hopelessly overcrowded, in which prisoners awaiting trial mingled with those already sentenced. Prisoners were expected to pay for what they wanted, and those who could not pay did without – sheets, clothes, even food. There was little furniture and no attempt to provide constructive activities. The place was a beargarden of fights, abuse, drunkenness and restless turmoil, and after dark the warders were bribed to allow male prisoners to visit the women's quarter.

After considering and praying, Elizabeth was ready to act. To show she trusted the women, she insisted on entering the prison alone, and she spoke to the prisoners of their children, growing up with them inside. Speaking as a mother to mothers, she gained their confidence and their agreement to start a school. With great reluctance, the governor was induced to make a room available and an educated prisoner was elected as teacher. Elizabeth worked with the consent of the women, involving them in the planning and taking their ideas seriously. After the children's school was established, adults requested to be taught to sew and read. Slowly order and a sense of purpose emerged in the prison. By 1818, Mrs Fry had tamed Newgate. One of the fashionable sights of London was to go and watch her read and expound the Bible, speaking with earnest calm, while around her those who had recently been screaming, drunken criminals sat quietly sewing, or weeping as the gospel message came home to them.

Elizabeth tackled the long-term problems of the prisoners as well as ministering to their immediate needs. She organised outlets by which they could sell the products of their needles and lay by some money against their release. Many prisoners were transported to Australia, a journey peculiarly dreadful for female convicts, who were abused on the voyage and exploited on arrival. Elizabeth lobbied for barracks to be built to receive the convicts in New South

Wales and formed a committee to provide each woman with baggage for the voyage - clothes, sewing equipment and, of course, a Bible.

She became a celebrity, feted by the Royal family, but knew domestic trials. Her husband became bankrupt and the family had to be rescued by her brother. Her children rebelled against the Quaker ways as they grew older and she suffered the humiliation of being censured as a parent of delinquents. But as she died she was busy founding a school of nursing, based on the famous Lutheran Institute of Nursing at Kaiserswerth. Tradition has it that among the young girls to whom she spoke of this project was a certain Miss Florence Nightingale. Through triumph and failure, she referred everything to her faith in Jesus. Her dying words were 'I am safe!'

PART TWENTY-TWO. VIEWS OF EUROPE.

SERAPHIM OF SAROV (1759-1833) 2nd January.

For some pages now our story has centred on England and on the struggles of those who stood for faith there. The bulk of what we have yet to tell concerns the Church of England and the heroism of those who followed Christ in the reign of Queen Victoria and the years leading to the Second World War. The story will also bring glimpses of the missionary endeavours by which the gospel was brought to new lands in continents beyond Christendom. But before embarking on this huge but essentially anglo-centric task, we shall visit a handful of lives of Christians whose presence in nineteenth century Europe kindled faith and in two cases provided new national heroes.

The contrast between England in the fourteenth century and England as Queen Victoria ascended the throne is striking. But far to the east, in the vast empire of Russia, very little had changed since the time of St Sergius. True, Russia had grown from a beleaguered principality struggling against the Tartars, to a great continental Power. True, as we see them portrayed in Tolstoy's 'War and Peace,' the aristocracy in the age of Napoleon lived a cultured, Europeanised existence, chatting in French and reading all the latest ideas from the West. But as far as the Church and the peasantry were concerned, Russia was still a medieval country. There had been no Reformation, no Renaissance, no Industrial Revolution. To read the life of Seraphim, who lived through the stirring era of the Napoleonic wars, is to enter a world much closer to Sergius than to Voltaire or Robespierre.

Seraphim was the son of a builder, and spent his childhood on building sites. He had a dramatic early experience of faith when at the age of seven he fell off some scaffolding, injuring himself dangerously; he and his family were convinced he was saved by the prayers of the Virgin Mary. At twenty, Seraphim made his way to Sarov, the monastery which would be his home for the rest of his long life. He was an unconventional monk, who early knew that he needed solitude and silence to fulfil his vocation. In 1794 he obtained permission to leave the monastery and live alone as a hermit in the middle of the vast Russian forest. For twenty years, he grew his own food, prayed, and like the medieval hermits he imitated, learned to live in harmony with nature, so that bears and wolves were tamed by his gentleness. Human beings however were harder to quell. In 1804, Seraphim was attacked by brigands and badly beaten up. It took him days to crawl to the monastery, and he never again walked without the aid of a stick. His days as a hermit were over; he clearly no longer had the stamina for such arduous solitude. Instead he created an inner solitude by taking a vow of silence, a vow he kept for nearly twenty years, living amongst the monks but not with them. It took him nearly a lifetime of this self-imposed isolation to achieve the peace he sought, but in 1825 he finally forsook solitude and began to speak of what God had shown him. The last twelve years of his life were humanly speaking the most productive. He became a living oracle, sought out by pilgrims from all over Russia, to whom he spoke about the joy of Christ in such radiant terms that many visitors commented on the transfiguration of his face, which shone like Moses.

He was an exact contemporary of William Wilberforce. It would be hard to imagine two lives more different, yet each man communicated vividly the joy of life in Christ.

PETER CHANEL (1803-1841) 28th April.

As Seraphim worked out his salvation in silence, at the other end of Europe a young shepherd boy was growing up in the French district of Belley. Peter Chanel's piety was early noticed by his parish priest, who encouraged his parents to have him educated and trained for the priesthood. Chanel was ordained in 1827. Despite acquitting himself well both as a parish priest and as spiritual director to a seminary, Peter Chanel always longed to be a missionary. In 1836, he got his desire, and was sent out to the South Seas by the newly formed missionary order, the Society of Mary. He was assigned as his station the island of Futuna, near Tonga, where he lived with another priest and an English layman, who knew the island and something of the language. The two priests struggled to gain acceptance in an alien culture, but gradually conversions began. As the mission became more successful, it attracted the mistrustful attention of

Niuliki King of Futuna, whose own status as his people's priest was threatened by the new religion. The last straw came when Niuliki's own son asked to be baptised; the King ordered his son-in-law, Musumusu, to deal with the situation. In 1841, Musumusu and his men surrounded the missionaries' huts. Some say they gained admission by claiming they needed medical help. At all events, in the early hours of 28th April, Peter Chanel was hacked to death by an axe. His dying words, in the local language, were 'This is for my good.' After his death, the remaining missionaries were evacuated, but three years later the Bishop sent fresh missionaries. Peter Chanel's body was disinterred and reburied in a suitable shrine; he was venerated as the first martyr of Oceania. The people of Futuna became remarkably rapid converts to Catholicism and the killer Musumusu was himself baptised. A penitential dance, called the 'Eke,' was devised to commemorate and mourn Peter Chanel, and this is still performed on Tonga.

JEAN MARIE VIANNEY (1786-1859) 4th August.

Another lad from the French countryside was to make a huge impact on the church in this era, although he never left his native France and spent most of his adult life in one tiny village of less than 300 people. Jean-Marie Vianney, to become famous as the Cure d'Ars, was born in Ecully, near Lyons in 1786. His family, peasant farmers, had a traditional catholic devotion; the young Jean-Marie's favourite game as he tended the family cattle was to build shrines out of feathers and petals in a hollow tree. This simple rural piety was torn apart, for the Vianneys as for many French Catholics, by the French Revolution, which unleashed a torrent of anticlericalism and ideological atheism. Many French clergy signed the Civil Constitution of the Clergy, a decree which subordinated the church to the state and imposed an enlightenment worldview on the church; many more refused to sign and were exiled or executed during the Terror. Lyons was the scene of particular violence, as hundreds, including scores of priests and nuns, went to the guillotine, and many more were drowned in the Rhone. The Vianney family helped priests on the run to hide and attended illegal masses in remote barns. These events had a profound effect on Jean-Marie. As a teenager, he was conscripted by Napoleon and sent to fight in Spain, but he deserted on the march and spent the rest of Napoleon's reign hiding in a remote Pyrenean village, Les Noes. Claudine Fayot, who sheltered him, remained a lifelong friend.

In 1812, Jean Vianney was able to return home, and to pursue his dream of becoming a priest. Sponsored by a great priest, Balley, who bent over backwards to support him, the young man was nevertheless a failure at seminary. Having had little education in his childhood, he was unable to catch up and his efforts to learn Latin were pitiable. He failed his exams, was ordered to leave, and only the unremitting efforts of M.Balley, who recognised his outstanding qualities, enabled him finally to be ordained. In 1818, the Bishop sent his least promising priest to the tiny village of Ars, where he could do little harm. Fifty years later, Ars would be the most famous village in France.

Vianney walked to his new parish and got hopelessly lost in the snow. A shepherd boy put him on the right path, and the young priest told him 'You have shown me the way to Ars, I will show you the way to Heaven.'

The new Cure embarked on a formidable course of asceticism. Convinced that nothing but prayer could convert his parish, he offered himself as a living sacrifice for his people. His fasting was terrifying; he would often eat nothing more than half a cold potato a day. In expiation for the sins of the parish he flogged himself unmercifully and spent whole nights in prayer. He memorised his sermons so as to be able to deliver them fluently, a task which usually meant sitting up all Saturday night. Both the villagers and the neighbouring clergy considered him mad, and complaints were made. The Bishop's response was memorable: 'I could wish more of my clergy were afflicted by this madness.'

In the end, his holiness won first the respect, then the love of the village, and newspapers began to report the strange spectacle of a village where the church was full, while all the taverns had closed for lack of custom; where more than fifty people went to sing Compline in the church every night, where scores of labourers attended early mass on their way to the fields, where the Corpus Christ procession took all day to get round the village, so many were the flower-decked 'altars of repose' which every household made to invite the privilege of a visit from the Blessed Sacrament. Visitors came; what they told encouraged more visitors; a branch line to the railway was built to accommodate the crowds; the taverns reopened as hotels. At the end of his life Jean-Marie Vianney was spiritual director to the nation.

From about 1830 onwards, his daily life appears impossible, yet he went on living it, day after day. He would get up at midnight and ring the church bell at 1.00 to announce that he was ready to hear confessions. Women queued to speak to him until 6,00 when he went to the altar to say mass. His evident absorption in his task and love for Jesus moved those attending to tears. At 8.00 he had some milk for breakfast, and then said Morning Prayer, after which he heard confessions until 11.00. At this point he preached a daily sermon and taught the village children. He allowed himself one hour between twelve and one to eat lunch, have a nap and visit the sick of the parish – whenever he went into the street, people crowded around him asking for prayers. By two he was back in church to say Evening Prayer and hear confessions until 8.30, when he led the parish in Compline and returned home. He usually spent an hour reading or talking to specially privileged visitors, before retiring to bed for two or three hours sleep until midnight, when the whole routine began again. On some days he spent eighteen hours in the confessional, listening, encouraging, giving advice. When somebody asked him how he coped with the cold of the unheated church, he replied gravely. 'I am very fortunate; I do not feel my feet at all in the winter months.' It is not clear how the people of Ars ever got themselves married or buried with their church in such constant use.

Three times Vianney, exhausted by the demands made on him, attempted to leave Ars. Each time a coincidence, which he interpreted as divine guidance, drove him back to his work. He died of exhaustion in 1859, already venerated as a living saint. He is the patron saint of parish priests, very few of whom can ever have dared imitate his heroic devotion to the sacramental ministry.

JOHN BOSCO (1815-1888) 31st January.
In the year of John Vianney's ordination, another peasant boy was born in Piedmont, then an independent kingdom in a divided Italy.

John Bosco's father died when he was two and he was brought up in great poverty by his adored mother. From an early age John revealed his extrovert, charismatic nature – he used to put on magic and juggling shows for his family and was always good at making people laugh. He left home at the age of twelve to look for work and spent his early teenage years drifting, doing casual work in the local vineyards. His life changed when he met a priest, Joseph Cafasso, who discerned his vocation and, despite his lack of education (he was even less lettered than John Vianney) encouraged him to enter a seminary. Here he existed on charity, being unable to buy books or even clothes. In 1841, he was ordained and began work as chaplain to a girls' boarding school in Turin. As he taught local children their catechism on Sunday afternoons, he noticed groups of boys, too old for the classes, who gathered around the church, larking about and attempting to disrupt proceedings. Regarded as a nuisance, they were regularly chased away by church members, but Bosco began to talk to them, and to discover beneath their bravado both their unhappy, rootless state and their openness to Christian faith. His life's work was opening before him.

Bosco ran a club for his boys for two years in the Church of St Martin, but this was closed after the neighbours complained at the noise and disreputable manners of the members. At this point he decided to make street-boys his full-time concern. He and his mother rented a large shed and began providing accommodation, guidance and education for homeless lads, of which there were hundreds in Turin. Bosco was a pioneer of education by kindness; he won the friendship and trust of the boys, a radical strategy in a world where it was universally believed that boys needed a regular thrashing to keep them in order. The work grew and by 1856 Bosco was housing 150 orphan boys, employing ten priests as co-leaders and having regular contact with another 500 children.

Bosco was a controversial figure in an Italy where the church itself was a centre of controversy. The government of Piedmont was anti-clerical, fearing the influence of the Pope, still a political figure ruling a third of Italy, and moving to modernise the kingdom by closing down religious orders and confiscating their assets. At the same time, the King of Piedmont, like all the petty monarchs of the peninsula, dreaded the popular drive for a united Italy and maintained a large secret police force to track and smother dissent. An outspoken and eccentric priest with no proper parish of his own, attracting large crowds of young men from the worst social background, was suspicious both as a reactionary agent of Catholicism and a potential cover for revolutionary politics. Bosco was harassed, intimidated, even physically attacked.

He persisted with his work, developing his educational theory, which involved bringing boys, who had known only ugliness in their lives, into contact with beauty. Music played a big part in the work, as did regular trips out into the country for picnics, sports and worship in little country churches. In 1859 he was able to regularise his work, founding the society of St Francis de Sales, whose gentle, humane approach to mission he greatly admired. By the time of his death in 1888, the Salesian Order had 64 houses world-wide, and was educating thousands of boys. Bosco also founded a sister order for nuns, which worked with a similar philosophy among girls. His funeral was attended by virtually the entire population of Turin, and when he was canonised in 1934, his feast day was declared a national holiday for Italians.

THERESE OF LISIEUX (1873-1897) 1st October.
In the second half of the nineteenth century, Catholicism had something of a renaissance in France, as many people reacted against the French Revolution and the anti-clerical tradition it had fostered. The Martin family of Alencon were devout even by French provincial standards. Both father and mother had considered entering religious orders before they married, and their five daughters all became nuns. The youngest, Therese, became one of the most influential saints of the modern era.

Outwardly, the life of Therese of Lisieux was unremarkable and short. She entered a Carmelite convent at the early age of fifteen, and died of consumption before her twenty-fourth birthday. What makes her remarkable is her spiritual autobiography 'The Story of a Soul,' which was published after her death by her sister Pauline, who was Mother Superior of the Convent. The book became a best-seller and is still widely read.

Therese was a tenacious little girl with an astonishing memory. The great tragedy of her life was the death of her mother when Therese was five, but her book contains vivid and detailed memories of her life with her mother. She was wilful and charming and petted by her entire family. Her mother's death had a catastrophic effect on her; she became nervous and tearful, perpetually craving the affection of her big sisters, hating school and in many ways a very unhappy little girl. But she was fearsomely intelligent, and saved by two things. One was her love for her father, whom she called 'The King of Navarre' and to whom she was always 'My little queen.' The other was the omnipresent catholic faith which shaped every details of the family's life. After Mme Martin's death, they moved to Lisieux to be close to relatives who could help bring up the orphaned girls. Sunday mass, prayers at home, the rhythm of fasts and feast-days, all this formed the world in which Therese grew up. She early decided that she was going to be a saint.

One by one her sisters left home and entered the Carmelite convent. Each departure filled Therese with grief, as she experienced the loss of her mother-substitutes, but also intensified her desire for the Carmelite life for herself. The Bishop rejected her application; she was far too young to know her own mind. In 1887 Therese and her father joined a diocesan pilgrimage to Rome, where the fourteen-year old girl broke with all protocol and, in front of her scandalised clerical tour organisers, asked the Pope for his personal intervention, so that she could enter Carmel before the regulation age. 'If God wishes it, it will happen,' was all the reassurance Leo XIII would give, but sure enough, on their return to Normandy the exceptional permission was given. M.Martin, who had gladly given all but one of his girls to God, was left alone and died after a stroke, nursed by Celine, the only Martin girl not to be accepted at Carmel.

Within the convent, Therese accepted a life of unremitting hardship, very different from the cossetted bourgeois comfort of her childhood. Here she evolved her 'little way.' She longed to be a priest, a missionary, a martyr. Deprived of any opportunity for greatness, she decided to do every little thing perfectly for the love of Jesus, and to welcome every discomfort, slight and disappointment as a gift from him. Some passages in her book are almost comical as she describes her efforts to receive with gratitude the clattering of false teeth, being splashed by dirty laundry water or being grumbled at by a bad-tempered, bedridden nun. But her project worked. By making every trifling incident an opportunity for a victory over self-pity or pride, she worked out her holiness.

The last years of her life were painful, as she succumbed, slowly and with only the most rudimentary medical assistance, to consumption. Spiritually she was in darkness, with the delight in prayer and communion with God almost entirely withdrawn. Still she persisted in her 'little way,' affirming her trust in Jesus no matter what suffering she endured, and turning her feelings of emptiness and desertion into prayer for atheists, whose condition she was privileged to share. Her last words, as she gazed at a crucifix, were 'My God, I love you.'

The publication of 'The Story of a Soul' set thousands of Catholics searching for the Little Way. During the First World War, more French soldiers wore medals of Therese than of Joan of Arc, and even today virtually every French church contains a statue of her. She is shown in art holding a bunch of roses, from her celebrated boast that after her death she would let fall a thousand flowers upon the earth.

Our survey of Roman Catholic piety has carried us forward in our story. It is time to return to England, and to Oxford in the 1830s, where a new movement was about to reopen the question of the catholicity of the Church of England.

Part Twenty-Three. The Oxford Movement.

JOHN KEBLE (1792-1866) 14th July.

The Oxford Movement, as it came to be called, was in essence an attempt to rediscover the idea of the church as a mystical, corporate entity, the principal means by which the work of Jesus Christ was carried on in the world. All the principal leaders of the Movement owed their souls to Evangelicalism, and carried over from their Evangelical roots a passionate love for Christ and a desire to see lives transformed by faith in him, but they came to mistrust the individualism of the Evangelical movement. The Wesleyan stress on personal conversion, an experience of intense emotional 'conquest' by the Holy Spirit, seemed too subjective as the basis for a Christian life, and the Oxford Movement men were driven back to examine baptism and the sacramental system as the source of salvation and power in a person's spiritual life.

Much more than a reaction against evangelicalism, however, the Oxford Movement was born out of an anxiety about the identity of the Church of England. The church had always been closely aligned to the state, and particularly the Crown; we have seen how some of the holiest Anglicans, men like Thomas Ken and William Law, were prepared to sacrifice their careers to a conscientious loyalty to their ordination vows of obedience to the king. Throughout the eighteenth century, Anglicans could maintain the pretence that the Church of England simply was the English nation, regarded from a spiritual viewpoint, but by the early nineteenth century this pretence was becoming unsustainable. Successive Toleration Acts had long made it possible for members of Free churches to hold public office and sit in Parliament. The Catholic Emancipation Act of 1829 extended the same rights to Roman Catholics. Meanwhile the historic ability of the church to govern itself through the Convocations of Canterbury and York had been reduced to a toothless formality. In practice, the Church of England could only effectively be regulated or reformed by Parliament, and Parliament might now consist of only a minority of practising Anglicans. The situation where the church could be governed by laws devised by men who were not even members of the church was deeply disturbing to thoughtful clergymen. Was the Church not a supernatural society, with an apostolic authority of its own? Or was it merely a department of State, to be directed by a purely secular agenda? These anxieties were crystallised in a sermon preached at Oxford on 14th July 1833. The preacher was John Keble, and the sermon came to be regarded as the beginning of the Oxford Movement.

Keble was the son of a clergyman, who had made his name by a book of verse, 'The Christian Year,' a series of poems inspired by the Sundays and Festivals of the Church Year. 'The Christian Year' is not much read nowadays, though a couple of the poems have become well-known hymns ('New every morning' and 'Blest are the pure in heart'). In its day it was one of the best-sellers of the nineteenth century. Many were moved by the book's simple meditations on the central truths of Christianity, and were turned back to re-examine the Book of Common Prayer which had inspired it. Readers were also stirred by the undertow of melancholy expressed in many of the poems; a sense that the church was in danger, was losing the beauty and holiness which were her birth-right. On the strength of 'The Christian Year' Keble was elected Professor of Poetry at Oxford. It is significant that he made his name as a poet rather than a theologian, for much of the power of the Oxford Movement derived from its appeal to the feelings as well as the intellects of the early Victorians. It was an age of nostalgia, with writers like Walter Scott and Lord Byron leading an imaginative journey back to an idealised Middle Ages, when the ugliness and complex social upheaval of the Industrial Revolution had not yet disrupted a society dominated by knightly chivalry and priestly piety, where beautiful churches filled with colour and music inspired a grateful peasantry to live a life shaped by the church's seasons and gladdened by her festivals.

Keble was a member of Oriel College and in the Common Room there he met and befriended two younger men, both of whom came to regard him as their father in God. They were John Newman and Edward Pusey, and the three were the founding fathers of the Oxford Movement. Though firm friends, they were very different men.

John Keble, for all his intellectual gifts, was primarily a pastor. With a wide, flexible mouth and deep, melting eyes, he impressed contemporaries by his tenderness and by his trustful goodness of spirit. To know Keble was to love him. In those days married men could not hold fellowships of colleges, but after his marriage it seems to have been no sacrifice to him to leave the university and devote himself to parish work, first supporting his father in his declining years, then as Vicar of Hurley near Winchester, a village where he was able to express the ideals of the Oxford Movement in the redecoration of the parish church and in a model life of preaching, teaching and pastoral care.

John Newman was a much more complex character with a highly original mind and a quick, impatient thirst for truth. The life of the mind was everything to him, and into his intellectual life he poured a spirit thirsty for love and security. He was a celibate by conviction, but a man who loved his friends passionately. His enemies he hated with a similar passion, for he was remarkably thin-skinned and took all criticism of his work and ideas extremely personally.

Edward Pusey was an aristocrat and a man of considerable private means. Physically slight and frail (in his twenties he weighed eight and a half stone), he was nevertheless regarded as a better shot than his older brother, and drove his carriage horses with a flourish. He had spent time in Germany, examining the new criticism which was calling into question traditional interpretations of the Bible, and knew both Hebrew and Arabic. His was the most profound scholarship of the three, but lacking either Keble's poetic turn of phrase or Newman's nervous originality, his writings and preaching never made so great an impact on the popular mind.

Keble's 1833 sermon was triggered by Irish politics. The government proposed to suppress ten Irish bishoprics and divert their income to other purposes. In itself this was a sensible idea. The Church of Ireland was the established church in a land where the overwhelming majority of the inhabitants were Roman Catholics, but were obliged by their tithes to support a church to which they did not belong. What bothered Keble was not the reform itself, but the way the decision had been made. A non-Anglican parliament assumed it had the right to abolish bishops and redeploy funds, and the church had no means of standing against the abuse. Keble preached passionately about national apostasy, about an England where the apostolic nature of the church had been forgotten, and holy things were debased in the service of a utilitarian, secular vision of life.

Shortly after the sermon was preached, a group of academic clergy met and decided that their mission must be to re-educate the English people about the nature of their church. They planned to do this by issuing a series of short papers on church topics, the 'Tracts for the Times.' A new name, the Tractarians, shortly attached itself to the new party. Keble had begun a movement which would transform the Church of England.

JOHN NEWMAN (1801-1890) 11th August.
The excitement generated by the 'Tracts for the Times' was considerable. The authors went back to the golden days of Anglican scholarship, to Lancelot Andrewes, Richard Hooker and William Laud, and asked questions about the very nature of the Church of England. To most English people it was evident that the church was a Protestant body, defining itself against the corrupt superstitions of Roman Catholicism. The Tractarians declared that the church was catholic, the Catholic Church of England, reformed indeed of medieval accretions, but miraculously preserved from the errors of Calvinism, with the historic catholic orders of bishops, priests and deacons still ruling it, the catholic sacraments still celebrated, and, in the Book of Common Prayer, a catholic liturgy still at the heart of its common life. As they read further back, the Tractarians attempted to link the life of the church to that of the Fathers before the division between East and West. Pusey sponsored a 'Library of the Church Fathers,' providing English translations of Augustine, John Chrysostom and Athanasius, the great Christian treasures to which the Church of England was heir.

Or was it? Newman was increasingly unsure. Outwardly the late thirties and early forties were the years of Newman's triumph. He was Vicar of St Mary's, the University church, and his sermons drew crowds of hero-worshipping undergraduates, entranced by his vision of a church truly catholic, a Christian life truly a sacramental extension of the Incarnation. Young preachers imitated not only Newman's matter, but his manner – his pulpit voice, his delicate gestures were copied by fans in a burst of what his enemies called 'Newmania.' But within, Newman could find no rest for his hyper-sensitive conscience. Some of his friends, some of his disciples, pushing his arguments to logical extremes, converted and became Roman Catholics, despising the Church of England and its Protestant manners. Newman deplored their departure, wrote against it, but doubted. He read of St Augustine and the Donatists; those North African separatists, so certain of their own righteousness, so contemptuous of those who maintained communion with the Bishop of Rome, how different were they from the Anglicans of his own day?

The issue came to a crisis when Newman published what was to be the last of the 'Tracts for the Times,' the notorious Tract 90. Published in 1841, the Tract was an attempt to prove that the Thirty-Nine Articles, the Elizabethan statement of belief to which every Anglican clergyman had to declare his loyalty, were not the Calvinist documents they appeared to be, but could legitimately be read in a catholic sense. Newman's arguments were certainly ingenious. For example, where the Articles declared that 'the Romish doctrine of Purgatory, pardons, the veneration of images…. is a fond thing, vainly invented,' Newman interpreted 'Romish doctrine' to refer to the excesses of late medieval superstition. The Article could not refer to the official doctrine of the Roman church as expressed in the Council of Trent, for the Council's findings were not published until after the Articles. While Anglicans must abjure the *Romish* doctrine, there was nothing to prevent them believing the *true, Catholic* doctrines of Purgatory, pardons etc. Evangelicals and ordinary church-people, brought up to regard the Pope as Anti-Christ, read such clevernesses with outrage. Newman was trying to trick the church into accepting popery. He was undoing the Reformation. Most Bishops wrote to their clergy condemning the Tract, and the University of Oxford officially censured it as teaching false doctrine. Heart-broken, Newman recognised that the majority of Anglicans rejected his belief in the catholicity of the church. The 'Tracts' were abandoned, and in 1842 Newman surrendered St Mary's to his curate, left off preaching, and retired to the village of Littlemore. Here he built a quadrangle of monastic style buildings, and with some chosen disciples, attempted to live a life of retirement and prayer.

It took him three years of anguished self-examination to make up his mind, but in 1845 he finally asked to be received into the Roman Catholic Church. The decision broke the Oxford Movement in the short term. Newman's conversion vindicated terribly those who had always claimed that the Tractarians were Jesuit traitors, out to ensnare victims for the embraces of the Scarlet Whore of Babylon. Keble, Pusey and Newman's other friends were grieved and bewildered. As a means of reforming the Church of England, the Oxford Movement had lost all credibility. In the following years, many other prominent Anglicans, including Manning, archdeacon of Chichester, and three of the sons of the great William Wilberforce, became Roman Catholics.

Newman himself never doubted that he had made the right decision, but his conversion brought him no happiness. He had cut himself off from his friends and his beloved Oxford, but found he was mistrusted by many of his fellow-Catholics as one who thought too much and asked too many questions. He founded an Oratory in Birmingham, attempted to work in a seminary training Catholic priests, but felt himself isolated and underused. In 1864, he was stung by an article written by Charles Kingsley, author of the 'Water Babies,' in which that hearty Anglican declared 'Truth for its own sake had never been a virtue with the Roman clergy. Father Newman informs us that it need not, and on the whole ought not to be.' The repeated slur of trickery and guile stung Newman into writing his great autobiography 'Apologia pro Vita Sua.' This work regained him the respect and even admiration of the Victorian public, as he laid bare the agonies of doubt which had led to his conversion. In his last years he was made a cardinal and was received by the public with something approaching veneration. Even those who disagreed with him could honour a man of transparent integrity. His great poem, 'The Dream of Gerontius,' was set to music by no less a person than Sir Edward Elgar, and his hymns 'Lead kindly light,' 'Firmly I believe and truly,' and 'Praise to the holiest in the height,' were sung by Roman Catholics and Anglicans alike.

EDWARD PUSEY (1800-1882) 16th September.
The departure of Newman left Dr Edward Pusey as the most prominent leader of the Tractarian Movement. In fact the Movement soon gained a new nickname – Puseyism. Pusey deplored the name, for he was a retiring man of massive integrity, who dreaded nothing more than a reputation as head of a sect. But that very integrity, together with his enormous scholarship, made him the person to whom troubled High Church clergy turned for advice and guidance. His steadiness and faithfulness ensured that there would still be a home for catholics within the Church of England.

Pusey was an ascetic, who fasted rigorously and helped to establish confession as a widespread practice in the Church of England. He knew personal tragedy when his beloved wife Maria and three of his four children predeceased him; for the rest of his life he had to battle with melancholy and a morbid tendency to believe that Maria's death was a punishment for his sins. He was lavishly generous with his large personal fortune, giving up his carriage horses in order to be able to donate £5,000 to a fund for building new churches in London, and anonymously founding and funding St Savour's, Leeds, as a model Anglo-catholic church. This foundation mired him in controversy, as two of the earliest clergy of the new parish seceded to Rome.

Pusey depended on Keble, who was his spiritual director, and was himself the inspirer and guide of many in the next generation who strove to rediscover the riches of the catholic tradition. He faced opposition. In 1843 the University banned him from preaching for two years following a sermon in which he had taught the Real Presence of Christ in the Eucharist. In his later years, he was involved in University reform and in the founding of Keble College, Oxford, as a memorial to his beloved mentor John Keble. Pusey's own memorial is the library and priestly college, Pusey House, which continues an Anglo-Catholic mission to the University.

In 1865, the three friends, Keble, Pusey and Newman met for the first time since Newman's conversion twenty years earlier.

Bizarrely, Keble and Newman entirely failed to recognise each other when Newman first knocked on the door. After some awkwardness, Newman records that they were able to converse with 'the old tone of intimacy, as if we had never parted.' But they never saw each other again.

JOHN MASON NEALE (1818-1866) 7th August.
Newman, Pusey and the Tractarians had been interested principally in catholic ideas. Pusey and Keble were certainly satisfied personally with an expression of these ideas in a Prayer Book tradition of worship which would now be considered quite 'low church.' But the next generation of clergy inspired by the Oxford Movement sought increasingly to incarnate the catholic ideas of the movement in visibly catholic worship. The centre of controversy shifted from 'Puseyism' to 'Ritualism' and to a war over what were the limits of legitimate Anglican worship.

John Mason Neale was educated at Trinity College, Cambridge, and became interested in church ritual not directly through the Oxford Movement but through his fascination with church architecture. In 1839 he and some Cambridge friends founded the Camden Society, which promoted an understanding of medieval church architecture and defined the canons of correct taste for church builders and restorers. It is to the Camden Society that we owe the Victorian church interior which most people believe is the traditional shape of a church. The box pews and huge three-decker pulpits, from which eighteenth century clergy had read Matins, were ripped out of church after church and were replaced with 'correct' medieval fittings: gothic arches, stained glass windows, a decorated altar as the focal point at the east end, a chancel full of stalls for a robed choir, a stone pulpit and stone font, and plenty of brass and dark, polished wood.

In 1842, Neale married Sarah Webster, who gave him five children, and became Vicar of Crawley in Sussex, but his hopes for a parish ministry were blighted by a diagnosis of that curse of the early Victorians, consumption. Neale was advised by his doctor to seek warmer climes, and spent half of each year in Madeira. In the event, he lived more than twenty years longer, but his health was always delicate and the ardours of parish work were beyond him. Instead he accepted the wardenship of Sackville College in East Grinstead. This was a charitable institution providing a retirement home and a chapel for local elderly people. In this safe environment Neale was able to experiment with his increasingly extreme ideas about how proper worship should look. He was mistrusted as a popish innovator, and the Bishop of Chichester went so far as to remove his licence to preach and conduct worship, but Neale persisted. He founded the Society of St Margaret in 1854, at first to provide nurses for his elderly charges, but later developing it into a full-scale convent of nuns, one of the first in England since the Reformation. All this was highly controversial and even resulted in a full-scale riot when one of the nuns died young and Neale was accused by her father of inviegling her into the order to secure her fortune.

Meanwhile his heart was in his writing – he wrote fiction, children's books, verse and most importantly church history. He was a leading expert on the orthodox church, and his 'History of the Eastern church' was for many years the standard work on the subject. His lasting legacy to the church is his hymnody. With antiquarian passion he rediscovered and translated for Anglican use the hymns of St John Damascene and St Ephraim of Syria, together with many of the great Latin hymns of the Middle Ages. His most famous hymn, however, is an original composition, 'Good King Wenceslas,' a carol which bears no relation to the historic St Wenceslas at all. Even antiquarians have their flights of fancy.

LYDIA SELLON (1921-1886) 20th November.
The Society of St Margaret at East Grinstead was not in fact the earliest Anglican order of nuns. That honour goes to the Society of the Most Holy Trinity, founded in Devonport in 1848 under the leadership of a naval officer's daughter, Lydia Sellon.

Pusey had long dreamed of seeing vowed religious life restored in the English church, and in Lydia Sellon he found a kindred spirit. She was already active in Devonport as a school worker and visitor of the poor, and was inspired by Pusey's vision. Her father gave land for the convent and built a chapel, and the new order was promoted by Bishop Philpott of Exeter, one of the few bishops to give enthusiastic support to the Tractarians. Pusey designed the habit of the sisters and helped Miss Sellon draw up their rule of life. He had the greatest respect for her, and declared that she would have been a bishop had she been a man.

In their early days, the sisters worked with the poor under the direction of the parish clergy. They proved their mettle during a cholera epidemic, but remained mistrusted by most good Protestants and were often pelted with potatoes and even plates. Lydia Sellon had her extravagances, liking to be known as 'Mother in God,' even by nuns much older than herself, and imposing a ferocious discipline of self-denial on the little community. It was the outbreak of the Crimean War which finally earned her sisters the respect of the wider community. For the Victorians, nuns had to be proven to be useful before they ceased to be sinister.

HARRIET MONSELL (1811-1883) 26th March.

In Victorian England you did not have to be upper-class to succeed, but it certainly helped. The Hon. Harriet O'Brien was the sister of an Irish peer and, despite regretting her lack of formal education, carried into her adult life a jaunty, easy self-confidence which stood her in good stead in her life's work, the founding of another Anglican sisterhood. Neale at East Grinstead and Lydia Sellon at Devonport may have allowed their zeal to lead them into imprudences; this would never be the case with the woman whom Neale himself called 'The most sensible woman I ever met'.

In 1839 she married Charles Monsell and accompanied him to Oxford where, as he trained for the ministry, he fell under the spell of Pusey. Husband and wife became convinced Tractarians, although they resisted the tide of conversions to Rome which followed Newman's departure. The conventional life of a clergyman's wife was not to be Harriet's for long. Her husband caught consumption and died in Naples in 1850. By his deathbed, Harriet offered herself to God for whatever work he saw fit.

During her widowhood, she stayed with her brother-in-law and sister at their home in Clewer, near Windsor. Here she became involved in that classic staple of early Victorian philanthropy, a Refuge for Fallen Women. Prostitutes haunted the consciences of the

Victorians, and as she worked with Rev. T .Carter, the Rector of Clewer, to give a home and a new direction to those trying to escape 'the oldest profession,' Harriet Monsell knew she had found what she had prayed for, a work to which she could give her life.

It was Carter who suggested that the House of Mercy could best be supported by an order of dedicated sisters, and in 1851 Harriet Monsell agreed to become the first superior of the new community. Her bishop was Samuel Wilberforce of Oxford, the only one of William Wilberforce's sons not to become a Roman Catholic, and as such, he was excessively nervous about allowing a nunnery to be formed in his diocese. It is difficult to appreciate the extent of the horror with which most English people regarded Roman Catholicism in the years following Newman's conversion. Fear of the wiles and treacherous intrigues of Catholic priests focussed above all on the fantasy of celibate men gaining a secret power over the consciences of women, asking them intimate questions under the seal, and then inviegling them into the Gothic horror of a life vowed to silence, fasting and solitude. Wilberforce wanted whatever happened at Clewer to be wholesome, open and English. Harriet Monsell agreed, and with a shrewd sensitivity to public opinion, managed to create a convent which could escape the suspicions of those reared on Guy Fawkes and Mrs Radcliffe. Wilberforce insisted that Pusey must not be involved in the project, that crucifixes and books by Roman authors be banned, that the nuns should not take life vows and that they should retain control over their property and be entitled to leave it to their relatives.

Harriet Monsell was exactly the right person to lead this controversial experiment. With her common-sense, positive attitude, sunny disposition and cheerful determination, she made the House of Mercy an open, joyful place. Many of the fallen women who found refuge there joined the community; many more were able to begin life anew with the support they received at Clewer. Visitors were agreeably surprised by the atmosphere, and Clewer gained many more vocations than any of the other early convents. Harriet Monsell disarmed parents and guardians by the straight-forward way in which she discussed the needs and desires of her novices, and by her open encouragement to the sisters to take regular holidays at home. The seal on the respectability of the House was put by a visit from no less a person than Queen Victoria, who was most impressed by what she saw. The Queen had desired to tour the house incognito, and was a little put out by the deferential curtseys which greeted her in every room she entered. 'But Your Majesty,' explained Mrs Monsell, with a twinkle in her Irish eyes, 'they are not curtseying to you, but to me.'

In her old age, Harriet Monsell retired from the House and lived at Folkestone, where she gave herself to prayer.

CHARLES LOWDER (1820-1880) 9th September.
As more and more idealistic young men left Oxford University fired with the ideals of Puseyism to begin their work in ordinary English parishes, so popular anxiety grew over the Oxford Movement's attempts to reclaim the catholic heritage of the Church of England. At parish level, this anxiety surfaced over attempts by pious young Puseyites to change the ritual practices of the church services. Paradoxically, the catholics claimed to be re-introducing what was commanded in the Book of Common Prayer. The notorious 'Ornaments Rubric' ordained that clergy should wear the robes which were in use in the second year of the reign of Edward VI; these consisted, antiquarians like Neale were able to inform the public, in the full Eucharistic vestments of a catholic priest, garb which had not been seen in English churches for over two centuries. Other practices which offended were the custom of preaching in a surplice, the use of candles on the altar, flowers to decorate the church, coloured altar frontals which were changed to mark the church seasons, the use of wafer bread and wine mixed with water for Communion, and the eastward position, where the priest stood with his back to the congregation as he celebrated, rather than taking the traditional north end, standing sideways on to the people. It says much for the success of the Oxford Movement that these practices, regarded as provocatively and shockingly popish at the time, are now the standard, boring practice in middle of the road churches with no pretensions to catholic piety. For the disciples of Pusey, these ritual changes expressed a catholic devotion to Christ really present in his sacraments. For many ordinary, English church-goers, they were

outrageous attempts to subvert the nation's Protestant heritage. In 1858, the tensions came to a head at St George's in the East.

St George's lay in the heart of London's docklands, an area of dreadful slums and unbelievable poverty. Most local people earned a pittance doing casual labour at the docks and under constant threat of unemployment. The only businesses which flourished were taverns and brothels, of which there were 154 within four streets of the parish church. The vicar of St George's, Bryan King, with his curates Charles Lowder and Alexander Mackonochie, believed that the visual richness of catholic worship would speak effectively to a population without education or any experience of church. Many members of the regular congregation disagreed and were dismayed by altar candles, chanted services, and King's smart new white embroidered chasuble. Trouble was sparked by the appointment of a low-church lecturer, who attacked the vicar's ritualism from the pulpit. Attracted by rumours of a fight, many local lads with no interest in religion started attending the church for the sheer pleasure of causing disruption in the name of 'no popery,' For over a year, the Sunday services became a joke, with hooting, jeering, parodies of the music, fireworks and dogs let loose, and physical abuse of the clergy and choir. The hooligans had a lot of fun; at one time fifty police officers were posted to maintain order, at another a squad of gentlemen from the West End, led by Tom Hughes, the amateur boxer and author of 'Tom Brown's Schooldays,' formed a bodyguard around the pulpit to protect the vicar from attack. Eventually King suffered a breakdown and left for an extended holiday, accompanied to the station by the mockery of a local brass band. But Lowder and Mackonochie were made of stronger stuff. St George's, the mother church of the parish, subsided into a genteel, uncontroversial pattern of services. But Lowder and Mackonochie had pastoral charge of two mission chapels in the heart of the slums, and here they were able to establish both the ritualistic worship they loved, and more importantly, an amazing work of conversion in the heart of London's poorest. Mackonochie soon left to become vicar of a flagship ritualistic church, St Alban's, Holborn. Charles Lowder gave the rest of his life to what eventually became the separate parish of St Peter's, London Docks. Beginning with nothing, in an area with no tradition of church-going at all, he created over twenty-two years a new church building, three schools, a refuge for fallen women, a working men's club and library, youth clubs and guilds, a pipe band, a string band and a choir. Everything centred on worship. Lowder and his team of curates held four services daily, with additional services on Sundays and in Lent. The style was uncompromisingly catholic, with vestments, processions, candles, incense, veneration of the sacrament and regular hearing of confessions. From being regarded as a ludicrous side-show, Lowder gradually gained first the respect, then the love of his people by his devoted care. The clergy lived together in a mission house, scarcely less poor than their parishioners; one curate recalled how their cook thought him remarkably fastidious when he complained at finding a cockroach in his cocoa. During a cholera epidemic, the clergy were the first at every stricken house, and bore the burden of the parish's grief and terror. Reporters who came to write satirical articles about Romish mumbo-jumbo were impressed against their will by the sight of hardened prostitutes in tears as Lowder led a procession of crosses and banners round the streets on Good Friday, to preach the Stations of the Cross.

Money was a constant problem and Lowder exhausted himself fund-raising. His reputation as a ritualist meant that his Bishop, Tait, mistrusted him and would never visit the parish for fear of seeming to approve the excesses of the ceremonial.

The many Anglicans who hated the innovations introduced by men like Lowder, could find no remedy except prosecution. Throughout the 1850's and 1860's the protestant Church Association prosecuted ritualist clergy in an attempt to get a legal definition of what was permissible worship in the Church of England. In 1868 Mackonochie was founded guilty of illegal acts: elevating the bread and wine at Communion, using incense, genuflecting before the sacrament. Although he attempted to find compromises, he was eventually obliged to leave St Alban's. Other ritualist clergy went to prison rather than obey the courts, whose jurisdiction in spiritual matters they would not recognise.

In 1878, Lowder was finally attacked, when three parishioners were found who were prepared to complain to the bishop about his practices. In his defence, he was able to send the

Bishop a memorial signed by 1,680 parishioners, thanking him for his care of the parish and begging him not to modify the services which they loved. Faced with this impressive evidence of Lowder's success, the bishop used his right of veto, and forbade the prosecution to proceed. This was an important milestone in the history of parish worship, as it conceded the principle that the desires of parishioners and the traditions of a parish are more important than legal definitions in determining what forms of worship ought to be used in a parish church.

Lowder was free, but exhausted. He took an extended holiday in 1880, went walking in the German Alps, saw the Passion Play in Oberammergau, where he stayed in the house of the actor playing Christ, and died quite suddenly in a hotel in Austria. It was many months before his parishioners would consent to remove the wreath of white flowers which they placed on his stall. He remains an outstanding example of a slum-priest, whose heroic labour reclaimed a godless area for Christ.

PART TWENTY-FOUR. THE REIGN OF QUEEN VICTORIA.

ELIZABETH FERARD (1825-1883) 18th July.

Although Bishop Tait never understood Charles Lowder and persisted in regarding his ritualism as infantile play-acting, he was too wise a man not to be impressed and moved by Lowder's missionary work amongst London's poorest. But could this work be done without the Anglo-Catholic trappings? Tait found an answer to this question in a young woman with an unusual vocation.

Elizabeth Ferard was an earnest Christian who deplored the way Puseyites were changing the church, and longed to be of use. In 1858, she visited the famous Lutheran Deaconess Institute at Kaiserswerth and was impressed by what she saw. In a thoroughly Protestant tradition, women were trained as nurses and pastoral workers and sent out to assist both hospitals and parishes. Elizabeth was certain that something similar would work in England. Back in London she contacted Bishop Tait and in 1861, with his blessing and support, the North London Deaconess Institution opened at King's Cross, with Elizabeth Ferard as head sister. The idea of women being ordained was not remotely dreamed of, but the Order of Deaconesses gave Christian women a role in church work and volunteers came quickly forward. Unlike Lydia Sellon and Harriet Monsell, Elizabeth Ferard eschewed Puseyism and refused to let her ladies play at being nuns. Deaconesses were Protestant, which is not to say that their training and regime was any less demanding than that expected at the fledging convents.

When her health failed Elizabeth resigned her leadership of the Institute and in her last years ran a convalescent house for sick children. Deaconesses continued to play a valued part in the life of the Church of England until nearly a hundred years after her death. In 1987, legislation was passed enabling women to be ordained as deacons, and the lay order of deaconesses went into almost immediate decline, as most of its members sought holy orders.

CAROLINE CHISHOLM (1808-1877) 16th May.

The history of the Oxford Movement and the controversies over ritual is essentially a history of change and conflict within the Church of England, and may seem parochial to any who do not particularly value either the sacramental life which the Tractarians were trying to revive, or the simplicity of worship which the Evangelicals were trying to retain. But Great Britain in these early years of Queen Victoria's reign was anything but parochial. Her naval power unrivalled since the end of the wars with Napoleon, her moral prestige enhanced by the abolition of the Slave Trade, which that navy was able to enforce, her national wealth magnified astronomically by industrial revolution, she was gradually increasing that Empire which by the end of Victoria's reign would cover a quarter of the earth's land mass. With Empire came both an awareness of the world beyond Christendom, and a sense of responsibility for it. So it was that the missionary became the new ideal of Christian service and Christian sacrifice.

Australia, discovered by Abel Tasman in 1759 and mapped by Captain Cook a few years later, was the farthest flung of the new lands which owed allegiance to the British crown. European settlement there had begun as part of the penal system. Convicts were transported to Australia, sometimes for life, sometimes for fixed periods of years. But many convicts, on their release, decided to make a new life for themselves in the new continent, and the farms and cattle ranches of free men were spreading out into the bush.

We have seen how Elizabeth Fry extended her concern for prisoners to transported convicts as well; through her influence a barracks for female prisoners had been built in Sydney. But by 1838, this barracks had been allowed to fall into decay.

It was in this year that Archibald Chisholm, an Indian army officer, brought his wife Caroline and his two young sons to spend a holiday in New South Wales. The Chisholms were Roman Catholics and struck up an acquaintance with a party of Scots highlanders, who had recently arrived in Australia as emigrants. Through their new friends, they realised the terrible plight of many new arrivals in Botany Bay. Most poor emigrants had spent what capital they had on their passage, and arrived destitute in a new world. Women were especially vulnerable. As the majority of convicts were male, young women were actively encouraged to emigrate in the hope of finding domestic work and perhaps husbands on the new farms. In practice many were met off the ships by the proprietors of brothels and tricked into prostitution.

Caroline Chisholm was determined to establish a safe haven where female emigrants could rest on landing. She badgered the Governor-General into letting her re-open Elizabeth Fry's barracks, took up residence there, cleaned it, poisoned the rats which infested it, and began welcoming the women. Before long she was helping them to look for situations, and eventually found herself at the head of a network of contacts, by which the women were placed with respectable families, then taken up country, and found homes and livelihoods on the farms. She took the utmost care to place each woman somewhere suitable, and held employers to account for the way her girls were treated, though she had no authority but moral authority. Although she resented being treated as a marriage bureau, inevitably many happy marriages did result from her work. She was the only person attempting to do anything for these women; the authorities denied all responsibility.

In 1846, she and her children returned to England, armed with dossiers of eye-witness evidence, and determined to stamp out abuses in the emigration system. Faced with signed and dated evidence of women abused and raped on the emigration ships, of children, supposedly orphans, in effect stolen from their parents out of workhouses and sent to Australia as cheap labour, of the waste of human lives perpetuated by the lack of proper finance or organisation, the Government was obliged to act. But impatient at the slow pace of official reform, Mrs Chisholm started her own Family Colonialisation Loan Society, which advanced money to poor emigrants and helped them establish themselves on new land in Australia. The great philanthropist Lord Shaftesbury, of whom we shall hear much more, was Chairman, and Charles Dickens wrote enthusiastically about the Society's work; he even went so far as to send Mr Micawber and the Peggotty family out as emigrants at the end of 'David Copperfield', although moved by the domestic chaos of the Chisholms' home and the 'dirty faces' of the children, he also lampooned Caroline as Mrs Jellyby in 'Bleak House.' Caroline Chisholm became a national heroine, with poems written in her honour, a ship named after her, and a gold medal presented by the

Pope, one of the few times when he and Lord Shaftesbury agreed about anything.

Caroline Chisholm's fame and popularity was important. It set the pattern for new opportunities for women to serve in public life, from which they were excluded by being thought unfit for any public office. We shall soon meet many other women who imitated her energy, her obstinacy, her refusal to be put off by male establishment inertia. Victorian earnestness was producing a new type of female saint.

ALLEN GARDINER (1794-1851) 6th September.

Beginning with a simple naval supply station at Cape Town, British power and influence gradually extended along the shore of South Africa, and from the time of the Napoleonic war South Africa was governed as a British Colony, although the bulk of the population was made up of native Xhosa Africans and Dutch Boer settlers. Over all three peoples, African, English and Dutch, loomed the threat from inland of the mighty Zulus, whose fearsome chief Shaka, sometimes called the Black Napoleon, had welded them into the most formidable army in Africa. In 1828 Shaka was murdered by his brother Dingaan who took his throne and his power. To the small European settlement of Durban in Natal there came in 1834 one Captain Allen Gardiner, perhaps the most unfortunate missionary who ever lived, though certainly one of the most zealous. Captain Gardiner had served in the navy during the Napoleonic wars, and had visited South Africa, China and South America. On the death of his beloved wife, he had vowed himself to God as a missionary, and it was in fulfilment of that vow that he now appeared in Durban. His objective was nothing less than the conversion of the King of the Zulus. Travelling inland, he made two visits to the Zulu capital and established amicable personal relations with Dingaan. The Zulu king even made Gardiner a grant of land as a token of his esteem, a grant which Gardiner persuaded him to transfer to the British Crown, thus transforming himself for a short time into a colonial administrator. But though the Zulus were immensely curious about the Christian gospel, and asked many intelligent questions, Gardiner was unable to persuade either king or people to convert. Nor was he any more fortunate with his compatriots in Natal. The English colonists were traders, fortune hunters and adventurers, no more interested in framing their lives after the Sermon on the Mount than were the Zulus, and Gardiner made himself very unpopular through his attempts to impose Sabbath observance, public prayer and Christian morals. The Zulu mission finally ended when war broke out between the white settlers and the Zulus, and Gardiner quit South Africa.

Over the next years he made repeated attempts to establish a mission in South America. In Brazil and Bolivia, he was opposed both by native apathy and by the hostility of Jesuit missionaries, who did not welcome a Protestant on their patch. Gardiner was unable to persuade any of the principal missionary societies to fund his schemes, which were more hopeful than practical, so he founded his own Patagonian Missionary Society, a body which lurched from crisis to crisis for lack of funds. In 1848 a lady in Cheltenham made the large donation of £6,000 to the society, and armed with this, Gardiner and six companions set out on what was to be their last voyage.

They headed to the very south of America, to Tierra del Fuego, where Gardiner had already made one fruitless landing. The territory was bleak and treeless and the natives difficult. They hung around the missionaries' encampment, ostensibly friendly but constantly demanding gifts and attempting to steal what they were not given. Gardiner had experienced this friendly hostility before, and his strategy was to keep his mission sea-based, storing their equipment on their two small boats, and sailing from point to point. But everything possible went wrong. One of the ships ran aground and was irreparably damaged. A cave was flooded and their winter clothes and even Gardiner's Bible were washed out to sea. A campfire set fire to a tent and destroyed much of their dry food. Most ominously, there was no sign of the relief ship which was expected to bring fresh supplies. Back in England, the Patagonian Mission had been unable to find a ship willing to make the voyage, and in desperation a naval frigate was commissioned to go and rescue Captain Gardiner. By the time the ship reached Tierra del Fuego, it was too late. The entire party had starved to death. The journals found with their bodies bear pathetic testimony to the unshakeable faith in God with which the wretched men prepared for their slow and inevitable death. In a lifetime of heroic travel, Gardiner had not made one convert or undertaken one journey which did not end in disaster. Yet his quixotic efforts were not entirely futile. His sad tale moved many and led to the founding of the South American Missionary Society.

The main lesson of Gardiner's tragedy was that faith and good intentions are not enough. To be successful, Christian mission needs to be organised. And organisation was one thing at which the Victorians excelled

HENRY VENN (1796-1873) 1st July.

JohnVenn, the Rector of Clapham and co-founder of the Church Mission Society, died in 1813, at which date his eldest son Henry was seventeen and about to begin his studies at Cambridge. The boy had already lost his mother ten years earlier, when she sustained fatal injuries falling off a stool. Now his father on his deathbed told his six younger children that he felt every confidence in leaving them to the care of their brother. He thus left Henry a huge responsibility, besides the Venn name, which had been borne by three generations of clergymen in the very heart of the Evangelical movement.

Fortunately young Henry, a serious methodical boy, was capable of bearing the responsibilities thus thrust upon him. His aunt in Brighton gave a home to his brothers and sisters; at Cambridge Henry Venn benefitted from the friendship and guidance of the great evangelicals of his father's generation, William Wilberforce and Charles Simeon, who confided in each other by letter how nice it was to see the next Venn growing up so satisfactorily. Venn had a great sense of family loyalty. His early tasks included publishing his father's sermons and writing a biography of his grandfather and namesake Henry Venn the vicar of Huddersfield (evangelical of course). He also felt an immense loyalty to the family Missionary Society, C.M.S., and after ordination and marriage (to the usefully wealthy Martha Sykes of Hull), he made the C.M.S his life's work. He was devoted to Martha and heartbroken when she died young of consumption, forcing herself to sit up in bed and smile brightly, so that her tiny children should not be haunted by bad memories of their mother's last illness. Henry did not find being a father easy. Another generation of orphaned Venns were brought up by aunt-power, and Venn, rendered independent by his wife's fortune, gave up parish work and from 1846 worked full-time as honorary secretary of the C.M.S.

Venn was an excellent administrator and a man of vision. No mission funded and backed by his society was going to go the way of the hapless Allen Gardiner (to whom, incidentally, C.M.S. refused a grant). Not reckoned a great speaker, the committee room was his kingdom, where he ruled by command of detail, utter lack of interest in his own prestige, and clear focus on what the society needed to achieve.

His analysis of the priorities of missionary work was both thoroughly evangelical and ahead of its time in an appreciation of what it meant for one culture to enter and convert another. His principles were that preaching must centre on Jesus Christ and on salvation, not on the church; that missionaries must communicate effectively in the local languages (missionary trainees who failed their language exams were not sent out by Venn); that translation of the Bible into local languages must be a priority; that as soon as possible native leadership must be developed in the new churches; that the mission churches develop self-reliance, and the C.M.S. must not act in rivalry to other missionary organisations. C.M.S. missionaries were expected to respect and work with local cultures. Venn saw clearly the danger of racism in a situation where missionaries represented the imperial power in the colonies; he warned his missionaries not to get involved in politics, not to mistake adoption of European manners for conversion to Christianity, to work for the development of a Christianity which would be truly national to its people, and to remember that the missionary was a temporary figure, working towards the point where he could hand over authority to an indigenous leadership.

As an avowedly Anglican Society, C.M.S. did much to develop the Anglican Communion. In 1837, there were nine colonial bishops. Thirty years later there were fifty-one. This number included, in 1864, the consecration of Samuel Crowther as bishop of Sierra Leone, the first black African bishop, trained and inspired by

Henry Venn. During his long years of dominance of C.M.S., Venn built up an unrivalled knowledge of affairs in West Africa and India, and was not afraid to use this knowledge to criticise the colonial authorities. There were some who criticised him as autocratic, none who doubted his sincerity or his expertise. He resigned his post only a year before his death.

ANTHONY, LORD SHAFTESBURY (1801-1885) 1st October.
Nothing illustrates so well the smallness of the closed, aristocratic circle which effectively governed mid-Victorian Britain and determined public opinion, as the surprising fact that Edward Pusey, the figurehead of the Tractarians, was the cousin of Lord Shaftesbury, the great evangelical philanthropist, whom we have already met supporting Caroline Chisholm's work for emigrants. Pusey and Shaftesbury differed on virtually every possible subject, given that personal loyalty to Jesus Christ was the cornerstone of each man's life. Shaftesbury hated and feared the Oxford Movement and lent every support to the Church Association in its prosecution of ritualists. Yet Pusey, the hermit of Christ Church, and Shaftesbury, the champion of chimney sweeps and factory children, shared an aristocratic outlook on the world, a social conservatism and a sort of nostalgia for a pre-industrial Britain where everybody knew their place and was happy there.

Shaftesbury had another famous relative by marriage. His adored wife Lady Minnie Cooper was the daughter of Lady Palmerston, the wife of the Prime Minister. Given that Minnie's mother had been Palmerston's mistress for years, before the death of her husband freed her to marry him, it is quite possible that Minnie was the daughter of Lord as well as Lady Palmerston. Though Shaftesbury had even less in common with Palmerston than with Pusey, the connection, and the shared aristocratic values it implied, led to Palmerston consulting his stepson on religious policy, with the result that all the bishops appointed by the Palmerston administration were Evangelicals, to the fury of Oxford and Dr Pusey.

But we run ahead of ourselves. Anthony Ashley Cooper, son and heir of the sixth Earl of Shaftesbury, had a famously unhappy childhood. His parents simply did not like children and not all his wealth and privilege could save Anthony from growing up lonely and unloved. He was neglected at home and bullied at Harrow; here one of the formative events of his life was his witnessing a pauper funeral, the coffin carried by drunken undertakers' men who swore and laughed as they dropped it. The unhappy lord realised that whole classes existed whose wretchedness made his own loneliness a trifle. Relieving that wretchedness became his life's mission.

As Lord Ashley, the young man had no difficulty in securing a seat in the House of Commons, and on his father's death in 1851, he inherited the Shaftesbury title and a seat in the Lords. In both houses he worked long, unpaid hours, to improve the condition of society. As a convinced Evangelical, many of his crusades were religious – the conversion of the Jews, the defeat of ritualism, the observance of the Sabbath. He chaired meetings of Venn's C.M.S, as he chaired meetings of virtually every other philanthropic society. He was instrumental in creating the Church Pastoral Aid Society, which provided grants to pay extra curates in busy urban parishes. But it was his work for the poor and those with no voice which did most to win the respect of his contemporaries. After Shaftesbury, nobody could say that Evangelicals were only concerned with personal salvation and lacked a social conscience.

His first great battle was for reform of the treatment of lunatics. The madhouse is one of the staple scenes of early Victorian horror fiction, and with good cause. Asylums were nightmare places, where no effective treatment of mental illness was attempted, and where the mad were kept under control by harsh methods, and often exploited by corrupt warders. Often persons merely eccentric or embarrassing to their families were incarcerated for life in these places, which were not properly regulated or inspected. It took Lord Ashley nearly twenty years to secure the Lunacy Act (1845) which provided commissioners to inspect asylums. The Act could not have passed without the evidence which Ashley had painstakingly gathered by years of visiting asylums and questioning staff and inmates. This patient, hard work was the source of his power.

Other pieces of legislation introduced by Shaftesbury included the Factory Act (1833) forbidding the employment of children under nine, and limiting the working hours of older children;

an Act (1842) to prevent the employment of women and children underground in the coalmines; the Public Health Act (1848) improving water supplies and sewerage; the Common Lodging Houses Act (1853) regulating the doss-houses in which the poorest found lodgings; the Chimney Sweepers Regulation Bill (1864), forbidding the practice of sending small boys up chimneys to clean them, an abuse only finally ended after further legislation in 1875. Each of these reforms was pushed past strong vested interests and the grudging apathy of a Parliament wedded to laissez-faire economics as the key to national prosperity. Each enactment involved laborious months of evidence gathering, and the awakening of the public conscience by publicity campaigns – the lesson of the anti-slavery campaign had been well learned.

Shaftesbury was not loved by many who knew him personally. He was too socially awkward, too harsh in his expression of inflexible religious beliefs, to be an entertaining companion. But he was venerated by thousands who never met him and who knew that his rigid conscience made him the champion of all who had lost by Britain's transformation into the 'workshop of the world.' The crowds who lined the streets for his funeral remembered him as a man of pity, and the sublimely inappropriate nude statue erected in his memory at Piccadilly Circus, though popularly known as Eros, is supposed to represent the Angel of Compassion.

CHRISTINA ROSSETTI (1830-1894) 27th April.

Perhaps no way of life has ever been devised at once so privileged and so stultifyingly limited, as that of a Victorian middle-class unmarried woman. Every profession, all participation in public life was barred to her. A married woman, an Elizabeth Fry or a Caroline Chisholm, might, with her husband's support and approval, make some effort at worthwhile work beyond her family circle. A woman with no husband had no presence beyond her parents' home, where she was kept in genteel comfort and expected to do nothing but amuse herself and soothe her relatives all her life. Yet three of the great names of mid-Victorian Britain found different ways to escape the gilded cage and, in doing so, redefined for others what might be expected of a woman.

Christina Rossetti lived outwardly a life purely conventional in its nullity. Her brother Dante Gabriel was a rebel and a pioneer, founding the pre-Raphaelite brethren and making a name for himself as a controversial artist. Christina stayed at home, went to church, nursed her mother. Two little love affairs came to nothing. She got poorer, darned her gloves, sent presents to her nephews and nieces, died. She is remembered for the rich quality of her inner life, made available to us in her poetry.

Her Christian faith was the source of much of her power as a poet. Sympathetic to the ritualist movement, she loved the richness of the liturgical year and wrote imaginatively on the themes of the great feasts – 'In the bleak midwinter' is by far her most famous verse. She also wrote convincing fantasy – one of her longest, earliest poems, 'Goblin Market' creates a genuinely spooky fairy world. Much of her work concerns the strife between earthly love and divine love, the grief of bereavement versus the serenity of the hope of heaven. Her love poetry is all about loss, separation and disappointment, yet even at her most melancholy she reaches after Christ with living faith. She is a testimony to how the most limited of circumstances can be turned to gold for a Christian who is prepared to see Christ in everything and to receive even disappointment and heartbreak as gifts from a God who tries us but never ceases to love us.

FLORENCE NIGHTINGALE (1820-1910) 13th August.

To another young woman of the same generation as Christina Rossetti, but of very different temperament, the life of a lady was so unendurable in its tedium as to drive her to the verge of madness. Florence Nightingale lived a privileged existence, driven by carriage between her father's London house and his two country seats, taken on long, culturally rich tours of the continent, entertained at all the best balls, taught French and Italian by the best masters, bored to tears by having nothing to do. Her heart was set on becoming a nurse, a profession which was then so disreputable that her mother and sister deluged her with blackmailing tears in an effort to divert her from her course. She was thirty before her father finally intervened and allowed her to visit the famous Institute at Kaiserswerth to be trained and to set herself up as head of a nursing home for decayed gentlewomen in London. That was in 1853. The following year came the Crimean War and with it Florence Nightingale's great opportunity.

The war was fought by Britain and France against Russia to prevent the latter dominating the ailing Turkish Empire and threatening the interests of the western nations in the middle- east. The centrepiece of the campaign was the long and arduous siege of Sevastapol, Russia's main military installation in the Crimea. The first war to be reported by modern-style newspapers, it appalled the public at home, who read with horror of the incompetence of the War Office and the unnecessary sufferings of the soldiers in the Russian winter due to the breakdown of supplies and medical services. Sidney Herbert, the Secretary at War, knew Florence Nightingale and asked her to go out and help. She took a band of nurses, including some of Lydia Sellon's sisters from Devonport, and established herself at Scutari, the military hospital near Constantinople to which wounded soldiers were ferried over the Black Sea. This place was a hell-hole, dirty, reeking and lacking the most basic medical resources. Men died in scores and often even so simple as task as removing the dead from the wards was delayed for days. Miss Nightingale was effectively ostracised by the military authorities, who resented being taught their business by a pack of women. With iron self-control, she refused to be drawn into a power-struggle, kept her nurses busy preparing bandages, and did not interfere until at last, in desperation at the horrors which were unfolding, the authorities asked her to help. Within months, Scutari was transformed. Stores were efficiently unpacked and distributed. Wholesome meals were cooked and served. The whole building was cleaned, and bedding and dressings regularly changed. Above all, the men were treated with respect and kindness. The legend of the 'Lady with the Lamp' portrays a romanticised vision of Florence Nightingale as a ministering angel, soothing pillows with a woman's gentle smile. The reality was far from gentle. Florence Nightingale had no mercy on her staff, worked impossible hours herself, and proved herself a formidable administrator; whenever an army surgeon declared that something could not be done, Miss Nightingale had the statistics and the plans to prove that it could be and must be.

She returned to England a national heroine, for many years honoured by being portrayed on the Ten Pound Note. She also returned physically and mentally exhausted, but determined to effect a thorough-going reform first of army, then of national medicine. She refused to take the celebrity role which the public wanted to give her; addressed no meetings, led no campaigns, embarrassed no-one with publicity stunts. Instead, pleading chronic ill health, she shut herself away in her sick room and read and studied and made herself the country's leading expert on matters medical. The Royal Commission on the health of the Army, chaired by Sidney Herbert, was directed by her. Its members came to her bedside to be given the facts and instructed in their strategies. The battle against vested interests was so unyielding that it drove Herbert to premature death, which filled Florence Nightingale with bitter remorse; she had been contemptuous of his complaints of fatigue and regarded his taking sick leave as treachery.

Her achievements were a reformed medical service for the army, and for the nation a new training college for nurses and a new status for the profession, which thanks to her became an honoured and loved calling. Spiritually, she pursued a very personal path of holiness, inspired by heroines like Joan of Arc and Teresa of Avila, who like her had had to fight for recognition in a man's world, and angry with the Church of England for its failure to give its women worthwhile work to do.

FREDERICK MAURICE (1805-1872) 1st April.

Lord Shaftesbury and his cousin Dr Pusey agreed on very little, but on one point they were in full accord. Those who disobeyed Christ and turned their backs on his grace must expect an eternity of pain in the flames of Hell. If people stopped believing in Hell, there would be no effective check on their consciences, and immorality and crime would run rife. Thus when in 1853, the Professor of Modern History at King's College, London, published a set of 'Theological Essays' in which he appeared to question whether hellfire was in fact 'eternal,' Pusey and Shaftesbury exchanged letters and found themselves for once on the same side. The man was a heretic, a danger to the young, and must resign.

The professor at the centre of the controversy was Frederick Denison Maurice, a large hearted, idealistic man, who had been baptised into the Church of England at the age of 25, after breaking with his childhood Unitarianism. He made his name with his first big book 'The Kingdom of Christ,' which takes the form of a dialogue with a Quaker. The book considers the main branches of Christianity in turn and asks how capable each is of expressing within human society the kingdom of God as preached by Jesus. In the end, the Church of England appears to be the best expression of God's kingdom and the Quaker is duly converted.

Recently widowed, Maurice was not only a Professor at King's, but Chaplain of Lincoln's Inn, and thoroughly immersed in the life of London. He held open house, particularly for intelligent working men, for whose benefit he was always working. It was an age of political unrest, with the Chartists campaigning for universal suffrage and the first stirrings of the Trades Union movement disturbing capitalists and respectable people. So rare was a gentleman, and a parson, who sympathised with the aspirations of working men that Maurice, vague, impractical, academic, and always kind, became a somewhat unlikely rallying point for what came to be known as Christian Socialism.

For Maurice, the heart of Christianity must always be, not doctrine, or church system, but universal love. 'The Church is the Family of all mankind,' he preached. 'We dare not refuse to any member of that family a share in the beauty and riches and responsibilities of the world which God created.' Preached amidst the shabby ugliness of London's backstreets, this unexceptional sentiment seemed revolutionary. Maurice and a group of friends fired by similar ideals attempted to organise working men's co-operatives, in which the workers would own their businesses and share the profits. The organisers being stronger on noble ideas than on business experience, these early experiments were largely commercial failures, but they cast a long shadow.

Maurice's troubles came about because he found abhorrent the traditional belief in Hell as a place where God maintained in perpetual and hopeless pain all who rebelled against him. Maurice speculated on other possible interpretations – was 'eternal' the same as 'everlasting' in Greek? Might not 'eternal death' mean annihilation rather than ceaseless torture? How did Hell serve a God of love? Public protest, led, as so often, by many who had not actually read 'Theological Essays,' did for Maurice's academic career and he was obliged to resign form King's College. His working-class friends remained loyal and he retained the post dearest to his heart, that of Principal of the Working Men's College, where he continued to work for the education of those shut out by class from the universities. Around the College gathered a galaxy of generous hearted gentlemen, too liberal minded to be confined by either Evangelicals or Tractarians. Charles Kingsley, Newman's opponent, was a firm supporter. John Ruskin taught art. Christina Rossetti's brother, Dante Gabriel, taught painting. Tom Hughes, who protected Lowder from hooligans, taught boxing in an attempt to build the physique of the lower orders – well-fed gentry from the country were frequently shocked by the pasty, unhealthy little men bred in the slums of the capital. Maurice was more secure on education than on commercial business, and the college survived and prospered. In his old age, his virtues were recognised and he became Professor of Moral Philosophy at Cambridge.

Although his achievements were patchy, Maurice is justly remembered as a pioneer in helping the Church of England discover its social conscience. After him, church workers were readier to recognise that salvation was not a purely spiritual phenomenon, but must affect the environment and social conditions in which people lived as well as their souls.

OCTAVIA HILL (1838-1912) 13th August.

Frederick Maurice did not only help working men through his college: women too found an inspiration in his scholarly kindness. In 1851, he prepared for baptism and confirmation a thirteen-year old girl, like himself from a Unitarian family, who was already a veteran promoter of his Christian socialist ideals. Octavia Hill's father was ruined when his bank failed. His family, provided with a home by his wife's father, lived in poverty rather less than genteel; they even lacked that essential badge of middle-classness, a servant. Mrs Hill educated her daughters, expected them to do housework and encouraged them to earn their own living. At the time of her confirmation, Octavia was managing a little toy factory, training children younger than herself to make the toys and working out how to market them and save the profits for the good of all the workers. It was a Christian Socialist co-operative in miniature. Deeply devoted to Maurice, she became administrative secretary for all the women's classes at the Working Men's College and burned with indignation when he was obliged to resign from King's College. Her other great mentor from Maurice's group was the art historian John Ruskin, who was much impressed by her talent, and trained and employed her as an illustrator for his books. Ruskin had money and one day was talking to Octavia, lamenting the lack of usefulness in his life. Octavia's reply was 'I know what I would do – something to provide better homes for the poor.' Intrigued, Ruskin asked more questions and between them they began a remarkable experiment in social housing.

The housing of the London poor was deplorably squalid. Families lived crowded into single rooms and cellars with no light, water supply or sanitation. Private landlords had no interest in improving their properties, knowing that no matter how wretched and run down they became, there would always be someone desperate enough to rent them. Octavia had lived amongst this degradation and wanted to change things. Her idea was that if tenants were given a stake in improving their homes, they would respond positively to the challenge, and that enlightened policy by the landlord could also be proved to be commercially viable. With Ruskin's capital she bought three houses in Marylebone and promised Ruskin that he would receive 5% interest on his investment. She collected the rents herself, insisting on business-like punctuality but treating the tenants with marked courtesy. In return all the houses were repaired, cleaned and decorated. A portion of the rent was set aside for repairs and the tenants decided for themselves what improvements should be made. Tenants responded as she had hoped, and she was able to declare her experiment a success. Ruskin was receiving his promised profit, giving the lie to exploitative landlords who claimed repairs would ruin them. The tenants were taking a pride in keeping their homes clean and orderly, giving the lie to defeatists who argued that slum-dwellers were incorrigibly dirty and feckless. Octavia became a celebrity, much to her own disgust, and her houses were visited by the great and good, including members of the royal family. Her business rapidly expanded: indeed, the Octavia Hill Trust has remained a feature of London's social housing to this day.

Octavia Hill was obsessed by fresh air. She longed to provide her tenants with room to breathe amidst the smoke and crowds of the capital. One of the first amenities she provided when funds allowed was a children's playground, and she always preferred cottages to flats, believing that even the smallest garden or backyard improved the quality of family life by giving children somewhere to play, and husbands space to pursue hobbies and keep out of the pub. She campaigned for open spaces to be available for the poor, invented the term 'Green Belt,' spent her leisure time walking footpaths to preserve their rights of way, and in 1894, helped to found the National Trust.

She is interesting because she was on the losing side of the long debate about social provision which ended, fifty years after her death, in the creation of the welfare state. She believed fiercely that grants of money kept the poor poor by stripping them of dignity and a sense of responsibility for their own welfare. Even the poorest person must be expected to contribute to any scheme for relief; only so would they be able to grow and take control of their own life. She opposed the introduction of old age pensions and would have been horrified by much of today's social provision via universal benefits. One of her creations was the Charity Organisation Society, which reformed local charities by enquiring carefully into the circumstances of each case before any money was granted. People who had contributed to their own troubles by irresponsibility, drunkenness and vice ought not to expect a charity to bail them out. The invidious concept of the 'deserving poor' began to shape attitudes. It is fascinating to speculate how different modern Britain would be had Octavia's principles prevailed.

She never married, regarded hard work as holy and a privilege, loved natural beauty and treated everyone she met with respect.

JOSPEHINE BUTLER (1828-1906) 30thMay.
Octavia Hill addressed the physical squalor of the Victorian city. Most middle-class observers were horrified by its moral squalor. The prostitute epitomised the dark side of Victorian respectability and prosperity, and Britain's cities teemed with them. Men tended to marry late as they must be able to support a wife and children and, as unmarried sex with social equals was unthinkable, it was tacitly accepted in many circles that resort to prostitutes was both inevitable and natural. Women, trapped in a system where opportunities to earn their living respectably were bleak, were easily drawn to the streets. The double standard in sexual morality meant that a servant girl or shop assistant who 'fell' lost position and reputation, while her male partner escaped blame. For such girls without characters prostitution was the only resource. Fear of sexually transmitted disease led to a premium being placed on virgins, and very young girls were routinely trapped or bought to be raped by clients and then left to the mercies of the brothel. The fallen woman is a stock figure of Victorian fiction, and guilt about her existence haunted the respectable. We have seen how redeeming prostitutes formed a central part of the ministries of Charles Lowder and Harriet Monsell. The work of challenging the whole system, and the degraded moral assumptions on which it rested, fell to a headmaster's wife from Liverpool, Josephine Butler.

When George and Josephine Butler arrived at Liverpool College in 1866, they had already known heart-rending tragedy in their marriage. Their five year old daughter Eva, remembered ever after as an angelic child, had fallen through the banisters of their home in Cheltenham and had been picked up dying from the hall floor. Josephine found it hard to speak of her adored daughter for the rest of her life, but her unassuageable grief drove her outwards to others who suffered. The gap made in the mother's heart was filled by girl after suffering girl, who found in her compassion and practical help. From early days in Liverpool, horrified by the city's poverty, she was visiting poor girls and even offering them beds in her own home. Inevitably many she tried to help were prostitutes.

In that same year 1866, the Contagious Diseases Act was passed (extended in 1869). The Act purported to be concerned for the health of the armed forces, and provided for the compulsory testing of prostitutes in garrison towns for sexually transmitted diseases. Every feature of this legislation horrified Josephine Butler. It assumed that young soldiers and sailors were incapable of continence. The special police appointed to effect the regulations were not subject to the local authority and had power to arrest any woman they had 'good cause' to believe was a prostitute – the opportunities for corrupt misuse of a power outside normal legal structures were evident. The test itself was brutal, degrading and very painful, and its application laid the whole blame for sexual misconduct on the prostitute, not her client. And since those who passed the test were given certificates permitting them to entertain service personnel, the effect of the system was state licensing of prostitution. A Christian country was issuing permits to sin. Josephine began to campaign for the Act's repeal, a fight that consumed her whole life.

Her work took the familiar shape of a Victorian reform campaign; publicity and the gathering of evidence. Josephine spent hours interviewing prostitutes, hearing their horrific stories of abuse at the hands of the police and of the cold-hearted hypocrisy of upper-class men. One girl, sent to prison for refusing to endure examination, had a few days before her arrest entertained the magistrate who sentenced her. Her story was not untypical. The Great Crusade, as Josephine called it, involved a demanding round of public meetings, leafleting, lobbying and eventually the giving of her evidence to a Parliamentary Commission.

Nothing illustrates the double standard more graphically than public reaction to the Great Crusade. People were shocked, not by the facts Mrs Butler uncovered, but by her knowledge of them. Respectable married women ought not to know about the sordid world of prostitution, still less speak about it, still less address public meetings about it. Josephine was vilified in the press as a voyeuse, a sick woman obsessed with filth, a threat to the purity of Britain's homes. She was spat at, pelted in the streets, had her meetings broken up by roughs employed by the brothel-keepers. Not the least painful element in her situation was the knowledge that many of the men in public life who opposed her campaign were themselves regular users of prostitutes. One woman informed her about a client, a clergyman, who had told her that he dined with the Butlers. Josephine never discovered his name, but the knowledge made her feel that even her own home had been defiled by hypocrisy and exploitation.

In the end, her doggedness, integrity and the incontrovertible nature of what she discovered earned for Josephine public respect, and for her causes success. The Contagious Diseases Act was repealed in 1886. It had taken twenty years of fierce campaigning to overthrow a system which, Josephine observed, 'stripped every woman of her civil rights that men might sin with impunity.'

Josephine Butler drew her inspiration from her Christian faith, and in her leisure hours composed a biography of her heroine, St Catherine of Siena.

MARY SUMNER (1828-1921) 9th August.
In 1882, just as the Parliamentary campaign for repeal was entering its final, arduous phase, George Butler was preferred by Gladstone to a canonry in Winchester Cathedral, and the Butlers moved south. Settled in the Cathedral Close, they quickly became friends with their neighbours George and Mary Sumner. George was the son of the late Bishop of Winchester, and in those days when nepotism was not a crime, had been made archdeacon in his father's declining years, later going on to become Bishop of Guildford. The bulk of his career, however, had been spent as Rector of Old Alresford, and it was in this quiet Hampshire village that his wife Mary began a work which was to rival Josephine Butler's in its impact on the life of British women.

Mary Heywood was such a gifted musician that her father was advised to make her an opera singer, but she chose instead marriage and the life of a clergyman's wife. In 1876, when her children were grown up and she had energy for work outside the home, she began inviting groups of women to meet at her house and learn together how they might best discharge their duties as mothers. A remarkable feature of these meetings was that women of every social class were invited, and expected to meet and discuss as equals. This village club was the very first Mothers' Union. It began as a practical, down-to-earth club to spread the arts of child-rearing and encourage mothers in the best practice of their vocation. Among the promises made by the first members were that they would not allow their daughters to roam about unescorted after dark, that they would not send their children to fetch liquor from public houses, and that they would attend church 'when my domestic duties allow.'

After the Sumners moved to Winchester, Mary was invited in 1885 to sit on the platform of a meeting held in Portsmouth for working women, part of that year's Church Congress. The chairman, to her horror, asked her to speak and describe her Mothers' Union. She plucked up her courage and gave a memorable speech on the high privilege of mothers: 'The hand that rocks the cradle rules the world.'

In 1887, the Bishop of Winchester made the Union a diocesan organisation, and from there, its spread was irresistible. It became a national and international institution. Mary Sumner edited the 'Mothers' Union Journal' and found she and the Union had a voice on a range of social issues affecting mothers – divorce, the education of women, the causes of infant mortality. Often mocked in modern Britain for its old-fashioned (and wholly undeserved) image, the Mothers' Union remains a potent force in Christian Africa, where it empowers women struggling to better their lot.

Mary Sumner was an aristocrat who treated everybody as equal. She was opinionated, great fun, and opposed to modern life: she would never have a telephone or a car, and refused to let guests smoke in her house. In extreme old age she addressed the Mothers' Union conference in the Albert Hall, and her tiny, clear voice, unamplified in that vast arena, was said to have been heard by every person present.

PART TWENTY-FIVE. MISSION AT HOME AND ABROAD.

GEORGE SELWYN (1809-1878) 11th April.

If we ask why women played such a prominent part in campaigning for social reform in Victorian England, a flippant reply, with a grain of truth in it, might be that all the idealistic men were having far too much fun establishing the British Empire. For a certain sort of active, out-of-doors man, the Empire provided both a sphere for duty and a huge adventure playground, where Victorian propriety could be abandoned in favour of exploration of uncharted wilderness, encounters with strange tribes, and all the intrepid improvisation of ways and means that pioneering life demands. A man formed for just such an adventure was George Augustus Selwyn, who became first Bishop of New Zealand in 1841.

Selwyn was at prep school with John Newman and his vision for the church was formed by the Oxford Movement. He went on to Eton, which remained in many ways his spiritual home, and then to Cambridge, where he was a rowing blue.

New Zealand was officially annexed to the British crown in 1840; the Maoris who lived there acknowledged Queen Victoria's overlordship by the Treaty of Waitangi, which, source of bitter controversy though it has been over the years, did at least secure them more respect and equality with the white settlers than was granted to the Australian aborigines or the native tribes of South Africa. The establishment of the colony was quickly followed by the establishment of a colonial bishopric and Selwyn was the ideal person for the job - restless, dissatisfied, with a creative energy and a love of outdoor pursuits and sport. He spent five years travelling around New Zealand and getting to know his people, both Maori and white. For the sons of the Maori chiefs, he founded St John's College, Christchurch, a boarding school modelled as closely as possible on Eton, and with the same aim of creating Christian gentlemen with an ethos of service and duty and the ability to lead. In a more innocent age, Selwyn had no self-doubt about transplanting a generation of boys so decisively from one culture to another, and in fact, seems to have been loved by his pupils and respected by their parents. Just as it had been for Anglo-Saxon kings 1300 years earlier, so in the nineteenth century conversion to Christianity was seen by the ruling classes of Africa and Australasia as a gateway to everything that was modern and desirable.

Selwyn was an architect of what was to become the Anglican Communion. He lost no time in slackening the ties which linked the churches of New Zealand and England, and under his leadership, New Zealand was the first colony to hold church synods, a gathering of Bishops with representative clergy, which had the power to legislate for the new church. This became a prototype for the establishment of self-government in all the Anglican provinces, and influenced the slow growth of a similar system in the mother country.

By a typographical error, the letters appointing Bishop Selwyn defined the limits of his diocese using the wrong longitude, so that on paper he was responsible for missionary work far to the east over thousands of miles of the South Pacific. Selwyn was quite ambitious enough to welcome this additional challenge. But if he was to bring Christ to the hundreds of tiny islands and archipelagos, he was going to need men, young Englishmen with his own love of sea-faring, adventure and danger.

JOHN COLERIDGE PATTESON (1827-1871) 20th September.

In 1841, as he was setting out on his great adventure, Bishop Selwyn preached at his beloved Eton. Among those who heard him speak about the sacrifice and the joy of a missionary calling, was fourteen-year old John Coleridge Patteson, known as Coley to his friends; a boy who combined great sensibility to literature and music with a love of adventure to rival Selwyn's own. The boy never forgot the sermon and when in 1854, Patteson, now a country curate near Exeter, met the missionary bishop again, he was ready to respond to Selwyn's invitation to join him in evangelising the islands of Melanesia. The younger and older man got on famously and Patteson was soon one of Selwyn's most trusted and loved assistants.

Selwyn's evangelistic strategy centred on his yacht. This vessel, which he helmed himself, made voyages around the Pacific, stopping at every island and attempting to make contact with the natives. Most were friendly, if shy; some were cannibals; some attempted to drive off the visitors with poisoned arrows. When friendly relations had been established, Selwyn and Patteson persuaded the chiefs to send their sons to St John's in New Zealand. The plan was to send back the next generation of leaders as committed Christians to their home islands.

Though often homesick, Patteson loved this life. He had a natural gift for languages and was soon fluent in many of the Pacific tongues. His manner to everyone was open, courteous and easy; he was almost immune from the insidious racism which bedevilled the relations of the British with the peoples of their Empire. Melanesians found him lovable and approachable and admired his courage, which was dauntless. For his part, Patteson developed a love for his people which included respect for their traditions and way of life. Although he didn't quite see how Christian Melanesians could continue to walk around completely naked, he could appreciate that to put the graceful islanders into top hats and frock coats was to rob them of their natural beauty and dignity. In 1861, Selwyn divided his diocese and consecrated Coleridge Patteson as first bishop of Melanesia. Five years later Selwyn left New Zealand and returned home as Bishop of Lichfield, where he found the midlands squires and archdeacons less compliant than Maori chieftains, and was frustrated by the resilience of the British constitution in baulking his attempts at introducing New Zealand style synodical government to his diocese.

Patteson meanwhile continued his mentor's cruising style of evangelism, spending six months of the year at sea, and six months at St Barnabas' College on Norfolk Island, founded in imitation of St John's. Here he had the great joy ordaining the first Melanesian deacons and priests.

Tragically, the bishop was not the only European sailing the Pacific in quest of promising young men. Patteson's mission was overshadowed by a wicked parody of his methods. Plantation owners in Australia and Fiji needed workers, and the so-called 'black-birders' toured Melanesia to recruit them. Young men were lured on board the ships with promises of a better life. As the islanders got wise to what was happening, more blatant trickery was employed, and at last the traders practised undisguised kidnapping. The slave trade was being re-established in all but name, and it was inevitable that Melanesians saw a connection between the friendly bishop inviting their sons to attend his boarding school, and more sinister visitors on the prowl for indentured servants. Patteson was infuriated, both by the cruelty of what was being done, and by the contamination by association of his own work in Melanesia. He campaigned vigorously for the British government to end the abuses, abuses which were in the end to cost him his life.

On 19th September 1871, Patteson's mission ship anchored off the island of Nukapu. The next day, the bishop, as was his custom, set off with a party in the boat to be rowed ashore. They were met by a party of natives in canoes, who at first seemed friendly, so much so that Patteson agreed to board one of the canoes and speak to them. After half an hour or so of conversation, the natives without warning stood up and began to shower the mission boat with arrows. When three men had been wounded and the boat had withdrawn out of range, the canoes made for shore, taking Patteson with them. By the time the missionaries had organised a rescue party to land, it was too late. They found Patteson dead, laid out formally on the beach, his body covered with a mat, on which was a palm leaf with five knots in it. These knots represented five men of Nukapu who had been abducted by the blackbirders; Patteson's murder was an act of revenge, in which the innocent European had paid the price for the guilty.

George Selwyn's son John succeeded Patteson as Bishop of Melanesia, and he was able to return to Nukapu in 1884, where he talked with one of the five men whose kidnapping had provoked the martyrdom. The islanders erected a cross to mark the site of Patteson's death, and accepted baptism.

The work of developing an authentic indigenous Christianity in Melanesia continued for the next fifty years: we shall have occasion to return there.

EDWARD KING (1829-1910) 8th March.
Dr Pusey died in 1882. The old man had outlived his era and was a relic – to some a holy relic, to others a symbol of suspicion, but, whether revered or reviled, he was alone. The church for whose catholicity he had stood so unflinchingly was now facing new challenges, and in his last years Pusey's ventures into print seemed

dated, almost quaint. None doubted their sincerity, but his thought seemed often irrelevant. The party to which he had unwillingly given his name was, however, established as an important part of the English church. The question now was, who would be Pusey's heir? Who would commend catholic Christianity to a new generation? Three great bishops in the late Victorian era offered three very different answers to this question.

Edward King became Bishop of Lincoln in 1885. He had made his reputation by his pastoral heart. He had come up to Oxford to Newman's college, Oriel, in the year Newman converted to Rome, and his spirituality was formed by the Oxford Movement. In 1858, he accepted the post of vice-Principal of Cuddesdon Theological College. Set in a village outside Oxford, the college was a new venture – until recently, it had been supposed that a university degree was all the preparation a man needed for ordination – and a controversial one. Regarded as a bastion of Tractarianism, rumours were rife of the unhealthy Romish practices and unmanly passionate friendships cherished behind its secluded walls. Edward King proved exactly the right person to dispel such a reputation. With an unwavering vision of simple holiness and an unerring pastoral touch, he established Cuddesdon as a place on which those trained there looked back as the happiest place they had ever lived, a small Paradise on earth. King became Principal in 1864, and in 1871, with much heart-searching, returned to Oxford as Regius Professor of Divinity. He was not an academic and had written little, so his appointment caused some stir, but his gentleness won over the opposition. His lectures on Pastoral Theology were crowded. The undergraduates responded to the warm humanity of the man, and his appointment to Lincoln was greeted with undisguised sorrow in Oxford. 'King is ideal for Lincoln,' wrote Charles Gore, the principal of Pusey House, 'but, oh! the blank it will be here ,'

Lincoln was considered a low-church diocese, and King a high-church bishop, but he again disarmed opposition by his charm, humility and determination to know his enormous diocese. Abandoning Riseholme, the country house which was the traditional home of the bishop, he established himself in the medieval Old Palace, right next to Lincoln Cathedral. His motive was pastoral and practical: 'It isn't every poor parson who has half a crown for a cab out to Riseholme.' King wanted to be accessible to all his clergy. Dressed in shabby black, with patched boots, he travelled by train around the diocese, visiting, preaching, confirming. A famous anecdote tells how, when the chaplain of Lincoln prison came to see him in distress about a prisoner facing execution, King himself took the chaplain's place, spent the night in the condemned call, brought the poor criminal to pray and trust Christ, and accompanied him to the scaffold.

Controversy over ritual was still troubling the Church of England. The bishops had continued their policy of avoiding scandal by vetoing any attempt to prosecute clergy for illegal ritual. Thus thwarted, the Church Association changed its strategy. If bishops vetoed prosecutions, they would prosecute a bishop. In 1888, Archbishop Benson received a petition against Edward King for illegal acts perpetrated at St Peter-at-Gowts, Lincoln. King was charged with facing east to celebrate, with mixing the Communion wine with water, having candles on the altar, using the sign of the cross in absolution, and allowing the 'Agnus Dei' to be chanted before Communion – a prayer which does not occur in the Prayer Book. Even at the time, these were recognised as fairly minor transgressions; extreme Anglo-catholics used incense, genuflections and a wide range of additional prayers. Hoping to avoid the scandal of a public trial in the regular courts, the Archbishop decided to try the case himself in a special court convened at Lambeth Palace. The spectacle of a man regarded as one of the holiest in England put on trial on such charges, disgusted and shocked many; after King's trial it became increasingly difficult to rally public opinion to prosecute Anglo-Catholics, and the ritual objected to has since become normative in Anglican churches.

In the Anglican calendar only two Victorian clergymen are granted the honour of a Festival, with their own collect. Edward Pusey was learned and John Newman was a genius, but John Keble is honoured more than they. Bishop Westcott was learned and Charles Gore was a genius, but Edward King is honoured more than they. The reason in both cases is the same. Both Keble and King were men of such transparent humility and holiness, that all who knew them loved them.　Their gentleness and courtesy, as well as their uncompromising devotion to Christ, give them lasting value as examples of priestly vocation.

BROOKE WESTCOTT (1825-1910) 27th July.
Edward King embodied the simple gospel holiness which stood at the heart of the Tractarian Movement at its best.　The world in which that gospel must be proclaimed was however far from simple.　It is a common assumption that it was Darwin and the Theory of Evolution which made faith complicated for thoughtful people at the end of the nineteenth century, but while scientific advances undoubtedly compelled Christians to revise the way they read the Bible, it was the textual criticism of scripture, originating in German universities, which wreaked the most havoc with the traditional beliefs.　As scholars subjected the biblical text to analysis, using the historical critical method, alarming claims began to be heard: that the New Testament was not penned by the apostles, that its miracles, particularly the Resurrection, were constructed fables, not historical records, that Paul had falsified the simple religion of Jesus with mysticism imported from Greek religion, that Jesus himself was deluded in thinking himself to be Son of God and died on the cross defeated and disillusioned.　To meet the challenge of such claims, something more was needed than simple faith.

Brooke Foss Westcott was above everything a scholar. Born in Birmingham into a family not particularly religious, his early enthusiasm was for science, and as a boy he collected ferns, butterflies and fossils. At Cambridge in the 1840's he read Keble and F.D. Maurice, and recognised a call to ordination.　His early career was in teaching, at Harrow, where one of his most promising pupils was Charles Gore. But teaching was not really what he was made to do, and he was most preoccupied at this time with his marriage and family (he and his wife Louisa had ten children) and with his writing, which secured him a national reputation as a scholar.　His life's work really began when in 1870 he became Regius Professor of Divinity at Cambridge.　Here he worked with two other great New Testament scholars, Lightfoot and Hort, and the three made a formidable team.

Westcott's powers of analysis, his ability to read the nuances of the Greek text of the New Testament, were exceptional, and his commentaries on the Bible were among the most profound and readable of the nineteenth century. Westcott, Lightfoot and Hort showed the reading world that textual criticism, far from being inevitably destructive, could illuminate the Bible and make a reader more, not less reverent. It was not surprising that all three men were appointed to the commission charged with revising the English Bible. This was the first attempt at a new translation of the Bible since the Authorised Version 250 years earlier, and, such was the respect in which that great translation was held, the new translation was conservative to the point of timidity. The project was necessary because textual criticism had revealed how inadequate were the texts from which King James' scholars had worked, but the Revised Version was never loved or much used beyond academia. It is hard for us, used to a new translation of the Bible appearing every other year, to appreciate the shock and outrage which greeted the alteration of loved and familiar phrases, however impeccable the scholarship which lay behind the changes. Westcott himself was dissatisfied with the work; in his heart of hearts, he recognised that attempts to patch the Authorised Version and imitate its archaic style had failed to produce a readable new version.

Though Westcott made his name by his academic work, he was far from a dry scholar. In 1884, he became a Canon of Westminster Abbey, and was directly exposed to the realities of urban life in the squalid slums which then surrounded the Abbey. He began to re-read the works of Maurice and to preach the message of Christian Socialism. In 1890, he was appointed Bishop of Durham. This great diocese was one of the most industrialised dioceses in England, and the Cambridge biblical scholar found himself spiritually responsible for the coal miners of the north-east. The last years of the nineteenth century were troubled ones for industry, with the fledgling Trades Union movement challenging the power of pit and factory owners, and much political controversy over the best way to improve the lot of working people. In 1892 occurred a three month miners' strike which heightened bitterness and anger on both sides of industry. On 1st March, Westcott invited representatives of both miners and pit owners to Auckland Castle, the seat of the bishops of

Durham, where he acted as go-between, and persuaded the miners to go back to work in return for a Conciliation Board to adjudicate on fair wages. In itself, the agreement did not perhaps settle very much, but it was an iconic moment. A Bishop of Durham trusted and respected by both working men and capitalists was a powerful image of the role of the church in society, working for social justice, but transcending faction to bring about peace. Westcott became a hero to the miners of Durham, who gathered in thousands to hear him speak. He died in 1901, a year after his youngest son, and just two months after his beloved wife.

CHARLES GORE (1845-1932) 17th January.
If you had asked the question, Who was Pusey's heir? in 1885, the year of King's consecration, most churchmen would have pointed to Charles Gore. Five years later, they would not have been so sure. We have met Gore as a pupil of Brooke Westcott's at Harrow. As a boy he attended St Alban's Holborn, and was entranced by the ritual and splendour of an extreme Tractarian church. He made a reputation at Oxford as a man formidably intelligent, with a genius for friendship but with a mischievous delight in shocking the conventionally minded. On being offered some tea by a respectable lady, he declared 'Thank you, but I never drink anything but alcoholic beverages.' After ordination, he secured King's old post of Vice-Principal of Cuddeson, where he revealed a genius for befriending and counselling the young; to such an extent did the students flock to Gore with their problems, that the Principal of the college wrote to him plaintively that he himself had no work to do.

After Pusey's death, it was decided to establish a theological library in his memory. Pusey House opened in 1883 and Gore was its first Librarian. He was established as spokesman of the Anglo-Catholics, but Gore was never an easy man to pigeon-hole. He once said of himself 'I was born radical-minded' and all his life he believed in the power of reason to uncover truth. A colleague once observed that Gore not only wanted you to agree with him; he wanted you to agree with his reasons. At Pusey House he took three steps which neatly symbolise his lifelong preoccupations. He founded the Society of the Resurrection, an experiment in establishing a modern, missionary religious order; the society was eventually to settle at Mirfield, Yorkshire, where its members distinguished themselves in theological training and in African mission. With his dearest friend, Henry Scott Holland, Gore helped to found the Christian Social Union, with Westcott as first President; this organisation sought to bring Christian principles to bear on the social questions of the day, and consciously built on the work of Maurice and the Christian Socialists. Finally, Gore published a book of essays, 'Lux Mundi,' which made him notorious and lost him the loyalty of many of Pusey's disciples. 'Lux Mundi,' was an attempt to face honestly the questions raised by historical criticism of the Bible. Gore's own contribution dealt with the nature of Christ's incarnation. A common argument against the critical readings of the Bible was that Christians ought to believe what Jesus believed. If he thought that the story of Jonah and the Whale was historical and believed that King David wrote the psalms, Christian scholars had no liberty to question these hallowed assumptions. Gore argued that by becoming man, the Son of God had submitted to all the limitations of being human, including the limitation of his knowledge. As man, Jesus of Nazareth accepted the common beliefs of his time and culture, and as such was as liable to errors of fact as anybody else. The idea shocked many, and Gore was marked as a dangerous liberal who polluted Pusey House. 'Lux Mundi,' declared Canon Liddon, Pusey's great friend, 'is a proclamation of revolt against the spirit and principles of Dr Pusey and Mr Keble.'

Suspicion continued to dog Gore, so much so that when he was nominated as Bishop of Worcester in 1901, a legal challenge was launched against his consecration. The agitation was unnecessary. As a bishop, Gore was conspicuous for his high-principled defence of Christian orthodoxy. Despite his personal love for the Blessed Sacrament, he fought a long rear-guard action against attempts to make the reserved host a focus for devotion and prayer, believing that such devotion was disallowed by the Prayer Book. He was also rigorous in maintaining that no one could honourably serve as a priest who could not assent to the plain meaning of the creeds it was his duty to recite. Gore's own later writings were an impressive restatement of Catholic Christianity in the context of modern knowledge. He was one of the founders of the modern liberal catholic movement, uniting a profound theological orthodoxy and love for catholic liturgy with a commitment to social radicalism and a willingness to think intelligently and use the fruits of scholarship and science.

He hated being a bishop but was a very good one, taking pains to get to know his clergy and dealing wisely with the large amount of administrative work. He drove though the division of the diocese of Worcester and became first bishop of the new diocese of Birmingham, which his efforts had created. He was greatly loved in the city but when his people presented him with a memorial in thanksgiving for his leadership, his response was 'Now I know that I am a greater hypocrite than I thought I was.' In 1911, he was transferred to the diocese of Oxford, where he was much less happy than in Birmingham. Pinned to his post by a ferocious conscience and an intellect which would not suffer fools gladly, he was often on the point of resigning. 'The position of a bishop in the English Church,' he once said, 'is an impossible one,' and after meetings his chaplain would sometimes retrieve from under his chair scraps of paper on which Gore had written 'I cannot stand this for more than another two minutes.' He was kept sane by his wicked sense of humour and by his love for people; clergy and their families in trouble were amazed by his kindness and gentleness.

Of the three great bishops King, Westcott and Gore, Gore is perhaps the most impressive, though he was undoubtedly the most exasperating to deal with. At his death, a famous headmaster said 'For forty years I have known no better argument for the truth of the Christian religion or for the doctrines of the English Church than that they satisfied the intellect and strengthened the heart of so great a saint of God as Charles Gore.'

MARTYRS OF UGANDA (died 1886) 3rd June.
During the last quarter of the nineteenth century occurred the unseemly historical process known as the 'Scramble for Africa.' Anxious to outmanoeuvre their competitors, the European powers, Britain, France, Germany, Italy and Belgium, extended their reach beyond their trading posts and colonies on the African coast,

claiming vast tracts of hinterland for their empires. By the end of the century only Abyssinia and the republic of ex-American slaves in Liberia were free of European control.

In this rapid expansion of colonialism, Christian missionaries found themselves in an uneasy position. Their principal concern was to bring Christ to peoples who had never heard of him, and in this endeavour they heroically faced long journeys into unmapped territory, coping with a lethal climate and the dangers of meeting unknown tribes. Yet as Europeans, they could not help but bring with them European cultural prejudices, often tightly interwoven with their Christian faith, and they were often perceived by African rulers as precursors of the imperialists, softening up territories which would subsequently be annexed. As a result, African rulers tended to have a highly ambiguous relationship with missionaries, in awe of the new ideas and technologies they brought with them, but suspicious and fearful that to get too involved would be to be trapped into ceding power to the forces behind the missions.

Nowhere were these tensions more evident than in Buganda, a district of what is now Uganda on the shores of Lake Victoria. Christian missionaries had been active in the area for some time. The C.M.S had a station there, headed by the Scots missionary Alexander Mackay, and the French Roman Catholic White Fathers had made many converts among the Bugandans. Muslim missionaries were also competing for the allegiance of the Kabaka, the local ruler, who attempted with some skill to play off these various visitors to his kingdom without committing himself to any of them. The situation became unstable with the accession of a new young Kabaka, Mwanga. Mwanga was unpredictable and hot-tempered, out of his depth but furiously anxious not to let anyone see his inadequacy. He was also an enthusiastic (though not exclusive) homosexual, and it was this side of his personality which triggered disaster.

Mwanga's practice was to use the young pageboys of his court as sexual partners. A number of these boys had been baptised as Catholics and decided that they must in conscience refuse the royal advances. Infuriated, Mwanga swung violently against the Catholic mission, prowling his palace and demanding of any boy he met 'Do you read book?' The Catholic pageboys were rounded up and burned at the stake, dying with conspicuous courage and singing hymns.

JAMES HANNINGTON (1847-1886) 29th October.
Alexander Mackay and the Protestant mission had not been directly threatened by the attack on the Catholic pageboys, and they watched uneasily to see whether the Kabaka's anger would extend to persecution of all the Christians in his kingdom. Shortly after the boys had perished, Mackay received news that an Anglican bishop was making his way to Buganda. James Hannington had been consecrated first Bishop of East Equatorial Africa in 1884, and he was intent on opening up a more direct route from the coast to Buganda, travelling though the district of Busoga. Mackay sent urgent warnings to him to retrace his steps; not only was the situation in Buganda volatile, but a local prophecy warned that a stranger coming from Busoga would bring trouble for the whole kingdom. This message never reached Bishop Hannington, who continued on his ill-fated journey in all ignorance.

James Hannington was a Sussex man, born in Hurstpierpoint, and like Selwyn and Patteson, a hearty outdoors-loving Christian, fond of riding and yachting. His wife Blanche had received the news that he felt called to missionary work, as a death sentence - mortality among Europeans in the tropics was very high and understanding of tropical disease in its infancy – but she gave her husband to God and saw him off to Africa, fully expecting never to see him again. As he made his way to Buganda, Hannington was indeed extremely ill, carried in a litter by his bearers, but undaunted in his determination to press on.

At the border, Hannington's party was stopped by the Kabaka's guards and confined to a circle of huts, where they could get no news of the outside world. After several anxious days, during which Hannington's diary records what it cost him to keep his faith, they were led out into the open and murdered.

From Mwanga's perspective, the martyrdom of Hannington was a disaster, precipitating exactly the catastrophe he was trying to avoid. The news that an English bishop had been murdered made the annexation of Buganda by the British Empire inevitable. Uganda proved a fertile mission ground and today over 90% of its people profess the Christian faith.

APOLO KIVEBULAYA (1864-1933) 30th May.

Among the witnesses of the deaths of the Catholic page-boys of Buganda was a young Ugandan from Mengo. Apolo Kivebulaya had accompanied his chief to the coronation of the Kabaka. The martyrdoms sufficiently impressed him to make him seek out Alexander Mackay and under cover of darkness, in that highly charged atmosphere of danger, the missionary and the boy had a conversation which Apolo never forgot. Apolo's path to Christian faith was a twisted one, but the memory of Mackay provided him with his centre of balance.

On his return home he was conscripted to fight in a Muslim army attempting to dominate Uganda; while in the field with them he had an experience of Jesus Christ calling him. He deserted and returned home, only to be made a refugee as his family fled the British army advancing to avenge Hannington. He went through a period of depression and unsettlement, on the one hand reading assiduously the New Testament in Mackay's Lugandan translation, on the other becoming addicted to opium. He was conscripted again, this time by British engineers seeking a labour force to build new roads, and finally he made the decision to be baptised. 'Today,' he declared, 'I arose from the dead.'

Apolo immediately longed to be a missionary himself, and sufficiently impressed the C.M.S team to be trained and commissioned as a Reader. He wanted to take the gospel where it had never been heard before, and set off alone, heading west into lands which now form part of Rwanda and Congo. On arrival in the kingdom of Mboga, far beyond the reach of Western missionaries, he set about preaching, at first with spectacular lack of success. He made a total of one convert, a woman called Debola, but his activities aroused the hostility of the King of Mboga who set his house and prayer hut on fire, had Apolo dragged before him, and ordered him to be beaten to death. The guards, believing they had obeyed these orders, left Apolo for dead in the bush, but Debola, creeping out in search of him, discovered that he was still breathing. For a month she nursed him back to health, and at last he was fit enough to return to the town. His appearance was regarded as a miracle; to both king and people he seemed to have returned from the dead, and conversions and baptisms quickly followed. Mboga became a Christian state, one of the earliest places to be converted without the input of Western missionaries, though these soon gave Apolo back-up and resources.

While hiding in the bush Apolo had caught glimpses of pygmies, the tribesmen of the jungle, gradually making contact with its elusive inhabitants. They showed him the shrine where they sacrificed to God and told Apolo how they feared him because he hated them and could only be appeased by offerings. Apolo spoke to them of a God of love, and by ones and twos brought them to faith and baptism. He built no churches, for buildings and settlements were alien to their nomadic lifestyle, but he translated Mark's gospel into their language and taught them to read it.

Even as a very old man, Apolo Kivebulaya spent long months walking into the Congo, keeping in touch with the network of Christian pygmies he had built up. He is remembered as a true pioneering missionary and one of the first generation of indigenous African evangelists.

ISABELLA GILMORE (1842-1923) 16th April.
The problem of urban poverty continued to disturb Christian consciences as the nineteenth century drew to a close. Church people were conscious that slum-dwellers had virtually no connection with their parish churches, and that desperate poverty bred moral and spiritual squalor. These were years when the Labour movement was growing and socialism was articulating an alternative vision to that provided by laissez faire capitalism. The noblest souls of the age were drawn to the slums of England as surely as they were to the mission-fields of empire.

Isabella Morris was one of ten children of which the most famous was her artist brother William. In 1860, she married a naval lieutenant, Archie Gilmore, but was left a childless widow by his early death in 1882. She took stock of her life and decided to train as a nurse, but her true vocation emerged in 1886, when she was head-hunted by the Bishop of Rochester and asked to begin an order of deaconesses within his diocese, which included some of the worst slums of south-east London and the docklands. As we have seen, parish work for women in the mid-nineteenth century had usually been modelled on the structure of a religious order, with sisters of mercy and deaconesses living a common life not dissimilar to that of nuns. Isabella Gilmore's vision was rather different and in many ways more modern. She certainly, in partnership with her bishop, created a diocesan order of deaconesses, just as Elizabeth Ferard had done in north London a decade earlier. But Isabella meant the order to train and resource women, not to be their primary focus of loyalty. Her deaconesses were to be parish-based, reporting to their own vicar rather than to a superior in the order, and, proviso still shocking to a world which expected lady volunteers, they were to be paid, professional and financially independent. Her work took a step closer to the day when women in the church could expect professional respect on a par with men.

Isabella, a true Morris, loved beauty and lavished care and attention on her Institute chapel, which had all the bright colour and medieval charm of her brother's work. But her heart was with the poor whom her deaconesses served. William Morris once observed, rather enviously, 'I preach socialism: you practise it.'

SAMUEL BARNETT (1844-1913) and HENRIETTA BARNETT (1851-1936) 17th June.

Octavia Hill attracted a team of younger women to help her run her charitable enterprises. One of these was Henrietta Rowland, the daughter of a wealthy business man of Clapham. Henrietta was high-spirited, pretty, fond of riding, and possessed of a formidable social conscience. Through Octavia Hill and the Charity Organisation Society she met the young curate of St Mary's Bryanston Square, Samuel Barnett, and in 1873 they were married. To many it seemed a marriage of Beauty and the Beast.

Henrietta, fascinating and cultivated, had chosen a husband who was clumsy, rather gauche and prematurely balding, not to mention socially a little beneath her. But in choosing Samuel

Barnett, Miss Rowland knew what she was doing. Each of them desired nothing more than to bring liberation to the slums of London and together they made an impressive team.

In the year of his marriage Samuel Barnett was offered the parish of St Jude, Whitechapel, frankly admitted by the bishop to be the worst parish in London. It was during Samuel's incumbency that Jack the Ripper became active in Whitechapel and the parish was a byword for degradation and criminal activity, a warren of narrow streets and airless courts, where a seedy glamour was contributed by gin palaces, brothels and opium dens. As good disciples of Octavia Hill, the Barnetts began their ministry on Charity Organisation Society principles. Indiscriminate alms-giving demoralised the poor; assistance should only be given to the deserving poor after careful enquiry into the circumstances. To the population of Whitechapel, these principles destroyed the only point of having a vicar, a gentleman who could be trusted to hand out blankets, coal and soup in hard times. The Barnetts were thus unpopular with their parishioners from the start. But they aimed for more than popularity.

Unlike earlier slum priests like Charles Lowder, Barnett did not regard his church solely or principally as a place of worship – he wished to bring culture, intellectual enquiry and beauty into the slums, to awaken consciences by enlarging minds. He displeased traditional Christians by offering oratorios instead of sermons on Sunday afternoons, and he and Henrietta began an annual tradition of exhibiting art in their church, a tradition which led to the founding of the Whitechapel Art Gallery.

Just as Barnett felt it important to open the slums to beauty, he was determined to bring about understanding between the classes by enabling them to meet and share their lives. In 1884, he founded Toynbee Hall, in memory of his friend Arnold Toynbee. Toynbee Hall was a university settlement, in which students from Oxford came to live alongside Eastenders so that each party could learn from the other. Octavia Hill was alienated from the Barnetts by their perceived lack of orthodoxy; she felt they had lost sight of the church's spiritual work in their quest for cultural and social improvement, and she ended up sponsoring a rival, more explicitly Christian university settlement at Oxford House, Bethnal Green. The split encapsulates a perennial dilemma for the church in the twentieth century: should Christians ally themselves with people of goodwill of all faiths or none, in order to improve society, or do such alliances fatally disable a distinctive witness to Christ?

It was not only in theology that that Barnetts grew apart from Octavia Hill. Their experience of the intractable problems faced by the London poor estranged them from Octavia's classical liberalism, with its emphasis on self-help and responsible choices. The Barnetts increasingly aligned themselves with the solutions proposed by the Labour Party and the Trades Unions, and came to believe that only state power and state money could deal with poverty adequately.

Samuel Barnett left London in 1893 and ended his days as Canon of Bristol Cathedral. His wife had her own projects which she pursued during her long widowhood. She founded the Children's Country Holiday Fund, to give children of the inner city some country space and air, and was involved in the Garden City Movement, which sought to plan and build new towns for the poor without the structural faults of the old cities.

WILLIAM BOOTH (1829-1912) and CATHERINE BOOTH (1829-1890) 20th August.

While Samuel Barnett sought to reform the slums with a social gospel, other Christians still held to the classic evangelical conviction that only a personal encounter with the living Christ could save a sinner. Perhaps no one had more impact on working class spirituality than William Booth, founder of the Salvation Army.

Booth knew poverty at first hand; as a teenager he worked as a pawnbroker's assistant to keep his mother and sister. He had a conversion experience at fifteen and began to preach in Methodist chapels, but the followers of John Wesley had become respectable, and were horrified when Booth, blazing with zeal, swept up the riff raff of the streets and led them into the chapel, seating them in the pews reserved for church members. He broke with the Methodists, convinced that the world of the chapel was too churchified to have any chance of reaching the lowest of the low; and it was these he longed to rescue. In 1852, at the age of 23, he met and fell in love with Catherine Mumford. She first noticed him when he was reluctantly compelled to recite 'The Grog Seller's Dream' at an evening party. The temperance poem offended the moderate drinkers present, and as Catherine defended the socially inept, passionate young man, both of them realised they had a special bond. They were married in 1855, despite the fact that they had almost nothing to live on; Booth was still a Methodist preacher at this time. In some ways Catherine was the more radical of the two. In their early married life Booth would not hear of his wife speaking in public, until one day when, impelled by the Spirit, she stood and spoke in a chapel in Gateshead. Booth was overwhelmed and convinced, and from then on championed women's preaching ministries, outraging Victorian propriety and Evangelical interpretation of the New Testament, and earning from no less a person than Lord Shaftesbury the title of 'Anti-Christ.'

Increasingly frustrated by Methodism, the Booths moved to London, where William preached in the open-air outside the 'Blind Boy,' a pub in Mile End, graduating to a tent and then to a hired dance hall. His methods were crude, direct and successful: fiery preaching with an uncompromising message of hellfire, redemption, the Saviour's blood and glory, followed by a call to sinners to come forward and make a public acceptance of Jesus. Booth found he could touch the roughest and the most degraded; the meetings were stormily emotional, as jeers and anger gave way to hysterical weeping, shrieks of joy and uninhibited singing. Booth ruthlessly jettisoned every aspect of 'church' which he felt kept the gospel fenced off as the possession of the respectable – he would have no decorated halls, no vestments, ceremonies, organ music, harmonies. He even abandoned as legalistic the sacraments. The people he went to find needed a simple gospel of powerful, personal conversion, and alcoholics, criminals and wastrels responded. The movement became the Salvation Army in 1878, and adopted the military metaphor in its uniforms, its terminology and its discipline. Booth was an autocrat and Salvation Army officers were trained to obey. At about the same time the trademark brass bands began to appear, playing hymns set to popular music hall tunes. 'Champagne Charlie is my name' became 'Bless His Name, he sets me free.' Army preachers shamelessly used any gimmick to grab attention and gather a crowd; Bramwell Booth,

William and Catherine's eldest son, once had himself carried into a meeting in a coffin, from which he arose to preach on 'O death where is thy sting?' The preaching was from the first backed by tireless practical help; the Army organised clothing exchanges, cheap cafés, soup kitchens, furniture loan schemes. The movement spread throughout England and was soon finding new outlets in Canada, the USA, continental Europe and India.

As the Army began to have an impact on the most deprived, the people beyond the reach of every conventional church, so it provoked opposition. A vicious parody, The Skeleton Army, was a gang of roughs, dedicated to breaking up Salvationist meetings, and Booth's officers met persecution similar to that visited upon the early Methodists. Bizarrely, the worst violence occurred in Worthing, most genteel of seaside resorts. Here the rioting and the attacks on sympathisers of the Army reached such a pitch that cavalry were brought over from Brighton to clear the streets. The court cases which followed this riot established the right of the Salvation Army to parade peacefully and to expect police protection as they did so.

The incident which first threatened to destroy the Army and ended up enhancing its reputation was provoked by Bramwell Booth's decision to get involved with the cause celebre of 1885, William Stead's newspaper campaign to end 'the maiden tribute of the modern Babylon.' The scandal of child prostitution continued to defile Victorian Britain, with the connivance of many outwardly respectable gentlemen. One Harley Street doctor was said to deflower a hundred virgins a year. Stead, the editor of the Pall Mall Gazette, decided that the trade in young girls could only be exposed by a fully documented enactment, demonstrating the ease with which children could be sold into prostitution. He enlisted the help of Josephine Butler, who introduced him to a reformed madam she was assisting, one Rebecca Jarrett. He also enlisted Bramwell Booth and the Army. The plan was that Stead and Jarrett, posing as client and procuress, should buy a girl from her parents and smuggle her to France, where the Salvation Army would protect her. The plan worked perfectly and Stead was able to electrify his readers with a first-hand account of how easy it was to buy a child for rape. In the short term, public anger was vented on the reformers. As the child's parents claimed they did not know that Stead was intending to violate their daughter, the courts formed the opinion that a real offence of kidnapping had occurred and Stead and the hapless Rebecca Jarrett were sentenced to prison. For a time it seemed that both Josephine Butler's campaign and the Salvation Army would be tarnished by association with the scandal. But truth prevailed in the end. Parliament was compelled by public opinion to raise the age of consent to sixteen (it had been thirteen) and the Army gained a reputation for protecting the children of the poor.

In 1888, Booth was involved in another celebrated campaign for social justice. Workers at Bryant and May's match factory in the East End were being poisoned by the yellow phosphorus used to make matches. After attempts to persuade the factory owners to change their practice had failed. Booth decided to start his own rival match factory, using the less harmful red phosphorus, and incidentally paying the workers two pence an hour more than they got in the commercial factories. Effective publicity made sure Booth's 'Lights in darkest England' outsold their rivals, and factory owners were compelled to reform their working practices to remain competitive. By 1901 Booth was able to close his factory, having effected a lasting reform.

Meanwhile, in 1890, Catherine Booth had died painfully of cancer. She bore her illness with an entire lack of self-pity, resolutely refusing to allow her husband and children to spend time nursing her, which ought to be given to the Salvation Army.

By the time of his death, General Booth was a hero across three continents. He was an autocrat who refused to share power and ran his great organisation on truly military lines, but he was deeply loved by those who knew him best. He left behind a force for Christian witness which has always proved able to penetrate the worst and most deprived of places with the gospel of Jesus.

WILSON CARLILE (1847-1942) 26th September.
The success of the Salvation Army impressed many in the established churches, and got people asking whether the same unorthodox methods might not be used in the Church of England's own mission to the slums. The most famous Anglican imitation of the Salvation

Army was the Church Army, founded by the irrepressible Wilson Carlile.

Carlile was born in Brixton, and though a delicate child, possessed an enormous fund of energy – the instruments he chose to learn as a teenager were the trombone and the banjo, which is an accurate indication of his character. His parents were devout Congregationalists (William and Catherine Booth were married at their church) but the young Carlile had no particular interest in religion. He left school at fourteen, having set himself a different goal: by the age of 25, he would have made £25,000. This he achieved, working in his grandfather's silk trading company from 7.30 am to 10.00 pm, and becoming head of the firm at eighteen. He was married at twenty-three and had made the fortune he promised himself. To overcome his childhood ill health, he ran five miles to and from the office every day, using the omnibus as his pace-setter, while the passengers cheered him on.

In 1873, all the achievements of this gallant workaholic disintegrated when a bank crash destroyed his business. He became ill, began to read devotional books, and had a conversion experience. From now on his energy and creativity would be devoted to spiritual work. Carlile began to worship in a Brethren church, but was drawn to the Church of England and confirmed at Clapham Church. In 1875, he played the piano for Moody and Sankey, the American evangelists, during their mission to London; applied for ordination; was trained at the London College of Divinity. He served at first in the parish of Kensington, which in those days had a vicar and ten curates. Carlile was the oldest and the only married man in the team, and he became frustrated by what he perceived as failure in his ministry. He was given responsibility for Evensong and found the consistently poor attendance at traditional worship deeply discouraging (most Sundays there were only two hundred people at Evensong). Carlile began to discover his happy talent for thinking outside the box; he struck up friendships with soldiers at the local barracks, with the workhouse, with the police station, and began holding services outside the church in local halls. His youth club was a riot, in every sense. Carlile used his showmanship and sense of humour to draw in un-churched young hoodlums from the streets; he found the cheek and backchat of these boys so funny that he had difficulty maintaining order, but no difficulty maintaining his hold on their affection. At last he began to hold open-air services at which ordinary church members, often the footmen and grooms of the big houses in Kensington, would give testimonies. Both the police and the Skeleton Army, from different motives, attempted to break up these meetings, but Carlile had found his true sphere of action. He linked up with other Anglican groups which were experimenting with open-air mission, and in 1882 the first Church Army mission was held. Carlile's vision was of an enthused laity able to work with the clergy in evangelism and teaching. No clergyman was allowed to be an officer in the Church Army, but no Church Army officer was allowed to operate without the invitation and authority of the clergy.

Opposition was as violent as anything experienced by the Salvation Army. On an early mission in Westminster, Carlile was so badly beaten up by a petty criminal alarmed by the conversion of his mates, that he was put out of action for six months. The lad responsible wrote to Carlile from prison and subsequently became a Christian.

Important developments in the Church Army's work were the establishment of a Training College in Oxford, and the launch of its trademark Mission Vans, which took the Church Army's mission out to remote rural parishes. From 1889, the Church Army was distributing food to 2000 homeless people on the Embankment, and by 1926, when Carlile retired, there were over 900 trained workers for the Army. It continues to do much for the social mission of the Church of England.

BERNARD MIZEKI (1861-1896) 18th June.
While such creative evangelism was taking place in the slums and backstreets of England, missionary efforts continued in Africa.

In 1886, a young African was baptised at the Cowley Fathers Mission in Cape Town. He was Bernard Mizeki, who had migrated to Cape Town from Mozambique, looking for labouring work. He was encouraged by the mission to get educated and trained as a catechist, and revealed brilliant talent as a linguist. He could speak four European and eight African languages.

Since the days of Allen Gardiner, British rule in South Africa had expanded enormously. Under Cecil Rhodes, British fortune-hunters and traders had penetrated far beyond the Boer republic of the Transvaal to establish a protectorate over Matabeleland (now Southern Zimbabwe). In 1891, Bernard was chosen to accompany Bishop Knight-Bruce to establish a mission to the Matabele. At first all went well for him. He settled in a village of the Nhowe tribe, gained the trust of the Marwende, the local chief, married his daughter Mutwa, who became a Christian, and established a routine of daily prayer, gardening and work with the local children, which seemed to win him the goodwill of his neighbours.

But as so often, the close association of missionaries and imperialists led to resentment and suspicion. Bernard offended the local witch doctors by cutting down some trees in a sacred grove where the chief's ancestors were venerated. When rebellion broke out against the British, white settlers were massacred across Matabeleland and all church workers were advised to escape to South Africa. Bernard refused to leave his post despite the obvious danger. In the middle of the night on 18th June 1896, he was woken by a loud knocking on the door. He went to answer, and was attacked and stabbed by two men, uncles of his wife. He dragged himself to the stream where Mutwa and a friend found him in the dark. They returned to the hut to fetch dressings for his wound, but as they returned to the place where he lay, they reported seeing a dazzling light and hearing wings beating. Bernard Mizeki's body had disappeared, and though it seems likely that the assassins had returned to drag him away, it was widely believed that a miracle had occurred.

Today Bernard Mizeki's shrine is one of the most prominent places of pilgrimage in southern Africa.

MARY SLESSOR (1848-1915) 11th January.
The British colonies in South and East Africa grew to eclipse the oldest British settlements in Africa, those on the West coast, infamous haunts of slave-traders of old. The climate in Uganda and Rhodesia was better suited to European settlers than the West coast, which was notorious as the 'White man's graveyard,' and was

impenetrable because of the dense rainforest which covered it. Nevertheless, British colonists continued to visit West Africa, partly in quest of the wealth of its forests, partly out of a guilty desire to atone for the ravages of the slave trade. In the land now called Nigeria, there once lived one of the most extraordinary of all missionaries. A self-educated mill-girl from Aberdeen, Mary Slessor made herself uncrowned queen of Calabar. In her childhood, dominated by an alcoholic violent father, the Presbyterian chapel was the only source of light for a young girl desperate to make something of her life. She was enthralled by stories of missionaries and longed to be one. After her father died she was able to settle her mother comfortably and applied to the Church of Scotland's Foreign Mission Board for training and a post. In 1876, aged twenty-eight she set off for West Africa, in a ship loaded with spirits for trading with the natives. 'Scores of casks', she commented, 'and only one missionary.'

The estuary of the Calabar River contained several small towns, where Christian churches were well-established. Upriver it was a very different story – a wild, jungle country without roads, towns or communications. The Africans who lived there had contact with the coast through trade, but they imported only the most destructive elements of western civilisation: rum and firearms. While Mary learned the local languages, taught and preached, she always had her heart set on this untouched hinterland, where no white person went and where there were no churches. In 1888, she finally went up the river to Okoyong. She was alone and, despite many staunch allies, she remained essentially alone for the rest of her life.

The Okoyong people lived primitive lives punctuated by outbursts of savage violence. Their chiefs administered traditional law and expected to be followed to the grave by wives and servants, who would be ritually slaughtered as the funeral progressed. The main means of determining the guilt of an accused person was by a poison ordeal. Girls at puberty were initiated into all-female drinking clubs, which imposed a ritual circumcision. Twins were feared, as it was believed one of the babies must be the offspring of an evil spirit: the children were killed at birth and the mother became a social outcast. All social occasions were celebrated by heavy drinking, which often culminated in brawls, fights and murders.

Mary Slessor differed from most missionaries in the extent to which she identified herself with the local culture. She early abandoned all pretence at Victorian propriety and went bare-foot with her skirts hitched up for easiness of working. She ate local food, initially to save the expense of importing European foodstuffs. She built her own house in African style and her compound quickly filled up with waifs and strays. She was patient with local etiquette, spending long hours entertaining the wives of the chiefs and attending respectfully the palavers of the men. But she was determined to be a Christian presence. The Sabbath was kept with true Church of Scotland solemnity, although Mary was so isolated that she sometimes lost track of the calendar. Once a carpenter came up from the coast to help her with repairs and was rebuked for being willing to work on the Sabbath. 'But it's Monday,' he said. 'Monday?' exclaimed Mary, 'Well, it will have to be the Sabbath now. You see,' in a whisper, 'I was whitewashing the rooms yesterday.' The Sunday services continued with no one any the wiser.

By sheer force of personality, Mary gradually established an ascendancy over her adopted home. Again and again she intervened to stop the sacrifice of a slave, the administration of poison, the murder of twins. She was prepared to sit and argue for hours with drunken, angry men (her childhood experience of managing her father stood her in good stead) until she gained her point. She soon acquired a large family of adopted children, mostly twins rescued from death. Slowly young people started to come to her to 'learn book': slowly people began to attend her simple services. She became the court of appeal for miles around, asked to adjudicate disputes and respected for her unbribable integrity. To everybody she was 'Ma.'

In her old age, Nigeria became a British colony, and the country changed beyond recognition. Roads were driven through the jungle; instead of trekking along overgrown paths, Mary had the use of a government car. She was even appointed a district magistrate. She became 'Ma' to the young colonial administrators too, co-opting them to lead the singing at her carol services, and lecturing them about their drinking and Sabbath-breaking as imperturbably as she harangued her African young men. She was respected for her unrivalled understanding of local languages, folklore and customs, and at her death it felt as if a power had departed from the land.

Part Twenty-Six. The First World War.

EDITH CAVELL (1865-1915) 12th October.
In February 1914, Charles Gore, Bishop of Oxford, led a preaching mission to the university. Always delighted by the company of young people, Gore was in his element and his preaching filled the University Church to capacity. When his chaplain attempted to bring him routine diocesan administration, he was waved off. 'Go away, go away. I don't care if all the rural deans have murdered their wives. Let them, I don't care!' Many young men came to a living Christian faith that spring. A few months later, Britain went to war with Germany. For most of those bright young students, their conversion turned out to be a preparation for death.

The First World War brought to a hellish end the Victorian world of self-assured prosperity and progress. The competition between the great powers, manifested in the scramble for African colonies and in an expensive arms race, finally imploded in a series of declarations of war following the assassination by a Serbian hothead of the heir to the Austrian throne. Russia assisted its ally Serbia; Germany stood beside Austria and, in a fatal miscalculation, decided to knock out Russia's ally France by a quick strike. This meant attacking not along the heavily fortified French border, but through Belgium, whose neutrality had been guaranteed by all the Powers. The violation of Belgian neutrality brought Britain into the war and a British army landed in Belgium. In the early months of the war, victory went to the German army, which advanced to within fifty miles of Paris before getting bogged down in a stalemate of trench warfare which lasted for four years. So rapid had been the initial German advance that many British and French personnel got trapped behind enemy lines in Belgium. Wounded, out of touch with their units or just plain lost, hundreds of such men were being hidden and cared for by a network of Belgian resistance workers, ranging from aristocrats like the Prince de Croy and the Countess de Belleville to farm-workers, plumbers and postmen. Allied soldiers were smuggled across the Dutch border to safety, and a key figure in their rescue was Edith Cavell, the nurse whose tragic fate made her one of the first heroines of the war.

Edith Cavell was the daughter of a Norfolk clergyman, and grew up accepting that genteel poverty would be her lot. She served as that staple of the Victorian lady with no means of support, a governess, but when she turned to nursing she found her vocation. People did not find Edith Cavell easy to like; she was reserved, self-contained, giving nothing away. But she had iron self-control and a devotion to duty. In May 1907, she was invited to go over to Brussels and introduce Florence Nightingale's modern nursing system to Belgian hospitals, which were still largely served by Vincent de Paul's sisters of charity. Miss Cavell was put in charge of a nurses' training school. She was still in Brussels seven years later when the city was occupied by the Germans and she stuck to her post: it never seems to have occurred to her to attempt to escape to England. In November 1914, two British soldiers knocked on her door. She disguised them as patients, kept them for a fortnight and found guides to take them to the frontiers. They were the first of many. Edith Cavell's training hospital became one of the centres of the network by which men were smuggled to safety. As a secret operation, it was decidedly amateur. Some of the soldiers went out on the town and returned late at night, loudly singing English drinking songs. Servants and nurses gossiped cheerfully in public places. As strangers came and went, Edith Cavell inevitably made some wrong decisions about whom to trust. She was arrested on 5th August 1915 and tried by the military authorities on a charge of treason. Technically this was a crime of which she could not be guilty, as she was not a German citizen, but she frankly admitted the central fact, that she had helped enemies of Germany to escape. She was sentenced to death on 11th October and, as if the authorities anticipated the outcry they were to cause, the sentence was carried out with extraordinary rapidity. She was shot at dawn the next morning, wrong-footing the American ambassador and others who were negotiating for a pardon. The cavalier shooting of a woman and a nurse horrified worldwide opinion and Nurse Cavell's death, portrayed as judicial murder, was used to fuel anti-German propaganda. She herself met her death with calm courage. She received Communion in her cell, and spoke famous words to the chaplain who attended her: 'I realise that patriotism is not enough. I must have no hatred or bitterness towards anyone.' The words were later inscribed on her memorial in Trafalgar Square.

CHARLES DE FOUCALD (1858-1916) 1st December.
The War was truly a World War because the principal protagonists were colonial powers and the grim struggle in the trenches of Flanders spread out over all the continents where the British, French and German flags flew. War atrocities occurred even in the most remote villages of the Sahara Desert, among tribesmen who knew nothing of the Archduke of Austria or the neutrality of Belgium.

Few men can have lived lives so full of colourful extremes as Vicomte Charles de Foucauld. Every episode in his story would make a film As a young man he was a cavalry officer in the French army, living with gusto the life of an Offenbach operetta hero, dandified, filling his days with dinners at the best cafes, dalliances with grisettes, duels and gambling; he even had a mistress called Mimi. On active service in Algeria, then a French colony, he fell in love with North Africa, the starkness of its landscape and the fierce, simple truthfulness of its Muslim inhabitants. Disguised as a Jew, he made an excursion into the kingdom of Morocco and returned to Paris to publish a book about what he found there. In Paris he started dropping into churches. He was discovered by the saintly Abbe Huvelin, who helped him reconnect with the Catholicism of his childhood. Ever the extremist, Charles now entered the strictest possible monastic order, the Cistercian or Trappist. Unbelievably, he found the life of a silent monk too luxurious and easy; he wanted more renunciation. 'Jesus was poor,' he wrote, 'and shared the life of the poor. I should do the same.' He left the abbey and travelled to the Holy Land, seeking a physical closeness to Jesus. In Nazareth he attached himself to the Poor Clares as porter and handyman, but still found the life of the nuns too easy compared with the real poverty of the Arab population. He toyed with the idea of buying the Mount of Beatitudes as a site for a pilgrim community, but it turned out not to be for sale. He returned to France and was ordained, and in 1901 set sail once more for Algeria.

His plan was to live as a missionary among the Muslims, but there was nothing conventional about his mission. Settling in the far south of Algeria, in the desert village of Tamanrasset, he finally found a poverty extreme enough to satisfy him. The villagers were abjectly poor and Charles lived as one of them. He did some chaplaincy work for the local French garrison, but had no other contact with Christians. He filled his days with prayer and with gentle acts of kindness towards his neighbours, to whom he tried to communicate a basic sense of the goodness and greatness of God. He had enough French gallantry left to send to Paris for hair dye for the women, when he discovered how distressed they were at going grey. His great desire was to be hidden, as secret as Jesus was during the years in Nazareth when his soul was formed.

When the First World War broke out, Turkey, whose Sultan was nominally overlord of all Muslim lands, sided with Germany, and unrest broke out in all places under British or French rule. Algerian tribesmen rose in revolt, seeking their freedom. A party of raiders came to Tamanrasset to seize a cache of guns from the fort there. As they entered the building, one of them, casually and without realising who he was, shot Charles de Foucauld dead. He was granted the death he had prayed for, a death without publicity or heroic grandeur, a death in which he could identify finally and fully with the crucified Jesus.

During his life this man of passionate extremes had no followers. After he died, an order grew up inspired by his ideals. The Little Brothers and Sisters of Jesus still seek to live the hidden life of Nazareth amongst the poorest people of the world.

GEOFFREY STUDDERT KENNEDY (1883-1929) 8th March.

As the trench warfare in Flanders stagnated into a ghastly stalemate, it seemed as if the war could never end. For four years, huge amounts of resources were piled into the front by both sides, convinced that one big push could break the enemy lines and make victory possible. Millions died in futile assaults against positions fortified by machine guns, heavy artillery and miles of barbed wire. Daily life for the troops was damp, muddy, comfortless; and their nerves were torn to shreds by the ceaseless bombardment of the big guns.

The terrible slaughter not only destroyed a generation of Europe's young men, but dealt a fatal blow at much of the moral and cultural consensus of the Edwardian era. The superiority of an enlightened Christian civilisation could no longer be blithely assumed: Christian ideas and Christian world-views seemed dangerously naïve. Central Christian assumptions about God's providence, the power of prayer and the Fatherly love of the Creator, were inevitably challenged bitterly by those who endured the incomprehensible suffering which the War brought. In these dark times, among those who attempted to make a stand for decency, faith and sanity was an army chaplain, Geoffrey Studdert Kennedy, known because of his habit of giving out free cigarettes as 'Woodbine Willie.'

Kennedy was of Anglo-Irish stock, brought up in Leeds, where his father was a parish priest, and therefore familiar from babyhood with the mixture of squalor and resilience of a slum parish. He was ordained in 1908 and served in parishes in Rugby, Leeds and Worcester. Everywhere people were entranced by his infectious jollity and enthusiasm and amused by his chronic absent mindedness and untidiness. Respectable people were startled by a vicar who wore odd socks or turned up at meetings without a coat, having given his clothes away to a chance acquaintance. His housekeeper insisted on keeping his money and only issuing him with pocket money for each day, for he would recklessly give everything in his pockets to anyone with a claim on his sympathy. When war broke out he was newly married, with a young son Patrick whom he extravagantly adored. He went out to France as a chaplain in 1915.

His first service, in Rouen, set the tone for what followed. It was Christmas and the troops were drawn up in the pouring rain. After leading a rousing chorus of 'O Come all ye faithful,' Kennedy held the men spell-bound by his racy off-the-cuff preaching, spicing his message with anecdotes and slang phrases. Then, inviting those who wished to receive Communion to follow him, he withdrew to a nearby barn, where he used the manger as his altar. 'It was wonderful; no lights, no ritual, nothing to help but the rain and the far-off roll of guns, and Christ was born in a cattle shed on Christmas Day.'

His absent-mindedness was legendary. On one train journey, he was so busy chatting that he missed his station. At the last minute he jumped from the moving train while his companions threw his luggage out after him. Kennedy lay helpless with laughter on the platform while the railway staff ran down the line to retrieve his possessions. On another occasion when a friend met him at Amiens station he had lost all his luggage except three coats, two of which did not belong to him. But the troops adored his defiant courage, his willingness to take risks, his disrespect for authority and his constant challenge to them to live up to the best they knew.

Beneath the camaraderie and the devil-may-care gaiety, Studdert Kennedy was growing steadily angrier as he witnessed what war did to ordinary people. A turning point came when he stumbled across a recently killed young German in a wood and found himself wondering 'Where is Christ?' The answer, he found, was that Christ was in the dead man at his feet. The crucified Saviour was one with the millions who were dying all around him. Kennedy articulated a personal response to the war, centred on the idea that God suffered in and with his people. In terms of classical theology, the idea was heretical; the church fathers had established the doctrine of God's impassibility, his inability to suffer, as a buttress against ideas that God could change or that creation could damage the creator. The extreme horror of the First World War made it obscene rather than comforting to suppose that God was essentially unaffected by what was being done to his children. Studdert Kennedy's experimental doctrine of a suffering God enabled him to endure the horror and defy the meaningless blasphemy of what was being done. In passionate poems, some in a Kipling-esque soldier's dialect, he presented his vision of the war as a huge crucifixion, and his hope that Christ's grace would transfigure this suffering too and make it a source of regeneration and hope.

When the war ended, he threw himself with passion into the task of making new world, worthy of the sacrifice of those who had died. Working for the Industrial Christian Fellowship, he toured Britain unceasingly, enthralling vast crowds with his tumbling oratory, calling for an end to the poverty, injustice and class-distinction of the pre-war world, summoning his hearers to despise moral compromise and live Christ-like lives of self-sacrifice and love. He died prematurely, over-worked and exhausted, but never losing his angry, passionate charm.

EGLANTYNE JEBB (1876-1928) 17th December.

The First World War left a poisoned legacy. Not only the troops, but the civilian populations, had suffered unprecedented hardship. The military victory of Britain and her allies was hastened by a naval blockade which slowly starved the population of Germany and Austria into submission. With their own people exhausted and traumatised, there were few among the victors with sympathy to spare for a demonised enemy; the Boche had got his just deserts, was the common feeling; but conditions in central Europe were truly desperate. The German and Austrian empires were dismembered politically, ruined financially. In Vienna, abandoned babies were brought into the hospitals and stacked on shelves to die. There was neither food to feed them nor medicine to treat them. One of the few people prepared to do something in the face of this catastrophe was Eglantyne Jebb.

Eglantyne had an idyllic late-Victorian childhood in a Shropshire manor house, riding, dancing, climbing trees and performing plays with her five brothers and sisters. She grew up into a beautiful, stately, ironic and curiously aloof woman who oddly, given that she dedicated her life to helping them, rather disliked the company of children. She detested her short career as a teacher, by no means reciprocating the adoration of her class, who she recalled 'resemble pigs when they see their food coming. They beam up at me all the way to school just as though they didn't know that I was going to bully them all day.' Worn down by the drudgery of her role, her faith deepened as she looked at the crucifix on the schoolroom wall and identified with the hopelessness of the Saviour. In 1901, her idealism badly dented, she returned home exhausted and shortly afterwards moved with her mother to Cambridge, where she relished the company of intelligent adults and the stimulation of a University town. It would have been easy for her to collapse into the decorative life of an upper-class young woman, but Eglantyne's social conscience would not permit self-indulgence for long. She attempted to do good on the local committee of Octavia Hill's Charity

Organisation Society, but was repelled by the judgemental stance of fellow committee members attempting to discern which of the 'deserving poor' ought to receive grants; 'case after case read, case after case ticked off.... Stories of drunkenness, debt, disease: one goes on to the next tea party.' Her emotional life centred on a fellow charity worker, Margaret Keynes, the sister of the economist Maynard, but their passionate friendship cooled after Margaret married. Eglantyne came to believe that she was not fitted for close relationships: 'I want some work to do.'

In 1913, Eglantyne was invited by her brother-in-law to travel with him to the Balkans for the Macedonian Relief Fund, a charity providing aid for refugees following the 1912 Balkan War. It was her first encounter with Eastern Europe, with physical danger and with the peculiar horror of war damage. These experiences were to be formative.

The Great War shocked and radicalised Eglantyne. She joined the Labour Party and the suffragette movement and moved in circles highly critical of the British establishment and its perpetuation of the bloody stalemate. When peace came, Eglantyne joined the Famine Council and campaigned for effective help to be sent to the devastated cities of central Europe. The message was not a popular one and in her efforts to awaken consciences, Eglantyne was one of the earliest to use that standard tactic of modern charity work, the publication of heart-rending photographs of children dying of hunger.

Astonishingly, she was prosecuted and found guilty under the Defence of the Realm Act for distributing propaganda on behalf of the enemy. Her trial was held the same day as the state funeral of Edith Cavell, whose body had been disinterred and returned to Britain, and a huge wave of public revulsion against German atrocities was stirred up. Eglantyne, with considerable adroitness, managed to harness this for her cause, quoting Cavell's famous words 'Patriotism is not enough' and appealing to the public to honour the spirit of the murdered nurse by acting to save innocent children. Speaking at the Royal Albert Hall, she waved a tin of condensed milk and declared 'There is more practical morality in this tin than in all the creeds!' She collected celebrities to endorse her campaign: Freud, Einstein, Anna Pavlova, A.A.Milne and George

Bernard Shaw, who answered the German-haters by declaring 'I have no enemies under the age of seven.' The tide turned finally when the Pope came out in favour of the campaign and ordered collections to be made in all Catholic churches for Save the Children, on Holy Innocents Day 1919. From then on Save the Children became a major charity and Eglantyne's determination that no child must suffer for the sins and follies of its elders was translated into powerful action across war-stricken Europe.

From famine relief Eglantyne Jebb moved to the newly-born human rights movement. During the last years of the life, she was increasingly based at Geneva, where, on a sunny Sunday in 1922, she climbed Mount Saleve and sat at the top drafting a 'Charter for Children.' This was subsequently enshrined in international law as the 1923 Geneva Declaration of the Rights of the Child.

Cynics would say that those who opposed Save the Children were proved right by events. The innocent children saved by Eglantyne's collections grew up to be the bitter young people who served in Hitler's armies and air force. But her insistence that compassion must know no barriers has become normative. Sadly, Save the Children has never lacked work in the ninety years since she died.

PART TWENTY-SEVEN. INDIA.

MARY RAMABAI (1858-1922) 30th April.

In 1883, Charles Gore, then still based at Pusey House in Oxford, received an unusual request from the Anglican sisters at Wantage. A young Indian woman staying at the convent had recently been baptised, but needed guidance, the sisters thought, in forming a proper Christian character. Gore duly met and talked with the young woman in question, but Mary Ramabai proved unconvinced of the merits of liberal Anglo-Catholicism.

The years between the wars were for India the years of Gandhi and the struggle for independence from Britain. For Indian Christians, these years were a time of discovery, when an indigenous Indian Christian spirituality evolved, and the Indian church freed itself from colonial missionary trammels. We are now to examine the lives of three great Indian Christians (and one great missionary) which illustrate this transformation.

Mary Ramabai knew tragedy early in her life. Her father was a Brahmin, a high caste Hindu, who lived as a travelling teacher, supported by the alms of the devout. In the great famine of 1876, few Indians could spare food for outsiders, and Ramabai's father, mother and sister starved to death. Ramabai herself survived, and, thanks to her father's eccentric belief in women's education, was able to support herself lecturing on the Vedas, the sacred texts of Hinduism. She was increasingly disturbed by the ingrained antagonism to women which she discovered in the Vedas; some texts suggested that the only route to salvation open to her sex was to obey their husbands and pray to be reborn as a man. At the age of twenty-two Ramabai married, but her husband died of cholera two years later, leaving her with a baby daughter, Monorama. In 1883, she took the momentous decision to travel to England and study medicine. During this time abroad, much to her own surprise, she made the decision to seek baptism, although, as we have seen, her Christian mentors were anxious about her orthodoxy. She travelled to the States and published a book, 'The High Caste Hindu Woman,' which won her international fame. She returned to her homeland in

1888 recognised as one of the western-educated elite who were to bring to birth the new India.

Uncertain how to be authentically Indian and authentically Christian, Ramabai found herself drawn immediately to practical work for the relief of India's poverty, and particularly those marginalised by Hindu tradition. Widows in India became non-persons. The British had stamped out the practice of Suttee, whereby women sacrificed themselves on their husband's funeral pyres, but widows were often socially ostracised as people who were not supposed to exist. Many became sacred prostitutes in the temples and then starved when their looks faded. Moreover, because girls were married off very young, often to men much older than themselves, there were a lot of widows around. Ramabai, who had taken the Christian name Mary, founded at Poona her Sharada Sadan, or House of Wisdom, a place where young widows and orphans could find a refuge and the chance to learn skills and trades by which to support themselves. This house gradually extended to become a small town in itself, with school, hospital, workshops, farm and gardens, all run by members of the community. It was not overtly evangelistic, but Mary Ramabai made no secret of her own Christian faith and shyly, gradually, the women began to join her at prayer. In 1891, her own discipleship took an important step forward when she experienced a profound personal conversion: Christianity was no longer just a philosophy to live by but a personal relationship with Jesus, who had saved her from her sins.

In 1896 came another famine, as dire as the one which had destroyed Ramabai's family. She would turn away nobody and at the height of the crisis 1350 indigent people were camping out in Sharada Sadan's grounds. The work of mercy made its own statement and at the turn of the century 1,200 people were converted, being driven down singing in ox-carts to the river to be baptised. A whole new Christian village was built, Mukti, peopled by 'graduates' from Sharada Sadan and rehabilitated refugees, and centred around a huge new church capable of holding 5000 people. Here in 1905 occurred the 'Mukti revival' when scores of people experienced the charismatic gifts of the Spirit. Patiently and gracefully, Ramabai continued to administer her growing 'empire' of relief institutions.

Her great sorrow in old age was the premature death of her daughter, whom she had intended as her successor. She herself died peacefully in her sleep. She was the first woman in modern India to achieve a position in public life, and the work of Mukti continues to this day.

AMY CARMICHAEL (1867-1951) 18th January.

A British missionary whose work paralleled that of Mary Ramabai, was Amy Carmichael, an Irish Presbyterian who arrived in India in 1895. She had always felt called to missionary work. When quite a young girl she had helped found 'The Welcome,' a Christian outreach to factory girls in Belfast. But India became her true home. She was greatly moved by the plight of the 'Devadasis,' young girls who were betrothed as sacred brides to the Hindu gods, and whose lives as objects of reverence within the temples often shaded darkly into abuse and sacred prostitution. Settling at Dohnavur, Amy made it her life's work to rescue these girls. The home she built grew to house over a hundred children, but Amy was anxious it should remain a home, not an institution. As well as Christian teaching, she filled the place with flowers, pet animals, music and laughter. To her European contemporaries, some of Amy's choices seemed eccentric, if not shocking. Like Mary Ramabai, she realised that Christianity could only serve India if it lost its cultural association with the British Raj. She adopted Indian clothes and diet and was even said to dye her skin to make her appearance less British. She was not afraid to use Hindu customs in the many parties, celebrations and special days which she invented to enrich the lives of her children. Those who volunteered to help her were warned to expect no salaries, for the community lived by faith and no fund-raising was permitted. Amy never asked anyone but God for money.

The work at Dohnavur became internationally famous through Amy Carmichael's writing; she wrote thirty-eight books, many of which sold widely. Her campaign bore fruit in 1947 when the state government of Madras passed a law to outlaw the dedication of children at temples.

During the last twenty years of her life Amy Carmichael was a chronic invalid and unable to walk. Those who knew her in this last period of her weakness were moved by her unfailing sunny faith and serenity.

SUNDAR SINGH (1889-1929) 19th June.

The spread of Christianity in a land so spiritually sophisticated as India, with its venerable religious traditions, could not but be controversial, especially given its inseparable association with the colonial power. Educated Indians were prepared to tolerate the presence of missionaries because of the prestige and power they could win for their children by a Western-style education. The family of Sundar Singh was typical. Committed Sikhs, they had the oriental openness to religions not their own – as a boy Sundar Singh read both the Hindu vedas and the Koran, and when he went to school with the missionaries, he was of course exposed to the Bible as well. None of this was supposed to compromise his loyalty to his own faith; he was to study and understand other religions, practise his own.

The boy's life plunged into crisis when at fourteen he lost his adored mother. In bitter anger he expressed his hatred for the God he had been taught about by publicly burning the Bible in the school playground, feeding it page by page into the fire and daring God to strike him down. Three days later he resolved on suicide. His home was close to the railway line and one night, kneeling in the moonlight, Singh informed God that if he had been given no sign by the time the 5.00am express went past, he would throw himself under it. The sign he demanded came: the boy saw a man with pierced hands enter his room and say 'Why do you persecute me? I died for you.' His life transformed, Sundar Singh went to the church in Simla and in 1905 accepted baptism. His family immediately disowned him and his brother, with his father's connivance, went so far as to attempt to poison him. For the rest of his life Sundar Singh lived a life on the margins, rejected by his own people, yet unable to identify with the Westernised church of the missionaries. Four years after his baptism he did attempt to train as an Anglican priest, but he left the Anglican college in Lahore un-ordained and unimpressed by institutional Christianity. His own calling would be very different.

Singh became a 'sadhu' or wandering holy man in the established Indian tradition. He wanted to bring Jesus to India using Indian spirituality, and for the rest of his life he lived in poverty as a homeless wanderer, sustained by alms and refusing any personal property beyond his clothes and a few books. He was received with awe even by those who did not understand him, and many legends grew up where 'the apostle with the bleeding feet' had passed. Of course he was persecuted, stoned, driven out of villages, attacked on the road. In Nepal, in 1914, he was sentenced to death and put down a well to die, with the bodies of two criminals for company. The circumstances of his escape are obscure, but were regarded by his followers as miraculous. By the end of the First World War he was preaching to crowds of thousands all over India, and he achieved a cult status in a western world whose spiritual bankruptcy had been exposed by the conflict. In the years following the war, the Sadhu visited Japan, China, the USA, Britain, Germany, and the Holy Land, disturbing and inspiring many by his message, so alien to a materialist, scientific society and yet so closely echoing the kingdom preaching of Jesus himself. He was shocked and grieved at the worldly compromise and spiritual despair he found in lands that had been nominally Christian for centuries.

All his life Sundar Singh was fascinated by Tibet, the mountain kingdom with religious traditions as strange to Sikhs as to Christians. He made his first journey there as early as 1906 and periodically returned, craving the silence and clarity of the Himalayas. He set off on his last journey in 1929, and never returned. No trace of him was ever found, and it is uncertain whether he was killed, perished in a mountain accident, or simply died of exhaustion.

SAMUEL AZARIAH (1874-1945) 3rd January.
The last great Indian Christian from this period whom we consider experienced none of the anguish of conversion from one religion to another. Samuel Azariah was born in Andrha Pradesh, in that southern part of India where the church had the longest history: the area where Francis Xavier (and perhaps even St Thomas) preached and baptised. He came from a Christian family (his father was an

Anglican priest) and at the age of nineteen Azariah was already serving the church as a YMCA evangelist. Evangelism was his passion and to further the conversion of India he founded, while still in his twenties, the Indian Missionary Society, which in 1905 became the National Missionary Society. Membership of both these societies was restricted to Indians, for Azariah believed as passionately as Mary Ramabai and Sundar Singh that Jesus could only reach the hearts of Indians if the church lost its cultural association with colonialism and the British Raj. In 1909 he was ordained and in 1912 became Bishop of Dornakal, a new diocese created to accommodate the growing number of converts. As bishop, Azariah continued to work for an authentically Indian church. By 1924, his diocese contained only eight clergy of English descent, and fifty-three Indians. The cathedral Church of the Epiphany, very much a personal project of the bishop, was completed in 1936; it is a striking witness in stone to Azariah's vision of the church, combining harmoniously elements of western gothic, Mughal and traditional Hindu architecture.

Ecumenism was another area where Bishop Azariah was determined not to be trammelled by inherited western tradition. He found it hard to be patient with the historic divisions, Catholic, Anglican, Presbyterian, Baptist, which the missionaries had brought with them from their homelands. Many of the causes of division thus perpetuated seemed to him irrelevant to India's denominations. His efforts bore fruit after his death. At just the same time as the Indian people, led by Gandhi achieved nationhood and independence from the British Empire, the Church of South India came into being, a fully united body bringing together all the Anglican and Protestant churches. The mutual recognition of ministry by those who had and had not been episcopally ordained was a cause of distrust and the Church of South India still has a somewhat ambiguous status within the Anglican Communion, but this great work of unity was one of the earliest and most successful examples of churches working together to overcome historic divisions.

Part Twenty-eight. The Church in the Modern Era.

EVELYN UNDERHILL (1875-1941) 15th June.

While these efforts were being made to root Christ in the rich soil of India, Britain and Europe struggled with the toxic legacy of the First World War. In an atmosphere of weary cynicism and bitter disillusionment, Christians were in danger of losing their way; long gone was the almost bumptious confidence about the future displayed by late Victorian church-people in the age of church building and missionary expansion. In an époque which saw the spread of Marxist materialism, the rise of totalitarian states of the left and right in Russia, Germany and Italy, the mass unemployment of the Great Depression and a new art focussed on the shocking, the bizarre and the unorthodox, there was much to daunt and little to reassure traditional Christians. The church was stretched beyond its comfortable Victorian limits, as Christians engaged with the modern world on two fronts. Evelyn Underhill represents a renewed quest for inner integrity and growth in the life of prayer. William Temple represents a renewed determination to incarnate Christian truth in a practical response to the economic and social demands of his age.

Evelyn Underhill was the daughter of a Wolverhampton barrister, her family nominally Christian but not church-goers. Although as a girl she hero-worshipped Jesus (along with Mahomet and Joan of Arc) she had no time for organised religion and indeed after graduating from King's College, London, she considered herself an atheist. She was happily married to Hubert Stuart Moore and outwardly lived the pleasant existence of a middle-class lady of leisure, entertaining her husband's business friends, holidaying on their yacht or in the South of France, writing chatty letters to a wide circle of friends. Inwardly she was engaged on a lifelong pilgrimage which led her first to discover mystical prayer, then to become a committed Anglican, and finally to be one of the most sought after and admired spiritual directors in Britain.

Evelyn made her reputation in 1911 with the publication of her great work 'Mysticism.' The fruit of her wide reading, it gave an account of the phenomenon of mystical prayer throughout the ages, drawing on Christian writers and on spiritual masters from other religions. Using insights from the new science of psychology, the book made a persuasive claim for the experience of God in prayer to be taken seriously, not dismissed as self-delusion or mental aberration. Evelyn herself had at this time no settled spiritual home. After holidays in Italy and France she was strongly drawn to Roman Catholicism, the branch of Christianity which she felt had done most to preserve the wisdom of contemplative prayer into the modern era, but the Vatican's attacks on modern thought in all its forms repelled her by its illiberalism. She still had strong doubts about the historicity of the gospel miracles. However by 1920 she had become a communicant within the Church of England, which she described as 'a respectable suburb of the City of God.' She continued to write copiously on prayer and mystical experience, and soon found herself the recipient of dozens of letters, as people from all walks of life consulted her about their own 'peculiar' experiences. She conscientiously answered all her correspondence, with gentle wit deflating pomposity and cooling over-heated imaginations, and providing rational, deep insights into the workings of God within the soul. Gradually, she became spiritual guide to many people and was sought after as a conductor of retreats and conferences. In an age when women still had no recognised teaching role within the church, Evelyn Underhill's influence was immense. She did much to revive an awareness of the inner life and helped many who found the institutional life of the church stale and limited.

To her grief, she never had children and compensated for this by a rather English, doting relationship with her cats, who often 'wrote' letters to her friends and had their own Christmas tree. In old age she was chronically ill, but accepted this with serenity; those who loved her described how when she entered a room, a light seemed to shine.

WILLIAM TEMPLE (1881-1944) 6th November.
Charles Gore never quite forgave Frederick Temple, the archbishop who consecrated him Bishop of Worcester, for what he felt was an unfair pressure put upon him to take high office. No such shadow existed in his relationship with Archbishop Temple's son William, an

extraordinarily bright boy, just the sort of young man to attract Gore's interest and protection. William Temple became an inspiration to his generation as Gore had been to his. Both men brought a keen analytical mind to the task of commending orthodox Christianity to an age tempted to doubt; both wrote widely read and widely praised major books on belief; both were driven by a keen social conscience; both as new bishops were responsible for the creation of a great northern diocese – in Gore's case Birmingham, in Temple's Blackburn; both were renowned as wits and had a deserved reputation for loyal friendship. Yet the differences were marked as well. Gore was thin and angular; in the pulpit and in conversation he twisted his limbs into extraordinary knots as he became absorbed in his subject. Temple, even as a young man, was tubby. With his round glasses and wide, smiling face, he reminded contemporaries irresistibly of Billy Bunter.

Gore the celibate was, despite his gregariousness, a loner, his emotional world centred on a few male friendships, charged with a peculiar Victorian intensity. He valued company chiefly for intellectual stimulus, and though he delighted in the company of young people, he did not suffer fools gladly. Temple's happy marriage was the backbone of his life; he was fortunate to find a wife who accepted that her husband would work sixteen-hour days and would regard holidays as space for writing, and who supported him with unquestioning loyalty. His great gift was approachability – people of all classes, intellectual backgrounds and nationalities experienced him as a friend. Finally the two men's approach to their work divided them. Gore was always a maverick and a rebel. Although he achieved much, he hated the administrative slog of doing it. Repeatedly his first reaction, when his conscience clashed with the system, was to offer to resign, and retirement, when it came, was a joy to him, the gateway to a final, immensely creative phase in his life. He was once seen, after a stormy church meeting, to stop on Westminster Bridge and shake his fist at Lambeth Palace. Temple would never have made such a gesture. He was a master of committee work, a natural networker, one of those rare beings who can see the wood for the trees in a meeting. Where Gore doodled his frustration on his jotter in committees, Temple more than once pulled off the stunt of listening to impassioned arguments, then silently drafting and passing to the chairman a proposal which bridged the two sides of the conflict and gave the committee a creative, universally acceptable way forward.

With his privileged background, it was amazing how he managed to reach out to the common man. Brought up in Lambeth Palace, educated at Rugby and Balliol, he progressed rapidly through a series of plum church jobs; at each he worked so hard and intelligently that he achieved more in a few years than another incumbent might have done in many. He was Headmaster of Repton (1910), Rector of St James, Piccadilly (1913), Canon of Westminster (1919), Bishop of Manchester (1921), Archbishop of York (1929) and finally (1942) Archbishop of Canterbury. As well as performing creatively the routine duties of each of these offices, Temple was centrally involved in every important aspect of church life – the National Mission of Repentance during the First World War; the passing of the Enabling Act, the first important step to giving the Church of England self-government under Parliament; the process of liturgical reform which culminated in the 1928 Prayer Book; negotiation between miners and owners during the National Strike; ecumenical work worldwide, including the creation of the Church of South India; the Malvern Conference, a watershed in the church's social mission; the 1944 Education Act which laid the foundations of the modern partnership of church and state in primary schools – as well as the ceaseless production of memorable sermons, life-changing missions and significant books. Temple's social conscience was such that he became the first Archbishop to provoke the now standard complaint that senior clergy should keep their noses out of politics, but unlike some of his successors he had the analytical ability to put down on paper a persuasive argument for why in a modern state the church can and must speak in the political arena.

He became Archbishop of Canterbury when Britain was once again at war with Germany, and played his part in sustaining the morale of an exhausted people during the darkest days of the war. Becoming Archbishop of Canterbury literally killed him; even his limitless energy was ground down by the demands he put on himself. In 1944 he took some days off for quiet prayer: for once he actually admitted 'I need this retreat.' Two months later he was dead and even at a time when so many were dying, he was sincerely mourned by the whole nation.

PAUL COUTURIER (1881-1953) 24th March.
The trauma of the Great War demanded changes of the church in France no less than in England. While the classic tradition of French Catholicism, represented by revered figures like Therese of Lisieux and Charles de Foucauld, tended to encourage an ideal of hidden prayer and solitary renunciation, in the twenties and thirties the French religious orders began to explore more open ways of connecting with a world which had lost its way. In particular, ecumenism became a powerful force among French Catholics.

Paul Couturier, born in Lyon, had been ordained in 1906. After the Great War, he found himself working extensively with Russian refugees, who flooded into France after the Bolshevik Revolution. The Russian aristocracy spoke French as fluently as Russian, so Paris was a natural place of asylum for emigres fleeing the chaos of post-Tsarist Russia. Couturier learned much about the traditions of the Russian Orthodox Church and became an expert on eastern spirituality. The more he worked and prayed with Christians outside the Roman Communion, the more his heart burned with the pain which division had inflicted on the church.

In the 1930s, he became a Benedictine and in 1933 he began what was initially Three Days of prayer for Christian Unity. This quickly expanded to become a Week of Prayer, stretching between the feast of St Peter on 18th January and St Paul on 25th January. The movement spread rapidly to all denominations, and is now an important means of bringing Christians together throughout the world.

Paul Couturier was greatly influenced by his contemporary Teilhard de Chardin, with his visionary writing exploring Christ as an evolutionary force, and he believed that those who prayed and yearned for unity formed an 'Invisible Monastery,' a community of prayer which transcended national and denominational boundaries. He corresponded widely with Jews and Muslims, seeking common spiritual ground with them as well. His desire to see the church an open, welcoming place for pilgrims and enquirers greatly influenced the liturgy of the French church in the modern era, particularly the foundation of the Taize Community as a place where young people from all over Europe, Catholic, Orthodox and Protestant, can meet together to share a life of simple prayer and encounter.

MAXIMILIAN KOLBE (1894-1941) 14th August.

The new World War in the midst of which William Temple found himself elevated to Canterbury was a conflict even fiercer and crueller than the First World War. The bitterness felt throughout Germany at the peace terms imposed at Versailles in 1919 provided the context in which Adolf Hitler and the Nazi party could seize power. A propagandist of demonic genius, Hitler was able to present himself as a national saviour for an impoverished and humiliated land. Only after he was securely entrenched in power did the madness of his fanaticism reveal itself, as he first destroyed the democratic institutions he had exploited to win power; then set about his programme of purifying the German people by ostracising and eventually attempting the extermination of the Jews; and finally, in his quest to fulfil the destiny of the master race, unleashing a series of wars of conquest, fought with a savage brutality never before seen in Europe, and at first terrifyingly and rapidly successful. For a long time the democratic governments of Western Europe found it hard to believe that Hitler could be quite the unscrupulous menace he seemed. In 1939, Hitler invaded Poland and Britain and France were obliged once more to declare war on Germany.

The Nazis despised the Poles, whom they regarded as racially inferior, almost as low as the Jews. The invasion of Poland was accompanied by deliberately staged atrocities and its conquest by ruthless purges of anybody who might lead resistance to the occupation. Captured officers were shot in swathes and all social leaders arrested. In Poland, a country so devoutly Catholic, this included the hierarchy of the Roman Catholic Church. Priests, monks and friars were rounded up and assigned to the notorious concentration camps. Among those immured at Auschwitz was a Franciscan named Maximilian Kolbe.

Kolbe came from a passionately Catholic family; he and all his brothers entered the priesthood and his parents, when they saw their sons settled, ended their marriage and both entered religious orders. Maximilian had a deep devotion to the Virgin Mary and rejoiced when the Pope declared her 'Queen of Poland.' As a Franciscan, he founded a new community near Warsaw, which soon numbered over 500 brothers. He edited a Catholic newspaper and for five years did missionary work in Japan; the Franciscan house he built in Nagasaki was one of the few buildings to survive the atomic bomb. In his role as editor, he was fiercely anti-Nazi, and his arrest after Poland surrendered was inevitable.

In Auschwitz, Kolbe was singled out for ill-treatment by the priest-hating guard in command of his section. He was given loads of wood to carry far beyond his strength, and beaten viciously when he failed. He maintained a serene demeanour and was noted for his willingness to share his meagre rations with others who complained of hunger. On 31st July 1941, occurred the incident which has made Maximilian Kolbe an icon of Christ-like self-sacrifice.

Three prisoners had escaped, and Kolbe's section was informed that a group punishment would be imposed. Ten men were chosen at random to be shut in 'The Bunker', an underground cell where they would be starved to death. One of the doomed ten, a Polish officer called Francis Gajowniczek, cried out in despair 'O my poor wife, my poor children, I shall never see them again.' Maximilian Kolbe stepped out of the line and offered himself as a replacement for Gajownizek. The grisly bargain was agreed and the married man was spared. Kolbe and the other nine were marched away and immured. It took fourteen days for them to die. Kolbe led his companions in singing hymns and reciting the rosary until, one by one, they succumbed to hunger. Kolbe was the last survivor and was finally killed by a lethal injection. The man he saved was present in St Peter's Square in 1982 to hear the man who died that he might live declared a saint of the church.

DIETRICH BONHOEFFER (1906-1945) 9th April.
On the whole, the German Christian response to Hitler was not marked by heroic resistance. Church-goers in Germany proved as

susceptible as the rest of the population to his dangerous glamour and to the hope of national regeneration he held out. There was some excuse for this failure of perception. Ever since Martin Luther constructed his theory of the Two Kingdoms in order to deny political authority to the Pope, the German church had had a strong reverence for secular authority and had been exceedingly wary of bids by clergy and church institutions to usurp powers which God had appointed to be wielded by the State. To denounce the government as anti-Christian was psychologically extremely difficult for church leaders trained in this tradition; and Hitler was able in his early years to pose plausibly as a man who stood for traditional, moral values against the decadence of the Weimar republic and the atheistic excesses of Bolshevism. Nevertheless, there is something shameful in the spectacle of church leaders obediently excluding ethnic Jews from their congregations, persuading themselves that Jewish Christians really would be happier worshipping with their own; in the records of eager preachers doing violence to the New Testament to make it compatible with the Nordic master-race mythology of the Nazis; in the willingness of churches to take down the crucifix, that disgusting symbol of craven semitic surrender, and replace it with the swastika. Even so eminent a theologian as Niemuller at first gave cautious welcome to Hitler's regeneration plans, only to realise his error and, after speaking against the regime, to end up spending thirteen years in prison, where he wrote those famous words, 'They came for the Communists, and I did not speak out because I was not a Communist. Then they came for the Jews, and I did not speak out because I was not a Jew. Then they came for me, and there was nobody left to speak out for me.'

But even in the worst days of the Nazi tyranny, there were Christian voices raised, and raised fearlessly, to denounce what Hitler was doing to the soul of a Christian nation. Dietrich Bonhoeffer belonged to a family both socially and academically prestigious. His father Karl was one of the most eminent psychiatrists in Europe; his mother Paula came from a cultured aristocratic family whose daughters had in previous generations been taught piano by Lizst and Schumann. They represented the best of the old Germany which Nazism was to destroy. Though not a church-going family, the

Bonhoeffer children were brought up as cultural Christians, with carols around the Christmas tree and family performances of Bach's motets and chorales to celebrate anniversaries. Karl Bonhoeffer brought up his children above all to think rigorously and un-shrinkingly. He always supported their decisions if they could back them by a rational, well-thought-out justification. This devotion to truth at all costs was through his life a hallmark of Dietrich Bonoeffer; another was the selfless courage with which he acted in accord with what he had demonstrated to himself was right.

If Karl Bonheoffer was disappointed by his son's decision, first to study theology instead of science, then to seek ordination rather than academic honours, he never showed it. Bonheoffer could always depend on his parents' support through the difficult course he charted over his short life of thirty-nine years. Although rooted in German theological tradition, he found his soul in work overseas in the United States, where he was impressed by the vitality of the black-led churches with their witness against racism, and depressed by the anaemic liberal theology of the fashionable churches attended by well-to-do New Yorkers. As Hitler consolidated his grip on power, Bonhoeffer was fortunate to be working as chaplain to Lutheran congregations in London, where he formed a lifelong friendship with George Bell, the Bishop of Chichester. In England, Bonhoeffer was comparatively safe from interference by the German government or church, and was able to organise resistance, the so-called Confessing Church, which denounced the compromises of the German church and called both Germans and the international Christian community to recognise, name and oppose the rising evil. In 1934, he returned home determined to work to reverse the damage being done to German Christianity. His task was to found and direct a seminary for the Confessing Church. Thanks to contacts with the landowners of East Prussia, old fashioned Christian aristocrats appalled at what Hitler was doing, he was able to establish a remote base at Finkenwalde, a charming house lost so far in the woods as to escape Nazi vigilance. Here Bonhoeffer did his most lasting creative work modelling his ideal Christian community. The men he trained lived a communal life centred on the Word of God – each student was expected to spend an hour each morning meditating on a given verse of scripture. Varied by plenty of sport, music and outdoor work, the community's main function was prayer. The book he wrote in this period 'The Cost of Discipleship' is our guide to what he was trying to achieve. The book denounces 'Cheap Grace,' the perversion of Luther's doctrine of justification by faith into an easy, lazy assumption that God's forgiveness will always be available if we believe correctly. Bonhoeffer brought the gospels back to life as he outlined in his burning, carefully crafted prose the demanding life of kingdom freedom to which Jesus summons us.

When war broke out, it was clear that Bonhoeffer would be conscripted into the army, and as clear that he would in conscience refuse to fight. His friends moved heaven and earth to secure a lectureship in the United States, where he would be safe; but within days of arriving in New York, Bonhoeffer knew he had been wrong to acquiesce in these arrangements. He must be with his country in the hour of danger. After less than a month he cancelled his engagements in America and returned to Germany. He avoided military service by a move which surprised and upset many of his friends, taking a post with the Abwehr, the German military intelligence. Had the man who denounced compromise in church and state sold out after all? By no means. Bonhoeffer was working as a double agent, linked with the wide network of those within the German establishment who wanted to make an end of Hitler. Through Bishop Bell, Bonhoeffer contacted the British government, trying to get assurances that if Hitler was destroyed by a coup, the victorious allies would deal mercifully with a new German government. These assurances Churchill would not give; locked into total war, he was committed to the utter destruction of Germany. After agonised searches of conscience, the conspirators decided they must proceed. Even if the cost was the ruin of their country, the evil of Nazism must be destroyed.

But in 1943, Bonhoeffer was arrested. Nobody had any idea that he was a double agent – a journey into Switzerland to facilitate the escape of a party of Jews had been misinterpreted as private money-laundering, and it was on suspicion of corruption that he was arrested. He was not uncomfortable in prison; his uncle was military governor of Berlin and the guards allowed him privileges. He continued to write and to stay in touch with his parents and his fiancée, the young Maria von Wedemeyer. He also continued, through elaborate codes concealed in books and letters, to keep in touch with the conspiracy. His friends even tried to delay his trial and keep him safely in prison, believing that Hitler would soon be dead.

The Valkyrie Plot is one of the great missed moments of history. After two failed attempts, on July 20th 1944, Colonel Von Stauffenberg managed to leave a suitcase bomb under the table at which Hitler sat at Council with his generals. The bomb went off, but the brunt of the blast was taken by an enormous table leg which shielded Hitler, leaving him with minor bruises and his trousers torn to shreds like a cartoon bomb victim. The failure laid open to Nazi vengeance the huge network of German resistance. Dozens of people were arrested, tortured, condemned. Bonhoeffer, whose brother and brother-in-law were executed, was handed over to the Gestapo and, early in 1945, driven out of Berlin, south to the death camp of Buchenwald. The Nazi regime was in its death throes. It was already clear that Germany had lost the war. Nevertheless the brutal routines of the camps continued unabated. Bonhoeffer impressed his fellow prisoners with his lack of fear, his determination to treat even the guards as human beings, his cheerfulness. In the letters which survive from his last days he speaks about faith and the future, in a much misunderstood phrase talking of 'religion-less Christianity.' Radical theologians have claimed Bonhoeffer as a prophet of the 'Death of God' movement, the idea that humanity has outgrown the possibility of belief in an objective God 'out there.' But nothing else in Bonhoeffer's life concurs with this – it is more probable that he continued to fight against the comfortable, social religion which had colluded so easily with Nazism. After Hitler, Christianity could not be a hobby, a collection of religious practices which comforted without affecting the central flow of a person's life. Christ demanded disciples who would sacrifice their whole lives for him. 'Religionless Christianity' meant that Christianity must be much more than a religion; it must be an authentic life of faith.

As the regime collapsed, Bonhoeffer and other important prisoners were driven south in Bavaria in a nightmare journey which even the guards seemed to find pointless. But, it seems at the personal order of Hitler, now weeks from death himself, Bonhoeffer was detached from the group and brought back to Flossenburg, another concentration camp. There on 9th April 1945, he was shot. American troops liberated the camp only two weeks later. Bishop Bell preached at his memorial service at Holy Trinity, Brompton.

THE MARTYRS OF PAPUA NEW GUINEA (1942) 2nd September. The campaigns to contain and destroy the Nazi regime ranged over Europe, Russia and North Africa. The Second World War became truly a global conflict with the decision of the militarised government of Japan to enter the war as allies of Germany, first launching the notorious pre-emptive strike on the U.S.A Pacific Fleet at Pearl Harbour, then sending armies of conquest to occupy British and French possessions in south-east Asia and threaten Australia and British India. At first the Japanese advance was as rapid and terrifying as the German army's European conquests. Singapore fell to Japan, and Indo-China and Burma were occupied. In 1942, Japanese forces arrived in Papua New Guinea. This, the third largest island in the world, formed loosely part of the British Empire, being governed from the Dominion of Australia. Missionaries had been active on the island for a generation and an infant church was in existence, although, as the tragedy of the Japanese invasion was to reveal, there were many New Guineans who resented the presence and influence of the missionaries.

Bishop Strong, the Anglican bishop of Papua New Guinea, could see that invasion was imminent, but after long prayer, decided that it was his duty to request missionaries to remain at their posts. For this decision he was much criticised, but he believed that the church would have no credibility if local Christians saw their leaders desert them in the hour of danger. All the missionaries, with devoted courage, remained to face almost certain death.

On July 21st 1942, two women stood on the beach at Gona, watching Australian and Japanese planes fighting in the sky above. One was a schoolteacher, Mavis Parkinson, the other a nurse, May Hayman, who was engaged to a mission priest, Vivian Redlich. As the women watched unbelieving, they suddenly realised that landing craft were heading for the beach; the invasion had begun. They escaped inland, and wandered in the jungle for several nights before being betrayed to the Japanese. They were bayonetted beside the graves just dug for them. Inland, Vivian Redlich celebrated the Sunday eucharist in his village, when news of the invasion arrived. His New Guinean assistant, Lucian Tapiedi, had remained with him after insisting that native mission workers who were married should return to the comparative safety of their home villages. The two men attempted to hide, but natives hostile to the mission betrayed them. Tapiedi was struck down by a sorcerer anxious to preserve traditional religions, and Redlich with other Europeans was handed over to the Japanese, who beheaded them. Another missionary, John Holland, was also butchered and his priceless translation of the scriptures, his life's work, was shredded.

But Bishop Strong's words proved prophetic. The martyrs were remembered and after the defeat of Japan fresh missionaries returned under whose guidance the Christianisation of Papua New Guinea was consolidated.

INI KOPURIA (1900 – 1945)
For the peoples of the Pacific, the arrival of so-called allies could be as traumatic as that of enemies. As the U.S Army island-hopped its way across the great ocean, building up the forces and occupying the strategic positions necessary to push back the Japanese advance, the arrival of such huge numbers of cheerful, brash, technically sophisticated young men wrought havoc on the fragile, tradition-based host cultures; it was not all as jolly as 'South Pacific.' Among those who felt overwhelmed by the American occupation of Melanesia was Ini Kopuria, the dynamic founder of the Melanesian Brotherhood. It was twenty years since he had founded this most successful of all missionary orders.
His had been a schoolboy at one of Selwyn's Christian colleges and was early noted for his determined Christian conscience. One Lent, the young Ini took a vow of silence, and when challenged by his teacher, wrote him a letter defending himself rather than break his vow. As a young adult, he surprised friends by becoming a

policeman rather than a priest, but his true calling was to missionary work and the Melanesian Brotherhood.

The brothers took temporary, not life vows, and devoted themselves to spreading the gospel over the islands and archipelagos where Coley Patteson and George Selwyn had first preached. The Melanesian Brotherhood was a native order and had the advantages of living close to the thought-world of those to whom they were sent. Ini Kopuria led by example, inspiring others by his deep prayerfulness, his unfailing cheerfulness, his shrewdness in dealing with disputes in the order. He moved from island to island, establishing churches and baptising sometimes hundreds of new Christians in the icy waters of the mountain streams.

His relationship with European missionaries was always edgy. Physically alert, mentally agile, extremely intelligent, he could not but resent the patronising racism which unthinkingly infected the attitudes of all but the finest of his white colleagues; and he often lacked the tact to avoid displaying his resentment. But to his own people he was a charismatic leader, until the Americans came. Ini and Melanesia found themselves negotiating an encounter with Western materialism far more complex than even the unhappy history of colonialism had thrown at them. Under the strain, Ini appears to have lost his faith in the church, if not in God. He resigned from the Brotherhood and withdrew into solitude. Only towards the end of his life did he re-establish contact with his old colleagues and find a place where he could confidently stand as a Christian in the modern world.

The Melanesian Brotherhood has continued to flourish as a great sustainer of the church in the South Seas and, as we shall see, its members have continued to suffer for their witness to Christ.

GEORGE BELL (1883-1958) 3rd October.
George Bell, Bishop of Chichester, continued to mourn his friend Dietrich Bonhoeffer and to live true to the vision, which that friendship had encapsulated, of a Christian Europe united to heal the wounds inflicted by the monstrosities of fascist dictatorship and World War. Bell was to all appearance a quintessentially establishment figure; educated at Westminster and Christchurch, he

only served a brief curacy in Leeds before taking the path of preferment. In 1914, he became Chaplain to Archbishop Randall Davidson, whose biography he later wrote; and went on to be Dean of Canterbury (1924) and Bishop of Chichester (1929). But his acute social conscience put him at odds with those who, by upbringing, were his natural allies; not even with his university friend, William Temple, did he always see eye to eye.

As Dean of Canterbury, he distinguished himself by his encouragement of the arts, in particular drama. He commissioned Christian plays from John Masefield, Dorothy Sayers, Christopher Fry and, most famously, from T.S.Eliot, whose 'Murder in the Cathedral' was performed at the Canterbury Festival in 1935 as a thinly veiled statement of the cost to a Christian of taking a stand against tyranny. In these plays, it was claimed, drama was performed inside an English church for the first time since the Reformation, and they typified Bell's desire to bridge the gap between the arts and the church, and to restore the rich tradition of Christian artistic patronage. As Bishop of Chichester, he began a policy of commissioning works from leading contemporary artists, in particular encouraging the German refugee Hans Feibusch, who painted some of his finest works for the cathedral and diocese. Bell's tradition continues to live at Chichester, whose cathedral contains fine windows, sculptures and tapestries by Chagall, Sutherland and others.

We have already seen how vital was the friendship between Bonhoeffer and Bell in sustaining German resistance to Hitler. The two men met for the last time in 1942 in Sweden, where Bell promised to do what he could to win British support for the plot against Hitler. That support he was unable to obtain, to his own lasting bitterness. Churchill's government would not take seriously the existence of 'good Germans' and Bell blamed himself for the failure of Valkyrie and the death of Bonhoeffer. In the closing phase of the war, Bell stood against public opinion by denouncing the policy of total war which brought about such horrors as the fire-bombing of Dresden and the dropping of the atomic bombs on Japan. To Bell, the decision to use weapons of mass destruction to terrorise civilian populations dragged the allies down to the moral level of those they were fighting, but so grim was the struggle that his witness was rejected with indignation by most people. Many have believed that Bell would have been the obvious successor to Archbishop William Temple, had not Churchill vetoed the preferment of a man he regarded almost as an enemy.

After the war, Bell continued to work tirelessly for reconciliation and healing in Europe, while working equally hard to modernise his own diocese. He drove himself and his staff relentlessly, but earned their devotion by his unfailing kindness. He was supported by his wife Henrietta to whom he was devoted; it was their great sadness that they never had children.

GREGORY DIX (1901-1952) 12th May.

Paul Couturier's ecumenism, William Temple's social gospel, George Bell's work for peace and reconciliation; the generation which came to maturity in the thirties expanded the vision of the church. Reform was also needed with increasing urgency in the church's worship. Gore, Temple and Bell were all deeply frustrated by the failure of the 1928 revised Prayer Book to get through Parliament. The Book of Common Prayer, despite its beauty and venerable association with all that was best in three hundred years of British history, had its limitations and, as more was discovered about the origins of Christian liturgy, those limitations became more apparent. Among those whose work did most to pave the way for liturgical revision, few scholars were more influential than Dom Gregory Dix, Anglican Benedictine of Nashdom Abbey.

Educated like George Bell at Westminster and Oxford, Gregory Dix passed those turbulent years of the thirties and the Second World War in the timeless obscurity of a monastery. His one venture into the busy modern world of mission, a posting for his order to the Gold Coast, ended abruptly when his health gave way and he was sent home to England. Dix delighted to cast himself as the outsider and his scathing wit gave little quarter to the Anglican establishment. No one, he said, should be surprised at the spinelessness of the bishops: was not the sign of a bishop a crook, and of an archbishop a double cross? On another occasion he said that the trouble with bishops was that they were Edwardian: they had the theology of Edward VI, the mental capacity of Edward VII, and the approach to morality of Edward VIII. The desire of his heart was to see the English church reunited to Rome, and he devoted his great scholarship to elucidating the riches of the church's heritage before the divisions of the Reformation.

His greatest work, 'The Shape of the Liturgy,' brought about a sea-change in the approach of Anglicans to the Holy Communion. Dix examined in meticulous detail the development of the Communion rite from its New Testament origins into the high ritual of the medieval mass. He traced a fourfold action at the heart of the Eucharist, which derived from the action of Christ: he took the bread, blessed it, broke it and gave it to his disciples. Dix showed how both Cranmer's Prayer Book rite and the Tridentine mass in different ways obscured this central action; his work was foundational for those, both Anglican and Catholic, who revised the liturgy in the sixties and seventies.

Gregory Dix died prematurely of cancer; he had refused treatment for six months in order to fulfil preaching engagements in America, and when he finally consented to treatment, it was too late.

JANANI LUWUM (1922-1977) 17th February.
It would be easy to tell the story of the church in the fifty-odd years since Bishop Bell died as one of melancholy decline. In Western Europe, despite many lives of heroic sanctity, despite missions, campaigns, reforms and renewals, the institutional church has steadily lost numbers and influence. But Western Europe is not the whole church. Elsewhere, Christian communities have been pioneers of justice for their people, missionary work has continued to plant new congregations, and as a result, Christian leaders have been seen as a principal threat by those seeking to rule through corruption and fear. In the final part of this long story, we return to three areas of the globe, Africa, Latin America and the South Pacific, where the Christian church is stronger than ever. In each case we revisit a land where we have seen the church founded by missionaries in a colonial era, to witness heroic stands for Christ by unlikely people who found themselves called to be modern martyrs.

The British Empire in Africa ended in the sixties. In 1962, power in Uganda was handed back to the Kabaka of Buganda, heir of the man who martyred James Hannington, in the hope that his traditional prestige would furnish unity in a land riven by tribal rivalries. The hope was a vain one. In 1966, Milton Obote, the chief minister, took power and forced the Kabaka into exile. In 1971 a military coup ousted Obote in turn and power was taken by the army chief Idi Amin, under whose rule 300,000 Ugandans were to disappear without trial. Meanwhile the new archbishop of Uganda had been elected: Janani Luwum.

Luwum was the son of a Christian village teacher, who experienced a profound conversion in 1948 during the East African Revival. He spoke in tongues, climbed a tree to preach Christ, was imprisoned by the colonial authorities for public order offences. In maturity, he was a big, lovable man surprisingly reserved about his faith and passionate about unity, both national and ecclesiastical. In Amin's early years, Luwum was criticised for visiting the President too often; exposure to power would, it was feared, seduce him. But he believed it was his duty to use what influence he had to attempt to moderate Amin's increasingly erratic behaviour. In 1972, when Amin expelled all Ugandans of Asian origin from the country, Luwum was one of the few to protest. From then on he worked to collect evidence of atrocities and misuse of power, and in 1976 led a united protest by church leaders against Amin's regime. In February 1977, the church leaders were summoned to meet Amin in Kampala. They were accused of abetting resistance to the government and one by one ordered to leave. Luwum whispered to his neighbour 'They are going to kill me. I am not afraid.' Sure enough, he was left alone with the government agents and never seen alive again. It was believed that Amin personally shot him; his body was never released for burial.

OSCAR ROMERO (1917-1980) 24th March.
Latin America's liberation from Spanish colonialists came earlier than Africa's independence, but the continent continued to endure racial and social dislocation as extreme as anything in the days of Martin de Porres.

The small state of El Salvador was typical of the region; the gulf between the land-owning minority and the vast majority of landless, exploited peasants was vast, and in the seventies, when peasants tried to organise to win rights for themselves, their efforts were brutally suppressed. The civil discontent in the country became a proxy conflict in the Cold War, with middle class Salvadorans seeing peasant unrest as Marxist agitation and the United States justifying propping up a clearly corrupt regime, because it believed that the only alternative was a Cuban style communist takeover.

In this fraught, unhappy country, what was extraordinary was to find the Roman Catholic Church, a conservative, hierarchical institution with natural affinities to the landowners who built its churches and paid its priests, gradually taking on the role of champion of the oppressed. The career of Oscar Romero illustrates this change. Brought up in rural poverty, his way out was ordination. He returned from training in Rome in 1944, and gained a reputation as a good administrator and a theological conservative, certain that the church's job was to preach salvation, not encourage political agitation. In 1970, he was an uncontroversial, 'safe' choice as auxiliary bishop of San Salvador. His first action was to damp down a campaign by the Jesuit priest Rutilio Grande, who was calling for the church to preach a gospel for the poor, to stand with the peasants in their struggle, to empower people to resist unjust government. Romero disapproved of lay people being licensed to teach and organise congregations: that was a priest's job. When he was appointed archbishop in 1977, many in the liberation theology movement were disappointed that such a cautious, un-political figure had been chosen to lead the church. But within a hundred days of his consecration, it was clear that Romero was going to be a radical archbishop.

The turning point seems to have been the murder by security of forces of Rutilio Grande, now working as parish priest of Aguilares. Romero visited the village, saw the body of his old sparring partner and something seems to have shifted within him. To the shock of wealthy Catholics, he announced that next Sunday there would only be one mass in San Salvador. The churches would be locked as a sign of mourning and the mass would be celebrated on the steps of the cathedral. Thousands of the poor filled the square. The mass became a protest, a sign that the church stood with the oppressed.

From now on the military government became increasingly anti-clerical. 'Be a patriot!' went one slogan. 'Kill a priest!' Churches which were seen as centres of Marxist agitation were sacked and the Blessed Sacrament scattered in the streets. Romero's weekly radio broadcasts told the truth about the atrocities being committed by the security forces and appealed for a Christ-like response. He was by no means universally supported by the other bishops, many of whom believed he was becoming too confrontational, but he believed he had no choice but to speak out, faced with the human misery of dispossessed tenant farmers, mothers bereaved of their children, murdered priests. In 1980, the final straw came when he wrote and publicly read a letter to President Carter of the USA appealing to him to condemn the regime and stop sending arms to support it. On 24th March, he was celebrating a funeral mass for a friend in the chapel of the hospital where he was living. As he finished his sermon a shot was fired and the archbishop fell dead on the altar step.

It took another eight years of fighting before anything resembling peace was established in El Salvador, where poverty, crime and injustice are still rife. But Romero is remembered as one who gave his life for the life of his people.

THE MELANESIAN MARTYRS (2003) 24th April.

At the turn of the twenty-first century, the Solomon Islands were beset by ethnic strife and civil unrest. In the disorder, Ini Kopuria's Melanesian Brothers showed their mettle. Respected by all sides as genuinely impartial, they were able to broker a peace deal, the Townsville Peace Agreement, which held a prospect of lasting order.

Only one warlord, Harold Kebe, still held out and refused to relinquish violence. The head of the Brethren, Nathaniel Sado, who knew Kebe personally, took the risky decision to visit the warlord's camp, alone and unarmed, to appeal to him to sign the Agreement. He never returned. Six other brothers set off in quest of their missing superior. Their names were Robert Lindsay, Francis Tofi, Alfred

Hill, Ini Paratabatu, Patteson Gatu and Tony Siriki. All six were shot on their arrival at Kebe's camp, and the body of Nathaniel Sado, when it was recovered, showed signs of torture.

Kebe's crime shocked all parties in the Solomons, where the Melanesian Brothers were regarded as sacrosanct, and revulsion at the murders undoubtedly hastened the establishment of peace.

Part Twenty-nine. to Eternity.

ALL SOULS DAY. 2nd November

Our story is coming to an end, and yet of course it has no end, for the story of the church can only end when the story of the human race ends. Over the course of this book, we have shared in the lives and experiences of some of the most extraordinary Christians, who have helped to shape the church and the human race by their prayer, their work, their legends and their writings. Yet these, whom we remember by name, are only a tiny proportion of all the baptised people of God, and the entire baptised people of God are only a fraction of the great human family for whose salvation Jesus Christ lived and died.

The feast of All Souls, observed the day after All Saints Day, has changed its meaning over the years. In the traditional theology of the Roman Catholic Church, where the observance originated, there was a clear distinction between saints and souls. Saints were victors. They had arrived in Paradise and All Saints Day celebrated their presence with Christ and their power as intercessors for the faithful. Souls, by contrast, were 'work in progress.' Still languishing in Purgatory, their sins had yet to be cleansed before they were fit to see God face to face. So All Saints Day was a day of celebration, All Souls a day of prayer for the speedy release of souls in Purgatory.

Anglicans, of course, do not believe in Purgatory and All Souls Day, where it is observed in the Church of England, tends to be a day for mourning and personal remembrance. While All Saints is a day to celebrate 'people in history with halos,' All Souls is a day to remember personal friends and relatives whose deaths still grieve us.

It is also a day to reflect that God does not only care about the famous, the holy and the shining ones. Every soul created by God is precious to him; every human life was of unique value. The story of God's salvation will only truly be ended when every soul has achieved the completion for which God created it.

ST MICHAEL AND ALL ANGELS 29th September

And God's love and eternal purposes are not confined to the human race. We are also invited to remember the eternal spirits who surround God's throne with worship and are sent, according to the Bible, as his messengers, his angels, to earth. The Bible only affords occasional, brief glimpses of these bright beings, whose vision of God is clearer than our own, but who are destined to be subordinated to us because God shared our nature in Christ, thus bringing about a more intimate union for the human race than any angel has ever enjoyed.

We are given the names of three archangels. Gabriel is the messenger of peace, bringing good news to the prophet Daniel, to Zechariah and supremely to the Virgin Mary[96]. Raphael appears in the Apocrypha as the angel of healing, acting as guardian to the boy Tobias[97]. Michael is the captain of Israel, the fighting angel, who beats down the devil and guards God's people against evil[98].

TRINITY SUNDAY

What then is the final consummation, the joy towards which this strange, eventful history of the saints has been pointing us? From Ignatius of Antioch, joyfully welcoming the lions in the amphitheatre as his passport to Paradise, to the Melanesian martyrs, giving their lives to bring peace to their sisters and brothers, the saints have always known that there is another world which matters more than personal safety and prosperity here. The good news of Jesus, the experienced power of the Holy Spirit, has opened hearts in every generation to a realisation of the Father's love. Every life in this book, martyr, theologian, mystic, founder, reformer, campaigner, priest, is in a way a commentary on the central truth of the Christian faith – that God is three in one, a community of love given and received, a community into which every believer is invited by virtue of his or her adoption into the everlasting son-ship of Jesus. The saints reflected that love in so many different ways, but they all died expecting that they would be granted the ultimate happiness, to see God face to face and rejoice in him for ever.

---

[96] Daniel 8.16; Luke 1.19; Luke 1.26.
[97] Tobit 3.17.
[98] Revelation 12.7.

SAINTS AND MARTYRS OF ENGLAND 8th November

The Octave Day of All Saints turns our attention once more to our own country. Although the calendar of the Church of England offers us riches from many lands and many ages, it is the story of England and the English church which inevitably takes centre stage. England, with all its faults, is our country and England's saints are our saints. Their full story can never be told – the thousands in each generation who responded in faith to the preaching of Aidan and Cuthbert and Wilfrid; who peopled the monasteries of Hilda and Dunstan; who built the great cathedrals and parish churches; who watched in awe as protestant martyrs burned and Catholic martyrs hanged; who fought for King Charles and loyalty, and for Parliament and freedom; who read and memorised 'Pilgrim's Progress' and 'Saints Everlasting Rest'; who quaked at the sermons of Wesley and Simeon; who signed the petitions of Wilberforce and Shaftesbury and Josephine Butler; who died faithful in prayer in the fever-ridden mission stations of Empire; in the backstreets of industrial cities, in quiet village and market towns; who got on with the unglamorous business of being Christian, electing church-wardens, coughing through Evensong, going up to receive Communion, complaining at the length of sermons, paying for the repair of roofs, doing simple acts of neighbourly kindness and just occasionally glimpsing the glory and goodness of God and knowing that it was all worthwhile.

There are hundreds of ways to be a saint. If English readers of this work are inspired to seek and find their own holiness, if the list of the Saints and Martyrs of England should be enlarged by one or two names from among them, then your author will consider his labours more than amply recompensed.

THE CALENDAR OF THE CHURCH OF ENGLAND.

Feast days are differentiated, as follows:

PRINCIPAL FEASTS are the most important days in the church year.

Festivals are days on which Holy Communion would normally be celebrated.

Lesser Festivals are of saints who have their own collect (special prayer) for use on the day.

Commemorations are less important days, where the saint might be remembered merely in intercessions on the day.

Additional days in the Chichester Diocesan Calendar are underlined.

JANUARY.

1.	**THE CIRCUMCISION OF CHRIST.**
2	Basil the Great and Gregory Nazianzen
	Seraphim.
	Samuel Azariah.
6.	**THE EPIPHANY.**
10.	*William Laud.*
11.	*Mary Slessor.*
12.	Aelred of Rievaulx.
	Benedict Biscop.
13.	Hilary.
	Kentigern.
	George Fox.
17.	Antony of Egypt.
	Charles Gore.
18.	**The Confession of Peter.**
	Amy Carmichael.
19.	Wulfstan.
20.	Fabian and Sebastian
	Richard Rolle.
21.	Agnes.
22.	*Vincent.*
24.	Francis de Sales.
25.	**The Conversion of Paul.**
26.	Timothy and Titus.
28.	Thomas Aquinas.
30.	Charles I.
31.	*John Bosco.*

FEBRUARY.

1.	*Brigid.*
2.	**THE PRESENTATION OF CHRIST.**
3.	Anskar.
4.	*Gilbert of Sempringham.*
6.	*Martyrs of Japan.*

8.	<u>Cuthman</u>
10.	*Scholastica.*
14.	Cyril and Methodius.
	Valentine.
15.	*Sigfrid.*
	Thomas Bray.
17.	Janani Luwum.
23.	Polycarp.
27.	George Herbert.
28.	<u>Oswald of Worcester.</u>

MARCH.

1.	David.
2.	Chad.
7.	Perpetua and Felicity.
8.	Edward King.
	Felix
	Geoffrey Studdert Kennedy.
17.	Patrick.
18.	*Cyril of Jerusalem.*
19.	**Joseph.**
20.	Cuthbert.
21.	Thomas Cranmer.
24.	*Walter Hilton.*
	Paul Couturier.
	Oscar Romero.
25.	**THE ANNUNCIATION OF OUR LORD.**
26.	*Harriet Monsell.*
31.	*John Donne.*

APRIL.

1.	*Frederick Maurice.*
5.	<u>Ethelburga of Lyming.</u>
9.	*Dietrich Bonhoeffer.*
10.	William Law.
	William of Ockham.
11.	*George Selwyn.*
16.	*Isabella Gilmore.*
19.	Alphege.
21.	Anselm.
23.	**George.**
24.	*Mellitus.*
	Martyrs of Melanesia.
25.	**Mark.**
27.	*Christina Rossetti.*

28.	*Peter Chanel.*
29.	Catherine of Siena.
30.	*Mary Ramabai.*

MAY.

1.	**Philip and James.**
2.	Athanasius.
4.	English Saints and Martyrs of the Reformation Era.
8.	Julian of Norwich.
12.	Pancras
	Gregory Dix.
14.	**Matthias.**
16.	*Caroline Chisholm.*
18.	Eric
19.	Dunstan.
20.	Alcuin.
21.	*Helena.*
24.	John and Charles Wesley.
25.	The Venerable Bede.
	Aldhelm.
26.	Augustine of Canterbury.
	John Calvin.
	Philip Neri.
28.	*Lanfranc.*
30.	Josephine Butler.
	Joan of Arc.
	Apolo Kivebulaya.
31.	**The Visitation of the Blessed Virgin Mary.**

JUNE.

1.	Justin.
3.	*Martyrs of Uganda.*
4.	*Petroc.*
5.	Boniface.
6.	*Ini Kopuria.*
8.	Thomas Ken.
9.	Columba.
	Ephraim.
11.	**Barnabas.**
14.	*Richard Baxter.*
15.	*Evelyn Underhill.*
16.	Richard of Chichester.
	Joseph Butler.
17.	Botolph.
	Samuel and Henrietta Barnett.

18.	*Bernard Mizeki.*
19.	*Sundar Singh.*
22.	Alban.
23.	Etheldreda.
24.	**The Birth of John the Baptist.**
27.	*Cyril of Alexandria.*
28.	Irenaeus.
29.	**Peter and Paul.**

JULY.

1.	*John and Henry Venn.*
3.	**Thomas.**
6.	*Thomas More and John Fisher.*
11.	Benedict.
13.	<u>Henry II of Germany</u>
14.	John Keble.
15.	Swithun.
	Bonaventure.
16.	*Osmund.*
18.	*Elizabeth Ferard.*
19.	Gregory of Nyssa and Macrina.
20.	*Margaret of Antioch.*
	Bartolome de las Casas.
22.	**Mary Magdalene.**
23.	*Bridget of Sweden.*
25.	**James.**
26.	Anne and Joachim.
27.	*Brooke Westcott.*
29.	Mary, Martha and Lazarus.
30.	William Wilberforce, Olaudah Equiano and Thomas Clarkson.
	<u>Olave,King of Norway.</u>
31.	*Ignatius Loyola.*

AUGUST.

4.	*Jean-Baptiste Vianney.*
5.	Oswald, King of Northumbria.
6.	**The Transfiguration of our Lord.**
7.	*John Mason Neale.*
8.	Dominic.
9.	Mary Sumner.
10.	Laurence.
11.	Clare of Assisi.
	John Henry Newman.
13.	Jeremy Taylor.
	Florence Nightingale.

	Octavia Hill.
14.	*Maximilian Kolbe.*
15.	**The Blessed Virgin Mary.**
18.	Jane Frances de Chantal
20.	Bernard.
	William and Catherine Booth.
22.	Symphorian.
23.	Rose of Lima.
24.	**Bartholomew.**
25.	Louis King of France.
27.	Monica.
28.	Augustine of Hippo.
29.	The Beheading of John the Baptist.
30.	John Bunyan.
31.	Aidan.

SEPTEMBER.

1.	*Giles.*
2.	*Martyrs of Papua New Guinea.*
3.	Gregory the Great.
4.	*Birinus.*
6.	*Allen Gardiner.*
8.	The Birth of the Virgin Mary.
9.	*Charles Lowder.*
13.	John Chrysostom.
14.	**Holy Cross Day.**
15.	Cyprian.
16.	Ninian.
	Edward Pusey.
17.	Hildegard.
19.	*Theodore of Tarsus.*
20.	John Coleridge Patteson.
21.	**Matthew.**
25.	Lancelot Andrewes.
	Sergei.
26.	Cosmas and Damian
	Wilson Carlile.
27.	Vincent de Paul.
28.	Wenceslas.
29.	**Michael and All Angels.**
30.	*Jerome.*

OCTOBER.

1.	Therese of Lisieux.
	Remigius.

	Lord Shaftesbury.
2.	<u>Leodegar.</u>
3.	*George Bell.*
4.	Francis of Assisi.
6.	William Tyndale.
9.	*Denys.*
	Robert Grosseteste.
10.	Paulinus.
	Thomas Traherne.
11.	*Ethelburga of Barking.*
	James the Deacon.
12.	Wilfrid.
	Elizabeth Fry.
	Edith Cavell.
13.	Edward the Confessor.
15.	Teresa of Avila.
16.	*Nicholas Ridley and Hugh Latimer.*
17.	Ignatius.
18.	**Luke.**
19.	Henry Martyn.
	<u>Philip Howard, Richard Woolman and Lewes martyrs</u>
25.	*Crispin and Crispinian.*
26.	Alfred the Great.
	Cedd.
28.	**Simon and Jude.**
29.	James Hannington.
31.	*Martin Luther.*

NOVEMBER.

1.	**ALL SAINTS DAY.**
2.	All Souls Day.
3.	Richard Hooker.
	Martin of Porres.
4.	<u>Charles Borromeo</u>
6.	*Leonard.*
	William Temple.
7.	Willibrord.
8.	Saints and Martyrs of England.
9.	*Margery Kempe.*
10.	Leo the Great.
11.	Martin of Tours.
13.	Charles Simeon.
14.	*Samuel Seabury.*
16.	Margaret of Scotland.
	Edmund Rich.

17.	Hugh.
18.	Elizabeth of Hungary.
19.	Hilda.
	Mechtild.
20.	Edmund.
	Lydia Sellon.
22.	*Cecilia.*
23.	Clement.
25.	*Catherine of Alexandria.*
	Isaac Watts.
30.	**Andrew.**

DECEMBER.

1.	*Charles de Foucauld.*
3.	*Francis Xavier.*
4.	*John Damascene.*
	Nicholas Ferrar.
6.	Nicholas.
7.	Ambrose.
8.	Conception of the Virgin Mary.
13.	Lucy.
	Samuel Johnson.
14.	John of the Cross.
17.	*Eglantyne Jebb.*
25.	**CHRISTMAS DAY.**
26.	**Stephen.**
27.	**John the Evangelist.**
28.	**The Holy Innocents.**
29.	Thomas Becket.
31.	*John Wycliff.*

THE CALENDAR OF THE BOOK OF COMMON PRAYER.
Entries marked * do not appear in the revised calendar.

JANUARY.

1.	**The Circumcision of Christ.**
6.	**The Epiphany.**
8.	*Lucian.
13.	Hilary.
18.	*Prisca.
20.	*Fabian.
21.	Agnes.
22.	Vincent.
25.	**The Conversion of St.Paul.**

FEBRUARY.

2.	**The Purification of the Virgin.**
3.	*Blasius.
5.	*Agatha.
14.	Valentine.
24.	**Matthias.**

MARCH.

1.	David.
2.	Chad.
7.	Perpetua.
12.	Gregory the Great.
18.	*Edward King of the West Saxons.
21.	Benedict.
25.	**The Annunciation.**

APRIL.

3.	Richard.
4.	Ambrose.
19.	Alphege.
23.	George.
25.	**Mark.**

MAY.

1.	**Philip and James.**
3.	*The Invention of the Cross.
6.	*St.John at the Latin Gate.
19.	Dunstan.
26.	Augustine of Canterbury.
27.	The Venerable Bede.

JUNE.

1.	*Nicomede.
5.	Boniface.
11.	**Barnabas.**
17.	Alban.
20.	*Translation of Edward the Martyr.
24.	**John the Baptist.**
29.	**Peter.**

JULY.

2.	The Visitation.
4.	* Translation of Martin.
15.	Swithun.
20.	Margaret of Antioch.
22.	Mary Magdalene.
25.	**James.**
26.	Anne.

AUGUST.

1.	*Lammas Day.
6.	The Transfiguration.
7.	*The Name of Jesus.
10.	Laurence.
24.	**Bartholomew.**
28.	Augustine of Hippo.
29.	The Beheading of John the Baptist.

SEPTEMBER.

1.	Giles.
7.	*Evurtius.
8.	The Nativity of the Virgin Mary.
14.	Holy Cross Day.
17.	*Lambert.
21.	**Matthew.**
26.	Cyprian.
29.	**Michael and all Angels.**
30.	Jerome.

OCTOBER.

1.	Remigius.
6.	*Faith.
9.	Denys.
13.	Edward the Confessor.
17.	Etheldreda.
18.	**Luke.**

25.	Crispin.
28.	**Simon and Jude.**

NOVEMBER.

1.	**All Saints Day.**
6.	Leonard.
11.	Martin.
13.	*Britius.
15.	*Machutus.
17.	Hugh.
20.	Edmund.
22.	Cecilia.
25.	Catherine of Alexandria.
30.	**Andrew.**

DECEMBER.

6.	Nicholas.
8.	The Conception of the Virgin Mary.
13.	Lucy.
21.	**Thomas.**
25.	**Christmas Day.**
26.	**Stephen.**
27.	**John the Evangelist.**
28.	**Holy Innocents.**
31.	*Sylvester.

BIBLIOGRAPHY.
A. General Histories.
'The Early History of the Church', Abbe Duchesne. *Detailed account of the politics of the patristic period.*
'Pagans and Christians,' Robin Lane Fox, Penguin 1986. *Study of pagan and Christian culture and spirituality in the third century.*
'The Early Church,' WHC Frend, SCM 1965.
'The Making of the Creeds,' Frances Young, SCM 1991.
'The Conversion of Europe,' Richard Fletcher, Harper Collins, 1997. *Mission outside the Roman Empire 450 – 1000.*
'A Distant Mirror', Barbara Tuchman, Ballantyne Books 1978. *Fourteenth Century; contains an account of the papal schism.*
'The Stripping of the Altars', Eamon Duffy, Yale University, 1992. *The impact of the Reformation on churches and congregations.*
'Reformation,' Diarmaid MacCulloch, Allen Lane, 2003.
'Reformation Thought', Alister McGrath, Blackwell, 1993.
'The English Civil War,' Diane Purkiss, Harper Perennial, 2007.
'The Victorian Church,' Owen Chadwick. SCM Press, 1987.
'The Wound of Knowledge', Rowan Williams Darton Longman Todd, 1979. *Study of Christian spirituality from Ignatius to John of the Cross.*
'English Spirituality', Gordon Mursell, SPCK 2001. *Examines most of the English writer saints.*

B. Biographies of Saints
'The Golden Legend', tr.William Granger Ryan, Princeton University Press, 1995. *Great medieval anthology of saints' legends.*
'Far above Rubies,' Richard Symonds, Gracewing, 1993. *Brief lives of post-Reformation women saints.*
'The Terrible Alternative,' ed.Andrew Chandler, Cassell, 1998. *Short biographies of twentieth century martyrs.*
The Catholic Truth Society publishes pamphlet lives of Francis Xavier, Charles Borromeo, Philip Neri, John of the Cross, Martin de Porres, Vincent de Paul, Charles de Foucauld, Maximilian Kolbe, Oscar Romero.

'Alone of all her Sex,' *(The Virgin Mary)*, Marina Warner, Picador 1985.
'Mary Magdalen,' Susan Haskins, Harper Collins, 1993.
'St.George', Christopher Stace, SPCK 2002.
'Jerome' JND Kelly, Gerald Duckworth, 1975.
'Augustine of Hippo,' Peter Brown, Faber & Faber, 2000.
'Martin of Tours,' Christopher Donaldson, Canterbury Press, 1980.
'Aidan, Bede, Cuthbert,' David Adam, SPCK 2006.
'St.Wilfrid,' John Nankivell, SPCK 2002.
'Alfred the Great', Asser, Penguin 1983.
'Saint Anselm' RW Southern, Cambridge University Press, 1990.
'Aelred of Rievaulx', Walter Daniel, OUP 1950.

'Hildegard of Bingen,' Fiona Maddocks, Review, 2002.

'Life of Thomas Becket,' tr.George Greenaway, Folio 1961.

'Francis of Assisi,' Elizabeth Goudge, Gerald Duckworth, 1959.

'Francis of Assisi', Adrian House, Chatto and Windus, 2000.

'Clare of Assisi,' Marco Bartoli, Darton Longman Todd, 1993.

'St.Louis,' Sire de Joinville, Bowes and Bowes, 1910.

'Catherine of Siena', Don Brophy, Darton Longman Todd, 2011.

'John Wyclif,' GR Evans, Lion 2005.

'Margery Kempe', Margaret Gallyon, Canterbury, 1995

'Joan of Arc,' Vita Sackville-West, Penguin 1936.

'Luther,' Heiko Oberman, Yale UP, 1989.

'William Tyndale,' David Daniel, Yale UP, 2001.

'Thomas More,' Peter Ackroyd, Vintage, 1999.

'Thomas Cranmer', Diarmaid MacCullough, Yale University Press, 1996.

'Philip Neri', Antonio Gallonio, Family Publications, 2005.

'Teresa of Avila,' Rowan Williams, Continuum 1991.

'Martin de Porres,' Joan Monaham, Paulist Press, 2002.

'Saint Maker' *(Francis de Sales)* Michael de la Bedoyere, Sophia Institute Press, 1998.

'Vincent de Paul and Charity,' Andre Dedin, New City Press, 1993.

'Donne, the Reformed Soul,' John Stubbs, Penguin, 2007.

'Samuel Johnson,' David Nokes, Faber & Faber, 2009.

'John Wesley', Stephen Tomkins, Lion 2003.

'William Wilberforce,' William Hague, Harper Collins 2007.

'Elizabeth Fry,' Janet Whitney, George G Harrap, 1945.

'The Cure d'Ars,' Francis Trochu, Burns Oates and Washbourne, 1930.

'St.Therese of Lisieux,' Kathryn Harrison, Weidenfeld & Nicholson, 2003.

'John Keble,' Walter Lock.

'John Henry Newman,' Ian Ker, OUP 2009.

'Pusey, restorer of the Church,' AG Lough.

'Charles Lowder and the Ritual Movement,' Ellsworth.

'Shaftesbury, the great Reformer,' Richard Turnbull, Lion Hudson, 2010.

'Florence Nightingale,' Cecil Woodham-Smith, Bookclub Associates, 1972.

'Frederick Denison Maurice,' Florence Higham, SCM 1947.

'Josephine Butler,' Jane Jordan, John Murray 2001.

'Three Martyrs of the Nineteenth Century,' *(John Coleridge Patteson)*, SPCK 1886.

'Search for a Saint,' *(Edward King)*, John A Newton, Epworth Press, 1977.

'The Miners' Bishop,' *(Brooke Westcott)*, Graham A Patrick, Epworth Press, 2004.

'Life of Charles Gore,' Prestige.

'Lion Hearted', *(James Hannington)* EG Dawson, Seeley and Co, 1908.

'The General next to God,' *(William Booth)* Richard Collier, Fontana Collins, 1965.

'Mary Slessor of Calabar,' WP Livingstone, Hodder & Stoughton 1935.

'Edith Cavell,' Diana Souhami, Quercus, 2010.

'GA Studdert Kennedy, by his friends,' Hodder and Stoughton 1935.
'The Woman who saved the Children,' *(Eglantyne Jebb)*, Clare Mulley, OneWorld, 2009.
'William Temple,' FA Iremonger, OUP 1948
'Bonhoeffer, Pastor, Martyr, Prophet, Spy,' Eric Metaxas, Thomas Nelson, 2010.

Short biographies of all British born saints may be found in the Oxford Dictionary of National Biography.

C. Works by Saints.
'Early Christian Writings' Clement, Ignatius, Polycarp, Dorset Press, 1968.
'Born to New Life', extracts from Cyprian, New City, 1991.
'On the Incarnation,' Athanasius, Centenary Press, 1944.
'The Life of Moses', Gregory of Nyssa, Harper San Francisco, 1978.
'The Trinity,' Augustine, New City Press, 1991.
'Christian Doctrine,' Augustine, Bobbs-Merrill Education Publishing, 1979.
'City of God,' Augustine, Penguin, 1972.
'Confessions,' Augustine, Penguin, 1961.
'Households of God,' *(the Rule of St.Benedict)*, Darton Longman & Todd, 1980.
'Ecclesiastical History of the English people,' Bede, OUP 1994.
'Major Works', Anselm, OUP 1998.
'Twelve Steps of Humility', Bernard, Hodder and Stoughton 1985.
'Letters', Bernard, Sutton Publishing 1953.
'Spiritual Friendship,' Aelred, Liturgical Press, 2010.
'Selected Writings', Thomas Aquinas, Penguin 1998.
'The Fire of Love,' Richard Rolle, Penguin 1972.
'The Ladder of Perfection,' Walter Hilton, Penguin, 1957.
'Revelations of Divine Love,' Julian of Norwich, University of Exeter, 1976.
'Complete Works,' Teresa of Avila, Sheed & Ward, 1946.
'Complete Works,' John of the Cross, Institute of Carmelite Studies, 1991.
'Introduction to the Devout Life,' Francis de Sales, Antony Clarke 1990.
'Sermons,' Hugh Latimer, CUP 1844.
'Institutes of the Christian Religion,' John Calvin, Eerdmans, 1989.
'The Laws of Ecclesiastical Polity,' Richard Hooker, Everyman 1907.
'Before the King's Majesty,' extracts from Lancelot Andrewes, Canterbury Press 2008.
'Selected Works,' John Donne, Nonesuch Press, 1929.
'The Temple,' George Herbert, Everyman, 1927.
'Holy Living,' Jeremy Taylor, Clarendon Press, 1989.
'The Saint's Everlasting Rest,' Richard Baxter, T.Kelly, 1834.
'Pilgrim's Progress,' John Bunyan, Collins 1953.
'Grace Abounding', John Bunyan, Religious Tract Soc, 1907.
'Felicities of Thomas Traherne,' ed.Quiller Couch, Dobell 1934.
'A Serious Call to the Devout Life,' William Law, Everyman 1906.
'The History of Rasselas,' Samuel Johnson, Penguin 1976.

'Forty-four Sermons,' John Wesley, Epworth Press, 1944.

'Story of a Soul,' Therese of Lisieux, Tan Books, 1997.

'Selections', from John Keble, Rivingtons, 1890.

'Apologia pro Vita Sua,' John Newman, Longmans Green & Co, 1908.

'The Kingdom within,' John Newman, Dimension Books, 1984.

'Complete poems', Christina Rossetti, Penguin, 2001.

'The Kingdom of Christ,' Frederick Maurice, Everyman.

'Personal Reminiscences of a Great Crusade,' Josephine Butler, Horace Marshall 1911.

'Meditations on the Seven Last Words,' Edward King, Mowbray 1910.

'Spiritual Letters,' Edward King, Mowbray 1911.

'The Reconstruction of Belief', Charles Gore, John Murray, 1926.

'The Word and the Work,' Geoffrey Studdert Kennedy, Longman, Green & co, 1925.

'The Wicket Gate,' Geoffrey Studdert Kennedy, Hodder & Stoughton, 1935.

'The Fruits of the Spirit,' Evelyn Underhill, Lowe and Brydone, 1962.

'The Life of the Spirit and the Life of Today,' Evelyn Underhill, Mowbray 1994.

'Nature, Man and God,' William Temple, MacMillan 1935.

'Readings in St.John's Gospel,' William Temple, MacMillan, 1941.

'The Cost of Discipleship,' Dietrich Bonhoeffer, SCM 1990.

'The Shape of the Liturgy,' Gregory Dix, A&C Black, 1986.

Routledge publishes a series of anthologies of the works of the early Church Fathers: volumes include Athanasius, John Chrysostom, Gregory of Nyssa, Cyril of Jerusalem.

Paulist Press publishes a series of 'Classics of Western Spirituality.' Volumes include Bonaventure, Catherine of Siena.

INDEX.